Aristotle, Oedipus, and Greek Religion

LOUIS F. GROARKE

Aristotle, Oedipus, and Greek Religion

University of Ottawa Press
2025

Les Presses de l'Université d'Ottawa
University of Ottawa **Press**

Les Presses de l'Université d'Ottawa / University of Ottawa Press (PUO-UOP) is North America's flagship bilingual university press, affiliated to one of Canada's top research universities. PUO-UOP enriches the intellectual and cultural discourse of our increasingly knowledge-based and globalized world with peer-reviewed, award-winning books.

www.Press.uOttawa.ca

Library and Archives Canada Cataloguing in Publication

Title: Aristotle, Oedipus, and Greek religion / Louis F. Groarke.
Names: Groarke, Louis, author
Description: Includes bibliographical references and index.
Identifiers: Canadiana (print) 20250208954 | Canadiana (ebook) 20250209004 | ISBN 9780776642420
  (softcover) | ISBN 9780776642437 (hardcover) | ISBN 9780776642444 (PDF) | ISBN 9780776642451
  (EPUB)
Subjects: LCSH: Aristotle—Religion. | LCSH: Oedipus (Greek mythological figure) | LCSH: Peripatetics. | LCSH: Paganism—Greece. | LCSH: Greece—Religion.
Classification: LCC B491.R46 G76 2025 | DDC 185—dc23

Legal Deposit: Fourth Quarter 2025
Library and Archives Canada

© Louis F. Groarke 2025

Creative Commons Open Access Licence
Attribution-Non-Commercial-Share Alike 4.0 International (CC BY-NC-ND 4.0)

By virtue of this licence you are free to:
Share — copy and redistribute the material in any medium or format.
Attribution — You must give appropriate credit, provide a link to the license, and indicate if changes were made. You may do so in any reasonable manner, but not in any way that suggests the licensor endorses you or your use.
Non-Commercial — You may not use the material for commercial purposes.
No Derivatives — If you remix, transform, or build upon the material, you may not distribute the modified material.
No additional restrictions — You may not apply legal terms or technological measures that legally restrict others from doing anything the license permits.

All rights reserved.

This book has been published with the help of a grant from the Federation for the Humanities and Social Sciences, through the Awards to Scholarly Publications Program, using funds provided by the Social Sciences and Humanities Research Council of Canada.

Production Team
Copy-editing   Tanina Drvar
Proofreading   Robbie McCaw
Typesetting   Dany Lagueux
Cover design   Benoit Deneault

PUO-UOP gratefully acknowledges the funding support of the University of Ottawa, the Government of Canada, the Canada Council for the Arts, the Ontario Arts Council and the Government of Ontario.

 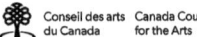  

About the Cover Design

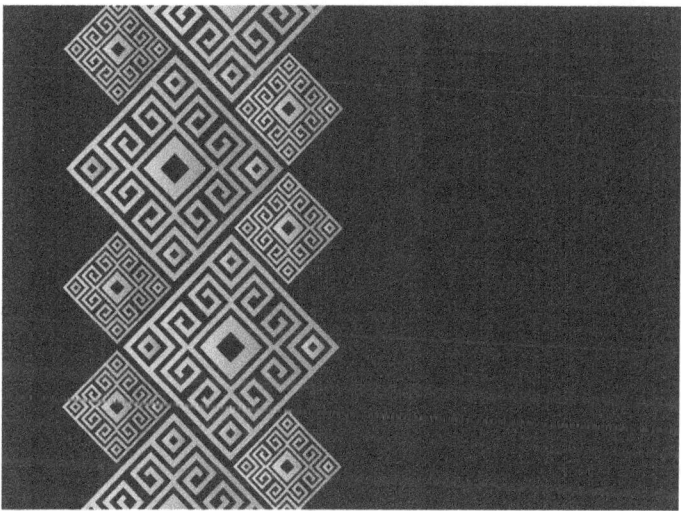

The Greek key or "meander" featured in the tiles on the cover is an archaic motif dating back to the Geometric period of Greek pottery (c. 900-700 BC). We find it on ancient Greek ceramics, frescos, textiles, and architecture. Put together in an unbroken band, the backward-curling motif represents stylized waves rising and falling. The key design is also modelled after interlocking fingers folded in a wrestling grip. The Athenians, in particular, were a seafaring people and similar representations of the wrestling grip may be found elsewhere in Greek pottery. The tile pattern recalls, as well, the role of the labyrinth of Greek myth. It was said to symbolize eternity, infinity, and the strength of community ties. Additionally, it was allegedly used to ward off evil spirits.

In Memoriam
Jude P. Dougherty (1930–2021)
Professor, Dean, Writer, Metaphysician, Public Intellectual

> Ond' io per lo tuo me' penso e discerno
> che tu mi segui, e io sarò tua guida,
> e trarrotti di qui per loco etterno.
>
> Dante, *Inferno*, Canto 1

Table of Contents

About the Cover Design v
List of Figures xiii
Acknowledgements xv
Note on Bibliographical Style xvii

CHAPTER 1
Method and Overview 1
   1.1. Introduction, Subject-Matter, and
       Methodology 1
   1.2. Chapter Summaries 10

CHAPTER 2
Did Aristotle Practise Religion? 15
   2.1. A General Picture: Ancient Greek Atheism? 15
   2.2. Aristotle and Disbelief 19
   2.3. The Religious Aristotle: A Minority Position 22
   2.4. First Textual Evidence 24
   2.5. Aristotle's Religious Practice 30
   2.6. Jaeger: The Old Developmentalism 36
   2.7. Melzer: The Esoteric Versus the Exoteric
       Aristotle 42
   2.8. Aristotle and Prayer Generally 49
   2.9. Aristotle and Petitionary Prayer 52

2.10. Aristotle's Self-Thinking God and Petitionary
   Prayer 55
   2.10.1. The Esoteric Reading 55
   2.10.2. Loose Theology 56
   2.10.3. A Caricature of Pagan Piety 60
   2.10.4. Friendship with the Gods 67
   2.10.5. A Religious Strategy: Intellectual Piety 70
   2.10.6. Petitionary Prayer and the Philosophical
      Tradition 78
2.11. Mythology and Pagan Revelation 81
2.12. The Scope of Inspiration 84
2.13. The Paranormal: Mystery Cults and
   Mysticism 88

CHAPTER 3
The Cosmos as a Hall of Mirrors 95
   3.1. Aristotle's "Theology" 95
   3.2. *Imago Dei* in an Aristotelian Vein 103
   3.3. Eternal Duration 106
   3.4. "Unmovedness" 112
   3.5. Unmixedness 127
   3.6. Immateriality 137
   3.7. Actuality 153
   3.8. Aristotle's God as Final and/or Efficient
      Cause of the Cosmos 159
   3.9. Incommensurable Wonder 171

CHAPTER 4
Aristotle and Fate 179
   4.1. Terminology, Determinism 180
   4.2. Τύχη, Science, and the Particular 190
   4.3. Τύχη in *Physics* II.4–6 199
   4.4. Bechler: Accidental Causality, Contrary
      to Reason? 210
   4.5. Four Levels of Accidental Causality 225
   4.6. Mayhew: Prayer, Τύχη, and Politics 228
   4.7. Inspiration and Supernatural Agency 232

CHAPTER 5
Oedipus and Aristotle.. 241
   5.1. Reasoning from Examples 241
   5.2. The Story of *Oedipus Tyrannos*......................... 242
   5.3. Aristotle's Opinion of Oedipus 246
   5.4. Esoteric and Exoteric Interpretations 251
   5.5. *Hamartia* 261
   5.6. Oedipus and *Hamartia*: Adkins.......................... 265
   5.7. Oedipus and *Hamartia*: Stinton 267
   5.8. *Hamartia* as a Term with Moral Colour............ 273
   5.9. Missing the Mark: The Aristotelian Mean 277
   5.10. Oedipus's Passion for Truth? 280
   5.11. Human Agency in Oedipus and Ancient
       Greek Culture.. 284
   5.12. Oedipus the Tyrant 290
   5.13. Oedipus Killing Laius 298
   5.14. Oedipus's Excusable Crimes? Aristotle's
       Ethical Exceptions 305
   5.15. Oedipus Furious.. 310
   5.16. Oedipus and *Akrasia* 314
   5.17. Was Oedipus Guilty of Parricide? 321
   5.18. Purity and Pollution (*Miasma*)........................ 326
   5.19. Guilt and Shame.. 334
   5.20. Bloodguilt and Oedipus 337
   5.21. Plato, Aristotle, and Catharsis........................... 343
   5.22. Sophocles's *Oedipus*: A Tragedy Without
       Hamartia? 353
   5.23. Oedipus and Hubris 355
   5.24. *Oedipus*, Theatre, and *Theôria* 365

CHAPTER 6
A Phenomenology of Discovery.................................. 373
   6.1. Aristotle and the New Testament....................... 373
   6.2. Aphrodite and Emmaus 375
   6.3. *Anagnôrisis*: Discovery 377
   6.4. Aristotelian Induction... 379
   6.5. Other Kinds of Aristotelian Induction 382

    6.6. Other Aristotelian Kinds of Quick-Knowing ... 384
    6.7. Putting It All Together: Formalizing the
         Flash of Understanding.. 387
    6.8. Rapid Insight in Homer and Luke...................... 389
    6.9. Complications 393
    6.9.1. Physical Resurrection? 393
    6.9.2. Can We Have Knowledge Directly from
         the Divine? 395
    6.9.3. Divine Visitation? 396

CHAPTER 7
Concluding Postscript 399
    7.1. An Overall View... 399

Bibliography... 405
Index 425

List of Figures

Figure 4.1. Nemesis (Indignation) and *Tuchē* (Fortune), red-figure ware (c. 430 BC), vase of the Heimarmene painter 185

Acknowledgements

Many people have supported and contributed to the completion of this book project. I owe a debt of gratitude to all of them but, unfortunately, I cannot name them all here. I would like to thank, in particular, my wife, Marie-Andrée, former teachers from the University of Waterloo, friends at St. Francis Xavier University, my close colleagues in the Philosophy Department, two anonymous referees who provided expert editorial and scholarly advice, Mireille Piché and the University of Ottawa Press for guiding the manuscript through the adjudication process, and Tanina Drvar and Martin Llewellyn for conscientious and thorough help during the final editing stages. Let me also thank Carmen Ruschiensky for her conscientious and careful efforts in putting together the index. I appreciate being part of the Philosophica Series at University of Ottawa Press, with its many distinguished prior contributors; philosophy in Canada needs a voice and a place in the national conversation. En espérant que ce livre ajoute quelque chose de valable à une longue lignée de recherches philosophiques au Canada.

Note on Bibliographical Style

As the texts of Plato and Aristotle are cited repeatedly, I only include the title of the primary source in the line reference. With Aristotle, I cite book, chapter, and Bekker number. With Plato, I cite Stephanus numbers. As a courtesy, I include translators' names in parentheses unless it is my own translation. I emend translations where necessary for grammatical consistency, to modernize style, or for contextual clarity. Relevant philological disagreement is disclosed.

This is a list of Aristotelian texts cited. Depending on the published source, some sources may be referred to by traditional Latinized names. (*De Anima*, etc.)

Categories
Constitution of Athens
De Interpretatione (On Interpretation)
Economics (Oeconomica)
Eudemian Ethics (Ethica Eudemia)
Fragments (of various sorts)
Generation and Corruption (De generatione et corruptione)
Generation of Animals
History of Animals (Historia Animalium)
Last Will and Testament
Magna Moralia
Metaphysics
Meteorology (Meteorologica)
Movement of Animals
Nicomachean Ethics (Ethica Nicomachea)
On Colours

On Divinations (On Divination in Sleep, or *On Prophesying by Dreams)*
On the Heavens (De Caelo)
On the Soul (De Anima)
On the Universe (De Mundo)
On Philosophy (fragments)
On Virtues and Vices
Parts of Animals
Physics
Prior Analytics
Posterior Analytics
Problems (Problemata or Problemata Physica)
Progression of Animals
Protrepticus
Poetics
Politics
Rhetoric (On Rhetoric)
Sense and Sensibilia (On Sense Perception)
Topics (Topica)

From the Platonic corpus, I cite from:

Apology (Defence of Socrates)
Crito
Epinomis
Euthyphro
Gorgias
Ion
Laws
Phaedo
Protagoras
Republic
Seventh Letter
Symposium
Theaetetus

Chapter 1

Method and Overview

> The image of Aristotle as a source of religious truth withered in the seventeenth century, the same century in which he ceased being an authority for natural philosophy.
>
> Craig Martin
> *Subverting Aristotle*

> Real historical understanding is not achieved by the subordination of the past to the present, but rather by our making the past our present and attempting to see life with the eyes of another century than our own.
>
> Herbert Butterfield
> *The Whig Interpretation of History*

1.1. Introduction, Subject-Matter, and Methodology

In Plato's *Symposium,* the drunk Alcibiades compares Socrates to statues of Silenus "sitting among the shops of those carvers of herms […] which once being opened up reveal they have gods inside."[1] He describes Socrates's arguments in the same

---

1. (Plato and Aristotle primary sources referenced in footnotes by title only.) *Symposium* 215a7–b3.

way.[2] Silenus was an ugly, pot-bellied, older companion of Dionysius who told the truth when drunk. Alcibiades is referring, then, to the difference between appearance and reality. Viewed from the outside, Socrates seems a ridiculous figure, just like a drunken old fool, but there is an image of the divine locked up inside himself, hidden from view. This is a familiar theme: What is beautiful on the outside is often ugly on the inside, and what is ugly on the outside is sometimes beautiful on the inside. So, while Socrates and his arguments may sometimes appear vulgar and even foolish, on closer inspection, they reveal something of everlasting worth and beauty. (Indeed, Alcibiades is the reverse of Socrates: beautiful on the outside and ugly on the inside; he is also drunk and telling the truth like Silenus.[3])

Socrates (with his good *daimon*) was a more overtly religious figure than Aristotle. Indeed, with Aristotle, the argument seems reversed. According to a familiar line of argument (discussed below), Aristotle played the role of a properly respectful religious pagan in his public life but secretly, as revealed in his esoteric texts, was a materialist atheist. He was religious on the outside, but atheistic and thoroughly secular on the inside. His public arguments, made to those outside his school, seemed friendly to established religion, but his technical, esoteric arguments, intended only for the inner circles, were resolutely scientific and even hostile to religious concerns.

This book, however, seeks to reverse that argument. I will argue for a religious Aristotle, a spiritual Aristotle, an Aristotle who is sincerely respectful of tradition, an Aristotle who has been hidden inside the effigy that secular philosophers have made of him. This Aristotle thinks that scientific

---

2. *Symposium* 221e1–222a6.
3. Alcibiades sees everyone double except for Socrates. Although we cannot trust Alcibiades's judgments about the other drunken (and perhaps duplicitous) companions, it seems he gets the ever-sober Socrates right.

knowledge has severe limitations; he views metaphysics as a mirror on divine transcendence, believes in a separable immaterial soul, takes religious ideas about fate seriously, sees tragedy as something with religious and moral implications, never definitively rejects the broader philosophical methodology of Platonism, and articulates an epistemology that is not altogether incompatible with mainstream Judeo-Christian tradition.

Although I present a detailed analysis of all these issues below, let us consider, first, why these topics require urgent reconsideration. The religious Aristotle I describe is not the Aristotle of the secondary literature. Or even the Aristotle of the public square. Since the Enlightenment at least, this is an Aristotle who has been largely ignored, pushed aside, disguised, put under wraps by mainstream commentary. But should the reader care whether Aristotle was a religious man or argued for religious doctrines? If one is a specialist in Aristotle, one might already have a view of such things, and if one is not, does it really matter?

Technical issues aside, there is a bigger reason for trying to recover the hidden religious Aristotle. Aristotle matters for contemporary philosophers, not just for historians, classicists, and philologists. In *De utilitate credendi* (*On the Usefulness of Belief*), Augustine (in sharp contrast to Descartes) insists that the first step to knowledge is finding a teacher so as to place oneself into a knowledgeable, authoritative tradition.[4] Aristotle is by no means always correct; he has his shortcomings. At the same time, he is—for contemporary thinkers interested in philosophy—a good place to start. For all his technical fastidiousness, Aristotle wanted a philosophical theory that we could live by; a worldview that incorporated all the major fields of philosophy: metaphysics,

---

4. Augustine has in mind the Catholic Church as teacher (as opposed to the Manichees) but the broader point is less restrictive: "every system of teaching, however mean and easy, requires, in order to its being received, a teacher or master." *De utilitate,* 35.

logic, morality, politics, what we would call epistemology, philosophy of language, science, history, and so on. But religious convictions are a regular part of the epistemological baggage most humans carry around. Aristotle did not share the Enlightenment animus against religion. Although he was not primarily a theologian, what he says about God, morality, justice, fate, music, art, and the myths has religious content that is, on its own terms, worth considering.

Aristotle's philosophy was not autobiographical in the manner of Socrates, who lived and died for a cause. In the eyes of the ancients, it was Socrates's way of life as much as what he said that mattered. Aristotle is more the systematizer, a scientifically minded collector of knowledge, a synoptic thinker that fits everything together, producing an overall view, not just for specialists but for a widely educated audience in the humanities, inside and outside philosophy. If we misconstrue his religious leanings, we misconstrue his views more generally. For what Aristotle says about one issue overlaps with other issues. As I explain in future chapters, familiar misunderstandings can be traced to an impoverished exegesis that does not take into account Aristotle's religious background.

This is a book in philosophy. I freely cite from historical, literary, religious, and even anthropological sources. But philosophy is driven by its own internal logic. It is held together by its own internal thread: What follows logically from what? The goal is always the development of a consistent position. The issue is not merely, what does this Greek word mean? Or what did this noted scholar say about this passage? Or what would we moderns like this theory to mean? Everywhere, logical inference holds things together. The goal, then, is to develop an accurate but also charitable picture of what Aristotle (and ancient Aristotelians) probably thought in a way that makes logical sense. There are dead ends and unresolvable questions, but relying on the principle of charity, we can make better sense of Aristotle if we judiciously add a religious dimension to his thought.

According to a traditional view, we become wise by returning to masters in the tradition and reconsidering what they believed, what they said, and why they said it. We may disagree with them, of course, even vehemently. But even the exercise of considering their beliefs and debating the reasons behind these beliefs has a way of elevating the conversation so that it extends beyond the biases and stereotypes of our own historical moment. I am not suggesting that we all become Greek pagans. But, as members of the educated public, we should take seriously what a highly influential philosopher such as Aristotle thought about such matters.

Reconsidering the religious elements in Aristotle is a way into another era's religious beliefs. Twentieth-century historian Herbert Butterfield complains about the "Whig interpretation of history" that "studies the past with reference to the present."[5] Something similar has often happened in the case of Aristotle. One cannot deny that something momentous happens when the proponents of a particular *zeitgeist* find traces of themselves in Aristotle. The medieval schoolmen saw Aristotle as almost Christian because they were fervent Christians. And they did a marvellous job explicating, developing, and extending his views. In specific fields, contemporary thinkers have developed more accurate accounts of Aristotle in virtue ethics, in philosophy of science, and in metaphysics. Nonetheless, there are limitations to this approach.

In this book, I am going to excavate an old Aristotle, more in keeping with his time period and his broad synoptic worldview. Butterfield's faithful historian does not study "the past for the sake of the present" but studies "the past for the sake of the past." The faithful historian attempts to study the past by looking at things "with the eyes of another century than our own."[6] This is what I am trying to accomplish here. Yet, paradoxically, we end up with an Aristotle that is *more*

---

5. Butterfield, *Whig Interpretation of History*, 11.
6. Butterfield, *History*, 31.

relevant to contemporary concerns because this historically authentic interpretation challenges the received wisdom of our own age; it presents us with an Aristotle who follows through the ramifications of his arguments in original and sometimes surprising ways, an Aristotle who is open to aspects of morality and metaphysics we and our contemporaries often overlook or even ignore. We can disagree with this older Aristotle but, even then, he serves as a useful foil to contemporary views. Trying to recover this Aristotle makes us work harder philosophically.

In studying Aristotle's religious views, we are studying the views of an entire school of philosophy. We talk about Aristotle as if there was one person who wrote all the texts that have come down to us, organized them, and oversaw their "publication." We say "Aristotle said this" or "Aristotle wrote this," but this is a useful convention. Philological opinion tries to distinguish, with varying degrees of success, between texts written by Aristotle, suspect contributions, and later additions. But no definitive overall answer is available on these sorts of questions.

Much of the original Aristotelian corpus has been lost. A substantial quantity of primary source material survives but this philosophical record remains incomplete and, in some important aspects, inconclusive. Some of the texts are clearly composed of scattered, even disconnected quotes stuck together at a later date. The corpus we have inherited is, then, a compilation from lost sources and the product of a group endeavour that—following the master's lead—was essentially collaborative in nature. Despite the usual references to Andronicus of Rhodes (and helpers), we cannot definitively know when, how, by whom, and to what exact purpose different passages were composed. One suspects that, on religious matters, there was disagreement in the Aristotelian school between individual students and colleagues. Although I begin the present book by examining the issue of Aristotle's personal religious convictions, most of the book is devoted to the place of religion within the ancient Aristotelian system as a whole. The precise level of commitment of Aristotle the person remains something of a mystery.

Aristotle was, then, the leader of a school of largely anonymous students and followers who must have added to his once mouldering and buried work while safeguarding, copying, cataloguing, and editing it over several hundred years. In the ancient world, writing something in the master's name or embellishing something already written while retaining the original attribution to the master was a familiar practice. Anonymous students in the Aristotelian school may have emphasized different aspects of the master's thought, or specialized in different fields, or edited books for different reasons. They must have tweaked texts, filled gaps, and added editorial comments or further technical distinctions to advance favoured interpretations of this or that point. Although there are many fine English translations, philological disagreement about such issues is forbidding and expansive. Despite serious exegetical problems, what Aristotle gives us is a general orientation, a broad, metaphysical framework within which the philosophical endeavour can take place.

This book does not adhere to the methodology of many other academic books on Aristotle. Current analytic philosophy, following in the path of science, prides itself in specialization. I do consider many technical treatments and engage with the secondary literature, but there is no end to second-hand commentary on Aristotle's views. (If one was so inclined, one could fill a book like this with thousands of footnotes.) My focus here is on the primary sources. There is no space in a wide treatment for anything approaching a complete review of specialist treatments on this or that contested point. I do highlight particular debates that impinge on Aristotle's religious views in insightful or in misleading ways. I consider the views of many present-day scholars but the argument of the book throws into question much of the secondary literature on pertinent points.

A familiar methodology in the journal culture and even in book-length treatments emphasizes isolated passages (and related commentary) chosen to prove a point. Call my methodology "big picture philosophy." I think that this is what Aristotle, a synoptic thinker par excellence, had in mind. I adopt, then, a more holistic approach than one finds elsewhere. Think of a jigsaw puzzle. There are many scattered pieces of evidence. The primary source material is incomplete and features choppy, divergent, obscure, and ambiguous passages. There are distinct gaps in the texts as well as additions, emendations, and amendments by later students and editors. The secondary literature remains fraught with disagreement. There are unresolved technical challenges of a philological nature. The goal of the present endeavour is, then, to put all these pieces together in a way that makes the best philosophical sense. In a way that makes the most logical sense. One wants to end up with the best big-picture readings of Aristotle.

Trying to recover what Aristotle thought about religion is not entirely different than other exercises in reading historical philosophy. Complications arise when we are faced with such diverse primary material and subtle (or not-so-subtle) variations in editorship and even authorship. But we can begin with the principle of charity. Aristotle, the man at the centre of all this philosophical endeavour, was a shrewd philosopher. He did not make obvious mistakes. He inspired an entire school of philosophy with a more or less consistent doctrine. How then can we piece together all the evidence in a way that turns Aristotle into the best philosopher possible—without falsifying or ignoring what the tradition says he says? From the incomplete record we presently have, how can we reverse engineer the original Aristotelian stance towards religion?

All this takes serious detective work. It makes for an exciting intellectual challenge because one has to sift through all sorts of conflicting evidence to come up with a surprising solution that, nevertheless, makes absolute sense. Holism is the best way to avoid partisan bias. It is rather like solving a crossword puzzle. It is not enough to find one right word or another right word—all the words have to fit together so that their letters and lengths and intersections match. Everything has to fall into place, so that we end up with a solution to all the individual words altogether. This means approaching the Aristotelian system as a system, not as a disparate group of individual editorial opinions. In the case of Aristotle, this results in a better understanding of an extremely influential thinker and his philosophical legacy.

W. D. Ross once complained that "much ink has been wasted" in Aristotelian scholarship "in the attempt to reconcile the irreconcilable."[7] This is, doubtless, true, but not everything is irreconcilable. Mapping out the landscape so that one knows where the swamps are located is already a big help. Because I aim at a "big-picture" approach, I will focus on primary sources including apocrypha, fragments, testimonies, and minor works as well as on celebrated passages. I also take into account the time period, the arguments of other ancient philosophers, and literary and historical works that touch on related issues. We need to respect other historical authors much closer to Aristotle's time period. They offer many clues to what Aristotle must have been thinking. Although Aristotle's theology is incomplete and his attitude towards religion remains, in some aspects, ambiguous, I will argue, nonetheless, that one can pick out repeating themes and a general orientation that helps illuminate the basic religious orientation of his synoptic philosophy.

This book presents an approach to philosophy *ad mentum* Aristotle. The aim is twofold: to accurately report on what Aristotle thought and to do it in a way that is relevant to philosophical concerns today. Although I bring together a wealth of detail from a very wide range of sources, I weave them together into an extended argument that should be fully accessible to anyone interested in historical Aristotelianism

---

7. Cited in Barbera, "On Music in Aristotle's Politics," 616–620.

and Greek thought generally. I argue against any sharp distinction between the esoteric and public doctrines. Aristotle is a synoptic philosopher who respects (with important qualifications) the *endoxa*, the commonly held views of the many and the wise in the community. But I turn now to the summary of the argument in this book.

1.2. Chapter Summaries

Following this introductory chapter, I turn to a longstanding, vexed question: Did Aristotle have religious convictions? Was he a practising pagan? Did he take religion seriously, not merely as an intellectual puzzle, but as a guide to how each of us should live our everyday lives? Was he a secret atheist; that is, a thoroughly secular thinker who, for political purposes, hid his anti-religious thought behind a veneer of superficial pagan piety?

Although Aristotle's convictions may have waxed and waned in the course of a long career, he never openly disparages Greek paganism. I suggest that Aristotle's religious views borrow more from Plato than generally acknowledged. The accepted corpus includes scattered remarks by Aristotle and his school on prayer, hymns, contemplation (θεωρία), marriage, politics, final cause, and fate (τύχη); these supply reasonable evidence of religious belief.

I argue, then, along with commentators such as Chroust, Bodéüs, and McClymont, that Aristotle shared in a sincere commitment to the Greek paganism of his time. Appealing to Simon Pulleyn's account of Greek religion, I criticize hermeneutic strategies such as developmentalism and esoterism, championed by commentators such as Jaeger, Melzer, Mayhew, and Broadie who seek to place as much distance as possible between the mature Aristotle and religious commitments. A familiar line of argument has it that Aristotle could not have believed in petitionary prayer because he posited a self-thinking philosophical god who paid no attention to anything outside himself. But other aspects of the extant corpus, carefully considered, suggest an Aristotle who conformed to Greek religious customs both in his personal life but also in his philosophy. Chapter 2 concludes in a consideration of Aristotle's epistemological stance towards religious mythology, the place he leaves for inspiration, and his attitude towards paranormal phenomena.

In Chapter 3, I argue that Aristotle's metaphysics revolves around a notion of divine imitation, unhelpfully glossed over in contemporary academic treatments. Although Aristotle remains more of a philosopher than a theologian, one can discern a ladder of divine imitation in Aristotle's cosmos that leads up to God as the final cause of the universe. If one looks carefully, one can find the properties of Aristotle's introspecting god reflected, however dimly, throughout the universe at many different levels of being. In Aristotle's epistemology, properties such as eternal duration, unmovedness, unmixedness, immateriality, actuality, and moral goodness can all be seen as part of a generalized striving by things in the universe to resemble God as closely as possible. The philosopher's theorizing (θεωρία) imitates the contemplation of God. The proper aesthetic response to such a god-drenched world is incommensurable wonder. I finish the chapter, which focuses mostly on primary sources, with a suggestive summary of results. Whether or not Aristotle's god deploys any efficient causality in the universe remains something of a mystery.

In Chapter 4, I consider Aristotle's account of τύχη, alternatively translated as luck, fate, or fortune. Mainstream commentators almost universally argue that the scientific Aristotle had little patience for the Greek religious notion of fate. They point to famous passages in his *Physics* II.4–8 where Aristotle seems to dismiss any belief in fate as the real cause of events in the world. I argue, in response, that this is a misreading of Aristotle's more subtle approach. Although Aristotle does not believe that fate is a scientific cause, Aristotle is not a positivist. He believes that there is a limit to scientific knowledge; in particular, he believes that there is a realm of particular (or accidental, or coincidental) causality that cannot be accessed by science. This leaves room for a particular causality that can be attributed to a divine plan that involves the rewarding of virtue and the punishment of evil.

In this chapter I engage with commentators such as Daniel Schillinger, Robin Smith, Tyler Huismann, Zev Bechler, Cynthia Freeland, Martha Nussbaum, Lindsay Judson, John Dudley, and Robert Mayhew. I argue that current debates about Aristotle and fate miss the point. Aristotle may be worried about an overenthusiastic religious reading of events that attributes too much to the direct intervention of the gods, but passages in the *Eudemian Ethics* and the *Magna Moralia* (as well elsewhere) go some way to reconciling religious notions of fate with deterministic science. While I do not provide a conclusive answer to all related questions, I do point to Socrates as a likely candidate, in Aristotle's eyes, for someone who made good decisions because he was divinely inspired.

In Chapter 5, I analyze Sophocles's play *Oedipus Tyrannos* (misleadingly known in English as *Oedipus Rex*) from an explicitly Aristotelian perspective. In contrast to most commentators, I argue that Aristotle viewed tragedy in religious and, therefore, moral terms. Although Sophocles depicts Oedipus as a fully autonomous individual and not as a plaything of the gods, one cannot appreciate what is happening without taking into account the religious and moral implications of the events described.

Oedipus was one of Aristotle's favourite tragedies. Although the play is not, in any simplistic sense, a mere didactic exercise, contemporary attempts to morally sanitize *Oedipus* misconstrue the religious and legal understanding that regulated homicide in ancient Greece. I criticize amoral interpretations of Oedipus's flawed character based on overstated but extremely influential claims (deriving from Dodds, Dawe, Stinton, Blondell, Golden, Adkins, Sachs, and others) about Aristotle's use of the Greek term ἁμαρτία (*hamartia*). Despite modern amoral interpretations to the contrary, Sophocles's play is an ingenuous restating of a familiar Greek trope: A hubristic personality suffers a self-inflicted downfall and is punished by the gods, those guardians of morality and law. Although Aristotle does make room for ethical exceptions in the *Nicomachean Ethics*, none of them apply to Oedipus, who suffers from a more honourable but highly blameworthy sort of *akrasia* (incontinence). Whether Oedipus was guilty of parricide is a more complicated question.

I argue here that Aristotle, in his *Poetics*, is responding to Plato's specific criticism of poetry as a source of religious pollution (μίασμα, *miasma*). We have to link his account of catharsis to temple rituals requiring liturgical absolution for even innocent homicide. Modern exegetes tend to misconstrue this aspect of the ancient debate because we now live in highly secular liberal societies that pay far less attention to the purity requirements imposed by religion as a key ingredient of morality. I conclude Chapter 5 by arguing that the experience of theatre can be thought of as a form of *theôria* in imitation of Aristotle's self-reflecting divine. What Aristotle means by theory is not a mastery of logical argument, but a state of contemplation accompanied by an epiphany akin to what literature provides.

In the final chapter, I argue that Aristotle's epistemology highlights the role of an often instantaneous burst of intelligence—pejoratively labelled "agitation of wit" by later authors—that operates in a wide variety of intellectual situations involving mental processes such as επαγωγή (induction), ἀναγνώρισις (discovery), and εὐστοχία (quick wit). Using an episode involving Aphrodite from the *Iliad* and the Emmaus story from the New Testament, I show that the old Aristotelianism is not violently opposed to a belief in the kind of knowledge described in religious scripture. There is ancient evidence inside and outside the corpus that provides some evidence of a friendlier perspective on even Judeo-Christian religious belief.

Chapter 2

Did Aristotle Practise Religion?

> In a certain sense Aristotle is, and in a certain sense […] is not, an atheist. If we mean by atheist one who denies the existence of a perfect intelligence subsisting of itself, and eternal in its essence, and the cause of all things else, Aristotle can hardly be called an atheist.
> […] [If] we mean by atheist one who ignores the reality of God's moral government, one who strips God of those attributes that vital and practical religion rest upon, […] who robs the fact of God's existence of its vivifying element for us in producing holiness,—if […] we mean […] one who, though he may allow the bare existence of a First Cause, yet invests that First Cause with none of those Divine characteristics that adorn it as a proper object of worship […] in such an acceptation of the term most indubitably must Aristotle be acknowledged an atheist.
>
> John M'Mahon, *Aristotle's Metaphysics*

2.1. A General Picture: Ancient Greek Atheism?

One erudite colleague, Christopher Byrne, believes that Aristotle's theism is so thin, so minimalistic, that it comes as close to being atheism as any theism ever could. This is not a rare view today. In this book, then, I am going to swim against the current and argue that ancient Aristotelianism was seriously committed to Greek pagan religion. At least that is what the admittedly elusive evidence seems to suggest.

Commentators sometimes present Aristotle as something of a positivist, a man with materialist scientific inclinations, religiously indifferent, secular, even skeptical and atheistic. But this is unfriendly (or friendly) caricature. Along with a few present-day commentators—in particular, the older author Anton-Hermann Chroust (1973), Canadian classicist Richard Bodéüs (2000), and, more recently, John McClymont (2010)—I will maintain that Aristotle was probably a rather typical ancient Greek, someone who took pride in his Greek religious heritage with its extensive mythology and pervasive culture of pagan temple worship.[1] The evidence for Aristotle's alleged atheism or even agnosticism is much weaker than generally acknowledged. Although a definitive answer on the question of Aristotle's personal religious involvement is not possible, much contemporary interpretation presupposes attitudes that are more modern than ancient.

Let us begin with a brief look at the polemical literature. There seems to be something of a recent trend featuring general-audience books by scholars who, in one way or another, emphasize the allegedly atheistic, naturalistic, secular, scientific, or liberal attitudes of ancient philosophers including Aristotle. I am thinking of publications like Edward Jayne's *An Archaeology of Disbelief: The Origin of Secular Philosophy* (2018), Mor Segev's *Aristotle on Religion* (2017), Tim Whitmarsh's *Battling the Gods: Atheism in the Ancient World* (2016), Stephen Greenblatt's *The Swerve: How the World Became Modern* (on Epicureanism, 2011), and Charles Freeman's *A.D. 381* (2009) as well as his *The Closing of the Western Mind: The Rise of Faith and the Fall*

---

1. Chroust, *Aristotle*; Bodéüs, *Aristotle and the Theology of the Living Immortals*; McClymont, "Reading Between the Lines: Aristotle's Views on Religion."

of Reason (2002). This literature (mostly) reassures us that the ancient philosophers and particularly Aristotle were (mostly) secularists like us before Christianity got in the way and ruined the party. I do not engage extensively with this literature here, but a brief comment is in order.

Segev confidently asserts: "When we discuss Aristotle's views of traditional religion, then, we must understand [that] Aristotle decisively dismisses and rejects these ideas. […] In the lost works, too, Aristotle seems to have insisted on his rejection of the content of religion."[2] I look more carefully at the evidence below, but this is overreach. Although Aristotle is a precursor for many contemporary attitudes, we cannot overlook decisive differences. Present-day commentators, accepting the supposed rivalry between religion and science, want an Aristotle that comes down on the side of science. However, this alleged opposition between science and religion is an Enlightenment trope. Aristotle's naturalism is not equivalent to the modern-day atheism that champions physicalist science as something that soundly defeats religion, providing an entirely areligious and materialist explanation of all there is to know.

Whitmarsh identifies the obscure pre-Socratic Hippo of Samos (fl. fifth century BC) as the first "real" atheist.[3] But reading modern "atheism" backwards into ancient Greek philosophy is a risky endeavour. First, the adjective ἄθεος (*atheos*) that Whitmarsh translates as "atheist"—as well as the more general noun ἀθεότης (meaning "atheism")—had pejorative moral implications. It was used to refer to the godless, the ungodly, those forsaken by the gods, as well as those that denied official belief.

---

2. Segev, *Aristotle on Religion*, 18, 70.
3. Whitmarsh, *Battling*, 63. Aristotle comments in the *Metaphysics* (Ross) I.3.9842–41: "I say nothing of Hippo, because no one would presume to include him in this company, in view of the paltriness of his intelligence."

Second, whereas contemporary atheists are usually rebelling against what they see as a defining orthodoxy imposed by church authority, the polymorphous religious impulses of Greek paganism were open to a very wide latitude of attitudes and interpretations. As Freeman points out, "For the most part, [...] Greek religion was undogmatic, its theology ever in flux. Myths and rituals were so interwoven into everyday life that no need was felt for an institutional hierarchy to defend them."[4] I say more about this below, but Greek paganism included a freewheeling literary phenomenon that spawned a diversity of belief without the level of doctrinal precision that was later worked out in, say, the medieval scholastic tradition.

Third, Whitmarsh points to the early pre-Socratic Hippo and his colleagues as exemplifying some sort of atheistic materialism. But the early Greeks have a much richer notion of matter, which is closer to animism. When Aristotle reminds readers that Hippo believed that "the seed, the primordial soul" that animates animals is water (not blood), it is hard to know what to make of all this.[5] Is Hippo thinking that moisture has some divinity in it that is able to organize things into life? The Epicureans as a school come closest to adopting a position akin to the modern atheism, but even they postulated the existence of the gods.

Finally, the atheism we know today is mostly an Enlightenment reaction against the Judeo-Christian tradition. Early Greek philosophy is situated outside this mental space. The philosophers inevitably complain about naïve and overly literal interpretations of the myths, but partly on the grounds that such interpretations are impious—i.e., they are not religious enough. The ancient Greeks were, as a rule, intensely proud of their religious poetry, their temple culture, their liturgical ceremonies and mystery cults, and their religious theatre. Aristotle seems to have been a proud Greek

---

4. Freeman, *A.D.*, 22.
5. *De Anima* I.2.405b2–4.

even though he was tied to the Macedonians and disliked by Athenians. Whatever his private philosophical opinions were on religious subjects, he did not publicly disavow the Greek religious tradition.

2.2. Aristotle and Disbelief

In his volume *An Archaeology of Disbelief*, Jayne paints a picture (mostly borrowed from Jaeger) of an older Aristotle who, as time went on, was increasingly influenced by "the various concepts of materialism advanced by pre-Socratic natural philosophers culminating with Democritus."[6] Jayne believes that the mature Aristotle grew more and more pre-Socratic as time went on, until he came to understand the world exclusively in material and empirical terms. If "in the beginning Aristotle served as a loyal advocate of Plato's spiritual teleology, [...] he later pursued a materialist alternative."[7]

Jayne comments: "Aristotle [gradually came] to realize that he preferred the various assumptions of pre-Socratic philosophers to Plato's concept of transcendence. [So] by the time he wrote *Physics* [he] seems to have almost entirely abandoned Platonism."[8] It is, frankly, odd to argue that Aristotle himself becomes something of a pre-Socratic when he himself complains about pre-Socratic materialism. For reasons I will not explore here, Aristotle is generally unsympathetic to atomism, the main branch of ancient materialism. In his own metaphysics, he takes a different Platonic route that privileges the role of form as something that decisively controls and shapes the material world, whatever his differences on specific points with Plato.[9]

As is so often the case, Jayne ends up contrasting the mystical Plato with the scientific Aristotle. I am going to

---

6. Jayne, *Archaeology*, 66.
7. Jayne, *Archaeology*, 66.
8. Jayne, *Archaeology*, 66.
9. For a very different opinion that turns form into a mere epiphenomenon, cf. Carrier, "Aristotelian Materialism."

introduce readers to evidence that seems to reveal a different Aristotle, one that is pious, mystical, poetic, non-reductionist, and an intellectual believer in religion as he knew it. Aristotle is always questioning and critical, but he does not seem to have been the minimalist theist he is so often made out to be. I will argue for an Aristotelianism that has its own particular take on philosophical issues but is much closer to Platonism than commonly believed.

If, as Jayne claims, the mature Aristotle was opposed in principle to religion, one might wonder why the surviving works mostly feature mild and rather noncommittal criticism on religious topics. But Jayne, like many other commentators, has a ready answer. Aristotle, he thinks, had to disguise his robustly secular perspective because he lived in intolerant times. After all, Socrates had been executed, in part, for being an "atheist." (Although this was, mostly, a political hit job and not a serious investigation into his religious convictions.) Other philosophers like Anaxagoras and even Aristotle did face various degrees of religious animosity.

This is how Jayne explains the situation:

> As for Aristotle's secular perspective, a major difficulty is that much of his analysis was in conflict with one or more orthodoxies, and censorship too often became a factor either through the destruction of texts or through their textual modification. To avoid censorship and the possibility of prosecution by the citizens of Athens, Aristotle reserved the full examination of his theories for his students and disciples, while his less offensive writings were made available to the public.[10]

This is a familiar enough strategy in Aristotelian exegesis, which I discuss further below, but contemporary exegetes who claim that Aristotle is a closet heretic do not seem to notice that this comes close to being an unfalsifiable thesis.

---

10. Jayne, *Archaeology*, 65.

To suggest that Aristotle was hiding his anti-religious beliefs comes very close to admitting that we cannot find strong evidence of any sharp rejection of Greek paganism in Aristotle's works. Perhaps there is little evidence because Aristotle was generally accepting of Greek paganism. It may be the editorial opinions of commentators that push this lack of evidence in an anti-religious direction.

Jayne claims that Aristotle shows little interest in religious topics. He concludes, "Aristotle specifically suggests the possibility of God in only one passage, and it occurs in an awkward sentence toward the end of the text that seems an interpolation at odds with everything discussed elsewhere."[11] This summary judgment is wholly misleading, but it is also out of step with the views of some older authors.

Boethius famously declared (when announcing a scholarly project he was never able to complete):

> I wish to translate the whole work of Aristotle. [...] Everything Aristotle ever wrote on the difficult art of logic, on the important realm of moral experience, and on the exact comprehension of natural objects, I shall translate, [...] I should also like to translate all Plato's Dialogues, and likewise explain them. [...] When this is accomplished, I will furthermore not shrink from proving that the Aristotelian and Platonic conceptions in every way harmonize, and do not, as is widely supposed, completely contradict each other. 1 will show, moreover, that they are in agreement with one another at the philosophically decisive points.[12]

Of course, Boethius never finished his project. And he exaggerated more than a little in declaring the *complete* agreement

---

11. Jayne, *Archaeology*, 92.
12. Boethius, *Second Commentary on Aristotle's De Interpretatione* (Hoffman), B. II. Praef. Cited in Von Campenhausen, *Fathers of the Latin Church*, 285–286.

of Aristotle and Plato. Nevertheless, I believe there is more agreement than we moderns like to think.

John Dillon of the Plato Centre of Trinity College, Dublin, once told me in conversation that Aristotle needs to be thought of as someone who continued working within the broad framework set by his predecessor. If we think of Platonism not so much as a belief in a series of dogmatic propositions but as a way of doing philosophy, it is easier to see Aristotle as a "scientific Platonist" who disagrees, obviously, with Plato on some very important points. Still, he can be seen as contributing to the same broad philosophical endeavour.

2.3. The Religious Aristotle: A Minority Position

No investigation of Aristotle's personal religious convictions will put scholarly debate to an end. One could venture that this is the nature of scholarly debate—but this is a special case. Aristotle is not a Socrates, a Boethius, a Kierkegaard, or a Nietzsche. He is a different kind of philosopher: more of an encyclopedist, a historian, a logician, a scientist, a collector of data, and a technician, who often keeps his own views in the background while articulating the views of others. I do think the collected evidence comes down on the side of personal commitment to religious belief of some sort (which may have varied at different points of his career), but we should keep in mind the limitations posed by this kind of inquiry. As McClymont points out, Aristotle's personal convictions may not even coincide with his "official" philosophy (for reasons we will explore below). Nonetheless, I believe that we can show that the notion of a religious Aristotle is not as far-fetched as many contemporary commentators assume.

Chroust, in an older study of the various *Vitae Aristotelis*, reports:

> Different scholars, often motivated by their own religious commitments, have come up with a great variety of widely conflicting suggestions and interpretations

> with regard to the religious content of the *Corpus Aristotelicum*. These suggestions range all the way from an allegedly complete religious indifferentism on the part of Aristotle, to his fervent affirmation as well as deeply felt awareness of certain fundamental religious problems faced by all thoughtful people.[13]

Although Chroust himself maintains that Aristotle was, indeed, "a profoundly religious man" and amasses evidence in support of this conclusion, most contemporary commentators gravitate to the opposite side of the question. There are, however, notable exceptions.

Canadian classicist Richard Bodéüs, in his controversial book, insists that Aristotle was, for the most part, a sincere believer. As Bodéüs points out, there is little or no textual evidence that Aristotle opposed pagan religious belief. He argues, for example, that Aristotle never doubted the efficacy of intercessory prayer, that he took it for granted that the gods were pleased by good moral behaviour and by pagan practices of piety, that he only uses the term *theologia* to refer to popular stories about the gods, and even that he believed that living gods had entered into direct contact with human civilization in the early stages of history.

McClymont, for his part, argues that "there is no good reason to doubt that Aristotle was sincerely pious."[14] He maintains that Aristotle followed largely in the footsteps of Plato and considered religious questions a matter of social convention and legal enforcement rather than a mainstream topic for philosophical consideration. McClymont points to the hymn Aristotle wrote for his friend Hermias as suggestive of a belief in personal immortality.[15] McClymont also cites Origen (c. 184–c. 253 AD) and Tatian (c. 120–c. 180 AD),

---

13. Chroust, *Aristotle*, see chapter XVI, "Aristotle's Religious Convictions," 221–231.
14. McClymont, "Reading," 45.
15. McClymont, "Reading," 41.

who had access to Aristotelian texts no longer extant, to the effect that Aristotle believed in a limited sort of providence that extended to the world in general but not to the specifics of human behaviour.[16] He relies on familiar evidence from *De Anima* that Aristotle believed in the immortality of the νοῦς (mind) and also suggests that Aristotle generally held Greek mythology in high regard, a perspective which, he thinks, is missing from the extant philosophical treatises but probably played an important role in Aristotle's lost dialogues.

2.4. First Textual Evidence

These interpretations seem, to the present author, about right. I consider details below. As McClymont suggests, Aristotle is rather reticent about what he believes; we have to "read between the lines" to get a sense of his overall attitude to religion. In reading Aristotle thoroughly, however, one never encounters any radical anti-traditionalism in politics or religion. In the *Topics*, he remarks, without the least hesitation, that anyone who wonders "whether we ought to honor the gods" stands in need of a whipping.[17] He seems to have written lost books interpreting and defending the poets and their accounts of religious mythology and the gods.[18] In a discussion of the friendship between the gods and men, he insists that the gods are "our greatest benefactors; responsible for our existence, our maintenance, and when we have grown up, our education."[19] He assures the philosophical reader that "whatever choice […] most readily produces the contemplation of God is best," and criticizes categorically, "any choice that […] hinders one from the contemplation of God or from services to God."[20] In an ambiguously worded

---

16. Specifically, Origen, *Contra Celsum* (*Against Celsus*) (c. 248 AD), 21, and Tatian, *Oratio apud Graecos* (*Address to the Greeks*), 5, 7.
17. *Topics* 1.11.105a1–10; Bodéüs, *Theology*, 8.
18. Cf. Menn, "Aristotle, Democritus and the Problemata," 10–11.
19. *Nicomachean Ethics* (Bodéüs) VIII.12.1162a4–7.
20. *Eudemian Ethics* (Solomon) VII.15.1249b17–21.

passage, he also suggests that God is not an authoritarian ruler but something we should approach as closely as possible and try to imitate.[21]

Aristotle does not seem to have been a revisionist in religious matters. In one fragment from a lost volume, he allegedly writes:

> We should nowhere be more modest than in matters of religion. If we compose ourselves before we enter temples [...] how much more should we do this when we discuss the constellations, the stars, and the nature of the gods, to guard against saying anything rashly and imprudently, either not knowing it to be true or knowing it to be false.[22]

This attitude of cautious reserve is not an enthusiastic endorsement of any particular system of theology, but neither does it involve a robust denunciation of ordinary religion.

If authors in the polemical literature like to think of Aristotle as a secular thinker, secularism was not much of an option in ancient Greece. In a discussion of the ideal political community, Aristotle insists that "temples must be distributed across the state."[23] A stern moralist, he proposes blanket censorship for public displays of a sexually suggestive subject matter *except* when they fit into religious festivities centred on fertility themes.[24] He recommends that the local temple be constructed in a prominent location beside the most important civic buildings. As he puts it:

> The principal common tables of the magistrates will occupy a suitable place, and there also will be the buildings

---

21. *Eudemian Ethics* VII.15.1249b 13–14.
22. *On Philosophy* (Ross) 87; also, Chroust, *Aristotle*, 223.
23. *Politics* (Rackham) VII.12.1331b17–18.
24. "Let the rulers take care that there be no image or picture representing unseemly actions, *except* in the temples of those gods at whose festivals the law permits even ribaldry." *Politics* (Jowett) VII.17.1336b14–20.

appropriated to religious worship (except for those rites which the law or the Pythian oracle has restricted to a [place outside the town]). The sight should be a spot seen far and wide, which gives due elevation to virtue and towers above the neighborhood.[25]

Several of the ancient vitae provide more tantalizing tidbits of biographical evidence. As Chroust points out, it is recorded that Aristotle "dedicated and inscribed an altar in honored memory of Plato," which suggests some sort of religious observance surrounding the memory of a deceased loved one.[26] In his *Last Will and Testament*, he directs his executors, as Chroust's reports, to "set up in Stagira life-size statues of Zeus and Athena in order to ensure, or show thanks for, the safe return of Nicanor […] [who] was abroad on a 'dangerous mission.'"[27] The specific passage from the *Will* reads: "Nicanor, if he is preserved (which is a prayer I have offered on his behalf) is to set up statues in stone four cubits in height to Zeus Saviour and Athena Saviouress at Stagira."[28] As Chroust explains: "To provide for such votive statues in a will was not an uncommon practice in ancient Athens and Greece [which shows] that Aristotle was a pious and god-fearing man."[29] Secular commentators tend to overlook these details because they never made their way into a philosophical argument. But why would someone who scoffed at intercessory prayer pay (extravagantly) for life-size votive statues to thank the saviour-gods Zeus and Athena for favours received?

We find further evidence of religious commitment among Aristotle's students in more peripheral texts. In the apocryphal *On the Universe*, a student or follower waxes

---

25. *Politics* (Jowett) VII.12.1331a24–7.
26. Chroust, *Aristotle*, 12.
27. Chroust, *Aristotle*, 218.
28. Chroust, *Aristotle*, 189.
29. Chroust, *Aristotle*, 218.

pious, describing God in the most extravagant terms. The text seems too effusively poetical to be from the original Aristotle, repeating themes and tropes in a highly embellished literary manner. If, however, this is not a work by Aristotle's own hand, we cannot discount the fact that it was included in the original corpus by later editors and must have captured their esteem. (I discuss some passages below.)

Again, in the *Economics*, a minor text sometimes attributed to one of Aristotle's students, the Peripatetic author describes marriage in distinctly religious, and almost sacramental terms. We are told that anyone who takes their marriage duties lightly "would seem to be slighting the gods for whose sake and in whose presence sacrifice was offered," that a man marries so that "he may obey the law of men and of gods," and that marriage is the principal means by which successive generations are able to "participate in immortality and to continue to offer petitions and prayers to ancestral gods."[30] The text further informs us that the gods will bestow "the greatest gift of all" on spouses that persevere, that Homer uses prayer to emphasize "the virtuous companionship of man and wife in marriage," and that the gods bestow on wives who stand by their husbands in times of adversity "the honor they deserve."[31] Quite apart from any philosophical content, such passages presuppose a religious framework for marriage and family life. The ancient vitae list two other books by Aristotle, *On the Common Life of Husband and Wife* and *Laws for Man and Wife,* dealing with similar themes.[32]

Aristotle and his school seem, then, to have accepted the social conventions of the times, whatever intellectual reservations a philosophical mind might harbour about the naïve folk details of Greek paganism. There is the further suggestion that the Platonism he was schooled in developed into

---

30. *Economics* (Armstrong) III.2. 100–110; 90–100; 80–90.
31. *Economics* (Gillies) III.4.190–200, 160–170; III.1.50–60.
32. From the list in the *Vita Menagiana*, in Barnes, *Complete Works*, 2386.

a philosophical-religious perspective with rites and sacred mysteries shared among the initiated. Lloyd Gerson reports:

> Platonism in antiquity had many features of a religion as well as a philosophical school. In this regard it was held to be open to the inclusion of truths—regarding the soul, divinity, and so on—handed down from nonphilosophical sources such as Pythagorean, Orphic, Hermetic, and Gnostic, as well as philosophical sources outside the Platonic tradition and even non-Greek sources.[33]

Whatever the mood at Plato's Academy when Aristotle was a student there, we cannot overemphasize the religious features of the cultural context in which Aristotle was working. Whatever reservations he felt about specific pagan beliefs, there is little sign of any overt or determined rebellion against Greek paganism. He may have been worried about accusations of impiety—we all know what happened to Socrates—but, mostly, Aristotle seems to value and even champion a robust sense of Greek identity, which would have included a cultural identification with Greek temple paganism.

As McClymont reports, Aristotle divides unanswered questions into three categories in the *Topics* (I.11.105a):

> He distinguishes three areas concerning which one may be puzzled: 1. One may be puzzled about issues of simple sensible fact, e.g. whether snow is white. In this case one solves the issue by perception; 2. one may be puzzled about some issue that is resolved by argument (presumably this would be a philosophical or scientific issue); or 3. one may alternatively be puzzled about whether or not to honour the gods or one's parents. In this case the issue

---

33. Gerson, *Other Platonists*, 26. Scholars often point to Diotima's mention of the mystery rites in *Symposium* 209eff. as evidence of some hidden religious meaning in Platonism.

is resolved not by argument, but by punishment. Both of these are matters of piety, and Aristotle clearly requires that punishment by law rather than philosophical discussion is the best means to resolve these things. The absence of a discussion of piety in Aristotle's treatises, comparable to his discussion of other virtues, is therefore by design rather than accident. For him, the spheres of philosophical argument and piety are separate and doubts in either area have separate means of solution.[34]

Plato, in the *Laws*, assigns the death penalty for acts of impiety.[35] Later in the same text, he calls the gods our guardians, insists that they are mindful of our interests, and recommends sentences of incarceration, re-education, and even death for alternate forms of atheism.[36] It would seem, then, from this Platonic *and* Aristotelian point of view, core questions about religious belief and practice are not open to debate. To question the general framework of Greek paganism would involve disloyal, anti-social (indeed, barbarian) behaviour. Religion was seen as a good thing, a unifying social force that inculcated virtue. Of course, there was a lot of latitude for disagreement about dogmatic details.

I am concerned, in this chapter, with Aristotle's personal attitude to religion. I think it is too strong to suggest that he was an atheist or a disbeliever and only going through the motions when it comes to Greek religion. Bodéüs maintains—correctly, I think—that Aristotle never thought of himself as a professional theologian defending religion or trying to sort through orthodox religious dogma. He is a physicist when doing physics, an astronomer when he does

---

34. McClymont, "Reading," 35.
35. Cf. *Laws* (Bury) IX.854e. "If any citizen is ever convicted of such an act,—of committing some great and infamous wrong against gods, parents, or State—the judge shall regard him as already incurable, reckoning that, [...] he has not refrained from the worst iniquity. For him the penalty is death, the least of evils."
36. *Laws* X.907aff.

astronomy, a political scientist when doing political science, a metaphysician when doing metaphysics. He discusses God in passing on his way to other sorts of problems. This complicates matters. It may be the case that Aristotle and his editors are sometimes, on religious matters, commenting on something in haste on their way to other more pertinent issues. But anyone who wants to discount Aristotle's religious commitment will be confronted with evidence, admittedly scattered, that requires some artful evasion.

2.5. Aristotle's Religious Practice

We do not really know the full extent of what Aristotle wrote about religious subjects. Most of the Aristotelian corpus is now lost. Diogenes Laërtius, to cite one source, lists 156 titles divided into approximately 400 books, including many books that could have touched upon religious matters.[37] None of this is very conclusive, but it seems that Aristotle comments on Homer and Hesiod, who were like scripture to the pagan Greeks. He argues with Xenophanes, a religious poet; he criticizes Pythagoreanism, a religious cult. He discusses hymns. He had a book on art (discussing statuary featuring the gods?); a book on Delphi, where the most important temple was located. There were various books on justice (including the requirements of piety?), as well as studies of foreign constitutions (commenting perhaps on their religious customs), and so on. I will discuss some details below.

The pagan Greeks were not a secular liberal society. The *Constitution of Athens*, compiled by Aristotle or by one of his students, describes a city-state operating according to a bewildering multitude of religious customs and rituals that would be unimaginable today. It contains, for example, a list of religious authorities and dignitaries that play a significant role in civic life. The list includes:

- the Commissioners of Public Worship "who are to offer the sacrifices appointed by oracle, and, in conjunction

---

37. Diogenes Laërtius, *Lives*, V.22–27.

with the seers, take the auspices whenever there is occasion";[38]
- the ten "Annual Commissioners" appointed "to offer and supervise sacrifices and administer all the quadrennial [religious] festivals";[39]
- the ten treasurers "who take charge of the statue of Athena, the figures of Victory, and all the other ornaments of the temple";[40]
- the "ten Commissioners for Repairs of Temples";[41]
- the higher Archon in charge of religious duties such as the supervision of religious parades and athletic contests, including those held "in honour of Zeus the Saviour";[42]
- the Polemarch (an Archon) who is to perform "sacrifices to Artemis the huntress and to Enyalius, [...] and [to make] offerings to the memory of Harmodius and Aristogeiton [old heroes of Athenian democracy]";[43]
- the "Superintendents of Mysteries" who supervise the mystery cults; and
- the "king" (another archon) who "administers all the ancestral sacrifices," reviews "indictments for impiety," and settles "any disputes [...] concerning priestly rites [...] as well as controversies concerning sacred rites for the ancient families and the priests."[44]

These officers are generally chosen by lot, which leaves their final appointments to fate, which is controlled by the gods.[45] Possible candidates are to be interviewed to see if they are sufficiently religious. Each is to be asked, for example, "whether he possesses an ancestral Apollo and a household Zeus, and

---

38. *Constitution of Athens* (Kenyon), 54.
39. *Constitution of Athens* (Kenyon), 54.
40. *Constitution of Athens* (Kenyon), 47.
41. *Constitution of Athens* (Kenyon), 50.
42. *Constitution of Athens* (Kenyon), 56.
43. *Constitution of Athens* (Kenyon), 58.
44. *Constitution of Athens* (Kenyon), 57.
45. *Constitution of Athens* (Kenyon), 55.

where their [public] sanctuaries are." One needs, so to speak, a private chapel at home if one is to accede to public office.

One way to capture the intense and all-embracing religiosity of ancient peoples is to read Livy's story of the founding of Rome (I.xviii–xxi) about Numa Pompilius's institution of an astounding array of Roman temple sanctuaries, public celebrations, priestly castes, and propitiatory and oracular rites set out in a distinctly pre-modern civic framework. The mindset at work in these ancient societies is about as far as one can go from modern secular humanism. For its part, the *Constitution of Athens* lays down specific rules governing the entry and use of each temple.[46] (For example, anyone accused of homicide is forbidden from entering a temple.[47]) Elsewhere (in a fragment), Aristotle identifies ten religious feasts that must be celebrated.[48] But the details are not so important here. In the *Politics*, Aristotle writes that "a constitution is the organization of offices in a state and determines what is to be the governing body and what is the end of each community."[49] Clearly, the aim, the goal of Athenian civil life is, to some very large extent, the practice of religion as a healthy regulating element in a well-run polis. Civic life in Athens was permeated with religious observance of all sorts. Throughout his report, Aristotle (or his student) does not seem determined to criticize or urge the reform of such practices but is more interested, it seems, in describing and preserving them for posterity.

Simon Price, in a comment on Xenophon's *Anabasis* (composed about 370 BC), describes the link between public life and religion in Aristotle's ancient Greece. He writes:

> Many aspects of [ancient Greek religion] are surprising to those reared on Jewish or Christian religious

---

46. *Constitution of Athens* (Kenyon), 47, 50. Cf. 39, 42.
47. *Constitution of Athens* (Kenyon), 54, 57.
48. "Fragments," F 637, R3 in Barnes, *Complete Works*, 2458.
49. *Politics* (Jowett) IV.1.1289a15–16.

assumptions. In place of one male god, [...] there is a multiplicity of gods, even unidentifiable gods. Gods are both male (Zeus, Apollo) and female (Artemis). There is no religious sphere separate from that of politics and warfare or private life; instead, religion is embedded in all aspects of life, public and private. There are no sacred books, religious dogma or orthodoxy, but rather common practices, competing interpretations of events and actions, and the perception of sacrifice as a strategic device open to manipulation. Generals and common soldiers, not priests, decide on religious policy. The diviners are the only usual religious professionals, and religion offered not personal salvation in the afterlife, but help here and now, escape from the Persians or personal success and prosperity. Religious festivals combined solemnity and jollity. Practice not belief is the key and to start from questions about faith or personal piety is to impose alien values on ancient Greece.[50]

Suffice it to say, then, that Aristotle lived at a time where religious practice permeated every aspect of public life. Whatever his personal religious convictions on specific points, to interpret his philosophy while taking for granted the kind of divide between religion and everything else in modern secular liberal society is anachronistic. As we shall see, however, some academic interpretations of Aristotle seem to rely on this sort of modern dichotomy.

I am not suggesting that there is no criticism of religion in Aristotle's work. Or that the religion of his time was never superstitious, or devious, or just plain silly. This is a culture that relied on hepatomancy (*haruspicy*), the reading of entrails, for divine assistance in war. In what now seems a ludicrous sounding passage from the *Problemata*, a text that has roots in the later Aristotelian school (up to the fifth or sixth century AD according to some experts), some unknown

---

50. Price, *Religions of the Ancient Greeks*, 4.

author contemplates "Problems Concerning the Nose." He asks the question: "Why do we regard sneezing as divine, but not coughing or running at the nose? Is it because it comes from the most divine part of us, namely, the head, which is the seat of reasoning?"[51]

Now, as strange as customs and ideas from other historical periods seem to us, it must be admitted that there is some basis for this kind of question in ancient Greek religion and culture. Price reports on an incident described in Xenophon's *Anabasis*:

> When Xenophon was trying to persuade the men that they had fair prospects for leaving Assyria safely, a man sneezed and the crowd took this to be a sign from Zeus of Safety (Soter) and immediately did obeisance [bowed or knelt] to him. Xenophon proposed that they vow to sacrifice in thanks to that god [...] as soon as they reached a friendly land. [...] When they reached the north coast, they duly sacrificed oxen to Zeus and the other gods, and celebrated athletic games, a moral component of Greek festivals.[52]

One cannot imagine any modern person thinking that a sneeze was something sacred or portentous in any quasi-mystical way, yet here we have a religious culture and even an Aristotelian passage taking this issue very seriously. But it gets worse. As if that is not enough, this pseudo-Aristotle returns to the issue a second time, asking: "Why is it that the emission of other kinds of breath, e.g. passing wind and belching, are not regarded as sacred, but that of a sneeze is so regarded?"[53] The answer is that those "emissions of breath" are a sign of ill health or come from the lower regions of the body associated with appetites. "Thus, sneezing is revered as

---

51. *Problemata* (Forster) XXXIII.7.962a21–24.
52. Price, *Religions*, 2.
53. *Problemata* (Forster) XXXIII.9.962a32–b7.

sacred as being a sign of health in the best and most sacred region of the body and is regarded as a good omen."[54]

Surely, no one could seriously write such a "scientific" passage today. Yet, here it is, inserted into a *scientific* part of the Aristotelian corpus. Clearly, this is not religion at a level that makes sense today (or perhaps ever). Aristotle has some important things to say about religion, but this is not one of them. Still, there is something to be learned from the inclusion of this odd tidbit in the corpus. What this shows is that the Peripatetics were not afraid to ask questions about all sorts of strange things and that the scientific paradigm they inherited and preserved over hundreds of years does not fit neatly into our own narrow understanding of science. One cannot divest what has come down to us as Aristotelian philosophy from some sort of wider, quasi-religious background. We should be wary, then, of any attempt to turn Aristotle or later Aristotelians into secular positivists. At least someone in the Aristotelian school (perhaps at an advanced date) wondered about such superstitious things.

If, however, religion was a more pervasive influence in ancient Aristotelian thought than commonly acknowledged, this was not to suggest that Aristotle (or his followers) was uncritical or naïve about religious phenomena. In the *Economics*, in the discussion on government revenue, the author explains how shrewd but sometimes dishonest political leaders can use religion to enrich themselves and manipulate the populace. In one case, the Ephesians, who worshipped the goddess Artemis (Diana), inscribe the names of citizens on pillars in the temple in return for donations to the public treasury.[55] In another, the ruler Dionysius of Syracuse, an unscrupulous character, claims that he has had a vision of Demeter, the goddess, who orders all women citizens to bring their jewellery to the temple, a convenient excuse for extra tax revenue. The same ruler, on another

---

54. *Problemata* (Forster) XXXIII.9.962a32–b7.
55. *Economics* (Forster) II.2.1349a9–1349a13.

occasion, "ordered that any women who wished to wear gold jewellery should dedicate a fixed sum in the temple."[56] As the Aristotelian author indicates, these are devious strategies that fleeced the gullible.

Still, such stories tell us something about the historical period and the grip religion had on ordinary people. This sort of devious manipulation was only possible (and only *is* possible) because religion is such a potent force in the world. We tend to view such things from the viewpoint of Dionysius, the crafty politician, but think of it from the woman's viewpoint. If my name is always on a pillar in the temple, if I heed a vision, if I pay the temple tax, is that not a form of submission to the divine, even a meritorious form of prayer? In these cases, this "prayerful" behaviour may be an embodiment of naïve gullibility, but it does not follow that all instances of intercessory prayer are a matter of political trickery.

Suffice it to say here that Aristotle and ancient Aristotelians did not live in a secular world but in a culture permeated with religious references; they took religion seriously, but they were not naïve and acknowledged the exaggerations and deviousness of many religious phenomena. It does not follow from all this that Aristotle or his students were not sincerely religious. I will argue that they were religious but, also, at the same time, critical thinkers.

2.6. Jaeger: The Old Developmentalism

Werner Jaeger's highly influential account depicts Aristotle as a somewhat pious young man who left behind Platonic religious notions mid-career and turned to science for the rest of his career.[57] Jaeger concludes, "when Aristotle had completed his destructive criticism of Plato's [theory of immaterial forms], exact thinking and religious feeling went separate paths in him. To the scientific part of himself there was no longer any such thing as an Idea [i.e., a Platonic form]

---

56. *Economics* (Forster) II.2.1349a14–1349a24.
57. Jaeger, *Aristotle* (Robinson), 20.

[...] but in his heart it lived on as a religious symbol, as an ideal. He [now] reads Plato's works as poetry."[58] Of course, to say that Aristotle thought of Platonism, with its immaterial aspects and spiritualist orientation as mere poetry, as something symbolic rather than true, is to transform Aristotle into a positivist sort of philosopher who considers religion as human decoration or an aesthetic embellishment with little epistemological merit. To separate religion from its truth claims is not to take religion seriously.

Jaeger may seem slightly dated but Gerson points out that his developmentalism "has been widely embraced" and "is seldom questioned even when the details are disputed."[59] Yet the exegetical problems are numerous and intractable. Jaeger's project imposes a template on these works that is largely fuelled by contemporary concerns. I will not respond in any detail because his interpretation is so speculative. There is no way we can know, in any precise detail, the sequence in which texts or passages in the Aristotelian corpus were written. (Plato's corpus is at least more open to this sort of investigation.) G.E.R. Lloyd comments: "Chronological studies—the examination of the relative dates of composition of the dialogues and the treatises—*cannot* and should *not* be expected to provide answers concerning the predominant characteristics or preoccupations of Aristotle's philosophy."[60] This seems sound advice. We can harbour pet theories, but Aristotle's extant works were revised and edited over many years by subsequent editors. What we have now is, apparently, Andronicus of Rhodes's (fl. c. 60 BC) later compendium. Whatever editorial spin later Peripatetic editors or contributors may have inflicted on Aristotle's work is very difficult to determine.

---

58. Jaeger, *Aristotle*, 118. This is in a discussion of Aristotle's previously discussed poem to Hermias.
59. Gerson, *Other*, 13. Cf. J. M. Rist's *The Mind of Aristotle* for a similar account of Aristotle's philosophical chronology.
60. Lloyd, *Aristotle*, 25 (my emphasis).

It is, in any case, Jaeger's overall approach that seems problematic. To sum up the problems with Jaeger's developmentalism, here is a heated Walter Wehrle who protests against the partisan nature of his methodology. Wehrle writes:

> One of the most objectionable tendencies I find in developmentalism is the sheer audacity on the part of commentators who shamelessly think nothing of correcting, at every turn, what they (erroneously) perceive as Aristotle's failures. [...] Developmentalism gives rise to a reckless tendency to dismiss anything that would seem to be an anomaly (i.e., anomalous to developmentalist interpretations), and so, armed with developmental theories, [scholars] become no longer interpreters but revisers, rather like scientists who would fudge or ignore altogether the flagrantly contradictory empirical evidence that fits ill with their a priori theorizing. [...] Developmentalism itself is just one more tool by which scholars can dismiss these anomalous texts by consigning them to some early period [i.e., the immature Aristotle]. [...] The revised view actually becomes the tail that wags the dog, by guiding the interpretation of the actual text. One may well wish that Aristotle had been more like us, a positivist, say, or a materialist, but when one allows this desideratum to become the arbiter of what we are supposed to read into the disputed texts, I begin to wonder if one has not again abandoned the role of interpreter and taken on the prescriptivist role of the dogmatizer. Examples could be multiplied indefinitely.[61]

The problem with developmentalism is that, rather than explaining Aristotle's diverse philosophical arguments according to some overall scheme that makes sense of them

---

61. Wehrle, *Myth*, 2–3. Cf., for example, his response to Irwin's revisionist account of "strong dialectic" over intuition.

as a whole, it tries to impose a contrived chronology on the text so as to omit or delete systematically passages that do not conform to the favoured template. This is not a fair exegetical strategy; the meaning seems projected onto the text rather than arising naturally from wide reading. In reading Aristotle thoroughly, one does not get a sense of a man changing opinions (like a Bertrand Russell character) but of someone who adheres to a methodology and a general worldview in a stubbornly consistent way.

If Jaeger is to turn the *mature* Aristotle into a modernist philosopher who believes in science instead of religion, he needs to extricate the Platonic elements from his thought. As Gerson colourfully explains:

> If one follows the Jaegerian hypothesis, then the inconvenient Platonic bits in the works that are otherwise determined to belong to the late, anti-platonic phase of development have to be dealt with somehow. There is considerable scope for resourcefulness here. For example, we discover that a Platonic passage is a "remnant" of Aristotle's discarded past, something like a permanent food stain on one's shirt that one must simply endure. More typically, we find that such a passage simply indicates the "background" of the discussion, as if Aristotle was just acknowledging the air he was forced to breathe. Sometimes scholars simply avert their embarrassed eyes. We also find suggestions of sloppy scissors-and-paste jobs or even of nefarious tampering with the texts by overzealous Platonists. All these interpretive strategies arise from a common assumption: since the "mature" Aristotle is opposed to Platonism, any Platonism in the works of his maturity must be there under false pretenses. This assumption is so widely and deeply held that it is seldom exposed to scrutiny. But it is still just an assumption for all that.[62]

---

62. Gerson, *Other*, 4.

Any exegetical attempt to hive off an exclusively scientific worldview from the religious content in Aristotle's work seems a simplification. Did, then, Aristotle slowly turn towards atheism, agnosticism, or religious indifferentism in his career as he devoted himself more and more to science? This Enlightenment trope—that science supersedes religion as intelligence progresses—has antecedents in ancient thought but not, seemingly, in Aristotle. Aristotle's interest in religious subject matter—what Greek poetry was mostly about—seems to have gathered momentum at the end of his life. The usual view is that Aristotle finished the *Poetics* in the last decade of his life, around 330–320 BC, after working on a list of winning playwrights and of plays at the Pythian and Dionysian festivals.[63] I argue, however, in Chapter 5, that we cannot understand Aristotle's literary criticism without reference to the morality presupposed by ancient Greek religion.

Neither does the *Constitution of Athens*, cited above, display any disinterest or hostility to Athenian religious practices. But the suggestion is that this work must also have been written by Aristotle or by a student under his direction, "not very long before his death" (c. 328–322 BC).[64] If, however, Aristotle is mostly a physical scientist by this time, uninterested in (and even opposed to) all things religious, why all the effort to record (without criticism) all this largely religious framework of Athenian civic life. And there is further evidence in the fragments.

Chroust reports: "In what appears to be an intimate confession made probably during the last years of his life, and [in] what might be called a 'baring of his soul,' Aristotle is said to have written to his friend Antipater, 'The lonelier and the more isolated I am, the more I have come to love the

---

63. *Poetics* (Lucas) xiii
64. Based on references to historical details in the text. "The treatise was written ... not very long before his death." *Constitution of Athens and Related Texts* (von Fritz and Kapp), 5. Cf. Moore, *Aristotle and Xenophon*, 144.

myths.'"[65] Chroust maintains that this interest in the myths can be taken as a sign of a deepening religious commitment. As Plato's Cephalus says, older people do sometimes turn towards religion.[66] Whether or to what extent this was the case with Aristotle, I argue that Aristotle's literary tastes have religious content later in this book.

Even if one wants to accept Jaeger's hypothesis that Aristotle became more focused on science as his career progressed, it does not follow that this shift in emphasis necessitates any disavowal of religion. In the *Posterior Analytics* (a major text), Aristotle comments that an event may have two simultaneous causes: It may happen to fulfill an end or be necessitated by brute nature. He gives the example of light shining through a lantern at night, which must naturally happen because of light passing physically through the material but which also happens in order to prevent us from stumbling in the dark. He then adds another example by way of a question: "If then, a thing can exist through two causes, can it come to be through two causes—as for instance if thunder be a hiss and a roar necessarily produced by the quenching of fire, and also designed, as the Pythagoreans say, for a threat to terrify those that lie in Tartarus?"[67] This is, granted, a fanciful pairing of parallel causes. Aristotle is no Pythagorean. But whatever religious arithmetic one wants to impose upon the world, there is no reason why it cannot operate hand-in-hand with natural, physical causes. To focus on the physical side of things (as a scientist, for example) does not preclude religious belief as another reason for things. (This is discussed in Chapter 4.)

Indeed, the *Posterior Analytics* question is not so different than the sneezing example in the *Problemata*: a religious comment thrown in pell-mell among more serious scientific material. The text continues, as if nothing odd

---

65. Chroust, *Aristotle*, 22. The fragment is from Demetrius, *De Elocutione*, 144.
66. *Republic* VI.330d ff.
67. *Posterior Analytics* (Mure) II.11.94b32–94b34.

had happened, to mention that there are "very many such cases, mostly among the processes and products of the natural world," which may happen either for a set purpose (as with the lantern or frightening souls in hell) and/or by brute necessity. Whatever else is going on here, it seems at odds with Jaeger's developmentalism.

2.7. Melzer: The Esoteric Versus the Exoteric Aristotle

But there are other ways of bolstering the argument for a religiously indifferent Aristotle. Commentators often distinguish between Aristotle's exoteric and esoteric writings. The exoteric texts, mostly lost, seem to have been dialogues written in an elegant, Platonic fashion, intended for a wider, non-specialist audience. The more technical esoteric works—called "acroamatic" or "acroatic" (the ἀκροατικά: literally "designed for being listened to")—were intended for advanced students in a classroom situation. Arthur Melzer argues, along with many others, that Aristotle purposely concealed his anti-religious, atheistic views from the public, restricting them to the in-house esoteric works that, mostly, compose the extant corpus.[68] To borrow the Silenus statue image used at the beginning of the book but in reverse, Aristotle is religious on the outside and at least agnostic if not atheistic on the inside. He cultivated a religious appearance (to avoid political trouble) but was secretly a religious skeptic.

Melzer borrows a trope from the sixteenth- and seventeenth-century authors Pierre Gassendi and Joseph Glanvill, calling Aristotle a "cuttlefish," because, as a defensive measure, the cuttlefish squirts out a brown pigment (that the Romans used as ink).[69] Borrowing a line from Leo Strauss,

---

68. Melzer, *Philosophy Between the Lines*, see "Aristotle as 'Cuttlefish,'" 30–46. Deriving inspiration from Leo Strauss's *Persecution and the Art of Writing*.
69. Melzer, *Between the Lines*, 38. Hence the English word "sepia," to refer to reddish brown ink, derived from the Greek and Latin word *sepia* for cuttlefish.

Melzer dismisses, then, some of Aristotle's announced religious opinions as little more than a public relations operation to avoid getting in trouble with the authorities.[70] In his firm opinion, "Aristotle [is] a multilevel writer who hides some of his doctrines through intentional obscurity […] [and] also propagates certain salutary fictions or noble lies […] in the exoteric writings."[71]

Like Jaeger, Melzer has found a way to discount any evidence that runs counter to his own hypothesis. He argues, for example, that Aristotle hid his dissatisfaction with religious doctrines about the immortality of the human soul and divine providence:

> On this most important issue of life, the exoteric writings clearly proclaim a quasi-religious doctrine of personal immortality that is more in tune with political needs as well as popular wishes and longings. By contrast the acroamatic or philosophical [esoteric] works studiously avoid any clear declaration on the issue. […] They seem to point, quietly and obscurely, towards a more skeptical view that, whatever its precise details, denies personal immortality. It seems clear that, in the exoteric writings, Aristotle is indeed willing to endorse fictions and to affirm and even argue for—with all his characteristic earnestness and precision—[religious] doctrines he does not believe.[72]

Melzer is also convinced that Aristotle did not believe in any form of divine providence. He comments, "It seems fair to say, in sum, that Aristotle probably rejects providence, but, if he does, he deliberately conceals that conclusion. He generally evades the subject as much as possible, but occasionally speaks exoterically (but tepidly) in favor of providence."[73] We

---

70. Melzer, *Between the Lines*, 43.
71. Melzer, *Between the Lines*, 46.
72. Melzer, *Between the Lines*, 44.
73. Melzer, *Between the Lines*, 45.

are left with an Aristotle who publicly says he believes what he does not believe. For this sort of commentator, Aristotle's true attitudes to religion are much closer to modern secular attitudes.

Melzer shores up his case by citing from Ross who also distinguishes between the Aristotle of the exoteric works who is "probably accommodating himself to common opinions," and the Aristotle of the esoteric works who has a minimalist idea of God "remote from popular ideas."[74] If, however, Ross argues that Aristotle "has no serious belief in divine rewards and punishments" and "no interest […] in justifying the ways of God to man," unlike Melzer, Ross believes that Aristotle is a firm monotheist who believes in an intellectualized god and only accommodates himself to popular opinions when he discusses polytheism.[75]

Melzer cites an amusing passage from *Sale of the Philosophers* by Roman satirist Lucian (117–c. 180 AD), where the auctioneer sells two Aristotelians, the exoteric and the esoteric, for the price of one.[76] He places great weight on a disputed quote from Alexander of Aphrodisias (c. 200 AD) "that in the lecture notes, Aristotle gives his own opinions and the truth, while in the dialogues he gives the opinions of others, which are false."[77] Melzer portrays rival ancient commentators who believe that Aristotle is sincerely religious as partisan ideologues who unwittingly rely on passages from Aristotle's popular writings.[78]

There are many problems here. If Melzer surveys the ancient evidence in some detail, even Jaeger dismisses "the

---

74. Ross, *Aristotle*, 186.
75. Ross, *Aristotle*, 186.
76. Lucian, *Sale of Philosophers* 2:503.
77. Melzer, *Between the Lines*, 39. This is Elias, in his commentary on *Aristotle's Categories*, 24b33. Elias is quoting Alexander and disagreeing with him.
78. Melzer, *Between the Lines*, 42. He is referring to authors such as Ammonius (c. 400–c. 520), Olympiodorus the Younger (c. 495–570), Elias (sixth century).

notorious tradition about the difference between the exoteric and the esoteric writings," identifying it as a late ancient invention "originating in the spirit of Neo-Pythagoreanism."[79] More importantly, when we consult Aristotle's own references to his more public writing in the esoteric texts, we do not discover any hint of hidden contradiction or duplicity. Here are all the relevant passages.

Leaving aside *De Anima* I.4, which is clearly a reference to non-Aristotelian texts (such as the *Phaedo*), Aristotle makes the following references to his public works in his technical corpus:

- in *De Caelo* I.9, he asserts that his popular discussions confirm what he is presently arguing;
- in *Politics* III.6, he mentions that "there is no difficulty in distinguishing various kinds of rule" because "often, they have already been defined in our popular discussions";
- in *Politics* VII.1, he suggests that "enough has been already said in discussions outside the school [i.e., in public] concerning the best life";
- in *Nicomachean Ethics* I.5, he confirms that the subject of the best life "has been sufficiently treated even in ordinary discussions";
- in *Nicomachean Ethics* I.13, he affirms that "some things are said about [the human soul], adequately enough, even in the discussions outside our school";
- in *Nicomachean Ethics* VI.4, he tells readers that when it comes to the difference between *technê* and *phronêsis* "we treat even the discussions outside our school as reliable";
- in *Eudemian Ethics* I.8, he asserts that the insufficiency of the Platonic Idea of the Good "has been considered in many ways both in our popular and in our philosophic discussions";

---

79. Jaeger, *Aristotle*, 32.

- in *Eudemian Ethics* II.1, he reminds students that the basic distinction between external and internal goods is a "distinction we make even in our popular discussions";
- in *Metaphysics* XIII.1, he notes that "most of what we have to say [about Platonic Ideas] has been repeatedly stated in popular works";
- in *Generation of Animals* II.3, he comments that "it is plain from the discussions elsewhere" why a vegetable soul must be acquired first in fetal development; and
- in *Physics* IV.10, he makes a methodological point that "the best plan" for understanding the nature of time "will be to begin by working out the difficulties, […] making use of current [i.e., public] arguments."[80]

This is the extent of the textual evidence. Throughout, Aristotle never hints at any fundamental disagreement between public and private doctrines. Almost invariably, he refers to the exoteric texts *in support of* positions he elaborates in the technical texts. As he puts it, "popular philosophy often propounds a view that […] confirms what we have said [in the technical discussions]."[81] Furthermore, Aristotle never claims ownership of ineffable doctrines or "unwritten teaching" like those he attributes to Plato in *Physics* 209b11–13.[82] If, then, we are to base our exegesis on what Aristotle says, the idea of conflicting double doctrines seems a made-up exegetical invention.

Why, in any case, would Aristotle dismiss popular views when he himself often takes popular consensus—the *endoxa*—as a starting point for investigation? Doubtless, technical discussion refines and extends knowledge, but Aristotle is not someone who thinks the truth is fundamentally at odds

---

80. See 407b 29; 279a 30–33; 1278b31–32; 1323a22–23; 1096a4; 1102a26–27; 1140a1–3; 1217b20–23; 1218b30–33; 1076a28–29; 736a36; 217b29–31.
81. *De Caelo* VI.9.279a 30–33.
82. As Plato mentions notably in the disputed *Seventh Letter*.

with widespread opinion. He argues, for instance, that we should (at least in many cases) rely on what "*everyone* would decide,"[83] that we can trust "that that which *everyone* thinks really is so,"[84] that whatever "*all* men have some conception of" must be true,[85] and that what "*all* of us do" indicates what we all should believe.[86]

So, Melzer's basic argument, that there is a secret, esoteric, atheistic Aristotle who believes the opposite of what the public Aristotle professes seems dubious at best. It goes against the general spirit of Aristotle's philosophy. Melzer makes three other arguments we can quickly mention here. First, he claims that Aristotle secretly rejects personal immortality, citing famous passages in *De Anima* (408b18–29, 430a23) where, in his words, Aristotle grudgingly "asserts the immortality of a *small* part of the soul."[87] But this is to turn the evidence on its head. Aristotle claims that the very best, the most powerful, the most important part of the rational soul is divine, which seems to indicate some sort of religious framework. The *De Anima* passages (which are difficult) may have something to do with Aristotle's opposition to Platonic reincarnation, but there are other passages that seem to suggest that the whole soul might be divine.[88] For example, in some difficult earlier passages in *De Anima*, Aristotle seems to suggest that it is the decay and injury of the body that causes our faculty for thinking to be impaired, but that the thinking soul (which must include the passive *nous*) is eternal and indestructible. He writes, "Thought seems to be an independent substance implanted in us and to be incapable of being destroyed."[89] Again, in *Generation of*

---

83. *Physics* (Hardie and Gaye) VIIVI.5.257a27–29.
84. *Nicomachean Ethics* (Ross) X.2.1173a1–5.
85. *On the Heavens* VI.3.270b5–17.
86. *Nicomachean Ethics* (Ross) VI.12.1102a3–5.
87. Melzer, *Between the Lines*, 42–43.
88. This is a complicated topic. Cf. Aristotle, *Nicomachean Ethics* X.7.1177b27–1178a8, and elsewhere.
89. *De Anima* (Smith) I.4.408a18–19. The distinction here is between the body and the soul, not between the active and passive *nous*.

Animals II.3, in a very strange and not entirely consistent passage, he seems to suggest something like an eternal soul that re-enters into each new body from the outside.[90]

Second, Melzer discounts the religious tone of Neoplatonist commentary on Aristotle. Although the details are murky, the Neoplatonist commentator Elias, for example, claimed Aristotle argued for personal immortality in his lost *Eudemus*, an early work modelled after Plato's *Phaedo*.[91] But, whatever is true about that particular text, the real divide in ancient metaphysics is not between Platonism and Aristotelianism but between Platonism and atomism. Aristotle, however, explicitly rejects atomism. He reserves an important place for form and leans to the Platonic side of things, whatever the specific differences that separate him from Plato. I will argue, in Chapter 3, that a rigorous account of Aristotle's metaphysics cannot avoid religious conclusions. If this means, in Gerson's phrase, "understanding Aristotle as a Platonist, or understanding Aristotelianism as a type of Platonism," so be it.[92]

Third, Melzer puts too much weight on Aristotle's brief comment that "Wishing may be for things that are impossible—for example, immortality."[93] This off-hand comment is not part of any extended discussion of such matters and is not intended as a serious inquiry into the issue. Who knows precisely what the isolated quip means? Perhaps Aristotle means that wishing for *physical* immortality—to age without dying—is to hope for the impossible. As we shall see, Greeks did believe in personal immortality of an inferior sort.

---

90. Cf. Aristotle, *Generation of Animals* II.3.736b23–736b29.
91. Aristotle (allegedly) argues, "the soul is immortal since all men instinctively make libations to the departed and swear by them, but no one makes libations or swears by that which is completely non-existent." Cited in Gerson, *Other*, 52–53. Cf. Ross, "Fragments," frag. 3; Elias, *Commentarius in Categorias*; Barnes, *Complete Works*, 2400.
92. Gerson, *Other*, 7.
93. *Nicomachean Ethics* III.2.1111b22.

But let us turn away from the secondary literature and look at what Aristotle himself says about some of these issues. In the rest of this chapter, I consider Aristotle's attitude towards prayer, the virtue of piety, religious mythology, inspiration, and the paranormal. In most cases, we find evidence—some of it of an admittedly peripheral nature—that Aristotle was a practising pagan. He had, no doubt, highly intellectualized religious attitudes, but that is not the same as saying he was devoid of religious belief.

2.8. Aristotle and Prayer Generally

Religious people pray. If Aristotle was religious, he must have prayed. Contemporary philosophers such as Broadie and Mayhew have argued, however, that Aristotle did not take prayer seriously. Such secularized interpretations seem implausible once Aristotle is historically situated.

Let us begin with a quick definition of prayer, of which there are many different types and many different ways of construing what it theologically entails. Thinking about the nature of God (as many theologians do) is not enough for prayer. To turn such intellectual exercise into prayer, it has to be joined to some purposeful attempt to enter into immediate contact with the divine. One has to address, in some sort, the Divinity. The person praying may send messages of love, devotion, or loyalty; he or she may ask for divine favours; he or she may seek refuge in some sort of mystical embrace. As we shall see, intercessory prayer plays an important role in the Greek pagan tradition, but Aristotle has little to say about the nature of prayer.

A quick look for passages concerning prayer in the extant Aristotelica turns up scant material. In a discussion of the literary technique of metaphor, Aristotle compares intercessory prayer and begging "for both are varieties of asking."[94] In the *Nicomachean Ethics*, he maintains that men should pray that what fate provides with will make them

---

94. *Rhetoric* III.2.1405a18–20.

better men.[95] In the *Eudemian Ethics*, he makes a cursory remark about praying for more friends.[96] In *On the Heavens*, he mentions "that we use the number three in the worship of the Gods."[97] And in *On the Universe*, the pseudo-Aristotelian author confirms that the gods must exist in the heavens "for we all stretch up our hands to heaven when we offer prayers."[98]

Aristotle does distinguish, however, between good and bad prayers. With respect to bad prayers, he mentions the King Midas who was done in by "the insatiable greed of his prayer" and Philoxenus, a famous glutton who prayed "for the gullet of a crane" so he could prolong the tasting of food sliding down his throat.[99] Aristotle also mentions the "good prayer" of the poet Phocylides: "In many things the middle have the best; Be mine a middle station."[100] In the *Politics*, Aristotle describes the ideal city-state as the kind of city we should pray for (εὔχομαι) or the city organized according to prayer (κατ' ευχήν).

Ancient sources mention one lost book *On Prayer*, which some commentators dismiss as a very minor work.[101] Mostly, Aristotle has little to say on the topic of prayer. He also says little about the religious virtue of piety. In one minor Aristotelian text *On Virtues and Vices* (*De Virtutibus et Vitiis*), a later Peripatetic author identifies piety "towards the gods" as "first among the acts of justice."[102] There is no

---

95. *Nicomachean Ethics* V.1.1129b5–6.
96. *Eudemian Ethics* VII.12.1245b20–22.
97. *On the Heavens* (Stock) I.1.268b6.
98. *On the Universe* (Forster) 6.400a16.
99. *Politics* (Rackham) VI.9 1257b14–17; *Eudemian Ethics* III.2.1231a15–16. The ancients misplaced the taste buds in the throat.
100. *Politics* I.13.1259b33–34.
101. Diogenes Laërtius (V.22); *Vita Hesychii* (X.9). Cf. Mayhew, "Aristotle on Prayer," 297, 300. Rist claims that the work never existed. ("The End of Aristotle's *On Prayer*.") Cf. Chroust's "Comments on Aristotle's 'On Prayer.'"
102. Chroust, *Aristotle*, 233; *On Virtues and Vices*, 1.1250b18 ff.

reason to suppose that such sentiments were dramatically at odds with the original Aristotle, who insists, as already mentioned, that those who do not honour the gods should be punished.[103] Aristotle does argue that τιμή (honour) "is the greatest of external goods," in part because it "is that which we render to the gods."[104] And, in making a moral point about charitable relationships with subordinates, he notes "one does not offer all sacrifices even to Zeus."[105] The lesser gods require, it seems, their tribute as well. But religious piety does not seem to be an overriding concern in Aristotle's virtue ethics. Although there is no hint of any deep rupture between Aristotle and the general framework of Greek paganism, the emphasis is squarely on human psychology and the building of moral character.

Aristotle was himself accused of impiety for his poem in honour of his father-in-law, the tyrant Hermias because "the hymn heroised and divinised Hermias, to an extent that ordinary Greek religion did not allow."[106] But, a closer look at the little hymn, dedicated to the Areta (the personification of virtue), reveals an edifyingly epistle that reassures readers that the virtuous win an eternal reputation. As R. Renehan comments, "the charge is an obvious sham. The

---

103. *Topics* 1.11.105a1–10; Bodéüs, *Theology*, 8.
104. *Nicomachean Ethics* (Ross and Urmson) IV.3.1123b19–23.
105. *Nicomachean Ethics* (Bartlett and Collins) IX.2.1165a15–16. Cf. *Eudemian Ethics* (Solomon) VII.10. 1243b12–13: "God is satisfied at getting sacrifices as good as our power allows." *Nicomachean Ethics* (Ross) IX.2.1165a14–1165a36: "We should not make the same return to everyone, nor give a father the preference in everything, as one does not sacrifice everything to Zeus, … but since we ought to render different things to parents, brothers, comrades, and benefactors, we ought to render to each class what is appropriate and becoming." *Eudemian Ethics* (Solomon) VII.11. 1244a1–1244a19: "Even to Zeus we do not sacrifice all things, nor does he have all honours but only some."
106. McClymont, "Reading," 41; Barnes, Complete F675 R3; Diogenes Laertius, *Lives* V.7; Athenaeus, *Deipnosophistae* 15. 696a–697b. Didymus, in *Demosthenem* col. 6; Jaeger, *Aristotle*, 118; cf. Ford, *Aristotle as Poet*.

poem reveals no trace of impiety against traditional religious beliefs."[107] Robert Parker explains, "it is all but universally agreed," that Aristotle's "supposed offense [...] lay neither in his theological beliefs nor his attitude to the Eleusinian cult but in a particular expression of his love of a tyrant."[108] A Macedonian tyrant, in particular.

So what are we to make of all this? Piety (in Greek, εὐσέβεια: literally, "to honour or worship well") was, for ancient Greeks, the height of virtue. But piety requires acts of devotion and submission to the gods. In particular, citizens were expected to pay special homage to the god or goddess that protected their locality. This was part of what it meant to be a good Greek citizen. Reverence for the gods was a matter of morality and law as well as religion. So why did Aristotle write so little about religious topics such as piety and prayer? Because he was a secret atheist and did not believe in religion? Or because he mostly took traditional religious beliefs for granted and did not feel any need to explore them further? I suggest the second alternative, though that is not always a popular position in the secondary literature. Consider usual arguments for a religiously indifferent Aristotle.

2.9. Aristotle and Petitionary Prayer

Most commentators construe ancient Greek religious practice in terms of petitionary prayer: The good pagan Greek citizen prays to the gods to ask for favours or prays in thanks for favours received. As we shall see, this is a highly simplified picture of Greek pagan practice but, as the generally accepted view, it does not fit easily into Aristotelian metaphysics. Aristotle famously defines God—at least his supreme monotheistic metaphysical god—as "thought-thinking-thought" (ἡ νόησις νοήσεως νόησις).[109] I discuss this concept further below, but for the moment, it is enough to note that the god of Aristotle's

---

107. Renehan, "Aristotle as Lyric Poet," 253.
108. Parker, *Athenian Religion*, 276–277.
109. *Metaphysics* XII.9.1074b34. Cf. XII.7.1072b20–23.

metaphysics is rather like a philosopher in the sky spending his time thinking (because thinking is the best activity). If, however, this god is a thinking being, what must he be thinking about? Surely, he must be thinking of himself for he is the very best thing possible.[110]

There are obvious problems with this picture of a self-contemplating god but, for the moment, note how egregiously it clashes with the traditional picture of petitionary prayer. Aristotle seems to posit a bodiless, self-absorbed god who is too busy thinking to do anything else. This is God as an eternal, changeless, philosophical principle that its entirely turned inwards on himself. How could such a god answer prayers? The Greek gods, as conceived for the purposes of religious worship, were like glorified human beings with specific personalities; they played favourites, answering prayers for honours received and persecuting the religiously indifferent for slights real or imagined. They took an active interest in the world. This bears little resemblance to the philosophical god of Aristotle.

The idea that prayer serves no purpose when we are dealing with a contemplative Aristotelian god who spends all his time thinking about himself and does not answer prayers, has a long historical trajectory. Nineteenth-century classicist George Grote argues that a consistent Aristotle "must have contended that persons praying could have no additional chance of receiving the benefits they prayed for," rendering the Greek concept of piety useless.[111]

More recently, Mayhew and Broadie have added their voices to the chorus. Mayhew comments, "Aristotle arguably rejects the conception of the gods that prayer requires. [...] The idea that the gods are anthropomorphic in that they can hear individual requests (i.e., prayers) from humans, and respond to them, is not [according to Aristotle] true of the

---

110. Cf. *Metaphysics* XIVI.7, 9.
111. Grote, *Aristotle*, vol. 1, 18, n. b.

divine."[112] For her part, Broadie is convinced that a man of Aristotle's intellectual acumen could not join with *hoi polloi* in their "childish" and "ridiculous" beliefs that the gods would reward pious prayer with "thriving crops and herds," with "successful economic and social ventures," and with "ships coming [safely] home."[113] On her account, Aristotle has no patience for ordinary, working-class, commonplace accounts of prayerful piety. He is really a covert secularist (or atheist) who uses religious terminology to promote his own technical agenda.

Broadie identifies two planks in Aristotle's naturalistic platform. First, she argues that Aristotle maintains that "Piety towards god is, in its truest form, the disposition for intellectual activity engaged in as by the *sophos*, i.e. purely for love of the activity itself."[114] And, second, that he believes that the "devoted" philosopher "is rewarded, not through any sort of divine intervention, but 'in bursts of understanding.'"[115]

Broadie's naturalized interpretation of Aristotle omits all the god-references that we find in Aristotle. She buys into the esoteric interpretation, thinking that the secretly secular Aristotle was (for political reasons) forced to hide his real meaning behind a religious façade.[116] There is, really, no need to mention God (or gods) in any of this, which is just cover for Aristotle's resolutely scientific naturalism. On her account, Aristotle's pious individual is a studious secular academic motivated by love of his or her discipline who enjoys it for its own intrinsic value. All Aristotle means when he talks about the philosophical life as a pious imitation of the philosophical god is that "pious" individuals who spend their time thinking about their academic fields—biology, chemistry, philology, metaphysics, whatever—will enjoy, in return, bursts

---

112. Mayhew, "Prayer," 307–308. I cite the passage he is referring to below.
113. Broadie, "Piety," 62, 64.
114. Broadie, "Piety," 67.
115. Broadie, "Piety," 67.
116. Cf. Broadie, "Piety," 69.

of divine-like understanding. Pious individuals do not pray. Academic research is to replace religious practice and epistemological success is to replace piety.

Broadie places the secular academic life on a pedestal as an intellectual exercise that is self-sufficient in and of itself. But her de-sacralization of Aristotle—although it may eliminate embarrassing religious overtones—is not the original Aristotle. There are many problems with her influential interpretation. I will make a list so as not to get lost in the details.

2.10. Aristotle's Self-Thinking God and Petitionary Prayer

In the academic literature, the question "was Aristotle religious?" is often posed as the question: "could Aristotle have had any belief in petitionary prayer given his introspective conception of God?" One cannot deny that the Aristotelian corpus is inconsistent on the god question. There are many references to traditional religious belief, but then, there is the self-contained immaterial god of his metaphysics, which is completely at odds, it seems, with traditional pagan sources. What are we to make of all this? I do not think any of this shows that Aristotle was not a sincere religious thinker. Consider (1) how secularist commentators rely on a partisan hermeneutic; (2) the unfinished state of Aristotle's so-called theology; (3) how ancient pagans actually practised religious piety; (4) the problematic nature of Aristotelian friendship with the gods; (5) Aristotle's reverent account of intellectual forms of piety; and (6) how the ancient philosophical tradition viewed petitionary prayer.

2.10.1. The Esoteric Reading

First, an author such as Broadie has to rely on an esoteric reading to eliminate all the religious content in Aristotle. This is already problematic. This splitting of Aristotle into an exoteric-esoteric, religious-secular, Dr. Jekyll–Mr. Hyde combination has a long history, but (as I have shown) it is not based on solid evidence. Broadie thinks that an atheistic-leaning Aristotle could not publicly say what he really thought, which might be true. If, however, impiety was a dangerous proposition in Athens, the spirit of her suggestion seems wrong.

Those who favour an esoteric interpretation write as if Aristotle sets out to correct a colossally mistaken religious tradition. But there is no indication that Aristotle ever believed that Greek paganism was colossally mistaken. He comes across as a moderate thinker, proud of his Greek heritage with its religious and mythological underpinnings and putting on display conservative leanings that respect traditional opinions. Unlike Socrates, he did not engage in *elenchus*, the public refutation of popular or conventional belief. He accepts, though not uncritically, the truth found in earlier traditional belief (the *endoxa*). His correction of prior consensus is measured, technical, precise, respectful.

Many of the tropes one finds in ancient Platonism—the soul as divine, God as immaterial, thought as god-like, God as pure actuality, the soul as self-moved mover, philosophy as close to mystical illumination—are also found in Aristotle. But Greek paganism was a sprawling, multi-tentacled sort of thing, mixed up with magic and superstition. There were worrisome extremes. Consider the curious practice of "curse tablets," (κατάδεσμοι *katadesmoi*), lead shingles with a written script, buried in the ground, thrown in bodies of water, or nailed to temple walls, which included a plea to the chthonic or liminal gods such as Hermes, Charon, Hecate, and Persephone to harm the person (or persons) in question.[117] Someone like Aristotle could not have condoned such practices. There was, then, lots of room for the criticism of specific pagan practices. To suggest, on the other hand, that Aristotle did not consider himself a loyal pagan Greek is extreme.

2.10.2. Loose Theology

But there is a second issue that needs to be explored. Ross believed that Aristotle focused on solving puzzles (*aporiai*)

---

117. Interestingly, tablets that include the (relatively common) name "Socrates" have been found. Gager, *Curse Tablets*, 145. Cf. n. 100.

rather than the elaboration of a coherent synthesis. This may not be the case for his metaphysics, but I think that Aristotle's approach to theology is mostly problem-solving. If the extant Aristotelian corpus says little about religion, this is unsurprising. One would not expect, say, a Christian biologist to spend his time discussing the relationship between the First and Second Persons of the Trinity while analyzing the difference between hawks and eagles. As Bodéüs suggests, Aristotle's philosophy has enormous scope; he generally enters into theological territory on the margins of other discussions. Unlike Plotinus or the medieval schoolmen, Aristotle does not aim to come up with any overarching theological framework that solves all problems in any definitive way. There are many religious problems he does not broach and apparent contradictions in the extant texts. He practises, so to speak, loose theology, not tight theology.

The argument we are considering is that Aristotle could not be sincerely religious in any Greek pagan sense because he has the "wrong" conception of God. In Broadie's case, Aristotle's "thinking God" is code for the basic principle of abstract thinking rid of any preternatural aspects. The academic, in thinking, rises up to the level of God, and is rewarded with bursts of secular understanding. There is no real divine, just thinking valued as an intrinsically pleasurable activity.

But, ironically enough, this sort of reasoning makes Aristotle out to be more of a theologian than he really is. It is as if Aristotle had one fixed idea of God and an entire system of philosophy that revolved around that fundamental point. Nothing could be further from the truth. Aristotle takes very seriously the idea of God-thinking-himself, but he also takes seriously the Greek pagan tradition. There is no overall orientation in his work that excludes traditional practices of Greek piety as somehow wrong-headed or misleading. If anything, there is a sort of bifurcation in Aristotle's work: metaphysically, there is a line of reasoning that leads us to this idea of a self-thinking god, but then there is a practical, moral, aspect of his thinking that leads to a respect for traditional religious authority. The problems here are philosophical rather than merely exegetical.

Does Aristotle believe in a self-thinking god who does not answer prayers? The answer seems to be yes and no. When we think of God thinking of the very best thing, we are led logically to the conclusion that he must be thinking of himself. This follows necessarily. But seen from another perspective, this seems to require a narcissistic god self-absorbed in himself.[118] But self-absorbed narcissism is not an admirable trait, and so it seems logically incorrect to attribute such a thing to God (who has to be the best in every possible way). Aristotle and ancient Aristotelians are fully aware of the problem. In the *Magna Moralia*, Aristotle (or his followers) follows the first line of reasoning but go on to conclude: "God will contemplate himself. But this is absurd. For if a human being surveys himself, we censure him as stupid. It is absurd then [...] for God to contemplate himself."[119] So, here, nestled, in the same Aristotelian corpus, we find a line of reasoning mocking the idea of a self-thinking god.

Is God a self-thinking being or not a self-thinking being? I do not think that Aristotle (or his followers) offer any definitive, adequate answer to such questions. Philosophy takes time. One can find an answer perhaps in Neoplatonism or scholasticism, but not in the earlier Aristotle. One can try to distinguish between better and worse texts—the *Metaphysics* being a more authoritative text or of an earlier strata than the *Magna Moralia*—but there is no neat solution to this kind of conundrum. Saying that Aristotle was not a practising pagan because he foresaw that a certain line of metaphysical

---

118. *Magna Moralia* II.15.1212b370–1213a7.
119. *Magna Moralia* (Stock) II.15.1213a5–7. There are, of course, other ways to arrive at the concept of a self-contemplating God. For Aristotle, activity is better than passivity; it follows that God, as the best possible being, must be pure activity. Cf. *Metaphysics* XII.7.1072b20–29 (Ross): "That capable of receiving the object of thought ... is active when it possesses this object. The possession rather than the receptivity is the divine element. [...]" And so on.

reasoning leads in a certain direction, is to simplify what is going on his work. If anything, it is to ignore the relevant evidence.

After all, as I have already mentioned, the extant records show that Aristotle himself engaged in petitionary prayer. To cite from his *Last Will and Testament*: "Nicanor, if he is preserved (which is a prayer I have offered on his behalf) is to set up statues in stone four cubits in height to Zeus Saviour and Athena Saviouress at Stagira."[120] Aristotle records that he has offered up a prayer on behalf of Nicanor. One could not be more explicit. Yet, the widespread consensus is that this is an authentic text. How, then, can scholars come to the conclusion that Aristotle was not a practising pagan because he could not have believed in petitionary prayer?

But it is not just the admission about prayer. It is also about the statues. A cubit is about 18 inches, which means that Aristotle is commissioning statues that were 6 feet high. A conspicuous display of piety that dovetails with ancient Greek models of religious piety. As Pulleyn reports:

> The best example of how acts of thanksgiving are compounded of prayer and offering is the colossal mass of *ex voto* inscriptions which survive from the ancient world […] This is an extremely important and central practice of Greek life. […] When one has received a favor from a god; it is only correct to give something in return.[121]

What one finds inscribed on the statues or objects of piety are things like "in commemoration of receiving a favor from Hermes" and "in fulfillment of a vow."[122] If, then, Aristotle asks that the statues be erected after Nicanor comes safely home, there is nothing unusual here. Pulleyn explains the pagan mentality: "If the prayer was answered, that was the time

---

120. Diogenes Laërtius, V.11–16; in Barnes, *Complete Works*, 2465.
121. Pulleyn, *Prayer*, 40. Nicanor was Aristotle's future son-in-law.
122. Pulleyn, *Prayer*, 40.

to erect a monument."[123] So Aristotle was, in this intimate detail from his practical life, conforming to the details of pagan religious customs. It would be a very unfriendly doctrine to suggest that Aristotle was disingenuous.

2.10.3. A Caricature of Pagan Piety

In any case, thinkers who discount Aristotle's religious convictions, usually rely on a secular caricature of pagan petitionary prayer. Here is a third reason to be wary of their conclusions. An author such as Broadie thinks Greek piety features self-interested and morally indifferent penitents buying favours from the gods through financial donations to temples and priests. But this is a strawman account akin to the argument that the cynical Glaucon makes in the *Republic* that the unjust man, whatever evil he pursues, will be able to win the gods' favour if he pays them off with magnificent sacrifices and temple offerings.[124] Glaucon depicts religious devotion as little more than an insurance racket: The gods will reward us handsomely if we pay high enough fees in temple buildsing and offerings. The more we pay, the better the insurance. If we buy enough insurance, the gods will look the other way whatever evil business we are about.

But mainstream Greek piety was not—as Glaucon's caricature has it—a matter of buying, say, a θυμιατήριον (thurible) filled with resin incense to burn at a temple and sending a commercial request up to the heavens for an expected benefit. It was about developing a relationship with the gods, like a relationship with a family member pushed up to a supernatural level. One honours one's mother, but one also expects one's mother to care for her children. That was how the Greeks approached their gods. (Granted there are all sorts of exceptional and contrarian exceptions in Greek tragedy and the myths, but the general picture is we are loyal to our gods and they are loyal to us.) Add to this the general

---

123. Pulleyn, *Prayer*, 37.
124. *Republic* 362c.

expectation in all religions that petitionary prayer should be accompanied by heartfelt reverence and moral behaviour. Thoughtful pagans did not believe that the gods could be bought off by pious bribery. Glaucon's suggestion that the best religion can offer is this kind of base commercial bargaining is intended by Plato as irreverent caricature.

In pagan Greek culture, the gods are the guardians of morality. They reward the good and punish the bad. (I will discuss fate in Chapter 4.) Aristotle believes firmly in the intrinsic value of moral behaviour. As he puts it, "A man is noble and good because he possesses noble goods for themselves, and because he practices what is noble for its own sake."[125] So one does not practise morality in order to seek favours from and avoid punishment at the hands of the gods. If, however, morality is good in itself, it does not follow that the gods do not require morality or that immoral acts will not be punished by the gods. Every sincere religious believer believes that divinity is on the side of the good and an enemy of evil and that morality is intrinsically valuable behaviour at the same time.

Authors such as Broadie treat this as an exclusive disjunction as if one has to believe either that morality is valuable for its own sake or that the gods are the guardians of morality. But one can embrace both beliefs at the same time (as every religious believer does). Certainly, in the ancient Greek mind, piety and morality coalesce. Plato points, for example, to temple thieving as a paradigm example of very serious evil because it is both sacrilegious and immoral at once.[126] It doubly offends against religion and morality. To feed his unruly appetites, the temple thief desecrates what is holy. So, intemperance and a lack of piety coalesce in a single wicked act. This is how the ancients thought of the relationship between morality and religion, not as separate but as

---

125. *Eudemian Ethics* (Solomon) VII.15. 1248b34–35. Cf., also, 1249a9–10.
126. *Republic* IX.575b; cf. *Laws* (Saunders) IX.853d: "The first law I will produce will deal with thievery from temples."

conjoined aspirations; one was to be moral and pious at the same time. One aspiration reinforced and complimented the other. (Plato's *Euthyphro* could be read as a philosophical challenge to this marriage of religion and morality, but I think it is a mistake to read any nuance of impiety into the work. Socrates is worried that Euthyphro is being impious by accusing his own father.)

What, then, did pagan petitionary prayer *fairly construed* entail? To begin with, we need to situate it in a wider historical context. In ancient Greece, prayer was everywhere. As Walter Burkert comments, there was "rarely a ritual without prayer, and no important prayer without ritual."[127] The Greeks celebrated and communicated with the gods through a wide assortment of practices: blessings before meals, hymn-singing, temple liturgies, animal sacrifice, consulting oracles, parades and processions, theatre festivals, pilgrimages, participation in the mystery cults, the erection of votive statues, the wearing of amulets and charms, libations, and so on. Petitionary prayer was not the only kind of prayer. As the pagan Greek mind sees things, there is another sphere of reality to which we secularized moderns have been desensitized. Prayer was a matter of turning attention to what supernaturally exists, acknowledging our dependence on that realm of existence, consulting it, revering it, worshipping it, and celebrating it.

It is true that the pagan Greeks petitioned the gods for whatever they needed. Why would they not? If one believes that the gods influence fate (or even that Fate [*Fortuna*] is a deity on its own account), it only makes sense to have recourse to petitionary prayer regularly. This was certainly the Greek way. But honest pagans tried to cultivate a personal relationship with their patron gods. There was a mutual sort of give-and-take with loyalty on both sides: the gods were to show a loyalty towards human followers by helping them through the difficult circumstances of their lives and

---

127. Burkert, *Greek Religion* (Raffan), 75.

believers were to show a loyalty towards their own gods by honouring them whenever they could. As Pulleyn reports:

> Whichever sort of prayer [we are talking about], the fundamental issues are χάρις [reciprocal goodwill] and τιμή [honour]. Either one tells the god he is already indebted to you for the τιμή you conferred on him in the past or else you promise to confer some more τιμή in the future if your request is granted. The relationship of the Greeks with their gods in prayer [...] can best be thought of as a continuum of reciprocal χάρις extending both forward and backward in time.[128]

As we shall see, Aristotle proposes a more intellectualized notion of piety, but does he dispute this general picture? It does not seem so.

If pious Greeks cultivated relationships with their patron gods, there is a neglected side to this sort of reciprocal exchange. Pulleyn explains:

> From the earliest times, characters in the works of Greek literature were in the habit of upbraiding their gods if they thought they were failing to live up to proper standards of behavior, by neglecting the claims of reciprocal obligation or by failing to show sufficient wisdom in their dealings with human kind.[129]

Believers could be "cranky" with their gods; they could not merely lament but complain outright in their prayers that their divine protector was not doing enough for them and had neglected their needs in their time of suffering. Or complain that their gods needed to do a better job wisely governing the world. In pagan Greek religion, the gods could be talked to, cajoled, taken to task, reproved, or honoured.

---

128. Pulleyn, *Prayer*, 37.
129. Pulleyn, *Prayer*, 215.

One could demand the loyalty—in both directions—that friendship entails. One could have, so to speak, an (unequal sort of) friendship with one's favourite gods.

But, along the same lines, one could also have a relationship with the dead, which paralleled the back-and-forth between penitents and their gods. As Pulleyn puts it:

> The dead were remarkably like the gods [...] in the cult they received. They were, however, not gods. Gods are extremely powerful. Heroes are rather less so, being subject to the power of the chthonic rulers, Hades and Persephone. The ordinary dead have an even more restricted sphere of influence. What is most significant, however, is that they were seen as part of a network of χάρις every bit as much as the gods.[130]

As with the gods, the pagan view of the dead in Hades involved the usual exchange of honour in return for favours. One prayed to the dead who, in return, were supposed to send good things back from the underworld. This is in keeping with traditional notions of piety.

But this highlights another point of possible contradiction between the practices of Aristotle as a pagan believer and his philosophical texts. As is well known, Aristotle suggests in *De Anima* III. 5 (408b18–29, 430a23) that only the active *nous* is eternal. Colloquially put, only the divine spark of intelligence that activates the rational mind continues to exist after death. The passage (which I discuss below) is obscure but it would seem to indicate that no personal individuality survives human death. If the passive part of the mind perishes at death (as this passage seems to indicate), this eliminates memory or even differentiated thought for we need a passive mind to engage in such things. All that seems to survive is the light in the mind that makes awareness possible,

---

130. Cf. Pulleyn, *Prayer*, Chap. 7, "Prayer and the Cult of the Dead," 116–131.

a general capacity for thought without any specific content (which is, perhaps, in part, why some commentators such as Alexander of Aphrodisias identified the active mind with God).[131] If, of course, no true individuality survives death that might also be an argument against Platonic doctrines of some sort of individual judgment after death; or it might be an argument (I think) against Platonic doctrines of recollection (*anamnesis*). If no memory or even differentiated thought remains, this would seem to rule out the possibility of innate knowledge and necessitate some empiricist theory of mind relying on induction (*epagôgê*). Aristotle's reasoning is not entirely clear, here, but he seems to want to say that only something that is pure actuality without passivity could be eternal. Perhaps this frustratingly incomplete passage is Aristotle following through on that particular line of reasoning.

Yet, in his *Last Will and Testament*, Aristotle takes care to fulfill all his obligations towards the dead in line with the ordinary conceptions of Greek piety. Along with the statues of Athena and Zeus, Aristotle leaves instructions to use funds from his estate to set up several statues for relatives: his mother, his brother (Arimnestus), and his brother-in-law (Proxenus). He piously dedicates the statue of his mother to Demeter, the traditional goddess of motherhood. But, in an ancient Greek context, this is very suggestive of the cult of the dead, which presupposed an immortal existence in Hades for souls that pass from this world. This was a deficient sort of personal immortality—as Achilles complains to Odysseus—for it meant living as a shade in Hades but it was, nonetheless, an eternal life for the individual who dies.[132]

Sappho (c. 630–c. 570 BC) captures the general Greek attitude in her poem "to a rich lady," cited by Plutarch, where

---

131. This commentator's understanding of Aristotle's theory with its discussion of a dispositional and a material mind seems deeply problematic but let us leave that aside here.
132. *Odyssey*, 1148–1491.

she upbraids the unknown woman for her lack of education and for her neglect of the poetry and the arts and condemns her as a person of no consequence:

> When you are dead you will lie in your grave, forgotten forever
> Because you despise the flowers of the muse; in Hades—as here—
> Dimly your shadow will flit with the rest, unnoticed, obscure.[133]

The poet is warning the rich lady of her impending fate but—notice—she does not say here that the lady will cease to exist after death. No, she will go to Hades, along with everyone else, where she will flit around like an anonymous shadow among the masses of the dead without any distinction and without anyone taking notice of her. This is in line with the cult of the dead that posited as the worst possible punishment, not the total destruction of human souls (which continue to exist in Hades forever), but neglect, oblivion, and abandonment by others. The rich lady will not have a statue erected in her honour. No one will pray to her; even the dead will give her the cold shoulder. (The cult of dead ancestors and all it entailed was common in early societies worldwide.)

Why, then, would Aristotle erect a statue to his dead mother in line with common pagan religious obligations unless he was participating in the cult of the dead, which presupposed some sort of personal immortality? McClymont writes: "Aristotle accepts traditional beliefs about the dead."[134] He points to Aristotle's somewhat odd insistence, in the *Nicomachean Ethics*, that we can be unhappy after we are dead. Aristotle reports: "for [the dead] not to be touched in any way by the fortunes of their descendants and all their friends seems excessively disagreeable and opposed

---

133. Sappho # 65, cited in Kitto, *Greeks*, 87.
134. McClymont, "Reading," 43.

to common opinions."[135] If, however, the dead continue to exist in Hades and watch what happens in the world from below (as the cult of the dead had it), they would presumably be happy or disappointed by the good or bad that befalls their living friends and descendants. The idea that our happiness can still be damaged even if we are dead seems to presuppose Greek beliefs about ancestral piety.

Aristotle's reasoning about the undifferentiated active mind as the sole survivor after death does not cohere with his apparent commitment to the cult of the dead. One can fill in the logical gaps in Aristotle's reasoning about the active mind: anything eternal must be entirely self-sufficient (independent of exterior factors); so the passive part of the mind cannot be eternal (because it depends on something outside of itself for its actualization). It follows that only the active part of the mind (which actualizes itself on its own) can be external. One can logically get to the same conclusion in other ways. But as is the case with the Aristotelian idea of a self-contemplating god, Aristotle (or his followers) never attempt to devise a complete theology that resolves all the attendant issues. (Other examples will be mentioned later.) It remains that Aristotle seems to have been a practising pagan with all the belief commitment that entails.

2.10.4. Friendship with the Gods

Once we understand this cultural background, we can make much better sense of some of the issues Aristotle feels the need to address in his philosophy. The familiar argument that Aristotle does not believe in petitionary prayer, for his god is too self-absorbed to pay attention to anything outside himself, ignores the larger picture. In the *Nicomachean Ethics*, Aristotle compares the gods to caring parents. He writes: "The friendship of children to

---

135. *Nicomachean Ethics* (McClymont, 43) I.10.1101a18; cf. 1101a34–1101b9. For a contrary view, cf. Thompson, *Ethics of Aristotle* (1956), 48–49.

parents and men to gods is a relation to something good and superior; for they have conferred the greatest benefits, since they are the causes of their being and their nourishment, and their education from birth."[136] The gods merit our friendship the way parents merit the friendship of their children. The gods are like our parents as the cause of our coming into being, our nourishment, and our education. They somehow take care of us and we, in turn, honour them the way we should honour our parents (another key tenet of Greek morality). I will not offer any extensive exegesis here, but this seems to be a rather typical expression of Greek χάρις (piety).

But, Aristotle, who takes philosophy seriously, notices a logical problem. In the aftermath of Christianity, it has become commonplace to think that we can have a reciprocal relationship with God. Aristotle believes that God is "a living being that partakes of knowledge."[137] But he also argues that friendship requires equality, which makes friendship with the gods an almost impossible ideal. In his own words:

> If there is a great interval in respect of virtue or vice or wealth or anything else between the parties, they are no longer friends, and do not even expect to be so. And this is most manifest in the case of the gods; for they surpass us most decisively in all good things. But it is clear also in the case of kings. [...] [where] it is impossible to define exactly up to what point friends can remain friends; for much can be taken away and friendship remains, but when one party is removed to a great distance, as God is, *the possibility of friendship ceases* [my emphasis].[138]

Aristotle suggests, here, that friendship with his monotheistic god—at least his supreme metaphysical god—is impossible.

---

136. *Nicomachean Ethics* (Ross) VIII.12.1162a4–7.
137. *Topics* V.4.132b13–14.
138. *Nicomachean Ethics* (Ross) VIII.7.1158b33–1159a5.

What we are supposed to think about lesser gods is perhaps harder to tell.

In the *Magna Moralia* we read: "it would be strange if one were to say that he loved Zeus."[139] Why? Because Zeus is a forbidding, even terrifying power? Because one is supposed to submit to Zeus, not love him? Because Zeus would not tolerate any equal? The text continues: "For friendship [...] exists only where there can be a return of affection, but friendship towards God does not admit of love being returned, nor at all of loving."[140]

This contradicts the earlier quote, but it even gets worse. Aristotle believes that friends should wish for the very best for their friends. But the very best thing for a friend would be to become a god. (This happened regularly enough in Greek mythology: for example, Asclepius, Hercules, Psyche, Ariadne, etc.) So, it seems that we should wish that our friends become gods. But we cannot wish this as that would mean we could no longer be friends for we cannot be friends with gods. A puzzled Aristotle continues:

> This is the origin of the question of whether friends really wish for their friends the greatest goods, e.g. that of being gods; since in that case their friends will no longer be friends to them, and therefore will not be good things for them (for friends are good things). The answer is that [...] a friend must remain the sort of being he is. [...] It is only so long as he remains a man that [a friend] will wish for [a friend] the greatest goods.[141]

But let us leave aside this strange aporia. We are interested, here, in Aristotle's attitude towards prayer and piety. And he does seem to propose an ingenious solution to this sort of dilemma, which we will consider in the next section.

---

139. *Magna Moralia* (Stock) II.11.1208b30.
140. *Magna Moralia* (Stock) II.11.1208b28–30.
141. *Nicomachean Ethics* (Ross) VIII.7.1159a5–11.

None of this shows that Aristotle was not a practising pagan. Indeed, he and his school seem to think that such questions are worth discussing, which would be a waste of time if there was nothing true or serious about religion. But, here as elsewhere, Aristotle is exploring the logical ramifications of belief; it is not as if he is proposing a definitive answer to all these questions. I do not think that Aristotle has a completely worked out system of theology to deal with all these problems and inconsistencies. If Aristotle was a pious pagan and if his position on friendship seems to distance us from the gods, this seems to undermine any orthodox notion of Greek piety. Except that Aristotle cleverly finds a way to insist on the importance of philosophy while respecting traditional Greek piety.

2.10.5. A Religious Strategy: Intellectual Piety
An author such as Broadie suggests that the secular Aristotle had no real interest in religion and believed that those of us who are smart enough should, in effect, forget about religious practice and pursue the academic life of philosophy for its own sake. But this is the wrong way to understand Aristotle's attitude, which gives us a fifth reason to be leery of such secularized accounts.

When Aristotle defines his supreme monotheistic metaphysical god as a thinking principle and philosophy as an imitation of that god, he is not rejecting religion; he is adopting a strategy that is intended to reconcile the practice of philosophy with traditional notions of piety. Aristotle proposes a *mimēsis* piety; we are to give honour and glory to God by imitating his nature as closely as possible. As they say, imitation is the best compliment. We pay respect to God, then, by doing philosophy. This rescues philosophy from the traditional accusation of atheism (a common trope in ancient Greece) and turns it into a religious activity par excellence.

Aristotle turns philosophy into something akin to religious observance. He does not refute Greek religion; he argues that the cultivation of the intellect—the best part of us—is the most noble service to the gods and, therefore, a higher form of religious piety for those with the requisite intellectual talents. Philosophy represents, if anything, an intensification of the religious impulse. Aristotle formulates an argument championing philosophy *because* it is religious. He emphasizes the *holiness*—the word is not too strong—of philosophy. Whatever this is, it does not sound like atheism.

Aristotle identifies what philosophers are engaged—in contemplation, literally, theory (θεωρία)—with the activity of the divine. Again, this follows from a certain line of reasoning. Aristotle thinks that the gods must spend their time doing whatever is best. But it seems, to anyone with a philosophical bent at least, that doing philosophy is the best. For philosophy is the apotheosis of thinking and knowledge and this is the best anyone can achieve. The gods, then, must spend their time, doing philosophy. To believe that they are on Mount Olympus feasting—drinking and eating—would be crass or tasteless; indeed, impious.

Aristotle asks: What would the gods do with their time? His comments here balance uncomfortably between polytheism—he speaks of the gods in plural—and his monotheistic metaphysics, a combination which is, admittedly, not easy to sort out. These complications aside, here is his way of arguing for philosophical gods:

> What sort of actions must we assign to the gods? Acts of justice? Will not the gods seem absurd if they make contracts and return deposits, and so on? Acts of a brave man, then, confronting dangers and running risks because it is noble to do so? Or liberal acts? To whom will they give? It will be strange if they are really to have money or anything of the kind. And what would their temperate acts be? Is not such praise tasteless, since they have no bad appetites? If we were to run through them all, the circumstances of action would be found trivial and unworthy of gods. Still, everyone supposes that they *live* and therefore that they are active; we cannot suppose them to sleep like

Endymion. Now if you take away from a living being action, and still more production, what is left but contemplation? Therefore the activity of God, which surpasses all others in blessedness, must be contemplative.[142]

When Aristotle defines God as "thought-thinking-thought" this description comes close to what the activity of philosophy is about: thought turned critically and reflexively inward, so to speak, peering back on itself.[143] If, then, God is reflection on reflection or intelligence about intelligence—or some meta-level inquiry of that sort—is this not the same as saying that the nature of God can be equated (in some superhuman sense, of course) with the act of doing philosophy? And if this is true, then, when we do philosophy, we are imitating God's nature, which seems (for all sorts of religious reasons) to be a pious thing to do.

And there are other reasons to opt for a more religious reading of Aristotle's meaning. As Andrea Nightingale reports, the root meaning of the word that Aristotle uses for theory, θεωρία (*theôria*), is largely religious. She explains:

> *Theôria* is generally defined as a journey or pilgrimage to a destination away from one's own city undertaken for the purpose of seeing as an eye-witness certain events and spectacles. In the classical period, *theôria* [...] involved pilgrimages to religious oracles or festivals and [...] travel[ling] abroad as a researcher or tourist. In the first and most traditional sense, a *theôria* was a civic embassy sent to an oracular center, generally for the purposes of consulting the oracle. The ambassador called the *theôros* was an official envoy whose role was to journey to the shrine, perform specific sacrifices and rituals, consult the oracle, and bear witness to the events or activities that transpired there. He was then required to return to his native city and give a complete and

---

142. *Nicomachean Ethics* (Ross and Urmson) X.8.1178b8–23.
143. Which almost sounds like a description of phenomenology.

honest account of what he had witnessed and heard. The *theôros* is thus charged with the task of communicating to the city what the god has unveiled to him. The *theôros*, then, is carrying out a transaction with divine as well as with human beings: this is a mission that must be done with religious correctness. […] *Theôria*, then, was a cultural practice that brought Greeks from different cities and ideologies into contact with one another in shared religious sanctuaries. […] [In] journeys to a religious festival or oracular center the *theôros* not only encounters foreign peoples and places but also interacts with the god who presides over a given festival or shrine (by participating in the sacrifices, prayers, and rituals). Here, the *theôros* encounters the ultimate and most distant "other," a divine being. Though he does not literally "see" this being, he does look at sacred images and symbols of the divinity and, by way of ritual, enters into a relationship with a god.[144]

Although the term *theôria* has a wider meaning, it originates in the notion of a pilgrimage involving long-distance travel to eyewitness something holy, like the Dionysia or the Olympic Games, in order to eyewitness something momentous and sacred.[145] Francis Cornford argues that it was the Pythagoreans who borrowed the word to mean something more strictly philosophical and epistemological.[146] Aristotle, in identifying philosophy as *theôria*, borrows from Plato some of these basic Pythagorean themes.

If, then, Aristotle tells us that God is doing *theôria*, he does not mean "theory" in the modern sense of accessing or assembling together a system of logical explanatory principles.[147] Aristotle's god has already arrived at truth. He does

---

144. Nightingale, "On Wandering and Wondering: *Theôria*," 29–30, 33.
145. Cf. Nightingale, "*Theôria*," 4, n. 3.
146. Cornford, *From Religion to Philosophy*, 200.
147. Again, cf. *Nicomachean Ethics* X.8.1178b20–4; 1178b32; *Protrepticus* B44.

not need to ask or answer questions. He is not engaged in data collection, what Aristotle calls *historia* (ἱστορία, from the Greek verb ἱστορέω: to inquire), nor is he involved in logical demonstration, what Aristotle calls ἀπόδειξις (*apodeixis*).[148] He is not writing books or journal articles. He is not arguing with interlocutors or trying to persuade them of anything.

Aristotle's contemplative god is directly apprehending the truth. Think, then, of the *theôria* of God as a kind of theatre. (The English terms "theatre" and "theatrical" derive from the Greek root *theôria*.) Theatre involves gazing upon a spectacle. Aristotle's god is, then, like a spectator, a *theôros* at a religious festival. Except, of course, according to the self-thinking line of reasoning, God is watching himself, because he is, so to speak, the best show in town.

But there are perhaps ways to interpret God's self-contemplation more broadly. We could posit that God is gazing upon himself as the ultimate explanatory principle for everything. In an effortless intuition, Aristotle's god sees why and how everything in the cosmos holds together because of his own nature. He is the apex where all general principles come together in an ultimate self-realization. The philosopher who inquires into the origin of things inevitably ends up thinking about the ultimate explanatory principles and, thus, shares in God's contemplation of himself. Someone opposed to religion could surely have chosen a different route, particularly in the esoteric teachings, to explain the nature of philosophy.

Later Neoplatonic authors such as Plotinus and Proclus are not so far from Aristotle when they situate divine reason in non-discursive intuition, what they call *nous*.[149] Suffice it to say here that ancient philosophers often conceived of logical argument as a ladder to be thrown away once the

---

148. As in his *Historia Animalium* or *History of Animals*.
149. Modern commentators in the analytic tradition are notably uncomfortable with non-discursive accounts of *theôria,* Cf. Sorabji, "Myths about Non-Propositional Thought."

truth seeker, like a *theôros*, arrives at the destination of truth. Hence, Plato's prisoner who escapes the cave and spends his time looking straight at the sun (epistemologically situated at the top of the Divided Line). Or the philosopher of Socrates's speech in the *Symposium* who climbs the ladder of knowledge until he gets to the top and can gaze on beauty in itself. Aristotle seems to have no problem accepting this general trope (although I cannot report on the specifics of his epistemological account here).

Commentators want to distinguish between the youthful and the older Aristotle (developmentalism) or between the private and the public Aristotle (esoterism). Here, however, is the youthful Aristotle, arguing in the *Protrepticus* (*Exhortation to Philosophy*), a public work, that doing philosophy is like being a spectator at religious rites or the Olympic Games. He writes:

> We don't claim that [philosophical endeavor] is [instrumentally] beneficial but that it is in itself good, and it is appropriate to choose it for itself. [...] For just as we travel abroad to Olympia for the sake of the spectacle itself, even if there is going to be nothing more to get from it (for the observing itself is superior to material wealth), and just as we observe the Dionysia [...] and as there are many other spectacles we would choose instead of money, so too the observation of the universe [*via* philosophy] should be honored above everything that is thought to be useful. For surely one should not travel with great effort for the sake of beholding people [as in festivals and theatre] imitating girls and slaves, or for the sake of beholding fighting and running [as in the Olympics], and think one should not [in philosophy] behold the nature of existing things, i.e. the truth, for free.[150]

---

150. Iamblichus (and Aristotle), *Protrepticus* (Hutchinson and Johnson), IX, 52.16–54.5.

Aristotle's wise philosophers, then, gaze upon the epistemological nature of truth like spectators at a religious event. They spend their time watching all the fundamental principles of reality somehow joined together in God. This is what philosophical *theory* means for Aristotle. We find passages on the same themes in works such as the *Nicomachean Ethics*, the *Eudemian Ethics*, and the *Metaphysics*.

In the *Nicomachean Ethics*, Aristotle claims that "the whole life of the gods is blessed" and that we can enjoy blessedness by imitating them.[151] Once again, in the *Protrepticus* he hits a similar tone in passages that seem to attribute immortality and divinity to the whole soul (not just the active *nous*). He writes:

> So nothing divine or happy belongs to humans apart from [...] as much insight and intelligence as is in us [...] this alone seems to be immortal, and this alone divine. And by being able to share in such a capacity, our way of life [...] [is] so gracefully managed that, in comparison with the other animals, a human seems to be a god. For "intellect is the god in us" – whether it was Hermotimus or Anaxagoras who said so – and "the mortal phase has a part of some god." So we must either do philosophy or say goodbye to living [...] since everything else [...] seems in a way to be [...] trash and nonsense.[152]

But this is not to repudiate religious belief; it is to value philosophy because of its religious content, because it is divine.

Aristotle's intellectualization of piety as a form of divine imitation is not so much a rejection of ordinary religious beliefs as an adaptation of those beliefs to a philosophical context. As I have already indicated, pious pagan Greeks entered into a

---

151. *Nicomachean Ethics* (Ross and Urmson) X.8.1178b33–4.
152. Iamblicus (and Aristotle), *Protrepticus* (Hutchinson and Johnson), 42; VIII 48.9–21. Cf. Hutchinson and Johnson, "The *Antidosis* of Isocrates and Aristotle's *Protrepticus*."

relationship with their patron gods. There was a give-and-take: human agents were to honour their gods; the gods were to take care of their devotees as if they were their wards. But Aristotle situates the life of the philosopher inside this sort of reciprocal relationship. The philosophers are to pay the gods proper homage and tribute by dedicating themselves to a life of divine imitation and the gods are to "reward" philosophers because they "honour and love" them. Aristotle writes:

> He who exercises his intellect and cultivates it seems to be [...] most dear to the gods. For if the gods have any care for human affairs, as they are thought to have, it would be reasonable both that they should delight in that which was best and most akin to them (i.e., intellect) and that they should reward those who love and honour this most, as caring for the things that are dear to them. [...] And that all these attributes belong most of all to the wise man [i.e., the philosopher] is manifest. He, therefore, is the dearest to the gods. And he who is that will presumably be also the happiest; so that in this way too the wise man will more than any other be happy.[153]

But this sounds very much like the traditional Greek notion of piety raised to the level of intellectual achievement.

It seems, then, that Aristotle may have genuinely believed that wise philosophers practised a higher form of piety. It is not simply, as on Broadie's secularized interpretation, that they are rewarded with increased understanding. Aristotle tells us, literally, that the person who is loved by the gods (θεοφιλής) will be happy; they will be εὐδαίμων: blessed with a good fate.[154] But Aristotle does not limit happiness—having a good fate—to bursts of understanding. He believes

---

153. *Nicomachean Ethics* (Ross and Urmson) X.8.1179a22–32; cited in Broadie, "Aristotelian Piety," 61.
154. The term εὐδαίμων, literally translated: "blessed with a good genius" or "with a good guardian spirit."

that no one can achieve happiness—*eudaimonia*—without external goods. "Without external advantage, life cannot be happy."[155] If, then, the gods are to reward philosophers with *eudamonia*—as he literally says—the gods must provide them with the necessary external goods. But, on Aristotle's account, external goods include things like prosperity, good health, longevity, children, friends, social standing, even good looks.[156] These things add up to a lot more than Broadie's "bursts of understanding."

We read in the *Magna Moralia*: "happiness cannot exist apart from external goods, and external goods result from good fate [εὐτυχίας]."[157] But, from a pagan Greek perspective, the gods are (in large part) in control of fate. This is, in part, why we are supposed to pray to them. On Aristotle's intellectualized version of piety, philosophers honour the gods by imitating them and they, in turn, take care of philosophers (almost like parents) by giving them what we need to be happy, which includes (it seems) external goods. As it turns out, then, that Aristotle's view of the philosophical life mirrors the traditional pagan view of piety much more than secular commentators suggest. (Note that Aristotle assumes that philosophers act "rightly and nobly" and that successful intellectual achievement requires moral virtues like temperance, diligence, patience, and industry. Ethics is, in Aristotle, always a means to *sophia*. So that philosophers are not only smart but morally good and deserve good things from the divine guardians of morality.)

2.10.6. Petitionary Prayer and the Philosophical Tradition
But there is another, sixth reason why we should be cautious when interpreting Aristotle's approach to prayer. If Aristotle

---

155. *Magna Moralia* I.8.1206b33–34. This is a constant theme in Aristotle's ethics. Cf. *Nicomachean Ethics* I.8. 1099a32–1099b8; *Eudemian Ethics* VII.15.
156. *Nicomachean Ethics* I.8.
157. *Magna Moralia* II.8.1207b17–18.

does not emphasize the importance of petitionary prayer in writing—however much he may have practised it in ordinary life—this attitude resembles other philosophers in the Hellenistic tradition. Pulleyn explains, "The most common theme among the later philosophers discussing prayers is that mortals being by nature less wise than the gods ought not to formulate specific requests because they do not know what is good for them."[158] This is a widespread attitude one finds among such diverse authors as Pythagoras, Socrates, and Epictetus.

According to Diogenes Laërtius, Pythagoras "forbids us to pray for ourselves, because we do not know what will help us."[159] According to Xenophon, Socrates "asked simply for good gifts, 'for the gods know best what things are good.'"[160] In the apocryphal *Second Alcibiades*, Socrates references the wise poet, "who, seeing his friends foolishly praying for and doing things which would not really profit them, offered up a common prayer on behalf of them all: 'Sovereign Zeus give us the good things necessary for us, whether we ask for them or not, and keep evil things away from us even when we ask for them.'"[161] Epictetus, in the *Discourses*, maintains, "My choice is one with God's choice, my desire one with His."[162] This seems to have been a common ancient trope. Perhaps Aristotle followed suit; this philosophical attitude seems in line with his intellectualist temperament. When Aristotle praises the "good prayer" of Phocylides—"Be mine a middle station"—he is favouring a prayer that lacks specifics, a prayer that leaves it entirely to the gods to decide how best that very general pious aspiration can be fulfilled.[163]

---

158. Pulleyn, *Prayer*, 37.
159. Diogenes Laërtius, *Lives of Eminent Philosophers* (Hicks) VIII.1; "Pythagoras," 9.
160. Xenophon, *Memorabilia* (Marchant) 1.3.2.
161. *Second Alcibiades* 142d–143a.
162. Epictetus, *Discourses* (Oldfather) 4.7.20.
163. *Politics* I.13.1259b33–34.

One could claim that Aristotle believes that studying philosophy is better (for capable minds) than the practice of the usual acts of pagan piety. Socrates provides a model for this sort of two-tiered approach. In Xenophon's *Symposium*, Socrates denounces lower levels of religious observance, distinguishing between two different Aphrodites who possess separate altars, temples, and rituals: "those of the Vulgar Aphrodite excelling in looseness, those of the Heavenly in chastity." Socrates praises the Heavenly Aphrodite as the patroness of "spiritual love, love of friendship and of noble conduct," belittling the Vulgar Aphrodite as the mere embodiment of fertility and carnal love.[164] An ancient Aristotelian could invoke perhaps a similar distinction between higher and lower levels of piety: that the usual rituals and practices incorporate (imperfectly) some aspects of proper reverence without being understood in some absolutely literal sense. This is, for example, what some later Neoplatonists do.

Andrei Timotin describes the way the later Porphyry distinguishes between higher and lower forms of prayer. Porphyry considers ordinary (theurgic) forms of prayer and sacrifices as an "inferior kind of prayer," which is, nonetheless, "a suitable tool to purify the souls of men who are unable to behave themselves according to the intellectual part of their soul." "The philosopher," on the other hand, who "love[s] according to the rule of the intellect," knows how to engage in contemplative prayer in imitation of the contemplative activity of God. It follows that "the philosopher [...] is the only person who knows how to pray to God appropriately and the only one able to do it."[165]

Porphyry's account of prayer is later Hellenism pushed in a certain direction. If, however, he criticizes lower forms of piety, he claims that philosophy should be respected because (as Aristotle argues) it embodies piety in an even purer form.

---

164. Xenophon, *Symposium* (Todd) 8.9–10. This is also a theme in Plato's *Symposium* introduced by Pausanias (180c ff.)
165. Timotin, "Porphyry," 96–97.

As Timotin explains, the philosopher "concedes [...] the efficacy of genuine [practical] prayers, but he subordinate[s] it to a superior, silent and intellectual kind of prayer, which corresponds to the act of contemplation of the νοῦς."[166] Porphyry's account of contemplation is not so distant from Aristotle's own notion of theory (*theôria*).

2.11. Mythology and Pagan Revelation

I have argued that the usual arguments stating Aristotle could not have believed in prayer because of his metaphysical conception of a self-thinking god are not as conclusive as some would have us believe. If, however, Aristotle and his ancient school were serious about religion, they must have had, it seems, some understanding of the pagan mythology associated with Greek religion and also, some belief in the efficacy of divine inspiration. I will consider the specific issue of fate later. Let us inquire now into what Aristotle specifically says about how to interpret the myths and how to make sense of the possibility of inspiration.

I discuss Aristotle's *Poetics* in the last chapter. For the moment, note that, in his *Rhetoric*, Aristotle comments that poetry "is an inspired thing" and, in a passage from the *Metaphysics* that deserves to be cited at length, he identifies traditional belief in God as inspired.[167] Aristotle reports:

> Our forefathers in the most remote ages have handed down to their posterity a tradition, in the form of a myth, that these [heavenly] bodies [planets and stars] are gods, and that the divine encloses the whole of nature. The rest of the tradition has been added later in mythical form with a view to the persuasion of the multitude and to its legal and utilitarian expediency; they say these gods are in the form of men or like some of the other animals, and they say other things consequent on and similar to

---

166. Timotin, "Porphyry," 103.
167. *Rhetoric* (Roberts) III.7.1408b18.

these. [...] But if one were to separate the first point from these additions and take it alone—that they thought the first substances to be gods, one must regard this as an inspired utterance, and reflect that [...] these opinions, with others, have been preserved until the present like relics of the ancient treasure.[168]

Aristotle seems to follow here a well-worn philosophical script. His teacher Plato spends much time complaining about the myths, insisting, nonetheless, that all men believe in the gods.[169] Aristotle, then, follows in his footsteps, positing the existence of the gods as a first principle, holding fast to the basic tenet of theism while repudiating metaphorical mythological exaggerations. Except that, in this particular case, theism has been communicated to the Greek culture, not through argument, not through observation or science, but through inspired utterance. This is, in effect, to presuppose some notion of revelation.

Greek religion started, it seems, as an oral mythological tradition. Aristotle, then, posits two standards of truth, one for literature and one for philosophy. He does not believe in the literal content of many of the myths. In an investigation of the distinction between perishable and imperishable things, he—rather impatiently—complains about the fanciful explanations of the poets. In one of the myths, the goddess Demeter fed ambrosia to Demophoon to turn him into a god. In response, Aristotle offers a *reasoned* argument as to why ingesting nectar and ambrosia cannot be the cause of immorality. He remarks:

The school of Hesiod and all the mythologists thought only of what was plausible to themselves. [...] For asserting the first principles to be gods and born of gods, they say that the beings which did not taste of nectar and

---

168. *Metaphysics* (Ross) XII.8.1074b1–13.
169. Cf., for example, *Laws* 886a.

ambrosia became mortal; and clearly, [...] what they have said [...] is above our comprehension. For if the gods taste nectar and ambrosia for their pleasure, these are in no wise the causes of their existence; and if they taste them to maintain their existence, how can gods who need food be eternal?—But into the subtleties of the mythologists it is not worthwhile to inquire seriously; on the other hand, [we, philosophers, scientists, and logicians] who use the language of proof must cross-examine and ask why things which consist of the same elements are, some of them, eternal in nature, while others perish.[170]

According to Aristotle, we cannot expect logical proof from poetry (or the myths). The literary conceit that the gods feast on nectar and ambrosia (the best foods) to achieve eternity is not to be taken literally. At least not by sophisticated believers. But Aristotle is very careful to suggest that the scientifically minded need not look for their answers in the myths (as some were wont to do). It does not follow that there cannot be gods or that we cannot point to elements of the universe that are eternal.

Aristotle himself claims: "The gods, as we conceive them, enjoy supreme felicity and happiness."[171] Poetic passages about the gods drinking nectar and ambrosia have to be understood metaphorically: the gods are supremely happy the way people are supremely happy when feasting at a banquet. Aristotle makes the point by drawing out a connection between what is happiness and what is divine. As Bodéüs points out, "in fifteen lines," and in what "is essentially his only exposition of theology, the only text that takes the gods as the object of investigation," Aristotle accepts the conclusion of "the most profane and elementary philosophy" that "the gods above all are happy."[172]

---

170. *Metaphysics* (Ross) IIVI.4.1000a8–21.
171. They are "μακαρίους καὶ εὐδαίμονας." *Nicomachean Ethics* X.8.1178b8.
172. Bodéüs, *Theology*, 155. Cf. *Nicomachean Ethics* X.8.1 178b8–22.

Stephen Bush comments that Aristotle sometimes uses the terms "blessed" (*makarios*) and "happy" (*eudaimôn*) interchangeably.[173] The former is, however, a word with deep religious resonances. As an older translator points out, "the word μακάριος, rendered 'blessed' or 'supremely happy,' is a derivative of μάκαρ, the adjective applied in Homer and Hesiod to the gods and to those of mankind who have been admitted after death to the Islands of the Blest."[174] This has occasioned debate about what Aristotle meant by happiness.[175] Suffice it to say here that Aristotle seems, on some occasions, to be linking human happiness to the supreme happiness he associates with the gods. Human beings—especially Greeks—are most happy when they are feasting. So, this provides a good analogy for the condition of the gods. Aristotle agrees, then, with the poets that the gods are supremely happy, but he is a philosopher, not a poet, and expresses this point about divine happiness through a reasoned line of thought, not through literary embellishment.

2.12. The Scope of Inspiration

What does Aristotle say about inspiration understood as the direct supernatural influence of the gods (or their spirit helpers) on human beings? What he says is surprisingly reminiscent of what Socrates says about poetic inspiration in the *Ion*, not that poetic genus is illegitimate but that it does not qualify as intellectual endeavour in a philosophical sense. Compared to Socrates's comment on rhapsodes, however, Aristotle has a much more expansive range of application in mind when it comes to inspiration. It is not simply artists and poets who are inspired, but heroes and

---

173. Bush, "Divine and Human Happiness," 58. He refers to X.8.ll78b8-33, 7.11.1152b. Cf. VI.11.1152b7 (Crisp): "Most people claim that happiness involves pleasure; this is why people call the blessed (*makarios*) person by that name, from *chairein* (to enjoy)."
174. In *Nicomachean Ethics* (Rackham) n. to 1098a (1934).
175. Cf. Lear, *Happy Lives*; Long, "Aristotle on *Eudaimonia*."

ordinary mortals who behave in noble ways that are above their natural capacities.

In the *Eudemian Ethics*, for example, Aristotle places "those who are inspired and prophesy" in the category of people who lifted up to a higher level of achievement beyond their own capacities. Although these people act thoughtfully, "they do not have it in their own power either to say what they said, or to do what they did."[176] Under the influence of divine inspiration, human agents do things that exceed any natural capacity they have. We must locate the cause for their exalted behaviour in something outside themselves.

Aristotle seems to associate inspiration with intense feeling and a lack of individual responsibility. In the *Magna Moralia*, the Aristotelian author identifies people who are brave because they "are inspired by the gods [οἱ ἐνθουσιάζοντες]."[177] (Literally, the god is in them: ἔνθους.) He explains that the inspired "are not really entitled to be named courageous, for if they lose the feelings [i.e., the inspiration], they cease to be brave; whereas true courage is permanent."[178] Courage, in these circumstances, is not a moral achievement because it is not a matter of fixed character but of divine help.

Aristotle believes, nonetheless, that inspiration is a positive phenomenon: it lifts up individuals to some higher capacity of achievement, filling the affected with the right impulses and leading to a much better outcome than could be expected if the human actors were left to their own devices. I should point out, however, that one encounters in Greek tragedy a more negative sort of "inspiration" when the vengeful goddess Ἄτη afflicts the guilty with ἄτη (*atē*), often translated as "folly," a spirit of delusion and obsession that leads to the downfall of the protagonist. This happens in the Oedipus story (discussed in Chapter 5) when the king relentlessly and recklessly—against better advice—blindly

---

176. *Eudemian Ethics* (Solomon) VI.8.1225a28–30.
177. *Magna Moralia* VI.20.1190b36–37.
178. *Magna Moralia* (Stock) VI.20.1190b37–1191a2.

(and against religious counsel) pursues a course of action that leads to his own downfall.

Aristotle, however, highlights the possibility of beneficial forms of divine intervention. He believes that individuals may accomplish great things, not because of natural capacities but because they have been visited by some divine force entering into them and guiding them towards what is good. Again, the author of the *Magna Moralia* explains:

> The fortunate man is he who apart from reason has an impulse to good things and obtains these, and this comes from nature. For there is in the soul by nature something of this sort whereby we are impelled, not under the guidance of reason, towards things for which we are well fitted. And if one were to ask a man in this state, "Why does it please you to do so"?—he would say, "I don't know, except that it does please me," being in the same condition as those who are inspired by religious frenzy; for they also have an impulse to do something apart from reason.[179]

Like those inspired by religious frenzy, the irrational (or non-rational) can be guided by a power inside them that pushes them to make the right decisions without the use of reason. Aristotle reiterates this explanation in the *Eudemian Ethics*, where he discusses the strange case of those who succeed by means of some uncanny insight that best works *when logic is relaxed*. These people succeed as if they were prudent and wise, not through any hint of logic, but through direct contact with a god. In words that almost repeat the *Magna Moralia* passage but make the divine connection even more explicit, Aristotle writes:

> Those are called fortunate [i.e., enjoying a good fate] who [...] succeed without being good at reasoning. Rational deliberation is of no advantage to them, for they have within

---

179. *Magna Moralia* II.8.1207a36–1207b4.

them a principle that is better than intellect and deliberation (which those with reason do not have): that is, they have inspiration [ἐνθουσιασμός] although they cannot rationally deliberate. Although irrational, they succeed, and like the prudent and the wise, their divination is speedy. And we must include within their understanding everything but the judgement that comes from reasoning; in some cases, their abilities are due to experience, in others to habit in investigation; and both experience and mental habit use God. This quality sees well the future and the present, and yet these are men in whom reasoning is relaxed. Hence, we have melancholic men, the dreamers of what turns out to be true. For the moving principle seems to become stronger when the reasoning power is relaxed, just as the blind remember better, being freed from their concern with visible appearances.[180]

This is a remarkable passage. Aristotle claims that some people make *more* intelligent decisions when they are not *distracted* by reasoning or by actual observation (like the blind). What is important here is that Aristotle leaves room in his philosophy for a supernatural impulse that pushes agents in the right direction.

For some, this may all seem far-fetched. But Aristotle situates the origins of human intelligence in the divine. Again, in the *Eudemian Ethics*, he reports:

The object of our search is this—what is the starting-point of motion in the soul? The answer is clear: as in the universe, so in the soul, it is god. For […] the divine element in us moves everything. The starting-point of reason is not reason but something superior to reason. What, then, could be superior even to knowledge and to intellect, except god?[181]

---

180. *Eudemian Ethics* (Solomon and Rackman) VII.14.1248a31–b4.
181. *Eudemian Ethics* (Solomon and Rackman) VII.14.1248a25–29. Cf. Dirlmeier, *Eudemische Ethik*, 498–500.

Aristotle makes a similar claim in his public lecture the *Protrepticus*: "For mind is the god in us [...] and mortal life contains a portion of some god."[182] These passages dovetail (*pace* Melzer) with Aristotle's description of the active *nous* as divine, as well as with other passages describing the soul as divine.[183]

2.13. The Paranormal: Mystery Cults and Mysticism

If Aristotle (and early Aristotelians) did believe that divine inspiration could move the souls of human agents, we may naturally wonder if they accepted the possibility of paranormal phenomena. In the minor manuscript *On Divinations*, Aristotle tries to articulate a naturalistic explanation of truthful prophesying that operates through dreams. One suggestion is that he attributes them to non-rational types who mostly operate according to animal instinct.[184] But, it seems rather, that he is worried about the suggestion that truthful dreams come, not to the educated and the aristocratic, but to mystics and seers who often come from the lower classes. In a passage where he wonders about the possibility of direct divine intervention, we read:

> As to the divination which takes place in sleep, and is said to be based on dreams, we cannot lightly either dismiss it with contempt or give it implicit confidence. [...] That divination in dreams should sometimes be genuine is not incredible. [...] Yet the fact of our seeing no probable cause to account for such divination tends to inspire us with distrust. For [...] it is absurd to combine the idea that the sender of such dreams should be God with the fact that those to whom he sends them are not the best and wisest, but merely commonplace persons. If, however, we abstract from the causality of

---

182. B110, Barnes, *Complete Works*, 416.
183. For example, *Nicomachean Ethics* X.7.1177b27–1178a8.
184. Cf. Struck, "Animals and Divination."

y that marks one for life. [...] For him, philo-
dically different from this.¹⁹⁶

ee that Aristotle did mostly think of religion in
experiential rather than philosophical terms, but
inimizes the epistemological content in religion.
learly believed, for example, that the gods existed
eve "the gods exist" is to affirm that the proposition
exist" is true. There is an epistemological side to
belief. Even the mystery cults operate on the assump-
at certain things are true, legitimate, praiseworthy,
Whatever the mystery cults were teaching, one cannot
find a way to hive off even this sort of specialized (and
uous) religious practice from epistemological content.
ut there is a bigger problem with any attempt to read
otle in this way. Bernabé's understanding of epistemol-
seems more in line with modern analytic philosophy
n original Aristotelianism. Aristotle never limits episte-
ology to deductive, discursive knowledge of the sort we use
arguments. He has a much wider view of reason, which
cludes induction, practical decision-making, and the
ormulation of first principles, all of which rely on a species
of direct intuition (*nous*) as Aristotle clearly indicates, for
example, at the end of the *Posterior Analytics*. (Even scientific
syllogisms originate in induction [ἐπᾰγωγή, *epagôgê*], which
relies on a species of empirically based intuition.¹⁹⁷) Bernabé
overlooks the fact that, for Aristotle, the most successful philosophical activity of all is *theôria* or contemplation, which
involves a non-discursive, intuitive sort of insight.

Bernabé differentiates sharply between Plato's and
Aristotle's view of mysticism. In the background is a familiar
stereotype: Aristotle was the scientist; Plato, the mystic. But
any such dichotomy is overly simple. Perhaps Chroust comes
closer to the truth when he writes:

---

196. Bernabé, "Aristotle and the Mysteries," 38.
197. Cf. Groarke, *Aristotelian Account of Induction*; "Aristotle: Logic."

God, none of the other causes assigned appears probable. That certain persons should have foresight in dreams [...] seems to be something [...] which surpasses the wit of man.¹⁸⁵

What troubles Aristotle is the idea that the gods would send prophetic dreams to commonplace people, but this is not quite the same as disavowing the epistemological possibility of truthful paranormal experiences altogether.

There are ancient authors who do suggest (with whatever degree of accuracy) that Aristotle approves of paranormal phenomena. Sextus Empiricus tells us that Aristotle maintained that belief in God could be traced to "the experiences of the soul [...] because of its inspiration and prophetic power in dreams."¹⁸⁶ Cicero relates an alleged incident where Aristotle describes three true prophesies in a dream of a friend (Eudemus of Cyprus).¹⁸⁷ (Cicero himself discusses the predictive power of dreaming in his *The Dream of Scipio*.) Still, the modern tendency is to understate Aristotle's interest in such things.

Aristotle was familiar with the mystic cults of ancient Greeks such as the Eleusinian Mysteries. In one fragment, he refers to Orphic "initiation rites" (which posited the body as the tomb of the soul) as a meaningful explanation of human imperfection and suffering.¹⁸⁸ In another fragment, he notes, "those who are initiated into the mysteries are not expected to grasp anything (discursively), but only to have a certain inner experience and thus be put into a particular frame of

---

185. *On Divination in Sleep* (Beare) 1.462b13–26.
186. F 10 R3 Sextus Empiricus, *adversus mathematicos* IX 20–23, in Barnes, *Complete Works*, 2391.
187. F 37 R3 Cicero, *De divinatione* I xxv 53, in Barnes, *Complete Works*, 2399.
188. B 106, F 55 R3, F 59 R3, F 60 R3, F 61 R3 (Iamblichus, *Protrepticus,* 45.4–48.21 Pistelli), in Barnes, *Complete Works*, 2416. Cf. Cornelli, McKirahan, Macris, *On Pythagoreanism*, 134–136.

mind."¹⁸⁹ Put in a more modern idiom, these religious events were not intended to produce an argument for anything but to make the mind receptive to the religious experience in which the cult specialized.

There is some older commentary that references Aristotle's purported beliefs on such matters. The medieval Byzantine scholiast Michael Psellus, in a reference to a missing Aristotelian text, suggestively tells his students:

> I undertook to teach you what I have learned, not what I have experienced [...] the one is matter for teaching, the other for mystical experience. The first comes to men by hearing, the second comes when reason itself has experienced illumination—which Aristotle described as mysterious and akin to the Eleusinian rites (for in these he who was initiated into the mysteries was being moulded, not taught)."¹⁹⁰

Another ancient commentary tells us: "Aristotle claims that those who are being initiated into the mysteries are not expected to learn anything but to suffer some change, to be put into a certain condition, i.e., to be fitted for some purpose."¹⁹¹

Aristotle does document the beneficial psychological benefits of mystical practices. In a comment about the healing power of religious music, he reports, "Some persons fall into a religious frenzy [...] as a result of the sacred melodies—when they have used the melodies that excite the soul to mystic frenzy—they are restored as though they had found healing and purgation."¹⁹² (This is not unlike the catharsis Aristotle identifies with tragedy.)

---

189. From the lost manuscript *On Philosophy*. F 15 R3 (Synesius, Dio 48A), in Barnes, *Complete Works*, 2392; Chroust, *Aristotle*, 224; cf. n. 6, 402.
190. *Fragments, On Philosophy* (Ross, vol. XII), 15, 87; Chroust, *Aristotle*, 224.
191. *Fragments, On Philosophy* (Ross, vol. XII), 15, 87; Chroust, *Aristotle*, 224.
192. *Politics* VIII.7.1341b 32 ff. See discussion below.

mind."[189] Put in a more modern idiom, these religious events were not intended to produce an argument for anything but to make the mind receptive to the religious experience in which the cult specialized.

There is some older commentary that references Aristotle's purported beliefs on such matters. The medieval Byzantine scholiast Michael Psellus, in a reference to a missing Aristotelian text, suggestively tells his students:

> I undertook to teach you what I have learned, not what I have experienced [...] the one is matter for teaching, the other for mystical experience. The first comes to men by hearing, the second comes when reason itself has experienced illumination—which Aristotle described as mysterious and akin to the Eleusinian rites (for in these he who was initiated into the mysteries was being moulded, not taught)."[190]

Another ancient commentary tells us: "Aristotle claims that those who are being initiated into the mysteries are not expected to learn anything but to suffer some change, to be put into a certain condition, i.e., to be fitted for some purpose."[191]

Aristotle does document the beneficial psychological benefits of mystical practices. In a comment about the healing power of religious music, he reports, "Some persons fall into a religious frenzy [...] as a result of the sacred melodies—when they have used the melodies that excite the soul to mystic frenzy—they are restored as though they had found healing and purgation."[192] (This is not unlike the catharsis Aristotle identifies with tragedy.)

---

189. From the lost manuscript *On Philosophy*. F 15 R3 (Synesius, Dio 48A), in Barnes, *Complete Works*, 2392; Chroust, *Aristotle*, 224; cf. n. 6, 402.

190. *Fragments, On Philosophy* (Ross, vol. XII), 15, 87; Chroust, *Aristotle*, 224.

191. *Fragments, On Philosophy* (Ross, vol. XII), 15, 87; Chroust, *Aristotle*, 224.

192. *Politics* VIII.7.1341b 32 ff. See discussion below.

God, none of the other causes assigned appears probable. That certain persons should have foresight in dreams [...] seems to be something [...] which surpasses the wit of man.[185]

What troubles Aristotle is the idea that the gods would send prophetic dreams to commonplace people, but this is not quite the same as disavowing the epistemological possibility of truthful paranormal experiences altogether.

There are ancient authors who do suggest (with whatever degree of accuracy) that Aristotle approves of paranormal phenomena. Sextus Empiricus tells us that Aristotle maintained that belief in God could be traced to "the experiences of the soul [...] because of its inspiration and prophetic power in dreams."[186] Cicero relates an alleged incident where Aristotle describes three true prophesies in a dream of a friend (Eudemus of Cyprus).[187] (Cicero himself discusses the predictive power of dreaming in his *The Dream of Scipio*.) Still, the modern tendency is to understate Aristotle's interest in such things.

Aristotle was familiar with the mystic cults of ancient Greeks such as the Eleusinian Mysteries. In one fragment, he refers to Orphic "initiation rites" (which posited the body as the tomb of the soul) as a meaningful explanation of human imperfection and suffering.[188] In another fragment, he notes, "those who are initiated into the mysteries are not expected to grasp anything (discursively), but only to have a certain inner experience and thus be put into a particular frame of

---

185. *On Divination in Sleep* (Beare) 1.462b13–26.
186. F 10 R3 Sextus Empiricus, *adversus mathematicos* IX 20–23, in Barnes, *Complete Works*, 2391.
187. F 37 R3 Cicero, *De divinatione* I xxv 53, in Barnes, *Complete Works*, 2399.
188. B 106, F 55 R3, F 59 R3, F 60 R3, F 61 R3 (Iamblichus, *Protrepticus,* 45.4–48.21 Pistelli), in Barnes, *Complete Works*, 2416. Cf. Cornelli, McKirahan, Macris, *On Pythagoreanism*, 134–136.

Alberto Bernabé argues, quoting from a chapter in the *Problemata*, that Aristotle believes that mystical states are caused by an excess of hot black bile.[193] But it is an overuse of Occam's razor to claim that because religious experience has a physical side, they are not genuinely religious.[194] Aristotle (unlike the atomists) never argues for physical reductionism. The text Bernabé cites mentions Hercules, Empedocles, Plato, Socrates, numerous well-known men, most of the poets and "all those who have become eminent in philosophy or politics" as suffering from similar conditions.[195] There is no suggestion, for example, that Socrates does not possess superior intelligence; the text is simply asking the question: Why was Socrates atrabilious (possessing a melancholic temperament thought to be caused by black bile)? We can all agree, for example, that the mere act of thinking is associated with some necessary physiological mechanism, but it does not follow that thinking has no immaterial aspect or that it has no epistemological content.

One might be tempted to argue that Aristotle accepted the psychological benefits or the social and political utility of religion (and even mysticism) without accepting any of its epistemological content. Bernabé writes:

> According to Aristotle, the [mystical] phenomena of μανία [mania] and Βακχεία [Bacchic possession] are subject to rational causes and for this reason he does not consider initiation [into the mysteries] as knowledge, for there are no texts transmitted in a discursive manner. Initiation does not affect reason and intelligence, since it is simply an emotional experience with a psychological effect; an unforgettable πάθημα generating *per se* a change

---

193. *Problemata* XXX.1.954a34.
194. Forster, *Problemata* (in the Ross collection, Oxford, 1927), vii.
195. *Problemata* (Forster) XXX.1.953a15.

of mentality that marks one for life. [...] For him, philosophy is radically different from this.[196]

One can agree that Aristotle did mostly think of religion in practical or experiential rather than philosophical terms, but Bernabé minimizes the epistemological content in religion. Aristotle clearly believed, for example, that the gods existed but to believe "the gods exist" is to affirm that the proposition "the gods exist" is true. There is an epistemological side to religious belief. Even the mystery cults operate on the assumptions that certain things are true, legitimate, praiseworthy, good. Whatever the mystery cults were teaching, one cannot neatly find a way to hive off even this sort of specialized (and ambiguous) religious practice from epistemological content.

But there is a bigger problem with any attempt to read Aristotle in this way. Bernabé's understanding of epistemology seems more in line with modern analytic philosophy than original Aristotelianism. Aristotle never limits epistemology to deductive, discursive knowledge of the sort we use in arguments. He has a much wider view of reason, which includes induction, practical decision-making, and the formulation of first principles, all of which rely on a species of direct intuition (*nous*) as Aristotle clearly indicates, for example, at the end of the *Posterior Analytics*. (Even scientific syllogisms originate in induction [ἐπᾰγωγή, *epagôgê*], which relies on a species of empirically based intuition.[197]) Bernabé overlooks the fact that, for Aristotle, the most successful philosophical activity of all is *theôria* or contemplation, which involves a non-discursive, intuitive sort of insight.

Bernabé differentiates sharply between Plato's and Aristotle's view of mysticism. In the background is a familiar stereotype: Aristotle was the scientist; Plato, the mystic. But any such dichotomy is overly simple. Perhaps Chroust comes closer to the truth when he writes:

---

196. Bernabé, "Aristotle and the Mysteries," 38.
197. Cf. Groarke, *Aristotelian Account of Induction*; "Aristotle: Logic."

> Aristotle's basic concern with the possibility of knowing God [...] through contemplation, wonder and awe, is to some extent mysticism—an attitude prepared by Plato's *Laws* (Books X and XII), [and possibly] by the *Epinomis*, [...] and by the general philosophical and religious mood which permeated the Academy during the last years of Plato.[198]

Chroust claims that Aristotle believes in an "inner illumination" whereby the individual directly intuits "the existence and reality of the divine as well as the immortality of his own soul."[199] Whatever else this means, it is hard to imagine a secular, atheistic Aristotle coming up with such religiously friendly ideas.

As we have seen throughout this chapter, there is much more evidence for a religious Aristotle or, at least, for pro-religious elements in the Aristotelian school than commonly acknowledged. Mostly, it seems that Aristotle's religious convictions, to the extent that we can know them, fit in with the intellectualized Pagan beliefs of his time.

---

198. Chroust, *Aristotle*, 229. The *Epinomis*, an alleged appendix to the *Laws*, is usually alleged to be spurious. For a dissenting opinion, cf. Altman, "Why Plato Wrote *Epinomis*."
199. Chroust, *Aristotle*, 225. See Chroust for relevant references.

Chapter 3

The Cosmos as a Hall of Mirrors

> [Aristotle] was a pagan philosopher whose unmoved mover did not even relate to the created world.
>
> Charles Freeman, *The Closing of the Western Mind*

> Even if Aristotle was not an atheist in the sense that he directly and openly attacked the divine. […] One could say that he was one in a broader sense, because his ideas on divinity indirectly tend to undermine it and destroy it.
>
> Denis Diderot and Jean Le Rond d'Alembert, *Encyclopédie*

> Among themselves all things
> Have order; and from hence the form, which makes
> The universe resemble God.
>
> Dante Alighieri, *Divine Comedy*, "Paradise"

3.1. Aristotle's "Theology"

In the previous chapter, I demonstrated that there is a good deal of scattered evidence that Aristotle was a moderate, intellectualized, practising pagan. At the very least, he took the religion of his age very seriously. It is, however, the religious content of his philosophy that will most concern us here. In this chapter, I show that when we consider Aristotle's worldview as a whole, rather than focusing on isolated passages friendly to this or that interpretation, we encounter repeated religious themes that structure his metaphysics. Aristotle sketches out a picture of the cosmos as a window on the divine that should inspire wise people with wonder. The textual evidence indicates that Aristotle did believe in an immaterial soul, although one intimately fused to the dynamic form of the living body. The overwhelming emphasis on the scientific aspects of Aristotle in contemporary commentary tends to obscure many quasi-Platonic elements.

Although Aristotle is a scientist with a determinedly empiricist outlook, I will argue that even his later work should be understood as an extension and modification of Platonism. One cannot make sense, for example, of Aristotle's mature comments about God in the *Nicomachean Ethics* or the *Metaphysics* without understanding Platonism as providing a framework for his thought. Lloyd Gerson does sketch out a picture of a Platonic-Aristotelianism in his provocatively entitled volume *Aristotle and Other Platonists* and I will argue, in a different way, that Aristotle's mature attitude towards metaphysics is more Platonic than we suspect. Although Aristotle is adamant that theological (or mythological) considerations should not interfere with the practice of natural science, although his account of material cause differs from other Platonists, his overall worldview includes a transcendental religious dimension. There is a religious element to what he is doing, which is, largely, a further extension of Platonic attitudes.

As I have already mentioned, a familiar developmentalist interpretation accepts, somewhat grudgingly, that the young Aristotle may have been momentarily influenced by the spiritualism of Plato's academy but insists that the older Aristotle left behind such immaterial exaggerations for more sober, physicalist, scientific ways of thinking. Theo Gerard

Sinnige takes issue with this "developmental" thesis. His basic stance seems sound: "there is no warrant," he declares, for "the current prejudice of a more empirically minded later Aristotle [...] who had finally lost hold of his theological principles."[1]

Anti-religious accounts of Aristotle have largely taken over public discussion. Harry Binswanger, Ayn Rand's editor, not atypically observes:

> Aristotle is the champion of this world, the champion of nature, as against the supernaturalism of Plato. [...] Aristotle's universe is the universe of science. The physical world, in his view, is not a shadowy projection controlled by a divine dimension, but an autonomous, self-sufficient realm. [...] In such a universe, knowledge cannot be acquired by special revelations from another dimension; there is no place for ineffable intuitions of the beyond. Repudiating the mystical elements in Plato's epistemology, Aristotle is the father of logic and the champion of reason as man's only means of knowledge.[2]

One finds similar attitudes reflected in much more technical arguments in the exegetical literature. I aim to show, however, that pushing the religious elements of Aristotle's thought to the margins is a serious philosophical mistake.

Bodéüs is right to worry about applying the term "theology" to Aristotle. Unlike Neoplatonists such as Plotinus and Proclus or schoolmen like Augustine and Aquinas, Aristotle is, for the most part, not in the theology business. His scattered comments on the divine pose myriad puzzles that have no uncontroversial solution. Was, for example, Aristotle a monotheist? In turning his attention to astronomy, Aristotle identifies a probable "god" with each of the 47 or 55 celestial spheres. Yet, only two paragraphs later, he

---

1. Sinnige, "Cosmic Religion in Aristotle," 34.
2. Rand and Binswanger, *Ayn Rand Lexicon*, s.v. "Aristotle."

argues (as elsewhere) that God "is one both in definition and in number."[3] He concludes this particular discussion with a quotation from the *Iliad*: "The rule of many is not good; one ruler let there be."[4] So, does Aristotle believe in one god or many gods? Is he a monotheist or a polytheist? Is Aristotle's god a ruler like Agamemnon in Homer? Or, as many commentators suggest, is he too busy with his own self-contemplation to bother ruling over others? How are we to reconcile such contradictory claims?

I think that we can go some way to resolving these tensions by considering the historical context. In pagan times, the use of the word "god" was rather more elastic than in later Judeo-Christian eras. The idea of a hierarchy of many supernatural beings of various sorts—gods? angels? demons? nymphs? muses? demigods?—would not have sounded odd or incongruous to a Greek pagan. Aristotle, who tends towards a moderate, middle position, might have found some truth in polytheistic religious belief while, at the same time, maintaining, philosophically, that there is one, supreme, perfect, and eternal principle that serves as an enduring archetype for the cosmos. Was Aristotle a henotheist? Both a monotheist and a polytheist? I am not sure he ever fully resolved such questions in his own mind. I will focus on his one philosophical god in this chapter. Nonetheless, he seems comfortable with the possibility of diverse manifestations of the divine.

Cicero, who was much closer to Aristotle historically, tells us about a passage from a now lost manuscript. He reports:

> Aristotle did well observe: "If there were men whose habitations had been always underground, in great and commodious houses, adorned with statues and pictures, furnished with everything which they who are reputed

---

3. *Metaphysics* XII.8.1074a38.
4. *Metaphysics* (Ross) XII.10.1076a.7. Citation from Homer, *Iliad*, Il.2.204.

happy abound with; and if, without stirring from thence, they should be informed of a certain divine power and majesty, and, after some time, the earth should open, and they should quit their dark abode to come to us; where they should immediately behold the earth, the seas, the heavens; should consider the vast extent of the clouds and force of the winds; should see the sun, and observe his grandeur and beauty, and also his generative power; [...] and when night has obscured the earth, should they contemplate the heavens bespangled and adorned with stars; the surprising variety of the moon, in her increase and wane; the rising and setting of all the stars, and the inviolable regularity of their courses. When [...] they should see these things, they would undoubtedly conclude that there are gods, and that these are their mighty works."

Is he worthy to be called a man, who attributes to chance, not to an intelligent cause, the constant motion of the heavens, the regular courses of the stars, the agreeable proportion and connexion of all things, conducted with so much reason, that our intellect itself is unable to estimate it rightly? When we see machines move artificially, as a sphere, a clock, or the like, do we doubt whether they are the productions of reason? And when we behold the heavens moving with a prodigious celerity, and causing an annual succession of the different seasons of the year, which vivify and preserve all things, can we doubt that this world is directed, I will not say only by reason, but by reason most excellent and divine? For without troubling ourselves with too refined a subtlety of discussion, we may use our eyes to contemplate the beauty of those things, which we assert have been arranged by divine providence.[5]

One can wish this away as Cicero's editorializing on an Aristotelian text of dubious provenance, but this may be

---

5. Cicero, *Nature of the Gods* [etc.] (Yonge), 78–80.

harsh. Philosophically, Cicero attributes to Aristotle an ancient version of an intelligent-design argument. We need not pursue this line of reasoning here; in part, because I think that Aristotle takes it for granted that divinity or divinities exist. What I want to show is not how Aristotle *proves* the existence of the divine but, instead, how his vision of the cosmos is a window on the divine, as a staircase to a sequence of ultimate transcendentals.

I will argue that the religious element in Aristotle's metaphysics is structural, not necessarily pious. Whatever the strength (or weakness) of Aristotle's personal religious convictions, we can catch glimpses of a philosophical god—intimations of divinity—in the architecture of Aristotle's cosmos. Granted, Aristotle's theology is hard to pin down in any unambiguous, definitive way. Some might argue that Aristotle's god is part of nature, at least inasmuch as they exist together in a symbiotic whole. This seems too extreme though it must follow, on Aristotle's account, that both God and nature are eternally necessitated (as there is no Creation). At the same time, he seems to conceive of them of separate forces, components, or elements of a whole with God always given metaphysical priority as final cause. But I will not try to sort out all the exegetical details here.

Suffice it to say that Aristotle posits a hierarchical world of parallel realities that strive to imitate his philosophical god on many different levels. If the resulting analysis sounds Neoplatonic that is unsurprising. Aristotle is earlier in the tradition but his scientific naturalism provides, on closer inspection, another road to God. As we have seen, Aristotle believes that the highest epistemological achievement is to be caught up in *theôria*, in a god-like appreciation of what is always and everywhere true. Aristotle's metaphysics serves as a window on God, and that is what Aristotle intended his metaphysics to be.

The treatise we now call the *Metaphysics*; that "farrago" or "hotch-potch" of ideas (Barnes's description) presents innumerable exegetical problems. My account tries to make overall philosophical sense of Aristotle's synoptic system. Although I do occasionally take issue with pertinent points of commentary, I cannot engage with an enormous secondary literature here. I will not limit my account to the perplexities of "Book Lambda" where Aristotle briefly waxes theological.[6]

In this chapter I focus, uniquely, on what I see as the logical structure of Aristotle's metaphysics. I want to show that Aristotle's metaphysical naturalism and his religious concerns coincide. Aristotle's achievement is not the elimination of religion in favour of science, but the articulation of a worldview that allows for the scientific and the religious to co-exist in some harmonious—indeed, interdependent—relation. Once we accept that Aristotle is a religious as well as a philosophical thinker, this opens up a new way of understanding his metaphysics.

I must sound a note of caution before beginning. I am not arguing that Aristotle sets up his metaphysical system in primarily theological terms. Aristotle is no Plotinus, no Aquinas. He does not write a summa of metaphysics. It is a mistake to think of the Aristotelian texts as being other than a compilation added to by many hands as time went on. What results is a rather scattered compendium; one has to piece together a systematic metaphysics from dense, competing remarks over many texts. There are not infrequent passages referring to the divine, to souls, to religious practices, and so on. What I want to do is show how those diverse comments add up to a system that, so to speak, mirrors the divine as the final cause of the cosmos. Aristotle never says that the world "mirrors" God (although he drops many hints). I aim to show, nonetheless, that this familiar Platonic trope, which later becomes explicit in Plotinus and Porphyry, is already there in an inchoate form in Aristotle. Although Aristotle himself never fits the pieces of this jigsaw puzzle together in any definitive or even entirely consistent way, a rigorous analysis of his rather scattered texts lends itself to this overall

---

6. Barnes, *Cambridge Companion to Aristotle,* s.v. "Metaphysics," 68.

picture. I want, then, to look at the systematic implications of his arguments for a larger religious worldview.

In a fragment from the *Protrepticus*, Aristotle argues along Platonic lines that only philosophers make good rulers because:

> the philosopher alone imitates that which is exact. [...] So presumably if a man either lays down laws for cities or performs actions by looking at and imitating other human actions or constitutions, [...] he is not a good or serious lawgiver; for an imitation of what is not good cannot be good, nor can an imitation of what is not divine and stable in its nature be immortal and stable. It is clear then that to the philosopher alone among craftsmen belong laws that are stable and actions that are right and noble. For he alone lives by looking at nature and the divine. Like a good helmsman he moors his life to that which is eternal and unchanging, drops his anchor there, and lives his own master.[7]

A commentator may complain that this is (allegedly) the young Aristotle before he (allegedly) turns more resolutely to materialist science. But what, then, are we to make of Aristotle's praise of the contemplative life in the *Nicomachean Ethics*, a major text, uncontroversially, by the mature Aristotle. In proving that "perfect happiness is a contemplative activity," he advances, as the key reason, "the activity of God, which surpasses all others in blessedness, must be contemplative."[8] It seems short-sighted to see this as anything other than a repetition of a common ancient trope, which the philosopher, in thinking deeply about reality, is somehow actively imitating the thought processes of God. If Aristotle never reached the stage where he set this eternal nature out as a definitive system, I want to show

---

7. Ross, "Fragments"; Iamblichus, *Protrepticus*, 54.10-56.12.
8. *Nicomachean Ethics* (Ross) X.8.1178b8, b21–22.

that the deep structure of Aristotle's metaphysics is liable to this kind of treatment. My focus here in this chapter is on philosophical analysis, not on a historical or philological treatment.

What results, then, is a metaphysics that resembles Neoplatonism more closely than we might suspect, while retaining important differences. Insomuch as Plato or Platonists render material particulars as mere images or reflections of the higher reality of a world of Forms, that is not Aristotle. If anything, Aristotle's metaphysics represents a reworking of this Platonic tradition in a way that takes particulars and individual materials very seriously on their own account, while retaining, however, a very Platonic metaphysical superstructure. At least that is what I will argue. Determining what the later Plato and Platonists believed about particulars is fraught with scholarly disagreement that I cannot enter into here.[9]

3.2. *Imago Dei* in an Aristotelian Vein

In *Genesis*, we read: "God said, 'Let us make man in our image, after our likeness.'"[10] Christian theologians use the phrase *imago Dei* (Latin for "image of God") to describe the way human nature is modelled on the nature of God. The pre-Christian Aristotle posits a parallel, not merely between human beings and God but between the entire cosmos and God. In Aristotle's universe, everything is striving, within the limits of its capacities, to resemble, as closely as possible, the transcendental nature of God. This includes human beings as rational animals, but it includes everything else as well. In Aristotle's metaphysics, the whole of (uncreated) nature rises up to fulfill itself in an exercise in imitation piety. This is why God is the final cause of Aristotle's cosmos.

---

9. Cf. White, *Plato's Theory of Particulars*; Buckels, "A Platonic Trope Bundle Theory."
10. Cf. Genesis 1:26–27; Genesis 5:1, 9:6; 1 Corinthians 11:7; Colossians 3:10; James 3:9.

In discussing where the soul is in the world, Aristotle recalls Thales's declaration that "everything is full of gods."[11] Patricia O'Grady traces the comment to Plato's Athenian Stranger, but the important thing for our purposes is the common Greek idea that the "divine" manifests itself everywhere in the world.[12] Aristotle's metaphysics is a much more sophisticated accounting of such notions. We find, if we look closely, a series of ontological levels—the precise number is not so important—that reflect various facets of the divine. Think of the universe like a Russian Matryoshka doll: each smaller doll fits inside a larger doll, which fits inside a larger doll, and, again, inside a larger doll, until we make our way to God, the largest doll of all. There is, then, a sequence of divine imitations, nestled inside each other, which eventually arrives at something truly, perfectly, genuinely divine.

Granted, Aristotle differs from Plato. If anything, he reacts to the exaggerated anthropomorphism of the Timaeus myth that has the Demiurge, aided by lesser gods deliberately designing and ordering things in the world for the best. As we have seen, Aristotle does not do away with divinity, however, as he points to prehistoric beliefs in the gods and the divinity of celestial bodies as "relics of an ancient treasure that have been preserved until the present."[13] He dismisses any depiction of gods "in the form of men or like some of the other animals" as a sort of noble lie directed towards the gullible multitude but, as we shall see, divinity plays an important role within the whole cosmos.

Stephen Menn suggests, plausibly, that Aristotle is engaged in constructing something of a rival "theology" to Plato.[14] Aristotle aims to strip the One God, then, of ignoble

---

11. *De Anima* III.5.411a7–8.
12. O'Grady, *Thales of Miletus*, 108–121. Cf. *Laws* 899a–b.
13. *Metaphysics* (Ross) XII.8.1074a38–b5.
14. Cf. Menn, "Aristotle and Plato on God." Menn's theory depends on a controversial reading of *Eudemian Ethics,* I.8.1217b31; *Nicomachean Ethics* I.6.1096a24–25.

anthropomorphic associations by emphasizing its unique role as final rather than efficient cause. Philosophically, this is a not an entirely successful strategy (as I discuss below). If, however, Aristotle believes that God has to be categorically different from finite beings in the world—he, rather cleverly, adopts an "anthropomorphism in reverse." God is not like things in the world; rather, things in the world are like God. God is not like the universe; the universe is like God. Things in the world continually strive to possess—however imperfectly or inchoately—the very properties that make God divine. (Whether that would logically entail that God must be like the world is an interesting question, but I think that Aristotle would have thought that was a wrong-headed way of asking the question.)

Aristotle's philosophical god possesses different properties such as eternalness, immutability, purity, immateriality, and thought. But we must never think of these properties as separate parts of God. God has only one property: divinity. All the different aspects of divinity coincide in some necessary nexus. But this also happens in the world. Wherever we find one divine property reflected in the world, we find reflections of other divine properties. As a rule, something that appears to have one of these divine properties must have the others, at least to some degree or in some sense.

Consider, for example, how Aristotle describes the active *nous*, which he identifies as a divine object in *De Anima* III.5. In that controversial passage, Aristotle tells us that the active part of the mind is "immortal" (ἀθάνατον: literally, deathless), "eternal" (ἀΐδιον), "unmoved" (ἀπαθὴς: immutable, i.e., cannot suffer change), "unmixed" or pure (ἀμιγής), and "separable" (χωριστός, i.e., distinct from the physical body and from anything else).[15] This is a deliberate attempt to depict the active *nous* as an intellectual image of God. If, then, Aristotle sees the entire universe as an image of God, one should also expect to find properties like (1) immortality or eternalness,

---

15. *De Anima* III.5.430a17–22.

(2) unmovedness or unalterableness, (3) unmixedness or purity, and (4) immateriality (separateness from the physical) elsewhere in the world. And, as we shall see, this is what we find if we look carefully enough. I will add other properties of God to this list later.

3.3. Eternal Duration

Ordinary Greeks commonly referred to the gods as "the immortals." (As Hesiod writes, "do sacrifice innocently and cleanly to *the immortals*."[16]) What is divine, by definition, must exist forever. In Aristotle's technical treatment of the One philosophical God, he describes him as "a living being, *eternal*, most good."[17] If, however, God is eternal, this is obviously not the case for the transient physical beings (such as ourselves) that inhabit the world. One can catch glimpses, nonetheless, of a striving towards eternity in the midst of the continual corruption and decay that characterizes the history of individual things in the universe.

Aristotle makes the point explicitly. He tells us that to "partake in the eternal and divine" is "the goal towards which all things strive and for the sake of which they do whatever their natures render possible."[18] In *Generation and Corruption*, he stipulates that the universe is in a state of *perpetual* becoming because this "is the closest approximation to eternal being [i.e., to God]."[19] Ever-changing and everlasting history is, then, an image of eternity. But let us set out this imitation of divine eternity in the cosmos in an orderly manner.

Let us begin with things closest to God. We could include, if we wish, the Greek gods of mythology, insomuch as they represent an admittedly ambiguous and figurative representation of the divine. These literary figures play little or no role

---

16. Hesiod, *Works and Days* (Lattimore), 337.
17. *Metaphysics* (Ross) XII.7.1072b29–30.
18. *De Anima* (Smith) II.4.415a26–b1; cf. *Symposium* 207b–d.
19. *Generation and Corruption* (Joachim) II.10.336b31–32.

in Aristotle's technical metaphysics. They may play a more serious role in Greek tragedy, which I discuss later. Still, Aristotle must be aware of them and even shows his respects (as when he pays for the *ex-voto* statues). In the *Politics*, he does suggest that there must be temples distributed throughout the land dedicated to *immortal* gods and heroes.[20] It is also clear from Aristotle's concept of *eudaimonia* that genuine heroes must, ideally, possess an *eternal* reputation for good. That is why he thinks their statues belong in public spaces.

But let us leave aside this "literary" level of interpretation and consider the level of existence closest to God in Aristotle's technical metaphysics. Let us begin, then, in Aristotelian astronomy, with a backdrop of eternal heavenly duration characterized by "the eternity of circular motion."[21] Aristotle believes that the heavens and the celestial spheres (all 45 or 55 of them) rotate forever. As he explicitly states, "The nature of the stars is eternal."[22] And again, "the movement of the planets is eternal."[23] Aristotle also insists that the ether that composes and fills everything in the heavens must be "ungenerated and indestructible."[24] This is why he attempts to explain how it is that this heavenly "stuff" never changes.

In the staircase of existence, we could place the subcelestial cosmos one level further down. The precise order of levels or steps is not at issue here. Aristotle is not an Augustine with any finished conception of a great "chain of being." Still, there are clearly higher and lower levels of existence in his metaphysics. Below the eternal celestial level, we have the sublunary sphere, which Aristotle believes (as the

---

20. *Politics* (Rackman) VII.12.1331b16–19. Cf. *Politics* VII.14.1332b16–21.
21. Cf., for example, Aristotle's discussion of logical necessity of "the eternity of circular motion" in *Generation and Corruption* I.11.
22. *Metaphysics* (Ross) XII.8.1073a35.
23. *Metaphysics* XII.8.1073a30–31.
24. *On the Heavens* II.3.270a13–15.

pre-Socratics taught) is everlasting. The sublunary sphere is a realm of changeability; it is filled with motion—growth, locomotion, decay, substantial change—all these different kinds of change fill up the sublunary sphere, which is a realm of becoming (that can be measured out according to the movement of the planets and stars). But Aristotle believes that "Motion [inside and outside the sublunary sphere] is eternal and cannot have existed at one time and not at another: in fact, such a view can hardly be described as anything else than fantastic."[25] It follows that change or motion in the sublunary world goes on forever.

If the physical, sublunary world is eternal, it seems that the physical elements or, at least, prime matter would also have to be indestructible. We may get changing mixtures of things (as Aristotle explains in his chemistry) but an eternal-perpetual world has to be made from something that never decays. If, for example, we were to come across a bronze shield that happened to exist forever, the stuff the shield was made of—i.e., the bronze—would have to exist forever. We cannot have an everlasting bronze object without everlasting bronze. But everlasting bronze has to be composed of physical elements that are also everlasting. So, the stuff of which physical things in the world are made—call it physicality, materiality, prime matter, the elements, or even being itself—whatever this is and whatever alterations it undergoes, it must be everlasting. Or we could not have an everlasting world. This everlasting stuff would constitute, then, another image of divine eternity.

Aristotle seems to push his belief in an uncreated everlasting world in strange directions, hinting at an understanding of history that resembles, more familiarly, the eternal recurrences of Stoicism. As if history were to endlessly repeat itself in cycles. He claims, for example, "that the same opinions appear in cycles among men not once nor twice nor

---

25. *Physics* (Gaye and Hardie) VIII.1.252a4–5.

occasionally, but infinitely often."[26] So the wheel of human history—forever spinning—would be another everlasting image of divine eternity in the world. But these are enigmatic comments, which I cannot explore further here.

Once we leave aside the cosmos and history as a whole, we discover other ways in which eternity manifests itself in the universe. As already mentioned, Aristotle claims that the active *nous* of rational souls is "immortal" and "eternal."[27] The status of the passive *nous* is more difficult to ascertain. In *De Anima III*, he claims it does not survive death. But, as already mentioned, things are not entirely straightforward for he also describes thought (which requires a passive *nous*) "as an independent substance implanted in us incapable of being destroyed."[28] This comment is located before discussion of the active–passive distinction; he seems to be talking here of the whole soul (with active and passive *nous*) as opposed to the physical body. But we cannot sort through the attendant complications here. Suffice it to say that at least in the best part of the best mind, we discover an image of divine eternity.

Lower animals lack a rational mind, but Aristotle (who had no knowledge of evolution) explicitly says that they are able to partake in immortality through the act of reproduction.[29] In his words: "Because nothing perishable can forever remain one and the same, an organism tries to achieve that end in the only way possible [through reproduction], and [...] continues its existence in something like itself [i.e., its offspring] which [...] belongs to the *same, one species*."[30] Biological species endure forever through reproduction. Cats and dogs strive towards eternity by making copies of

---

26. *Meteorology* (Webster) I.3.339b27–30.
27. *De Anima* III.5.430a23. Cf. Plato, *Phaedo* 64a ff. Here Socrates talks about philosophy as a training for death when the soul separates from the perishable body.
28. *De Anima* (Smith) I.4.408a18–19.
29. *De Anima* (Smith) II.4.415a26–b1; *Symposium* 207b–d.
30. *De Anima* (Smith) II.4.415b3–8.

themselves—their progeny—so that the species (the phenotype) continues on forever, staying the same; but this supplies another image of divine eternity.

More could be said, but what do we end up with? We find ourselves inside a universe with images, echoes, imitations of eternity, stacked one on top of another on many different levels: the mythological gods, the heavens, the physical world of becoming, the physical stuff the world is made of, the cycles of history, the active mind, biological species—all these things mirror eternity in imitation of the eternal god. Although physical beings come into and out of existence on a regular basis, the universe still manages to model and mirror the eternal divine. The structure of the whole cosmos conspires to imitate everlastingness, layer after layer, in a way that imitates God. And that is not all.

When we get to the level of individual humans, we find that Aristotle describes individual human agency as something that aspires to everlastingness. Although I will not investigate the many ramifications of these issues here, I should note that Aristotle's view of morality seems to revolve around the idea that we should pursue an eternal good and avoid an eternal evil. He describes happiness as *eudaimonia*, which amounts to the achievement of an *everlasting* reputation for goodness after we die (like Socrates achieved). If we are heroically good, people will tell their children who will tell their children, and so on, keeping us alive (so to speak) forever. We will become immortal like the gods—indeed, we will achieve a sort of divinity—not because we survive death in this world but because a copy of ourselves will perpetually extend into the future. The envisaged process is not unlike biological reproduction except that it creates an intellectual rather than a physical copy of the participating agents. Suffice it to say, then, that the importance of a lasting reputation for good after we die—a general feature of ancient and tribal cultures—has to do with a striving towards immortality and is properly seen as an imitation of divinity. Aristotle is elaborating on a very familiar trope here.

But there is a second way in which Aristotle's ethics could be seen as gesturing towards eternity. We usually think of Aristotle as a virtue ethicist—which he principally is. Less noticed, however, is that Aristotle places limits on moral behaviour that are fixed, immutable, and unmoved forever. Aristotle comments that "unjust, cowardly, and voluptuous behaviours" as well as specific actions such as adultery, theft, and murder "must *always* be wrong."[31] *Always* wrong. That is, *eternally* wrong.

Aristotle writes, "All these and similar actions and feelings are blamed as being bad in themselves; it is not the excess or deficiency of them that we blame. It is impossible therefore ever to go right in regard to them—one must always be wrong." [32] That is, these feelings and behaviours must be wrong at any point in time, past or future. They are intrinsically evil; that is, their badness derives from the nature of the act itself, not from the surrounding circumstances. That is why it is not possible ever to be right with them, whatever the circumstances. But this means that these limits on human behaviour are, essentially, eternal. It is not far to go from this realization to the idea that there is an image of the eternal goodness embedded in moral striving. In a world of perpetual becoming, there are fixed moral standards that provide, then, another image of an eternal god who stays good forever.[33]

If the astute reader of Aristotle can find an image of eternity in morality, one could readily pick out other examples. In Aristotle's logic, for example, the principle of non-contradiction is fixed and true forever. It never changes. Or, expressed more aptly, what the principle of non-contradiction reveals about the world never changes. We could say something similar about the truths of mathematics and geometry. So even here, one can find images of eternity as we did in the immortal mythological gods, in the movement of the

---

31. *Nicomachean Ethics* (Ross) II.6.1107a14.
32. *Nicomachean Ethics* (Rackham) II.6.1107a14.
33. I will discuss the goodness of Aristotle's god further below.

heavens, in the duration of the world, in human history, in the active mind, in biological species, in materiality. But we must consider other divine attributes.

3.4. "Unmovedness"

If we have already noted many intimations of eternalness in the world, turn to the complementary Aristotelian property of being unmoved or immutable. Aristotle is very clear about this. To be God is to be an unmoved mover: "The first mover must be unmoved."[34] But the property of being "unmoved" or immutable does not only apply to God but is echoed, over and over again, in the layered structure of Aristotle's metaphysics. Along with intimations of eternity, we can discern intimations of "unmovedness" all around us.

The technical Greek expression Aristotle uses to describe the immutability of God is: ἔστι τι ὃ οὐ κινούμενον κινεῖ.[35] Literally, this translates as: "there is something which, not being moved, moves." Aristotle's point is that the divine moves on its own initiative; it never has to be moved by anything outside itself. The divine has an internal source of motion; it always moves on its own power.[36] Nothing pushes or pulls God from the outside—nothing would be capable of this—and yet God moves.

More generally, then, to attribute the property of unmovedness to something is to claim that it has the remarkable ability of initiating movement on its own. Obviously, in a plain ordinary sense, things in the world move. Even the heavens move (for us and for Aristotle). In Aristotle's metaphysics, only his philosophical god (and perhaps the celestial intelligences?) are, in any absolute or unqualified sense, unmoving. But being unmoved in the technical sense intended here, means, more modestly, retaining the same

---

34. *Physics* (Hardie and Gaye) VIII.6.258b12–13.
35. *Metaphysics* 12.7.1072a25.
36. *Metaphysics* XII.8.1073a27. Cf. *Physics* VIII.6. Thanks to Paolo Biondi for a helpful discussion.

nature unchanged—i.e., unmoved—through time. Suppose a dog runs across the street. The dog moves in reference to the outside world, but the dog's nature is unmoved: that is the important thing. The dog is still a dog—on both sides of the street. Indeed, the dog's trajectory across the street depends on the dog: i.e., the dog is a self-mover, which means, in Aristotelian terms, it is an unmoved mover.

Aristotle believes that unmovers are self-initiators of action. Think of it this way. Aristotle's ultimate god is the original unmover. He cannot be moved by anything outside himself. The only movement we can attribute to Aristotle's ultimate god is thinking understood as an immaterial kind of moving and beholding. God cannot be subservient or even subject to the influence of anything outside himself. Any thought in his mind must be put there by his own (unchanging) will and nature; it cannot be forced upon him by anything foreign existing outside himself. Insomuch as other things in the universe imitate God's unmovedness, they do so in a much more partial or derivative way. Even when they can be moved by things outside themselves, they are still unmoved insomuch as they also possess—to varying degrees—a capacity for self-initiated movement; that is, they change according to a nature that resides inside themselves. The mythological gods, human beings, animals, even inanimate chemical compounds and intellectual objects are *unmoved* to the degree that any changes they exhibit derive from their own natures rather than from forces from outside themselves. Lesser beings are, of course, moved by forces outside themselves. Even the Greek gods of myth are influenced by things outside themselves; their behaviour is changed, for example, by the events of the Trojan War. Nonetheless, insomuch as one can detect some degree of self-initiated movement in whatever instance of being, we can identify this with the metaphysical unmovedness fully exemplified in Aristotle's god. Only God exists as a perfect paradigm of unmovedness, that is (in the proper sense) inaccessible to all external influence, but lesser beings are able to imitate him to some degree, in the measure of their capacities.

Unmoved things in the world possess agency. The unchanging (i.e., the unmoving) natures they possess give them the ability to act in self-directed ways. They generate their own behaviour. They are not passive playthings of merely exterior forces; they have an inward identity that is able to exert and express itself according to its own principles. In Aristotle's metaphysics, only God can originate movement in any completely independent sense. Nonetheless, if we look carefully at things in the world, Aristotle thinks that we can discern less perfect examples or degrees of "unmovedness" at different levels of existence. These unmoved movers generally possess some degree of self-directed agency. Being "unmoved" in this technical sense and being "self-moved" coincide.

The prospect may seem a bit odd but consider, first, the "unmoved" character of the mythological gods of traditional Greek religion. These immortals are unmoved only in the sense that they are not prey to the usual earthly forces that *move* the rest of us. You cannot move a god the way you move a brick, a table, or a cat. They are beyond the set of things that are, in any physical sense, movable. That is why they can appear out of nowhere and travel instantaneously to the most distant places. They move themselves (by an act of will, presumably) but they are external to the chain of natural causality that moves bodies in the world. At least in Homer, they do what they want heedless of the laws of nature; they intervene in natural causality and (efficiently) cause alteration anywhere in the world and, in this sense, are movers but they are unmoved movers in that they are themselves unmoved by anything outside themselves. They fly down from Olympia on their own independent initiative and change things in the world. This is at least suggestive of the possibility of a greater unmover behind everything. But, again, this relates to a level of ambiguous, poetic, practical piety.

Let us progress further to the second tier of metaphysics proper: the divine (or quasi-divine?) level of celestial spheres. Aristotle reports on their rotation as follows: "each movement also must be caused by a substance unmovable in itself and eternal."[37] Outside the One philosophical God, then, Aristotle posits the existence of a series of crystalline spheres that move the planets and stars while remaining unmoved themselves. "There must be heavenly substances," he concludes, "which are of the same number as the movements of the stars, and in their nature eternal, and in themselves unmovable."[38] These unmoved movers, in making the heavens revolve, imitate, then, the unmoved nature of the transcendent god. Their metaphysical significance is somewhat ambiguous; insomuch as they are productive of "physical" movement (rather than immaterial mental movement), they seem situated at a lower level in Aristotle's metaphysical scheme. Pushing something quasi-physical (like Aristotle's stars) seems to require an interaction with brute external forces that influence what results. But I will not try to resolve these cryptic issues here.

Aristotle also reports that the ether, "the primary bodily substance" that composes the quintessential celestial spheres, is "exempt from increase and all alteration," as an "unaging, unalterable, and unmodified" thing.[39] Put otherwise, the ether (whatever exactly its nature consists of) is unmovable; i.e., it cannot be changed from the outside. As the pseudo-Aristotle puts it in *De Mundo*, it must be "free from disturbance, change, and external influence."[40] Yet it also must possess agency (efficient causality) of some sort

---

37. *Metaphysics* (Ross) XII.8.1073a34.
38. *Metaphysics* (Ross) XII.8.1073a3–40.
39. *On the Heavens* (Stocks) I.3.270b25. Interesting enough, Aristotle argues that observation shows that the movements of the heavens do not change: "The mere evidence of the senses is enough to convince us of this, at least with human certainty. For in the whole range of time past, so far as our inherited records reach, no change appears to have taken place either in the whole scheme of the outermost heaven or in any of its proper parts"; 1.3.270b12–16. Aristotle thinks ether is completely different than air, water, earth, and fire. He complains that Anaxagoras misuses the term by identifying it with ordinary fire. *On the Heavens* I.3.270b25.
40. *On the Universe* (*De Mundo*) II.392a.30–33.

if it moves or aids in the movement of the heavens. So, this unmoved fifth element that moves the heavens supplies another image of the unmoved mover that is Aristotle's god. (Perhaps this fifth element moves along with the spheres [?] but the important point is that it must initiate its own movement: it would be, then, an *unmoved* mover.)

And there are further layers of unmovedness, at lower levels, in Aristotle's metaphysics. As I have already mentioned, Aristotle explicitly states that the active *nous* is unmoved. But he also insists that souls, in general, are like God in that each soul—even in the case of animals and plants—is an unmoved mover. "It is an impossibility," he writes, "that movement should be even an attribute of it."[41] What he means is that the soul cannot be moved by anything outside itself. We can relocate the living body in which a soul resides, but that is a different matter. Considered in terms of its own nature, we cannot pick up an immaterial soul—by itself—and move it somewhere else. The agency of the body has to be attributed to the soul, but the soul's agency cannot be attributed to something external, pushing or pulling it from the outside, so to speak. This explains the difference between organisms and artefacts. (And is wholly at odds with modern reductionism where the physicality of the body is acting as the agency that makes life do what it does.)

Aristotle is explicit about all this. In the *Movement of Animals*, he tells readers that there must be something in the organism "that causes movement without itself being moved."[42] He compares the soul to the centre of a wheel: "Just as in the case of a wheel, so there must be a point which remains at rest, and from that point the movement must originate."[43] The soul is like the centre of a spinning disk; the centre point is umoved but it is what makes everything

---

41. *De Anima* (Smith) I.3.406a1–2.
42. *Movement of Animals* (Forster) 9.703a1–3. Cf. *De Anima* (Smith) II.2.414a19–21.
43. *De Anima* (Ross) III.10.433b13–14, 25–28.

else spin. Less metaphorically, souls are "unmoved principles that impart motion."[44] They are the origins from which all the "motions" that characterize life—reproduction, nutrition, growth, locomotion, perception, even thought—derive.

When Aristotle describes souls as unmoved movers, he is not denying, of course, that animal souls, for instance, are lodged in physical bodies that move and are receptive to perception, changing desire, and circumstance.[45] Aristotle's souls are unmoved insomuch as the power of living originates from inside them. Life does not come from the outside; it comes from the inside. Souls are not moved by something else that endows them with life from an external source; movement arises from an internal perspective that always stays the same. The organism is the same organism because there is a soul inside it that never changes: i.e., that is unmoved. This is even true for an organism like a butterfly that passes through life-cycle stages with morphological differences: egg, caterpillar, chrysalis, butterfly. The point is that the changes in the organism "come from the inside"; they are self-initiated by the nature of the butterfly not by external forces. Nature does not make a butterfly the way humans make artefacts. In this technical sense, then, souls are the unmoved movers inside living things, orchestrating the living functions of the body (and thought). They represent, accordingly, another (imperfect) reflection of Aristotle's unmoved mover.

But there are other unmoved movers in Aristotle's cosmos as well. Consider, for example, the unmovedness of the biological species. In Aristotle's biology, the form of the species "dog" impresses itself, so to speak, on the individual matter of individual dogs. (A cat could be composed of the same matter but rearranged in a different way.) Aristotle has no inkling

---

44. *Physics* VIII.6.259bff; cf. Menn, "Aristotle's Theology," 436.
45. "The soul can be moved incidentally." *De Anima* (Smith) I.4.408a31.

of evolution.[46] Species remain eternally the same. Dogs are always dogs. Cats are always cats. So, the form "doghood" and the form "cathood" are eternally unmoved. Yet this unmoved form moves particular instances of matter to produce individual dogs and cats. So, we have something unmoved that moves something else which, thus understood, supplies us with another image of Aristotle's unmoved mover god.

As already mentioned, Aristotle views biological reproduction as a striving for immortality: Organisms produce offspring that belong "to the *same, one species [my emphasis]*."[47] Through reproduction, the biological species continues on—unchanged or *unmoved*—forever, in spite of the deaths of individual specimens. In the absence of evolution, dogs never become another species. The form of dog is, then, metaphysically fixed for all eternity; it is eternally unmoved and yet continually moves something: the matter that makes up all particular members of that species.

Aristotle is no Plotinus. I am not suggesting that Aristotle casts his observations in Neoplatonic terminology. But the structure of his metaphysics requires species to be unmoved things. If progeny are "not numerically but *specifically* one," this is because they possess the same form, which carries on in offspring, even when that form is housed in a new body and the individual matter changes.[48] So, the generalized form—i.e., the species—remains unmoved in the process of reproduction. New baby dogs are still dogs. They remain the same in terms of the species although they are not individually the same.

But the form of the biological species is not merely unmoving. That is not strong enough to capture all that Aristotle means. Aristotle leaves a very large place for his

---

46. As I have argued elsewhere, it does not follow that evolution is an empirical impossibility. It is rather that Aristotle does not seriously entertain that empirical possibility; it is off his radar, so to speak.
47. *De Anima* (Smith) II.4.415b3–8.
48. *De Anima* (Smith) II.4.415b8 (my italics).

notion of the soul as an unmoved *mover*. He observes that in all plants as well as animals, "natural bodies are organs of the soul."[49] He identifies "the soul as the cause or origin of the living body";[50] as "the source of movement, the end, and the essence of the whole living body";[51] as "the final cause";[52] and "as the source of local movement."[53] But to say that the soul is the origin of the living body, the ultimate source of movement, or the goal towards which the body aspires is to say that it is the unmoving form that is all these things, for the soul is the form of the body.

All this comes to the fore in Aristotle's discussion of sexual reproduction. Aristotle observes that the reason for the (sexual) generation of animals is that "soul is better than body,"[54] that "nature acts like an intelligent workman,"[55] that "nature uses the semen as a tool,"[56] and that "the material of the semen" [houses] "the principle of soul."[57] He asserts that the male seed alone contains the soul or form that is injected into the menstrual matter of the female. The discussion here is not entirely consistent but Aristotle (or his editors) explain:

> The menstrual fluids are semen, only not pure; for there is only one thing they have not in them, the principle of soul. For this reason, whenever a wind-egg [a sterile egg] is produced by any animal, the egg so forming has the parts of both sexes potentially, but has not the principle in question [the soul], so that it does not develop into a living creature, for this is introduced by the semen of the

---

49. *De Anima* (Smith) II.415b17–19.
50. *De Anima* (Smith) II.4.415b9.
51. *De Anima* (Smith) II.4.415b11–12.
52. *De Anima* (Smith) II.4. 415b15. "This shows that that for the sake of which they are is soul." II.4. 415b20.
53. *De Anima* (Smith) II.4. 415b22.
54. *Generation of Animals* (Platt) I.23.731b27.
55. *Generation of Animals* (Platt) I.23.731a25. Cf. I.22.730b10–31.
56. *Generation of Animals* (Platt) I.22.730b20–21.
57. *Generation of Animals* (Platt) III.3.737a7.

male. When such a principle has been imparted to the residue of the female it becomes an embryo.[58]

Unlike in modern reductionist theories where the matter does the real work and the form supervenes on biochemical operations, in Aristotle it is the other way around. In the case of the reproduction of dogs, for example, the doghood soul (the unmoved form) moves the passive matter to produce a new dog that preserves the same form of doghood despite accidental differences in the matter. The form doghood is unmoved, only the matter changes; the species stays the same while moving something else.

We should not misunderstand one side detail in Aristotle's theory of epigenesis (or fetal development). His theory bears some resemblance to the recapitulation theory championed by modern biologists such as Ernst Haeckel. Aristotle argues, most importantly, that human beings pass through plant, animal, and human stages. They first possess a nutritive, then an animal, and finally a rational soul.[59] But Aristotle never suggests that the same soul passes through plant, animal, and human stages. It is not as if the plant soul becomes an animal soul, which, then, becomes a rational soul. There are three separate principles that never mix. Indeed, Aristotle goes so far as to assert (strangely) that the rational soul enters into the embryo from the outside.[60] He explains:

> Those principles whose activity is bodily cannot exist without a body, e.g. walking cannot exist without feet. For the same reason [the vegetable and animal soul] cannot enter [the embryo] from outside. [...] It remains, then, for the reason alone to enter so and for reason alone to be

---

58. *Generation of Animals* (Platt) II.3.737a27–34
59. Cf. *Generation of Animals* II.3.736a31–736b3.
60. *Generation of Animals* II.3.737a7–10.

divine, for no bodily activity has any connexion with the activity of reason.[61]

This leaves us, of course, with an embarrassing question. If the rational soul enters into the embryo from the outside, where does it come from? The text offers no answer to this puzzling question, but what matters in the present context is that all this reinforces the picture of the soul as an unmoved mover.

On Aristotle's account, there are no cases of one form becoming another form for there is no evolution.[62] In this sense, then, each type of soul is an unmoved mover. Whether it is a plant or an animal soul that comes from within the body or a rational soul that comes from the outside, this unmoved species-form is something separate from and unaffected, it seems, by the ever-changing matter—even though it organizes the matter to produce the operations of life. The soul is not changed by the matter; the matter is changed by the soul. Even plant and animal souls, though more closely associated with the body, are unmoved movers like the rational soul that mysteriously comes from outside. So, here again, we have a persistent image of unmovedness that pervades several layers of existence in Aristotle's metaphysics.

Outside of biology, Aristotle's technical metaphysics revolves around a concept of unmovedness. His account of substance (the usual translation of οὐσία) and substrate or *hupokeimenon* (ὑποκείμενον) have sparked extensive disagreement in the specialist literature. I cannot do justice to those philological debates here. Suffice it to say that Aristotle proposes two accounts of change: (1) substantial change where one thing turns into something completely different (say, a person dies, and the living body decays and turns into dust: living body ≠ dust); and (2) mere alteration, where the

---

61. *Generation of Animals* (Platt) II.3.736b23–736b29.
62. Aristotle recognizes the existence of individual monsters but that is a different thing.

same thing takes on new properties (say a cup of water that was hot, now becomes cold).[63] His account of alteration presupposes something—a substance, a substrate, an entity, a being, a thing, a unit, an artefact—that persists and remains the same through change. But this "underlying something" is another instance of unmovedness.

Take one of Aristotle's many examples: A healthy Socrates becomes an ill Socrates.[64] What changes here is the condition of Socrates: It is the same Socrates throughout. But Aristotle presents many other examples of alteration: The pale man becomes dark (i.e., suntanned), the morally bad man becomes good, the lump of bronze becomes a sphere, the piece of stone is carved into a statue of Hermes, the cold water becomes hot, and so on.[65] In such cases, the identity of the subject—the thing altered—remains unmoved; it remains what it is without changing. This is movement forced on the object "from the outside," but even here, what changes are the metaphysical accidents, the variable properties the substrate may or may not possess. But the underlying nature remains the same: The water does not turn into fire, the marble remains hard, the suntanned man is still a rational animal. There is a self-directed preservation of the nature by the nature, which preserves itself despite surface changes. Aristotle's world is composed then of a plurality of unmoved individual things (primary substances, etc.) that, in each individual instance and in this technical sense, provide repeated images of Aristotle's unmoved god. The world is filled, it turns out, with identities that remain unmoved despite change.

Aristotle is not a Neoplatonist when it comes to matter. Whereas the later Neoplatonists depict matter metaphysically

---

63. Cf. *Generation and Corruption* I.4.319b7–32; *Physics* I.7.189b33–191a23; *Categories* 5.4b14–19.
64. Cf. *Categories* 10.13b12–11.14a14.
65. Cf. *Categories* 5.4.a10–21, 4b14–19; 10.13a21–31; *Physics* I.7.189.35ff; I.7.189.35ff; 190b30; 191a10; *Generation and Corruption* I.4.319a13–14. This is a recurrent theme.

as the absence of absence, Aristotle has a healthy respect for the positive reality of material things in the world. He often points to something material as the underlying, unmoved thing—the substance or substrate—that persists through change. He mentions things like bronze, wood, stone, and the living body. When one carves, for instance, a statue of Achilles out of marble, the shape changes but the marble remains the same marble. The marble, then, is unmoved despite the new shape it now displays. It retains the same nature. Even in the midst of change, in this case and others like it, there is an unmovedness at the centre of things, an identity that is fixed, that reflects the fixed nature of Aristotle's philosophical god.

But consider something even more basic and less complicated than most substances: the element fire. Aristotle notes that we call "simple bodies" such as "earth and fire and water" substances.[66] Except that an element like fire (a combination of the properties of hot and dry) is a very peculiar sort of substance because its nature is fixed and unmovable. Aristotle observes, "fire never becomes cold."[67] And again, "It is not possible for fire to be cold."[68] And again, "any part of fire that one takes will be hot."[69] Fire is always hot. That is, fire cannot, in this respect, suffer alteration. Although fire is constituted by a process of change, this changing remains unchanged (as Heraclitus might have said). Fire is self-directed in that it actively retains its form as fire through time. It represents, then, another instance of *moving* unmovedness in the world. Its hot nature is unmoved; it can never change.

The metaphysically disinclined might think that fire is the *moving* element: It is composed of dancing flames that devour fuel and send off smoke. It may seem, as Heraclitus indicates, a perfect symbol of becoming. Yet fire has an

---

66. *Metaphysics* (Ross) V.8. 1017b10–11.
67. *Parts of Animals* (Ogle) II.2.468b30.
68. *Categories* 10.12b26–13a2.
69. *Physics* (Hardie and Gaye) IV.9.217b14–15.

immovable metaphysical nature because fire is always the same in every instance (at least for Aristotle).[70] Fire can change into other elements (as Aristotle tries to explain in *Generation and Corruption*) but, then, it is no longer fire. Every particular instance of fire possesses the same hot property. A burning candle, a torch, a campfire, a forest fire: In each of these instances a particular instance of fire "aspires" to embody and put on display the fixed nature of fire. In this sense, one can think of the *form* (or actuality) of fire as an unmoved mover. (Aristotle says that a nature like fire is "actualized all the time."[71])

In Plato, the Forms are unmoved movers. Perhaps a particular instance of fire participates in something like the Form of Fire, or in the Forms of Heat, Symmetry, Beauty or Motion—however one wants to construe this. (This is a complicated question.) But in Aristotle, metaphysics is not like that. There is no other-worldly, ethereal Form of Fire or its properties outside the world. The Form is in the world— but the Form of Fire is still there, and the Form of Fire is an unmoved mover: It produces change in the world without being changed itself. Its nature is always the same. Like the nature of Aristotle's philosophical god.

If, however, Aristotle does not believe in Platonic metaphysical Forms, the closest he comes to some sort of belief in abstract immaterial forms is perhaps in his account of mathematics. Aristotle does not believe in the Platonic Form of, say, circularity. He does not think that circularity exists outside its physical instantiations (except perhaps in the mind of God). G.E.R. Lloyd explains:

> Aristotle's philosophy of mathematics differs radically from Plato's. […] He did not postulate separate intelligible mathematical objects. […] Aristotle agreed with

---

70. Aristotle does recognize different species of fire. Cf. *Topics* V.5.134b28–29.
71. *De Interpretatione* 13.23a2–4.

Plato that while physical hoops or rings come to be and pass away, circularity does not. But while the mathematician can study the circle in the abstract, circularity does not exist as a separate intelligible entity.[72]

If, however, Aristotle does not believe that circularity exists as a separate entity *per se* in the world (outside the mind of God), neither does he think that circularity is mutable. Circularity, understood as an abstract mathematical form, imposes fixed properties on particular circles. All circles require a curvilinear boundary; all circles must possess an area that is a function of π, and so on. In this sense, the nature of circularity never moves, like Aristotle's god.

As Lloyd points out, Aristotle explicitly states that mathematical objects (like squareness, circularity, triangularity, parallelness, equality) are not, in themselves, subject to change.[73] In other words, they are unmoved. Yet every physical object that instantiates one of these ideas conforms to specific requirements that derive from the nature of the mathematical form itself. There is a sort of "self-initiated" unchangeability here. To use a very simple example, imagine starting to draw a square—what will you do? As the line-figure takes shape, you will make sure it is composed of straight lines, equal sides, right-angle corners, and so on. Without this prescribed nature, which never changes in general principles, whatever the time or place, you cannot draw a square. The unmoved mathematical nature—the idea or form of squareness that belongs to squareness itself—defines the shape you draw.

All I want to say here is that, in such a situation, we have something eternally unmoved and, by extension, something that can be taken as an image of the unmoved mover that is Aristotle's god. This line of thought can be extended in perhaps surprising directions. If crystals take on certain

---

72. Lloyd, "Mathematics and Narrative," 392.
73. *Movement of Animals* 1.698a25–26; *Physics* II.2.193b34; *Metaphysics* I.8.989b32–33.

regular shapes—so salt crystals form cubes, for example—one can see this, from an Aristotelian perspective, as matter organizing itself according to the form of "cubeness," which functions like an unmoved ideal that always stays the same. If someone asked Aristotle why the world is this way—that crystals strive to be cubes—he would not say because a creator god designed it this way, but he might, very likely, say it is because things in the universe are all striving to resemble God as the final cause of the cosmos. In ordering themselves geometrically, salt crystals are submitting to a rational principle—cubeness—that is unmoved. What a cube is is always and everywhere the same, like Aristotle's unmoved god, which is always and everywhere the same.

I have already mentioned the eternally fixed standards of ethics. Moral first principles stay always the same—forbidding "unjust, cowardly, and voluptuous behaviours" as well as specific actions such as adultery, theft, and murder. These ground-floor standards do not move—they remain unchanged, down through the eons. Yet these unmoved criteria move moral agents to behave in prescribed ways in submission to them. They are, then, in this sense, unmoved movers. We could look elsewhere for examples of fixed standards that motivate human agents to emulate them but suffice it to say that one could find many other examples of unmoved movers in the human realm of Aristotle's cosmos.

To summarize, then: We discern in Aristotle's cosmos a sequence of unmoved movers providing image after image of the unmoved god. The lesser gods, the celestial spheres, the active *nous*, souls, biological species, even inanimate natural kinds, mathematical ideas, and ethical standards mirror God's nature by supplying more or less inferior copies of "unmoved-movingness." (This unmovedness is coming from the things themselves; whether God plays any role as an efficient cause of all this is a question for later consideration.) There are, of course, other ways to approach Aristotle's metaphysics. I only want to make the point that those images are lodged there, deep in the structure of things, stacked up on top of one another (so to speak). We will only see them if we take the trouble to look. In this loose sense, then, we could say that the structure of Aristotle's metaphysics is infused with theological content; it mirrors the nature of the unmoved god. But the images of God do not stop here. If Aristotle's god is eternal and unmoved, he is also "unmixed" or pure. Consider that divine property next.

3.5. Unmixedness

To say that God is "unmixed" or "pure" is to say that he is only composed of himself; his god-nature is utterly simple in that it excludes all foreign elements. As we have seen, Aristotle seems to think that God is pure thought and nothing else. Indeed, he tries to exclude all foreign content from that thought, describing God as thought thinking about thought itself and nothing else. Hence this picture of a self-thinking god. If, however, we look carefully, we can find this property of unmixedness mirrored, in a layer-like way, throughout the structure of Aristotle's metaphysics.

Again, it is important to point out that the term "unmixed" has a technical meaning here. Things in the world are generally mixed in that they are made up various ingredients. But in Aristotle, wholes that are greater than the sum of their parts possess a unity, a oneness that is unmixed insomuch as it maintains and preserves the very same "unmixed" identity over time. Return to our dog example. The dog that runs across the street has feet, fur, a tongue, eyes, a liver, appetites, perceptions, a soul, and so on. We can analyze the dog, dividing it into its various parts. But the dog is pure dog—that is, it is not half-dog and half-cat, or half-fire and half-dog, or half-dead-dog and half-living-dog. The dog is wholly, thoroughly, purely dog because its nature is unmixed: it is pure dogness, it is unmixed in this technical sense.

In Aristotle, only his philosophical god is, in any absolute sense, unmixed. That is, in part, why his ultimate god has to be always introspecting. Because, in some very strange way, God has to be unmixed with every other subject matter. When we speak of images of unmixedness in the world, we are not speaking of this sort of unqualified unmixedness. We mean that there is a oneness in things that makes them uniquely themselves and nothing else. The dog is pure dog just as Socrates is pure Socrates and fire is pure fire. They may be composed of different elements and perform different functions, but they are one thing and purely that thing in a way that mirrors the Oneness of God. This is not a perfect reflection of the divine unmixedness but images in the world are never perfect copies of the eternal prototype.

The Aristotelian author of *On Colours* reports: "We never see a colour in absolute purity: it is always blent, if not with another colour, then with rays of light or with shadows, and so it assumes a tint other than its own."[74] We may speak of "pure red" or "pure green," but no colour is, in any absolute sense, unmixed in the world. Still, *pure* red still provides an image of the purity of Aristotle's philosophical god. If, as I am arguing, the objects in Aristotle's world mirrors, in some imperfect sense, the attributes of his god, they are not God. Our Aristotelian author reports: "light may be a blend of many colours, though the sensation produced is not of a blend but of some colour predominant in the blend. This is why objects under water tend to have the colour of water, and why reflections in mirrors resemble the colour of the mirrors, and we must suppose that the same thing happens in the case of air."[75] Things in the world are in the world; they are not in God. As a Platonist might say, insomuch as things in the world mirror or share in god-like properties like unmixedness or purity, they do it imperfectly. They do this, nonetheless, by presenting an interior oneness or sameness that, at least on Aristotle's account, usually "emerges" a mix of more primordial things. But return to our step-by-step account of Aristotle's metaphysics.

---

74. *On Colours* (Loveday and Forster) 3.793b14–794a16.
75. *On Colours* (Loveday and Forster) 3.793b27–33.

In the case of the mythological gods we are presented with beings who, despite their anthropomorphic flaws, remain (for the most part) unmixed divinity. (The unruly Greek imagination did leave room for things like demigods and other mutations, but let us leave that aside here.) The Homeric gods are unmixed with anything mortal or inferior to themselves. Logic requires that Zeus (whatever he is) must be pure Zeus; Athena must be pure Athena; Apollo must be pure Apollo. And so on. These gods may disguise themselves in mortal form but that is only disguise. As gods they must be purely divine. Hence Xenophanes's philosophical criticism of the myths, which mix all these things up, giving the gods human attributes, and bad ones at that. But all this is literature, not technical metaphysics.

In Aristotle's account of astronomy, the heavens and the celestial spheres are composed of the fifth element *aither* (ether), which is, Aristotle tells us, "simple and unmixed."[76] That is why, he says, the motion of the heavens must be absolutely regular (circular): because they have no mixture of parts or properties. In a more literary turn, the Peripatetic author of *On the Universe* describes the heavens as a "*pure region*" "free from all the gloom and disordered motion" of "our troubled world" and inhabited by a "pure" God.[77] Which is only a less sophisticated, more poetic repetition of the general Aristotelian notion that the heavens are unmixed—a common Peripatetic trope. If, however, the heavens are pure and unmixed, this imitates the nature of Aristotle's unmixed God.

At the sub-celestial level, Aristotle claims (as we have seen) that the active mind is pure or unmixed. In a different book, he also seems to approve of Anaxagoras's more general understanding of *nous* or mind as a separate

---

76. *On the Heavens* II.6.288.b19–20. Hence his argument that the ether is everlasting because something simple (without parts or contrary properties) cannot change.
77. *On the Universe* (Forster) 6.400a5–10.

element, unmixed with all the others, to be added to the four unmixed physical elements—fire, water, earth, air—in the universe.[78] Aristotle comments, "Anaxagoras is right when he says that mind is impassive and *unmixed*, since he makes it the principle of motion: for it could cause motion in this sense only by being itself unmoved, and have supreme control only by being *unmixed* [my emphasis]."[79] So we end up with a general picture of mind or soul as unmoved and unmixed in imitation. This, once again, is a case of imitating the unmoved and unmixed nature of God. Whatever exactly that means, mind is pure mind; soul is pure soul. There is nothing foreign, nothing extraneous inside *nous*. If there was, this foreign object might exert some external influence on the intellect, which would lose its "supreme control" over itself.

Aristotle ridicules the idea that souls could be composed of ratios of opposing properties.[80] Echoing Socrates, he also dismisses the theory that the soul could be a harmony composed of different things. He explains, "the power of originating movement cannot belong to a harmony," meaning here that the ability to be the source of bodily motion cannot belong to something that has more than one part.[81] If the soul had internal parts, these parts could be moved or rearranged with respect to one another. So, the unmoved nature of the soul is logically connected to its unmixed nature. Unmovedness and unmixedness come together as one package; the soul is unmoved because it is unmixed.

---

78. There is no uncontroversial interpretation of Anaxagoras's famous account of *nous*. I tend to side with a minority who see his doctrine as similar to Aristotle. See Sedley, *Creationism*.
79. *Physics* (Hardie and Gaye) VIII.5.256b25–28. Cf. *De Anima* (Smith) I.2.405a16–18: "What [Anaxagoras] says is that thought alone of all is simple, unmixed, and pure. He assigns both characteristics, knowing and origination of movement, to the same principle."
80. Cf. *De Anima* I.4.
81. *De Anima* (Smith) I.4.407b30–31, I.4.407b34. Cf. *Phaedo* 853e–86d, 94b–95a.

In some difficult passages, in *De Anima* and *Sense and Sensibilia*, Aristotle reasons that the same soul can perceive different sense impressions at the same time *because* it is an undivided and dimensionless point-like thing.[82] Even though the colour red and the sound B flat are radically—indeed, incommensurably—different, the same soul that perceives them both "is an identical and numerically single thing."[83] Although colours and sounds are irreconcilably distinct (because of differences in the sense organs), "there must be some unity in the soul by which we perceive all things."[84] The soul is not like a bag of marbles but more like drops of water that run together to form an undivided continuum. Whatever precisely a soul or mind is, it must be a perfect indivisible unity like a geometrical point. It is not mixed with anything else inside itself but, somehow, remains a simple unmixed property or quality. (Of course, this might seem to cause a problem for the vegetable-animal-rational soul amalgam, or for the active-passive *nous* amalgam, but Aristotle does not seem to think so.)

If the soul is unmixed, this is not to deny, of course, that it has distinguishable aspects or faculties: imagination, memory, perception, conceptual thought, will. But faculties are powers of the same individual. If, for example, Aristotle famously distinguishes between the vegetable, the animal, and the rational soul, he does not think that the individual rational agent possesses three souls. There is one soul that, in operating, is capable of fulfilling different roles or functions.

The connection between the active and passive *nous* is more puzzling. In the famous passages in *De Anima* II.5, he makes it clear that the active *nous* is, as we have seen, unmixed. Aristotle also claims that the passive *nous* (the "thinking soul") must also "be pure from all admixture" (so

---

82. Cf. *De Anima* III.2.426b30–427a14; *Sense and Sensibilia* 7.449a5–19.
83. *Sense and Sensibilia* (Ross) 7.449a15.
84. *Sense and Sensibilia* (Ross) 7.449a10.

that it can receive any intellectual form).[85] So there is an unmixedness mirrored in both types of higher mind. (We could perhaps describe the relationship between the active and passive *nous* as a connection between full actuality and utter passivity. In the thinking mind, then, the unmixed presence of actuality exists side-by-side with the unmixed absence of actuality, so that both aspects of the soul are entirely unmixed but in opposite ways.)

On the other hand, precisely how the active and passive *nous* can relate to one another as different "parts" of the very same unmixed soul is something of a mystery. Perhaps one could solve this with some sort of double-aspect theory as if the two aspects of the mind were the two sides of a single sheet of paper, but I will not attempt to resolve this difficult issue here. Suffice it to say that, whatever Aristotle's precise meaning, he stresses the unmixedness of the passive and the active mind in the rational soul and in all the other levels of souls in imitation of his unmixed philosophical god.

If, however, souls provide an image of unmixedness, Aristotle also believes that the living species that are produced by different types of souls are unmixed. Jumbled-up species like centaurs (half-human/half-horse) and satyrs (part-goat/part-man) are not possible. In the *Posterior Analytics,* Aristotle comments that one cannot produce a scientific definition of a "goat-stag" (τραγέλαφος) because an animal that is both a goat and a stag is impossible.[86] It is not merely that a goat-stag cannot exist; a goat-stag is like a square-circle, as it is an impossible mixture of incommensurable essences. Different species have different natures; they cannot be mixed into one and the same thing. (Aristotle was aware of "monsters" such as infertile mules [a cross between a horse and a donkey], but he did not classify them as genuine species because they cannot reproduce.[87])

---

85. *De Anima* (Smith) III.4.429a19.
86. *Posterior Analytics* II.7.92b4–8.
87. Cf. *Metaphysics* VII.8.1033b30–1034a2.

In Aristotle's non-evolutionary biology, then, the essences of different species are unmixed. Dogs are entirely dogs. Dogs do not become dogs gradually—starting out as a different species that slowly transitions into dogs. Their "doggedness" nature remains fixed, unchanged, unmixed. Dogs are dogs from day one until they die and the next generation follows suit. So, the essence of "dog"—despite all the changes individual dogs are susceptible to—remains *unmixed* and eternal just like Aristotle's unmixed god. (The possible exception to this is the spontaneous generation of lowest-level life; but this is too complicated to discuss here.[88])

When we arrive, then, at nonliving things, we can discover further examples of unmixedness even though textual difficulties render any precise interpretation treacherous. Different scholars and even Aristotle himself in different works points variously to the elements (fire, air, water, earth), to the most fundamental chemical properties (wet/dry, cold/hot), or to mysterious prime matter as the *unmixed* substratum that makes up the simple bodies (τὰ ἁπλᾶ σώματα) that underlie physical appearances in the world. In whichever case, however, we end up with some unmixed physicality in resemblance to Aristotle's unmixed god. (Of course, Aristotle's god is pure actuality whereas prime matter is [at least in the Neoplatonic tradition] complete passivity, so there is, we could say, resemblance here in spite of utter difference. Prime matter [on this Neoplatonic account] is an *empty* reflection of God's unmixedness; whereas God is unmixed because he is only actuality, prime matter is unmixed because it is entirely empty; it is the pure absence of actuality.)

I cannot properly investigate the scholarly disputes here. Timothy Crowley, an unorthodox voice, reports "Aristotle seems to be quite clear on the point that the elements of bodies *are* the simplest material constituents of bodies."[89] Indeed,

---

88. Cf. *History of Animals* V.19, VI.15; *Generation of Animals* III.11.
89. Crowley, "De Generatione et Corruptione 2.3," 163. The paper has an extensive bibliography.

Aristotle, in the *Metaphysics* and *On the Heavens*, defines the elements (or the so-called elements) as matter that is "not itself divisible into bodies different in form."[90] That would seem to indicate that the elements are not composed of anything else. Except that, in *On Generation and Corruption*, he seems to claim that these elements are "blended" with more fundamental physical contraries. "Fire is hot and dry," he writes, "Air is hot and moist. [...] Water is cold and moist, and Earth is cold and dry."[91] Add to this account of elements being composed of something simpler, scattered references, which are often interpreted as referring to some sort of "first matter" or "prime matter" that is the universal underlying stratum of material existence.[92] Sometimes Aristotle seems to suggest that if we were to dig down deep enough, we would come across something (variously described) as the simplest material reality, which cannot be broken down any further. As Hugh King explains, "When we consider the [...] proximate matter [that specific objects are composed of], we may in turn analyze out its matter; and so on until we arrive at a first matter. This first matter is evidently the terminus of the analysis because it cannot be in turn considered as composite, i.e., it cannot be further analyzed into a form and some more primitive matter."[93] Suffice it to say for our purposes here that whether we consider the elements, contraries, or prime matter to be a most fundamental physical reality, we eventually meet with something simple and unmixed, which provides another image of the divine unmixedness.

We might point to some sort of emergent metaphysics as the answer to Aristotle's ambiguous account of different layers of material existence and material properties. That would mean, paradoxically, that a composite body could

---

90. *On the Heavens* (Stocks) III.302a15–19. For the same definition, cf. *Metaphysics* 5.3 1014a26–1014b15.
91. *On Generation and Corruption* (Joachim) II.3.330b2–5.
92. Cf. Cohen, "Alteration and Persistence."
93. King, "Aristotle without *Prima Materia*," 373.

create a new kind of matter that emerged as a new kind of simple substance. If this sounds odd, Aristotle himself posits the existence of *homoeomerous* substances that arise from a *true* union of more primitive materials and are made of the same "stuff" at every level of division. Water is, he suggests, an example of a homoeomerous compound, a mixture that "must be uniform" such that "any part is the same as the whole, just as any part of water is water."[94] Aristotle seems to think, then, that if we were to divide a body of water into drops, and then divide those drops into smaller drops, and then into smaller drops, and so on, indefinitely, however long this process of division continues, we will always find that even the smallest drop of water is composed of nothing but more water. In other words, at every level, water is *simply* water. But this means that water is unmixed with anything but water. So even here, on this other account of matter, Aristotle posits another image of unmixedness, which can be construed as an imitation of the unmixedness of God.

Let us take our bearings, then. At different levels in Aristotle's metaphysics, we find an image of purity or unmixedness that mirrors the purity or umixedness of God. We can discern unmixedness (or purity) among the mythological gods, in the heavens, in the active *nous*, in souls more generally, in biological species, in the four elements, in homeomerous compounds, and in prime matter. There is, doubtless, a similar metaphysical rationale in each case. It does not matter how natural kinds develop or emerge; what matters is that we end up with unmixed things that are purely themselves and distinct from things that are not themselves. This traditional Aristotelian approach offers solutions to pertinent questions about supervenience and "grounding" that have been raised in the emergent metaphysics now popular in the analytic tradition, but I do not

---

94. *Generation and Corruption* I.10.328a10–12.

have space to address those issues here.[95] Perhaps one could devise an alternative sort of metaphysics where everything is *mixed up* with everything else and there are no clear boundaries between kinds (*per* Anaxagoras, for example), but this would be very far from Aristotle.

I will not explore the issue fully here, but one should quickly note that one can also discern images of unmixedness or purity elsewhere in Aristotle. I have already mentioned the principle of non-contradiction. Aristotle conceives of the principle in metaphysical as well as logical terms. At least as far as he is concerned, there can be no contradiction anywhere, anytime, in the world. In contradictory relations, there is no possibility of something half-contradictory or of a 25 percent contradiction. The principle enforces (so to speak) a sort of umixedness on the world. We cannot have contradictions mixed up with non-contradictions (at least in Aristotle's logic). Here, then, if we look hard enough, we can discern another image of umixedness (or purity) in imitation of Aristotle's unmixed god.

Or consider the ethical or even political arena. In extolling the contemplative over the active life, Aristotle recommends philosophy as something that possesses "pleasures marvellous for their purity."[96] He seems to believe that *pure* thought—thought that is unmixed with anything else but is only thought (whatever precisely that means)—brings about the highest, most divine-like happiness. The purest happiness. So, the philosopher, lost in contemplation, offers another image of the unmixed god. One could perhaps point to virtue ethics ideals like unmixed justice, unmixed temperance, or unmixed wisdom (etc.) as other examples of hypothetical states that mirror the unmixedness of Aristotle's god, but this is to step outside the realm of metaphysics into something involving practical human endeavour. Let us return, then, to our focus on metaphysics.

---

95. For an example of this sort of approach that takes it in a moral direction, see Franklin, *Worth of Persons*.
96. *Nicomachean Ethics* X.7.1177a25.

3.6. Immateriality

Let us consider, then, how things in the world imitate a more controversial feature of Aristotle's god: his thoroughly immaterial nature. Although some Aristotelian-friendly philosophers are hostile to any metaphysical interpretation that includes immateriality as a real property of things in the world, I will argue that images of immateriality abound throughout Aristotle's metaphysics. We can best understand how these imitations of immateriality play a role in Aristotle's cosmos, not by citing individual passages from the corpus, which are often pushed in partisan directions, but by examining the nature of Aristotle's immaterial God.

Before turning to Aristotle's philosophical God, we might wish to begin with a definition of immateriality as something separate from materiality. Except that defining immateriality (or materiality) is no easy feat. The modernist preoccupation with the mind-body problem (since Descartes) has raised all sorts of difficulties but there is not the space here to delve into that kind of detail. Suffice it to say that immateriality, in the most primary metaphysical sense intended here, must be something more than a shadow, an image, or hallucination without any substance. It must possess some sort of real metaphysical "thereness." It has to be something more than a mere fiction or idea we project onto reality.

Immateriality, in order to be truly immaterial, must lack obvious physical attributes such as size, shape, solidity, divisibility, perceptibility, etc. Except that, in an Aristotelian cosmos, immateriality generally exists alongside, inside of, and entangled up with materiality. If matter is the potential for a certain type of change, immateriality is the actuality that operates that change. This is most obvious in the case of living organisms. Aristotle's philosophical god is pure immateriality without any physical insubstantiation, but that is a special case. Generally speaking, in Aristotle, the immaterial and the material cannot be hived off from one another (as in a modern thinker like Descartes).

Let us turn, then, to Aristotle's immaterial god. Although I cannot offer any finely grained textual exegesis here, the gist of the way Aristotle talks about such things suggests that there are important logical connections between divine properties such as eternalness, unmovedness, unmixedness, and immateriality. None of these four divine properties is metaphysically or logically prior to the others; they all exist together, coincidentally, in one and the same being. It is not that we have a god that is divided into four parts each with a separate property; no, we have one comprehensive property, divinity, looked at from four different perspectives. It is clear, however, that Aristotle's god has an immaterial existence entirely separate from physical things and this immateriality is logically connected to his other attributes.

Let us first consider Aristotle's description of God in Book Lambda (12) of the *Metaphysics*, where he examines the nature of divinity and the celestial spheres. Focus, for the moment, on the relationships between various divine properties. Aristotle writes that there is a god "which moves without being moved, being eternal."[97] And again "[divine] substances must be without matter for they must be eternal."[98] And, finally, he says that something that is a divine substance "cannot have any magnitude, but is without parts and indivisible (for it produces movement through infinite time) [...] [and] is impassive and unalterable."[99]

If, then, Aristotle's god possesses divine properties such as eternalness, unmovedness (impassivity and unalterableness), unmixedness (indivisibility), and immateriality, it seems that if God is to have one of these properties, he must have the others as well:

- So, for example, to say that the god "which moves without being moved" is, therefore, "eternal," is to posit a link

---

97. *Metaphysics* (Ross) XII.7.1072a24–25.
98. *Metaphysics* (Ross) XII.6.1071b21–22.
99. *Metaphysics* (Ross) XII.7.1073a5–12.

between unmovedness and eternalness. (Unmovedness + eternalness.)
- To say that because the divine substances "must be eternal," they "must be without matter" is to posit a link between immateriality and eternalness. (Immateriality + eternalness.)
- To say that the divine "cannot have any magnitude," "for it produces movement through infinite time" is, once again, to posit this link between immateriality and eternalness. (Immateriality + eternalness.)
- To say that the divine is "indivisible" and "without parts" because it "produces movement through infinite time" is to posit a link between unmixedness and eternalness. (Unmixedness + eternalness.)
- To say that the divine, which "cannot have any magnitude" is "indivisible" and "without parts" is to posit a link between immateriality and unmixedness. (Immateriality + unmixedness.)
- And, finally, to say that the divine, which "cannot have magnitude" is "impassive and unalterable" is to posit a link between immateriality and unmovedness. (Immateriality + unmovedness.)

I will not pursue this property-by-property analysis any further here. If, however, we add all this up together, we get a picture of God with: God = unmovedness + eternalness + immateriality + unmixedness. Suffice it to say that on Aristotle's analysis, these divine properties are interrelated and dependent on one another.

One would expect, then, that similar relations between these properties should exist in a world that is striving to resemble God as much as possible. Wherever one finds an image of one divine property, the discerning metaphysician ought to look to see if one can find an image of a complementary divine property. There are obvious constraints that limit the world's ability to imitate God. If, however, divinity requires "a substance that is eternal, unmovable and separate from sensible things," it should be unsurprising to find eternal and unmovable things in the world that are also "separate from sensible things."[100]

With this in mind, let us turn to various levels in Aristotle's metaphysics. Where do we find immateriality understood as something real that exists apart from any physical instantiation? It is hard to know what to do with the mythological gods, which Aristotle occasionally denigrates. Perhaps Aristotle was uncomfortable with their ambiguous material-like natures. Leaving aside those types of divinity, then, let us turn to obvious places in the cosmos where Aristotle explicitly mentions immateriality: (first) in the realms of the heavenly spheres and (second) in the active *nous* of the rational soul. Aristotle reports: "there must be substances which are of the same number as the movements of the stars, and in their nature eternal, and in themselves unmovable, and without magnitude."[101] "Without magnitude" here means immaterial. So, we have a series of eternal, unmoved, immaterial movers that turn the night sky with the stars.

But, further down in the sublunary sphere, we find Aristotle describes the rational mind as something that possesses a unity like the process of continuous thinking but "not a unity like a spatial magnitude."[102] The mind or intellect (*nous*), he further specifies, is "either without parts or is continuous in some way *other* than that which characterizes a spatial magnitude."[103] As we have seen, the active part of the soul, Aristotle's active *nous*, is entirely separate from physical things and immaterial. Except that Aristotle even insists that the passive *nous* "cannot reasonably be regarded as blended with the body."[104] So the

---

100. *Metaphysics* (Ross) XII.7.1073a3–5.
101. *Metaphysics* (Ross) XII.8.1073b36–39.
102. The rational soul is "one and continuous in the sense in which the process of thinking is so." *De Anima* (Smith) I.3.407a7–8.
103. *De Anima* (Smith) I.3.407a8–10 (my emphasis).
104. *De Anima* (Smith) III.4.449a25.

whole of the rational soul must be immaterial, which makes logical sense if we think of souls, more generally, as images of Aristotle's thinking god. In effect, Aristotle relies on the same sort of reasoning he uses about God: Because the soul is (in the precise sense already explained) unmoved and unmixed, it must also be immaterial. But turn next to souls in general (including plant and animal souls).

Despite brave attempts, it is very difficult to arrive at any plausible reductionist account of Aristotle's general notion of the soul.[105] Aristotle describes, not just the rational soul, but even the animal soul as something located inside a physical body but "distinct from a spatial magnitude."[106] In *De Anima*, he writes, "Hence the rightness of the view that the soul cannot be without a body, while it cannot *be* a body; it is not a body but something relative to a body."[107] To argue that the soul is not the body but merely the shape (or pattern) of the body seems, to the present author, to be an overly materialistic interpretation. Aristotle goes so far as to reiterate the common opinion of his time (current in Plato's Academy) that "it must be painful for the soul to be inextricably bound up with the body; and, as is frequently said and widely accepted [i.e., as the *endoxa* have it], that it is better for thought not to be embodied."[108]

Even when it comes to perception (which is a mental operation lower than thought), Aristotle seems to believe that it requires an immaterial mechanism. In discussing common debating mistakes in the *Topics*, he advises the reader to make sure that one's opponent does not conjure up a fiction to use in the place of something real. He gives the following example of such a mistake: "Suppose white is defined as colour mingled

---

105. To mention one older but substantial contribution that reviews much of the exegetical literature and its reductionist or physicalist tendencies, see Shields, "Soul and Body in Aristotle."
106. *Movement of Animals* (Forster) 9.703a3. Cf. *De Anima* (Smith) II.2.414a19–21.
107. *De Anima* (Smith) II.2.414a19–23.
108. *De* Anima (Smith) 1.3.407a35–407b6.

with fire." This is clearly mistaken, Aristotle claims, "for what is bodiless cannot be mingled with body, so that colour cannot be mingled with fire, whereas white does exist."[109] Put another way, we know that colours like white exist as qualia in the mind, but they cannot be mixed with a physical body like fire because they are immaterial phenomena; they can be caused by fire (as Aristotle explains in his account of vision) but the colour in the mind is a different immaterial, unmixed reality. And there is more evidence of this kind of thing.

In a surprisingly explicit passage in the *Generation of Animals*, Aristotle makes a distinction between activities that require or do not require a body. He is discussing how living things, when generated through sexual reproduction, come to have specific capacities. He suggests (although there is some tension in the passages) that the semen and the embryo come to develop, first nutritive (plant) capacities, then sensitive (animal) capacities, and then rational capacities in that order as ontogenesis progresses. Arguing that the semen (along with the sun) has a vital heat different from mere fire that is life-giving, he discusses "the material of the semen, in and with which is emitted the principle of soul," distinguishing two kinds of souls: "one is not connected with matter and belongs to those animals in which is included something divine (namely, the reason), while the other is inseparable from matter."[110] ("Inseparable" here does not mean "the same as.")

There are, then, two kinds of souls, an animal or plant soul that cannot exist without a body, and a rational soul that is entirely unconnected to matter. Aristotle makes a corresponding distinction between material (or bodily) and immaterial (or bodiless) activities and comes to the (somewhat mysterious) conclusion that the mind (or soul) must enter the body from the outside. As already mentioned above, he reports:

---

109. *Topics* (Pickard-Cambridge) VI.12.149b1–3.
110. *Generation of Animals* (Platt) II.3.737a7–10.

> Those principles whose activity is bodily cannot exist without a body, e.g. walking cannot exist without feet. For the same reason also [those bodily principles] cannot enter from outside. [...] It remains, then, for reason alone so to enter [the body from the outside] and alone to be divine, for no bodily activity has any connection with the activity of reason.[111]

Whatever precisely is meant here (and however unsettled Aristotle's biological understanding of reproduction), this is an unequivocal claim about the immateriality of the rational capacities of the soul. Aristotle believes the thinking of the divine rational mind transcends any material or physical instantiation. This is why a rational soul (but even, I will argue, the animal soul) must be immaterial.

Although Aristotle, who was a practising scientist, demonstrates a keen appreciation of material cause, we cannot ignore or overlook his repeated claims about the immateriality of the soul. The mind-body debate in modern philosophy has spawned epiphenomenalist interpretations that, from an Aristotelian viewpoint, miss out on the larger picture. There is, after all, a logic to Aristotle's position. It is not simply that the immaterial nature of the soul imitates or mirrors an immaterial god (which it does). It is that, in Aristotle's metaphysics, immaterial things are, in principle, indivisible and incapable of being moved. Something needs to have extension in space to be divisible. An immaterial thing without extension cannot be divided. There is nothing (physical) to divide. Nor can it be moved. Why?

We have to touch things to make them move.[112] Aristotle writes: "It is impossible to move anything [...] without being in contact with it."[113] All four kinds of Aristotelian movement, "pulling, pushing, carrying, and twirling," require an

---

111. *Generation of Animals* (Platt) II.3.736b22–28.
112. *Physics* VII.2.243a17–18.
113. *Physics* (Hardie and Gaye) VII.2.244a14–244b2.

application of physical force.[114] But this explains why the *unmoved* soul cannot be moved: *because it is not a physical thing*. How could we touch, be in tangible contact with, pull, push, carry, or twirl a bodiless thing? There is nothing (physical) to manipulate. Yes, living things always have a body, but when we talk about the soul per se—by itself—there is no way to reach out and touch immateriality and do any of these physical things. So, the immateriality of Aristotle's soul helps explain why it is unmoved and indivisible. This is perhaps why, at the end of *Progression of Animals*, which is a book about how animals move, Aristotle (or the Aristotelian author) says: "After determining these questions, it remains to investigate the soul."[115] As if to say, after looking at all the moving parts of animals, let us consider that part of animals—the soul—which exists without movement.

But Aristotle's soul is also unmovable inside itself. In the case of the rational soul, it can entertain changing thoughts; in the case of the animal soul, it can entertain changing perceptions. Of course, the soul can be activated by the will or by the sense organs. But the soul itself—i.e., the agency or actuality that makes all this possible—is without parts. This power is, so to speak, one single thing. To use a physical metaphor, it is like a room without furniture; the room is always the same because there is nothing to move around inside it. There may be changing scenery that one can see through the windows, or flickering shadows projected on the walls, but the room itself is a single immaterial thing. We mix water with our wine or sugar with our tea. But one cannot pour a part of the soul into another part of the soul. Because, being immaterial, the soul is, as Aristotle says, unmixed and partless.[116] This also explains why the active part of the rational soul is eternal; because composite things are destroyed when

---

114. Alteration, diminution, and growth all entail and are caused by locomotion on some level. *De Anima* (Smith) 1.3.406a12.
115. *Progression of Animals* (Farquharson) 14.714b22.
116. Cf. *Sense and Sensibilia* 7.449a20–21.

we pull them apart—but immaterial things like souls are without parts to be pulled apart and must therefore be eternal, a common ancient trope.

Granted these are difficult texts that have spawned widespread exegetical disagreement over details. But the important point here is that Aristotle seems to believe that the mind perceives and thinks by using *immaterial* forms. Hence his picture of the perceiving mind as a wax seal that receives the shape of the brass without the matter. As he puts it:

> Generally, about all sense perception, we can say that [each] sense has the power of receiving into itself the sensible *form* of things without the matter, in the way in which a piece of wax takes on the impress of a signet ring without the iron or gold: [...] in a similar way, the sense is affected by what is coloured or flavoured or sounding [...] insofar as it is of such and such a sort and according to its *form*.[117]

But this sort of immaterial transfer also happens in thought, where "the faculty of thinking thinks the *forms* in the phantasms."[118] As we shall see, in Aristotle's philosophy of mind, perception and conceptual thinking are parallel phenomena in that they both use immaterial forms in the mind. Aristotle states this explicitly.

In his discussion of human cognition, Aristotle maintains that the intellect *becomes* that which it perceives or that which it thinks. He also writes: "the intellect *is* in a way all existing things; for existing things are either *perceivable or thinkable*."[119] Both "faculties of knowledge and sense" depend on "perceptible forms," which activate those cognitive

---

117. *De Anima*, (Smith) II.12.424a17–23 [my emphasis].
118. *De Anima* (Smith) III.7.431b2 (my emphasis).
119. *De Anima* (Smith) III.7.431b21 (my emphasis), cf. III.4.430a3–4. Cf. Gendlin, *Commentary on Aristotle's De Anima Book III*.

powers without the matter. This is why Aristotle thinks that even conceptual thinking cannot occur without perception. As he explains: "Hence no one can learn or understand anything in the absence of perception, for when the mind is actively aware of anything it is necessarily aware of it along with an image; for images are like sensuous contents except that they contain no matter."[120] The images contain no matter; i.e., they are immaterial, but in Aristotle's epistemology, these phantasms are somehow identical with forms that exist out in the world.

Aristotle writes, "in the case of objects that involve no matter that which understands and that which is being understood are the same; for theoretical knowledge and its object are identical."[121] And, again, he twice insists "Knowledge in its actualization is identical with the thing known."[122] This requires some explanation. How are we to make best sense of this?

In ancient philosophy, the basic understanding is that the perceiving-thinking mind somehow reproduces the world inside itself. If you perceive a crow or think about an idea of a crow, the crow somehow enters the mind and exists inside your intelligence. However exactly this happens, Aristotle points out that the matter that makes up the crow is left behind—obviously, it does not enter the intellect—only the "form" of the crow exists inside the mind. In perception, it is the sensible image that enters the mind; in conceptual thinking, it is the essence, the nature of the crow that somehow enters the mind. Aristotle believes then that the mind can somehow strip off the immaterial image or the immaterial essence from material things and hold it in its powers of concentration. Except that he is a metaphysical realist. What the mind contemplates inside itself is *identical* with the form that really exists out in the world. Perception and cognition

---

120. *De Anima* (Smith) III.8.432a5–9.
121. *De Anima* (Smith) III.4.430a2–5.
122. *De Anima* (Smith) III.3.430a17–18; III.7.431a1.

are trustworthy because form (unlike matter) can exist in two places at the same time—in the world and in the reproduction of the world in the mind. The mind can reproduce (in perception) the image but also (in cognition) the essence of things inside itself. This is best explained by examples.

Suppose we have a sputtering candle flame. What is going on metaphysically? Seen from a quasi-Platonic perspective, we might claim that the candle's struggle to stay lit is an attempt by the candle (or the flame) to turn its nature into as perfect an image as possible of the universal form "Fire." The flame may be trying to "imitate" an unmoved, unmixed, immaterial, eternal mover: the "Form" of Fire. Or suppose we have a biological kind: say, ducks. Seen from a similar perspective, every duck in the world would strive to embody, to the best of its ability, what a duck is. The Form of "Duckness" (the "secondary substance") would be an immaterial, unmoved, eternal mover that acts as the essence or nature that all ducks share.

Aristotle does not think that things in the world are created or brought into being by some higher form acting as efficient cause. When it comes to living things, he believes the chicken comes before the egg: "what is primary is not the seed, but the complete organism; [...] the man is prior to the seed."[123] "The seed produces in the same way as efforts of craft do."[124] That is, the seed produces according to a predetermined plan. The blueprint is the form of the species being created. But it is not some disembodied Platonic form but the biological parent that does the work to produce the seed that gives rise to the individual organism: "the generator is sufficient to produce the thing and to be the cause of the thing in the matter."[125] In the case of the candle flame, it is the inorganic operation of the matter that strives to emulate the eternal Form of Fire; the direction is bottom-up not top-down.

---

123. *Metaphysics* (Irwin and Fine) XII.7.1073a1–2.
124. *Metaphysics* (Irwin and Fine) VII.1034a35–b1.
125. *Metaphysics* (Irwin and Fine) VII.8.1034a4–6.

We can use this Platonic template, which Aristotle inherited from his teacher, to try and explain what happens when a mind perceives or thinks: "fire" or "duck"? It seems, in Aristotle's theory of mind, that intellect is able to somehow pull away the form of fire or the form of duckness leaving behind the material instantiation of that form in concrete particulars. In perception, it pulls away the sensible image; in cognition, it pulls away the essence. (Aristotle distinguishes the perceptible from the conceptual.[126]) But these forms that enter the mind must be immaterial if they are able to enter the mind without the matter. And this is what Aristotle explicitly claims: "In so far as the realities that the mind knows are capable of being separated from their matter [i.e., in perception], so it is also with the powers of thought [i.e., when it comes to concepts]."[127] It follows that there must be immaterial forms of "fire-ness" and of "duckness" that somehow exist in the world. They are a mysterious part of the metaphysical structure of things; as immaterial forms, however, they provide more images of Aristotle's immaterial god.

It is important to emphasize that these immaterial instances do not exist uniquely in the mind. They exist—really—out in the world though always instantiated in matter. The mind goes out and takes them from the world and somehow appropriates them (while leaving them simultaneously out in the world). When the mind perceives a particular duck or conjures up an idea of a duck, the individual duck and the nature of duckness still exist in the world. This is not to say that duckness can happen without matter; it cannot, according to Aristotle. For duckness to exist in the world requires a material cause. Nonetheless, the *form* of duckness is another immaterial thing, which exists both in the mind and the world in imitation of Aristotle's immaterial god.

Aristotle's view of species is radically different from the modern picture where material cause and efficient cause (via

---

126. Cf. *De Anima* III.4.429b10–22.
127. *De Anima* (Smith) III.4.429b21–22.

natural selection and random mutation) organize themselves to produce the form of duck (which is really an epiphenomenon). Aristotle is a realist when it comes to species: The form is real and the form is fully in charge. The Duckness organizing the individual bits of matter is a real thing: it produces a sensory appearance but also a real instantiation of that nature. (Note that Aristotle has a bifurcated theory. Individual things are the object of perception; concepts are the objects of cognition, but both perceptions and concepts exist as immaterial forms in the mind. Hence, perhaps, the distinction between "substance" in the *Categories* where it is a matter of *perceiving* individual ducks as "primary substances" and "substance" in *Metaphysics* Zeta when, asking what something is, we identify the substance as a duck, where the concept of "duck" represents an understanding of its nature).[128]

Aristotle writes, "the soul is analogous to the hand."[129] The soul is somehow able to reach out and grab onto the appearances and the natures of things—the perceptual and the conceptual forms, we could say—and transport these forms inside itself. But this leaves us with immaterial forms in the mind *and in the world* as imitations of God's immateriality. Whether Aristotle's account here is correct is not the issue. Aristotle thinks of form, as sensory appearance or as nature, as an immaterial something we take out of the world. But this gives us another level of immateriality in the world that provides another image of the immateriality of God.

If all this seems strange to the modern mind, think of mathematics. As is well known, Aristotle believes that mathematics deals with abstraction. The mathematical sciences, he says, "cut off a part of being and investigate the attributes of this part."[130] There are technical debates about what exactly abstraction

---

128. For one mainstream account, cf. Wedin, *Aristotle's Theory of Substance*.
129. *De Anima* (Smith) III.8.432a1.
130. *Metaphysics* (Ross) IV.1.1003a25.

(ἀφαίρεσις) entails but let us leave those aside here.[131] Instead, think of triangularity. Triangularity is not a particular triangle; it is a universal ordering principle that "imposes" itself on all triangles. But Aristotle is a metaphysical realist. It is not as if the mind conjures up an idea like triangularity and imposes it on the world (as in post-Kantian metaphysics). It is rather that the form of triangularity has to be retrieved from the world so that, in truthful assertions about triangles, what exists in the mind corresponds to what exists in the world. There has to be triangularity in the mind and triangularity in the world for justified true belief on Aristotle's account. But triangularity—not individual triangles but triangularity itself—is an immaterial form. It follows, then, that triangularity exists as a concept in the mind but also as an immaterial form-in-the-world; i.e., as enmattered. Triangularity, in both places, constitutes another image of the immateriality of Aristotle's god.

More generally, we could say that, in Aristotelian metaphysics, form exists in the mind *and in the world* as a level of immateriality that has to be somehow included in any metaphysical accounting of what exists. We moderns tend to favour a reductionist account of form; Aristotle is more Platonic. Not that he believes in a separate realm of forms, but he does believe in form as a distinct ontological component of the world. Whatever form is—an appearance, a structure, a nature, a principle—it exists as something immaterial. So, for example, when he says that the soul is the form of the body, he does not mean that the soul is whatever shape the material body takes; no, he means that there is a thing called the human form that imposes itself on the matter to produce a human being. In the case of something like triangularity, this picture of form is perhaps harder to accept. It may not square with conventional accounts of Aristotle, but the notion of immaterial form in the world follows from his philosophy of mind and his metaphysical realism. (Granted,

---

131. Cf. Cleary, *Aristotle and Mathematics*; "On the Terminology of 'Abstraction.'"

the science of metaphysics sometimes ends in some strange places.)

Much more deserves to be said, but simply note, for our purposes here, that one can extend the same sort of reasoning elsewhere in Aristotle. I have already mentioned the role of the principle of non-contradiction in Aristotelian logic.[132] The principle of non-contradiction is, obviously, not a material object. (Logical principles are immaterial.) Yet everything in the world conforms to the principle of non-contradiction without exception. The principle of non-contradiction remains unmoved while controlling being in the world and thus constitutes, we could say, an unmoved mover in the image of Aristotle's *immaterial* god.

In Aristotle, logic is not only about what we believe. It is about being, about what actually exists. Logic has a metaphysical reach. Aristotle introduces the principle of non-contradiction:

> He whose subject is being *qua* being must be able to state the most certain principles of all things. This is the philosopher, and the most certain principle of all is that regarding which it is impossible be mistaken; for such a principle must be [...] non-hypothetical. [...] This, then, is the most certain of all principles. [...] It is impossible for anyone to believe the same thing to be and not to be.[133]

It is not that there is an immaterial idea that somehow "floats" above the world and forces everything to be a certain way (as perhaps in Plato); it is that things in the world have natures such that they *must* conform to basic logical (and mathematical) principles. These immaterial principles never change; they are eternally unmoved. They set out boundaries that beings cannot transgress. Although the efficient cause of the principle of non-contradiction is in the nature of things,

---

132. Cf. *Metaphysics* IV.3–6.
133. *Metaphysics* (Ross) IV.3.1005b10–30 [my emphasis].

it still constrains (i.e., puts a limit on) what can be true of beings in the world. It is in some sense a distant, pale reflection of a distant unmoved god, but there is still an image here for those who know how to look.

Aristotle ties logic to the nature of beings in ways that are largely foreign to modern formal logic. He writes, "in deductions [syllogisms], substance is the principle of everything; for deductions begin from what-it-is."[134] That is, the nature of being in the world is what imposes logical necessity on syllogisms. Conclusions follow necessarily from their premises because the forms or essences of things impose a strict necessity on instances of the same kind. The Forms of Fire or of Duckness are, as we have seen, unmoved movers. In Aristotle, these unmoved forms impose a logical necessity on things such that we can make valid syllogisms, not on the basis of enumerative principles (as in modern statistics), but in terms of necessary natural kinds. The logical principles that derive from this "essentialism" in the world may be a faint reflection of Aristotle's unmoved immaterial god, but they provide yet another image of unmoved immateriality.

I discuss God as final cause of the cosmos below. Simply note, for the moment, that the passive role of the principle of non-contradiction and other logical principles is a good image of God's final causality. It is not that there is an agent called "the principle of non-contradiction" forming things in the world in its own image (as on the Judeo-Christian model of a creator god). It is rather that other things are "aspiring" to conform to it, which is (on the standard view) how Aristotle's god moves other things in the world. Not by actively imposing a design on them, but by offering something they *must* aim at.

Although morality may not seem to present an image of divine immateriality, Aristotle's virtue ethics could be construed as an attempt to aspire to ideal standards that are universal and immaterial—placed outside any particular act

---

134. *Metaphysics* (Irwin and Fine) VII. 9.1034a30–3.

and yet providing a template in the mind for behaviour. So that, when it comes to morality, immaterial universals, which are unmoved movers, can also be seen to act as a final cause towards which human agents strive, which would provide another image of the immaterial unmoved god that acts as a final cause of the entire cosmos. But I will not pursue this line of thought here.

To sum up this all too brief inquiry into problematic property of immateriality, we can posit layered images of immateriality in Aristotle's cosmos: in the celestial spheres, in the active *nous*, in souls generally, in species, in the mental contents of perception and conceptual thought, in natures and sensory appearances in the world, in natural and mathematical kinds, and even, by extension, in something like the principle of non-contradiction or in universal moral standards. Just as we have images of unmovedness, unmixedness, and eternalness in Aristotle's metaphysics, we also have images of immateriality that mirror the immateriality of God.

3.7. Actuality

My purpose here is not to present a complete schematization of Aristotelian metaphysics. If, however, one can find imitations of divine properties such as eternalness, unmovedness, unmixedness, and immateriality throughout Aristotle's cosmos, other divine attributes make their appearance as well.

Aristotle champions actualization, the movement from potentiality to actuality, as the basic metaphysical achievement. There are many degrees and kinds of actualization (generally, ἐνέργεια, ἐντελέχεια). Aristotle writes, for example, that vision is the actualization of the eye, that chopping something with an ax is an actualization of the tool's potential, that being awake (as opposed to sleeping) is the actualization of our conscious capacities, that the wise man "exercising his wisdom" is actualizing himself.[135] He defines daylight as an *actualization* of the transparent (διαφανές)

---

135. *De Anima* (Hicks) II.5.417a27–28; *De Anima* II.I.412b27–413a.

that "turns potential colours into actual colours," the soul as "the first actuality of a natural body that is potentially alive," and physical motion as "the actualization of what potentially is qua potential."[136]

I will not try to sort out these different usages here. The important point is that Aristotle's god is pure actuality (that is why he does not have a passive intellect). God's nature supplies, then, the supreme criterion in all reality for actuality. When Aristotle's god, who is thought-thinking-thought, thinks, he uses his optimum nature to its optimum capacity to produce the best thoughts most efficiently. This actualization of God is supreme, perfect, effortless. And because Aristotle believes that rational thought is the highest achievement, it counts as the ultimate accomplishment.

All actualization requires an efficient and a final cause. Something can be said to be actualized if and only if the said agency effectively realizes its intended purpose. We find, then, a perfect manifestation of final and efficient causality in the thinking nature of Aristotle's theoretical god. It is not quite right to say that his god is trying to achieve something and succeeds as if he had to work at it or as if he had to overcome the possibility of him not achieving it. Aristotle's god just "is." At the same time, insomuch as God has a nature that can be mirrored in the world, we can say that he intends to think (final cause) and puts that aim into effect with his perfect thinking ability (efficient cause). But there are, of course, endless instances of efficient and final causality in Aristotle's universe; each instance is then an imitation, however remote, of God's efficient actualization of his final cause (thinking).

Dealing with divine attributes is no easy task. Here, then, is an inevitably clumsy way of putting it. Think of it this way: What is the activity of God? He is "doing" efficient cause and final cause. What is the activity of beings in the world? They are "doing" efficient and final cause. They imitate then

---

136. *Physics* III.1.201a11; cf. *De Anima* III.7.418b9-10; *De Anima* (Smith) II.1.412a27.

what God is doing; they mirror his successful actualization of final cause (thinking) through his efficient causality (thinking). Let us leave puzzles about God aside. (I do not think Aristotle adequately solves them.) What matters here is that any time something in the world actualizes its nature—when the celestial spheres successfully turn around the planets, when biological species reproduce, when a bird builds a nest, when an arrow hits a target, all these must be thought of as imitations of God's actuality.

The same could be said of any manifestation of efficient and final causality. There is no need to be overly sentimental or even pious about all this. When a lion kills its prey, this is efficient and final causality at work. This too is an imitation of the actualization of God. Every time hydrogen combines with oxygen to produce water (something Aristotle had no idea of), some kind of potentiality has been actualized. As the traditional formula has it, matter is potentiality, form is actuality.[137] When matter takes on the form of water, whenever powers are exerted in the attainment of an end, we have something that mirrors, however faintly, God's efficient and final causality. In every instance, we have an image, however far removed, of the actualization of God.

This is not to leave morality out of the picture. We moderns tend to put things like metaphysics and morality into different boxes: the is-ought distinction. But, for Aristotle, morality is part of reality. We act morally, not by submitting to external constraints, but by fulfilling the potentialities inherent in our own rational nature. As one reference work has it: "Living well consists [...] in those lifelong activities that *actualize* the virtues of the rational part of the soul."[138] This is standard virtue ethics. But, here again, we have another instance of an actualization in imitation of

---

137. "For the form exists actually, ... but the matter exists potentially; for this is that which can become qualified either by the form or by the privation." *Metaphysics* (Ross) XII.5.1071a7–10.
138. Kraut, "Aristotle's Ethics" (my emphasis).

the actualization of God. The morally successful agent successfully achieves human actualization understood as virtue (ἀρετή), which then leads to *eudaimonia*. Aristotle himself writes: "Happiness [*eudaimonia*] seems [...] to be among the most godlike things; for that which is the prize and end of virtue seems to be the best thing in the world, and something godlike and blessed."[139] This seems a frank acknowledgment that moral happiness—the *eudaimonia* produced by virtue— provides another image of the actualization of God.

Aristotle's philosophical god is, as we have seen, a thinking god. When we humans think, we are trying to be like God. The wise philosopher engaged in *theôria*, participates as closely as possible in God's actualization. Indeed, Aristotle points to the efficient and final causality of the active mind as the human phenomenon that most closely resembles the actualization of God. He describes the active mind as pure actualization: "τῇ οὐσίᾳ ὢν ἐνέργεια," "its being is activity."[140] It is like a light inside the intellect that never shuts off, making "potential colours into actual colours."[141] Its task, so to speak, is to actualize knowledge. Consider, ever briefly, how Aristotle outlines this mechanism of thought.

Aristotle distinguishes, of course, between the passive mind, νοῦς παθητικός (*nous pathētikos*)—literally, the "pathetic" mind, the mind that *suffers* alteration—and what is traditionally referred to as the active mind, νοῦς ποιητικός (*nous poiētikos*), the *making* mind—from Aristotle's use of the Greek verb "ποιέω" (*poieô*): to make, produce, invent, or create. He claims that the active mind "makes everything [τῷ πάντα ποιεῖν]" whereas the passive mind "becomes everything [τῷ πάντα γίνεσθαι]."[142] He compares the relationship between the two to the relationship between an

---

139. *Nicomachean Ethics* (Ross) I.9.1099b14–17.
140. *De Anima* III.5.430a18. Hence the Latin name: "agent intellect" (*intellectus agens*).
141. *De Anima* (Smith) III.5.430a16–17.
142. *De Anima* III.5.430a14–15.

artist and the medium.[143] Think of a potter and the clay. The potter can make anything: a vase, a plate, a cup, a candlestick, anything at all. But the potter needs clay. The active mind is like the potter; the passive mind, like the clay. The active mind uses the raw potentiality of the passive mind to fashion it into the content of thought.

As we have seen, Aristotle claims that the active mind is deathless, eternal, unmoved, immutable, unmixed, and immaterial—in effect, divine. But notice that the relationship between the active and passive mind is mirrored in the relationship between matter and form. In Aristotle's world, form organizes matter to produce different biological species, different elements, even different geometrical shapes. Every time this actualization happens, we have another image of God. Not that Aristotle's god designs the world; it is rather (as we shall see) that world that strives to resemble God as closely as possible.

I will not belabour the point, but one can find countless images of the efficient and final causality of God in the cosmos. There is a pedantic, literalist reading of Aristotle, but poetry is not at odds with Aristotle's picture of the world. If poets often speak of a world brimming over with intimations of the divine, this is how Aristotle's metaphysics functions. There is a normative side to his metaphysics: It is not just description; it also involves appreciation.

In discussing the generation of animals, Aristotle says that "being is better than not being," "living [is better] than non-living," "soul is better than body," and that things "eternal and divine" are better than things that "admit of existence and non-existence."[144] We get here, in abbreviated terms, a metaphysics of betterness—a stairway to heaven, so to speak—that moves up at every metaphysical level. We move from inanimate matter that is better than non-being, to living things that are better than inanimate things, to immaterial souls that are

---

143. Cf. "οἷον ἡ τέχνη πρὸς τὴν ὕλην." *De Anima* III.5.430a12–13.
144. *Generation of Animals* (Platt) II.1.731b22–31.

better than material bodies, to whatever is eternal and divine that is better than mortal, contingent beings. At each new level, we get a better image of what is good because we get a more complete level of actualization; journeying upwards until we arrive at the supreme good and the best actualization only to be found—completely and perfectly—in Aristotle's theoretical god.

Aristotle writes: "Nature always strives after the better."[145] Which is to say, any level of nature always strives to actualize itself more fully. This happens at every level of existence, except, of course, in the case of God. One could fill out, then, Aristotle's little "chain of being" to produce something along the lines of traditional schema.[146] One could add all sorts of smaller intermediate steps (as later thinkers did); to wit: prime matter, the elements, inanimate mixtures, plants, animals, rational animals, souls, the active soul, the heavenly spheres, and, ultimately, God as first mover. The result will be some sort of punctuated staircase of being towards a fuller and fuller actualization.

More could be said but suffice it to say that Aristotle's universe is like a hall of mirrors, with every case of actualization mirroring, more closely or more remotely, an image of God. There is considerable room for lyricism here. To cite only one brief example, Philipp Rosemann comments, in a discussion of Aristotle's metaphysics, that "the circular motion of the heavenly bodies, the cyclical transformation of the elements, and the circle of life" are all "different levels of imitation of the perfect self-identity and unity that belong to the divine."[147] Rosemann focuses on circularity because it involves a recurrent "return upon the self" that replicates, he thinks, the "self-thinking thought" of God.[148] He further points to Aristotle's comments about the cyclical nature of human

---

145. *Generation and Corruption* (Joachim) II.10.336b31.
146. Cf., for example, Augustine, *City of God*, XI.16,
147. Rosemann, *Omne Agens Agit Sibi Simile*, 49.
148. Cf. *Metaphysics* XII.9.

history and to human introspection as further "circular" (or inward turning) imitations of Aristotle's introspecting god.[149] So, with a little poetic push, even anything circular could be said to provide a glimmer of the efficient and final causality of the divine actualization that corresponds to God's perfect nature.

3.8. Aristotle's God as Final and/or Efficient Cause of the Cosmos

Let us turn, then, to the question of God's role in the world. That is, instead of considering how other beings imitate or copy God, let us define the role, if any, Aristotle's god plays in this staircase to heaven.

On the standard account, Aristotle identifies God, exclusively, as the final cause of the universe. God is not an efficient cause. God leaves a mark on the world only through final causality. Everything in the world is trying to resemble God as closely as possible. The goal is not to be God (which would be impossible) but to present as close an image to God as possible. Hence the exercise in imitation piety that pervades the entire cosmos, from top to bottom, so to speak. This is, accordingly, how and why God functions as the final cause—the aim or purpose—of the cosmos.

Menn expresses the conventional wisdom when he writes, "Aristotle agrees with Plato that a separate Good-itself [i.e., God] is […] the goal or model in imitation of which all good things, including the world-order, are produced"[150] What he means is that this "separate Good-itself" does not mix with anything else. He is enthroned in his own self-contemplation and, unlike the Judeo-Christian god, does not design the nature of things in the world or watch over earthly events with some caring providence.

---

149. "The same ideas, one must believe, recur in men's minds not once or twice but again and again." *On the Heavens* (Stocks) I.3.270b19–20. Cf. also, *Meteorology* (Webster) I.3.339b27–30.
150. Menn, "Aristotle and Plato on God," 573.

There is textual evidence for this interpretation. In the *Metaphysics*, for example, Aristotle comments that God as the unmoved mover "causes motion by being loved, and [thus] moves other things."[151] On this model, God (or the gods) are *unmoved* movers. The goodness of the divine supplies a purpose for everything that happens in the world, but the divine does not do any of the work. The divine is (so to speak) a stationary final cause. Everything else does the moving so as to approach as close as possible towards what is divine.

In the *Metaphysics*, Aristotle points out that the term "final cause" can apply to (1) a "being for whose good an action is done" or to (2) a thing "towards which the action aims."[152] He maintains that God can only be a final cause in the second sense. God cannot benefit from the actions of anything else in the universe so his good is not the final cause for which things are done in the universe. As a final cause in the second sense of the term, however, God can inadvertently benefit those other things. Imagine iron filings being pulled towards a magnet. The magnet is stationary, but the iron filings move—we could say, in Empedoclean terms, because they have a "love" [φιλότης]—the magnet. They propel *themselves* towards it. This is like the standard interpretation of Aristotle's god. God is the stationary magnet, and the rest of the world moves in his direction.

There are reasons why such a line of thinking would be attractive to an Aristotelian philosopher. In some extravagant paragraphs, the pseudo-Aristotle of *On the Universe* speaks of God as "the preserver and creator of all that is in any way being brought to perfection in this universe," but is careful to add, "he does not take upon himself the toil of a creature that works and labours for itself."[153] The text is largely a poetic gloss on Aristotelian ideas, but it places

---

151. *Metaphysics* (Gerson) XII.7.1072b4. (Cited in Gerson, *Other*, 200–201.)
152. *Metaphysics* XII.7.1072b1–4.
153. *On the Universe* (Forster) 6.397b21–25.

particular emphasis on the leisurely, unwearied nature of God's rule over the cosmos, which "is without toil or labour and free from all bodily weakness."[154] The same author compares God to earthly kings or emperors like "Cambyses and Xerxes and Darius" who have servants and underlings to do menial tasks for them. Such an aristocrat god will not be doing any work. He will remain eternally above the fray, enjoying pure contemplative leisure (σχολή) because leisure is better than work, being valued for its own sake and not as a means to some other end.[155]

And there is an epistemological advantage to this way of thinking about things. Supernatural explanations were common enough in ancient Greece. In a vulgar joke, Aristophanes has Strepsiades believing that rain was "Zeus pissing through a sieve."[156] As two commentators explain, "Strepsiades' joke about the sieve may sound irreverent and ignorant, but the idea that rain is sent by the gods was commonplace in fifth Century BC."[157] This is precisely the sort of *deus ex machina* religious explanation Aristotle wants to avoid. Aristotle is always a scientist; he wants to explain events in the world in natural terms, in terms of natures or essences. He does not want explanations by supernatural interventions as a substitute for science.

One could wish that this was all there was to it. But one can find evidence in the corpus in support of the idea that

---

154. *On the Universe* (Forster) 6.400b7–13.
155. *Politics* VIII.3.1138a10. Aristotle describes leisure as "the first principle of all action." *Politics* (Jowett) VIII.3.1137b33.
156. Aristophanes, *Clouds*, 373. Cf. Aristotle's discussion of whether rain falls with a purpose (*Physics* II.8.198b10ff.). Does rain have a *telos*: to make the crops grow or to complete its natural motion downward? (Aristotle gives an argument here against natural selection evolution: "It is impossible this should be the true view." *Physics* [Ross] II.8.198b35.) But the important point, in the present content, is that God is not sending the rain down to water the crops; nature by itself is doing whatever is being done.
157. Claughton and Affleck, *Aristophanes: Clouds*, 30.

Aristotle's god is the efficient cause of the cosmos as well. As Fred Miller suggests, there are obvious textual difficulties, maybe even inconsistencies with any god-as-exclusively-final-cause interpretation.[158] Let us consider them, briefly.

In Aristotle's astronomy, the celestial spheres are moved by the divine intelligences. The suggestion in *Metaphysics* XII is that the spheres are attracted to these unmoved movers, which operate solely as a final cause.[159] If the intelligences were efficient causes, they would presumably have to move in order to impart motion to something else (which would contradict their unmoved status). This is a standard Aristotelian account of *unmoved* movers. But later in the *Metaphysics* Aristotle strikes a different note. He makes the point that the way the parts of the universe are ordered reflects the goodness of God.

Aristotle writes:

> [The cosmos is] like an army; for the good of an army is found both in its order and in its commander, and more in the latter; for he does not depend on the order but it depends on him. And all things [in the world] are ordered together somehow [...]—fishes and fowls and plants—[...] they are all connected. For all are ordered together to one end, as in a house, [...] according to the principle that constitutes the nature of each member. [And] [...] there are some functions in which all share for the good of the whole.[160]

There seem to be two main claims here: (1) the universe is ordered like an army, and that (2) the universe is ordered like a household. But this makes it sound like God organizes the universe in the way a commander organizes an army or in the way a household manager (an important ancient role) organizes a house. And this would make God (at least to some degree) an efficient cause of the cosmos.

---

158. Miller, "Aristotle's Divine Cause."
159. *Metaphysics* XIII.7.1072b1 ff.
160. *Metaphysics* (Ross) XII.10.1075a11–18.

Aristotle uses the Greek word στρατηγός (*stratēgos*) to refer here to the commander or general of an army. But, as the term makes clear, army commanders devise and implement strategies—στρατηγήματα (*stratēgēmata*)—for defeating the enemy. They play an active role in determining what the army will do. They *command*; they tell everyone else what to do. The Greek term *stratēgos* was also used to refer to governors who, of course, *govern* their jurisdictions. It seems to follow, then, if the comparison is accurate, that Aristotle's god governs the universe like a military commander, playing an active role in the organization and strategic deployment of the "fishes, fowls, and plants" that are his forces. But this makes God a very busy efficient cause.

And what are we to make of the claim that the cosmos is like a well-ordered household? Thomas Aquinas, in his commentary on Aristotle's *Metaphysics*, compares Aristotle's god to a *paterfamilias* who lays down precepts that the family members obey.[161] This is a later gloss on Aristotle, but it highlights an important aspect of the original household analogy. If we turn to the *Oeconomica* (usually attributed to Aristotle's students or to Theophrastus), we encounter a description of the ideal household master or manager. The Peripatetic author writes, "There are four qualities that the head of a household must possess in dealing with his property. Firstly, he must have the faculty of acquiring, and secondly that of preserving. [...] Thirdly and fourthly, he must know how to improve his property, and how to make use of it."[162] But this sounds very much like a view of a household manager as an efficient cause. Again, the text advises:

> The master and mistress [working together as household managers] should, therefore, give personal supervision, each to his or her special department of the household

---

161. Aquinas, *Commentary on the Metaphysics*, Lesson 12.2634. Cf. George, "God Is Love?"
162. *Oeconomica* (Armstrong) I.6.1344b23–28.

> work. In small households, an occasional inspection will suffice; in estates managed through stewards, inspections must be frequent. For in stewardship as in other matters, [...] if the master and mistress do not attend diligently to their estate, their deputies will certainly not do so.[163]

It is not the details that matter. What matters is that household managers are very active people, constantly intervening in the running of daily household business. And if this is what Aristotle's god is like, he would have to be a very active efficient cause; someone who, so to speak, busies himself about the daily affairs of the world.

And there are more indirect indications that Aristotle (or his anonymous followers) are comfortable with the idea of God as intervening ruler and an efficient cause of reality. As already mentioned, Aristotle finishes a theological discussion with a quote from Homer: "The rule of many is not good; let one be the ruler."[164] But the term he uses for ruler is κοίρανος, which means, in the usual military sense, a ruler or commander who takes decisions and exerts power over others. The point in Homer is that it is better to have one person (and one intelligence)—i.e., Agamemnon—directing the Greek military effort than to have separate tribal groups making military decisions for themselves. But, again, this suggests a god governs the cosmos like a military commander directing a large-scale military operation. And that would turn God into an efficient cause that imposes order from above.

In *De Anima*, Aristotle writes, "the soul is also the final cause of its body" just as God is the final cause of the universe.[165] So far, so good. But Aristotle also "appoints" the soul as the "ruler" of the body. In the *Movement of Animals*,

---

163. *Oeconomica* (Armstrong) I.6.1345a6–12.
164. *Metaphysics* (Tredennick) XII.10.1076a5; the citation is from Homer, *Iliad*, 2.204.
165. *De Anima* (Smith) II.4.415b15.

he writes, "The animal organism must be conceived in the likeness of a well-governed commonwealth [...] and the soul resides in a kind of central governing place of the body."[166] If then the analogy is to hold true, should God not be the ruler residing in the central governing place of the whole cosmos and, thereby, be an efficient cause of the cosmos? For the soul is clearly the efficient cause of the living body; it animates and organizes the body—that is its function—but does that not mean, according to the analogy, that God should be doing something similar to the universe?

In the *Politics*, Aristotle argues that justice requires that the better rule over the worse: "Hence the ruler ought to have moral virtue in perfection, for his function, taken absolutely, demands a master artificer, and the rational principle is such an artificer."[167] But would this not apply to God? If God is the ruler of the cosmos, should he not also qualify as the "master artificer"? At least if these comments about being a ruler are to be taken seriously.

And there are other hints at God being something more than an aloof self-introspecting intelligence. In *On Generation and Corruption*, Aristotle writes:

> Coming-to-be and passing-away will [...] always be continuous. [...] Not all things can possess being, since they are too far removed from the [original] principle. God therefore adopted the remaining alternative, and fulfilled the perfection of the universe by making coming-to-be uninterrupted; [...] because that coming-to-be should itself come-to-be perpetually is the closest approximation to eternal being.[168]

But the claim that God *adopted* the remaining alternative and perfected the cosmos by making coming-to-be

---

166. *Movement of Animals* (Farquharson) 10.703a28–703b1.
167. *Politics* (Jowett) I.13.1260a16–19.
168. *Generation and Corruption* (Joachim) II.10. 336b25–336b34.

uninterrupted means that God intervened. This picture requires an active god who did something to make the cosmos a certain way; that is, it requires something more than a non-interventionist god that is only final cause. It requires a god that, to some degree at least, efficiently intervenes in the events of the world.

In the *Physics,* Aristotle comments that particular events in the cosmos "come *after* intelligence and nature." Even if the heavens came about due to random chance (αὐτόματον), he claims that "it would still be true that intelligence and nature will be prior causes of all this and of many things in it besides."[169] What does Aristotle mean by "intelligence and nature"? This is, granted, a rather mysterious declaration. But it sounds like the old Greek idea of material stuff (nature) being shaped and governed by the divine (intelligence). Where else can one find intelligence, except in a divine realm that somehow acts upon the world?

Aristotle distinguishes between intelligence and nature as if they were two different things. He says elsewhere that nature by itself is not a sufficient explanation for the universe. In the *Metaphysics*, he comments:

> It is not likely that either fire or earth or any such element should be the reason why things manifest goodness and beauty both in their being and their coming to be, [...] nor again could it be right to ascribe so great a matter as beauty and goodness to [random] spontaneity and luck.[170]

There are two claims here: first, the four elements (the material building blocks of nature) cannot account for a world charged with beauty and goodness; and, second, random physical chance cannot account for a world charged with beauty and goodness. It seems lame—as developmentalism might have it—to pass this off as a relic from an immature

---

169. *Physics* (Hardie and Gaye) II.6.198a9–14.
170. *Metaphysics* (Ross) I.3.984b14–15.

Aristotle enthralled with Plato. But the passage suggests, very strongly, that Aristotle's god is directly responsible for beauty and goodness in the world either as an exemplar that everything strives to model or in a manner analogous to the Platonic Demiurge. This is not out of keeping with Aristotle's larger philosophy.

As Miller points out, a god without efficient causality seems, at best, to move things in a very tenuous, purely symbolic sense.[171] Aristotle himself criticizes interpretations of Plato's forms that conceive of them operating purely as final cause. According to Aristotle, such passive forms should not be considered as the true cause of material events in the world for "we are everywhere accustomed" to identify efficient causality as the true cause of something.[172] Aristotle further complains that Platonists fail to recognize that it is the *particular* form embedded in a particular object that "is the *more* controlling cause."[173] Fire is hot because its internal nature (or essence) is hot, not because some otherworldly Platonic form causes fire to be hot. In such passages, Aristotle seems to disparage final-cause-imitation as a less important and very subordinate sort of causality. But how can God—the best being of all—be someone who only has access to final causality in the world. Indeed, if God is only the final cause of the cosmos and everything else is doing the work to resemble him as closely as possible, these other things would seem to be the ultimate cause of what happens, not God. They deserve all the credit for their own achievements; God seems largely cut out of the picture. (Something atheistic interpretations of Aristotle like to stress.)

In *Generation and Corruption*, Aristotle further claims that final causality is incapable of ever moving anything

---

171. *Aristotle's Divine Cause* (Miller) 280. He mentions Enrico Berti, Sarah Broadie, Carlo Giacon, and Menn in this connection.
172. "We in the products of nature and of art alike, to look upon that which can initiate movement as the producing cause." *Generation and Corruption* (Joachim) II.9.335b26–29.
173. *Generation and Corruption* (Joachim) II.9.335b35.

except in an empirically empty and purely figurative sense. He comments, for example, that the efficient cause of health, "the process from which it originates" (presumably, regular exercise, good nutrition, and proper rest) "is an active cause" but the goal of health, considered as the thing "for the sake of which" we exercise, eat well, and rest, cannot be considered as an "active power" "except metaphorically."[174] It follows, one might argue, that Aristotle has something much more assertive and dynamic in mind when he repeatedly refers to God as the prime *mover*.

In the *Physics*, Aristotle says that God "first imparts movement," that he is the author of a "continuous process of change," that he is "the cause of the fact that some things exist and others do not," and that he is the reality "that causes the motion of [all] other movers."[175] Marie George comments, "If God is a final cause alone, the unmoved mover of Bk. VIII of the *Physics*, who is clearly an efficient cause of all motion, would not be God."[176] But Aristotle clearly thinks that the unmoved mover *is* God.

In the *Eudemian Ethics*, as previously noted, he writes:

> What is the starting-point of motion in the soul? The answer is clear: as in the universe, so in the soul, it is God. For [...] the divine element in us moves everything. The starting-point of reason is not reason but something superior to reason. What, then, could be superior even to knowledge and to intellect, except God?[177]

It is difficult to reconcile such passages with any insistence that Aristotle's god only acts in the cosmos as a final cause. Aristotle seems to believe that God, somehow or other, gives

---

174. *Generation and Corruption* (Joachim) I.7.324b13–18.
175. *Physics* (Hardie and Gaye) VIII.6.258b11-12, 259a3–7.
176. George, "God is Love?" 3.
177. *Eudemian Ethics* (Solomon and Rackman) VII.14.1248a25–29. Cf. Dirlmeier, *Eudemische Ethik*, 498–500.

everything an initial push like the fundamental causal push, that push a parent gives to a child on a swing to get them going. If all Aristotle means is that our thoughts aim at God as the final cause of motion, that would make us the starting point of thinking, not God. We would be the *prime mover* of whatever happens. Aristotle seems to have something rather more divine and more dynamic in mind.

If we suppose that God is only a final cause, he would be like a target and everything else in the universe would be like an arrow aimed at the target. But the target does not seem to be the source of agency. To claim that the bullseye on the target is the mover, that it *causes* the arrow to hit the target in the right place, seems far-fetched. In the arrow example, surely, the archer is the first mover and he deserves the credit for the arrows hitting the bullseye. But that is because the archer is the efficient cause of the arrow's movement. If God is not an efficient cause in any sense, it is difficult to see how it makes sense to insist that he is the one imparting movement to the world.

Let us suppose, to use a thought experiment, that we have a bodybuilding enthusiast looking for inspiration. He hangs a poster of Hercules on his wall. Hercules's muscular physique represents the goal, the final cause our bodybuilder is aiming at. He is determined to look like Hercules in the picture. So, the bodybuilder bench presses, deadlifts, squats, follows a strict diet and a gruelling workout ritual. He works hard. At a certain point, he has bulked up so much he looks like a reasonable facsimile of Hercules. But suppose someone asks: "Well, what *caused* him to become so big?" Surely, the bodybuilder's muscles were caused by his exercise routine and diet. He was the one lifting all those heavy weights; that is the efficient cause that turned him into a new Hercules. Would it not be odd if someone were to point to the picture of Hercules on his wall and say that the picture is, in the best sense, *the cause* of his new physique? That the picture is a "mover"? Yet that is precisely what the standard interpretation of Aristotle's god does. It restricts God's agency to this one, very limited account of causality.

Again, suppose someone was to reason: "Well, the Hercules picture is like Aristotle's god. It's exclusively a final cause. It doesn't move anything as an efficient cause, but it 'moved' the bodybuilder, providing a model for him to aim at." Still, surely, it is the athlete, not the picture, that is "doing the heavy-lifting." Aristotle consistently suggests that God should get the most credit for everything. The divine is a cause, a mover, in the best, most robust sense of the word. If the role of God in the universe is akin to the role of the Hercules picture in our example, it seems far-fetched to credit God as the true cause and the mover of all beauty and order in the universe.

Let us turn to a more Aristotelian example. Consider a biological species, let us say, dogs. Aristotle believes that living things are the final *and* efficient cause of themselves.[178] The final cause of dogs is (more) dogs. Why do dogs exist? To make more dogs. But dogs only secure their existence by reproducing with other dogs. The efficient cause of dogs—what brings new dogs into being—is previous dogs mating. In the case of a biological species like dogs, then, we have something that is both the aim and the "mover" of itself.

As Aristotle's god is the final cause of everything, dogs must be striving to emulate the goodness of God. This is not so odd. Dogs embody many different types of goodness: speed, strength, loyalty, courage. (Plato compares his guardians to dogs.) Dogs could be said, then, to imitate the goodness of God as final cause. But, on the standard interpretation, God is only final cause. The *efficient cause* of dogs is dogs. Again,

---

[178]. The formal cause, as the definition of the living thing, is also equivalent to efficient and final cause. Cf. *De Anima* (Smith) II.4.415b8–28. "The soul is the cause or source of the living body. The terms 'cause' and 'source' have many senses. But the soul is the cause of its body alike in all three senses which we explicitly recognize. It is (a) the source or origin of movement, it is (b) the end, and it is (c) the essence of the whole living body."

it is dogs that are doing all the work. They seem to be the "prime mover" of canine goodness in the world. Unless God has some sort of role as an efficient cause—it seems strange to give him credit for whatever goodness dogs achieve.

As discussed below, we cannot understand traditional Greek religion or Greek tragedy without considering the notion of fate. But fate cannot play a moral role in the universe without some divine force that is able to reorder events in the cosmos according to moral merit. That would require some sort of divine efficient causality. The usual view is that Aristotle left no place for religious notions of fate, but I will argue, in the next chapter, that his account of fate is subtler than that. At the very least, Aristotle leaves room in his universe for fate understood in Greek pagan terms.

Is, then, Aristotle's god only a final cause or an efficient cause as well? Any conception of the divine that views the supernatural uniquely as final cause seems insufficient. Any conception of the divine as efficient cause clashes with standard interpretations. Perhaps Aristotle—or, better yet, the Aristotelian school—is simply inconsistent. Perhaps there are divergent points of view coming from different periods in Aristotle's career or from different students and editors. I can offer no definitive answer to these puzzles except to suggest that the Aristotelian corpus provides evidence that Aristotle and his school did, at times, consider God as an efficient as well as a final cause of reality. As the ultimate standard of intelligibility, it would seem that God might be responsible—somehow or to some ultimate degree—for how things are in the universe. Undeniably, he plays an essential role in Aristotle's metaphysics.

3.9. Incommensurable Wonder

Aristotle is endlessly perplexing. In presenting arguments against the supernatural origin of divination in dreams, he claims "Nature is mysterious though not divine."[179] If,

---

179. *On Divination in Sleep* (Beare) 2.463b15.

however, he busies himself trying to find a naturalistic cause for divination, he opposes those who would view divinity as another manifestation of nature. References to the operation of the divine in the world (which we find in many other Aristotelian texts) are references to something truly transcendental. In the corpus, language about the divine is not an embellished way of talking about what is only natural. The divine is something that, in principle, defies natural explanation.

The word "logical" derives from the Greek λόγος (*logos*), which means, among other things, a ratio. Aristotle believes that nature is intelligible because it operates in terms of finite ratios. He explains, "order always means ratio."[180] He applies his concept of an optimum ratio between opposing tendencies to many aspects of nature, to perceptions, to body parts, to chemical compounds, to biological reproduction, to morality, to politics.[181] In each case, the ratio measures something: A, in relation to something else, B. Aristotle explicitly advises, however, that God, understood as "the eternal beautiful, and the truly and primarily good [...] is too divine and precious to be relative to anything else."[182] In other words, we cannot fit God into any meaningful ratio. If, then, Aristotelian science explains the world through ratios, God is beyond that. Reason, logic, calculation, or measurement is defeated when it comes to God. Aristotle's god is incommensurable, transcendental, which is why he "compels our wonder."[183]

Aristotle's god is an actual infinity and just as an actual infinity, he is beyond comprehension.[184] In Aristotle's system, we cannot say, for example, that the beauty of the god is to the beauty of something in the world is as two is to one,

---

180. *Physics* (Gaye and Hardie) VIII.1.252a4–5.
181. Cf. Groarke, "Aristotle's Contrary Psychology."
182. *Motion of Animals* (Farquharson) 6.700b34–35.
183. *Metaphysics* XII.7.1072b24–26.
184. Cf., *Physics* III.4–5.

as ten thousand is to one, or, even, as one million to one. The beauty of God to the beauty of things in the world is as infinity to the finite but infinities are above number—indeed, beyond human calculation. Infinity does not compute; it is (for Aristotle) outside the human ken. No adequate description of the infinite is possible.

Aristotle's god (as the final cause of the cosmos) is the ultimate criterion according to which everything else has to be understood. But there is no way we can find a unit of measure—either quantitative or qualitative—to apply to God's nature. There is no logical formula, no template, no Pythagorean shape or number for Aristotle's god; he cannot be defined or limited or fully understood. The best we can hope for is an intimation, a hint, a likeness of what is partially grasped. In this chapter, I have tried to show, however incompletely, that Aristotle's cosmos is filled to the brim with things that resemble God. That imitate God. But the proper response to God is not quite logical understanding but wonder or astonishment at what exceeds any full or adequate explanation.

Aristotle does not view wonder solely as a prelude to the explanations of philosophy (as in the *Metaphysics*) but articulates an aesthetics of wonder in his *Poetics* where he discusses the aim and proper emotional response to literature. Joe Sachs protests that commentators have overemphasized the role of catharsis in Aristotle's treatment of Greek tragedy.[185] Sachs explains:

> The word *catharsis* drops out of the *Poetics* because the word wonder, *to thaumaston*, replaces it, first in chapter 9, where Aristotle argues that pity and fear arise most of all where wonder does, and finally in chapters 24 and 25,

---

185. The term only appears once in Aristotle's analysis. He writes, "Tragedy, then, is an imitation of an action ... through pity and fear effecting the proper purgation [catharsis] of these emotions." *Poetics* (Butcher) 4.449b22-28.

where he singles out wonder as the aim of the poetic art itself, into which the aim of tragedy in particular merges.[186]

Sachs identifies the *Iliad* as the "prototype of tragedy" and insists that "it is not a poem that aims at conferring glory but a poem that bestows the gift of wonder." Tragedy, he thinks, uses the familiar experience of hurt or despair to "lift" the audience up to a state of wonder. We are left with "the feeling of being washed in wonderment."

Aristotle does refer to wonder (θαῦμα from the verb θαυμάζω, *thaumazô*: to marvel at something) as a necessary ingredient of serious theatre. He insists, "The element of the wonderful is required in tragedy."[187] But wonder also has an epistemological side. To feel wonder is to appreciate the surpassing nature of something, but that requires some kind of intelligent judgment. It requires a *knowing* that cognitive limits are reached, touched, or even surpassed. The pianist regaling herself with Liszt's *Transcendental Études* provokes wonder because her uncanny virtuoso ability and expressive touch exceed what we could have hoped for. (Hence, the rumours about the original Liszt being possessed by the devil.) Wonder happens when understanding comes to a stop at the cusp of something much greater than the human. This presupposes an epistemological realization as well as an emotional response. Despite the overly rationalistic interpretations of many commentators, Aristotle's metaphysics is ripe for aesthetic appreciation.

When Aristotle famously suggests that philosophy begins in wonder θαῦμα (*thauma*), in the act of being amazed or astonished θαυμάζω (*thaumazô*), he is expanding on Socrates's earlier comment in the *Theaetetus* that "wonder is the feeling of a philosopher, and philosophy begins in wonder."[188] For his part, Aristotle maintains:

---

186. Sachs, "Aristotle: Poetics."
187. *Poetics* (Butcher) 25.460a13.
188. *Theaetetus* (Jowett) 155d.

> It is owing to their wonder that men both now begin and at first began to philosophize; they wondered originally at the obvious difficulties, then advanced little by little and stated difficulties about the greater matters. [...] And a man who is puzzled and wonders thinks himself ignorant; [...] therefore they philosophized order to escape from ignorance.[189]

Aristotle goes on to suggest that philosophy solves the problem of wonder by explaining the causes of things.[190] Read in a certain way, his comments might make it sound as if philosophy is a spoilsport that drains the world of wonder. A little like the know-it-all that tells everyone how the magic trick was performed so that the amazement evaporates. Heidegger takes it upon himself to "correct" Aristotle. He comments:

> [Wonder] is not left out in the process [of doing philosophy] [...] but the beginning rather becomes [...] that which governs. The pathos of astonishment thus does not simply stand at the beginning of philosophy as, for example, the washing of his hand precedes the surgeon's operation. Astonishment carries and pervades philosophy."[191]

This is a discerning comment. Except that Heidegger's "correction" misunderstands Aristotle. On Aristotle's account, philosophy does not eliminate wonder. It produces a learned amazement, a higher amazement about different things, which is better than an amazement based on sheer ignorance.

Aristotle accepts that there is this cognitive side to literature. He writes: "Even a lover of myths is a lover of wisdom, for the myth is made up of wonders."[192] Or, more literally,

---

189. *Metaphysics* (Ross) I.2.982b12–20.
190. *Metaphysics* I.2.983a12–20.
191. Heidegger, *What Is Philosophy*, 6.
192. Chroust, *Aristotle*, 402; the passage is from *Metaphysics* VI.2.982b16–17.

"the myth-lover is in a sense a philosopher, since myths are composed of wonders."[193] (Aristotle does use the word φιλόσοφος here.) But pagan religion is based on mythology. Even if the anthropomorphic accretions of poets go astray, Aristotle believes that there is something true and morally correct about these religious myths. It is not that they are literally or provably true. It is that they have philosophical content (as Aristotle comments in his comparison of poetry and history).[194] A successful story rings true, which is to say that it captures something reliable about human nature and the nature of the cosmos.

But we do not have to turn to poetry and the myths to find reasons for wonder in Aristotle's philosophy. Contrary to a familiar caricature, Aristotelian "essentialism" does not drain the world of mystery, of aesthetic feeling, of religious possibility. In Aristotle's philosophy, every manifestation of what is good, wise, valuable, or beautiful is an image of a god who is beyond rational understanding. As we have seen, metaphysical properties such as eternalness, unmovedness, unmixedness, immateriality, actuality, and efficient and final causality all imitate the divine properties of God. The suggestion that the universe is like a house of mirrors reflecting the divine is not a later (or earlier) Platonist theme revisited by the Romantic poets. It is already there, at the very heart of "essentialist" metaphysics in Aristotle.

Aristotle's overall worldview pushes us to a perspective on reality that keeps mirroring the divine. We could say that the life spent in metaphysical contemplation is the happiest life of all because looking on images of God has, after all, an inevitable aesthetic effect.[195] We have to take Aristotle seriously when he identifies contemplation as "a pleasure peculiar to itself," that "aims at no end beyond itself," that is "leisurely," "relaxing," and "self-sufficient," and has "and all

---

193. *Metaphysics* (Tredennick) VI.2.982b16–17.
194. *Poetics* IX.1451b5–7.
195. Cf. *Nicomachean Ethics* X.8.1079a31–32.

the other attributes of blessedness."[196] Anyone who engages in *theôria* the way Aristotle's god engages in *theôria* must arrive at some pinnacle of appreciation. Appreciating universal metaphysical truths, not as an emanation of the divine but as a mirror of the divine, must take our breath away and fill us with some kind of wonder. Aristotle does not dismiss, of course, physical reality. He believes in material cause, in observation, in science, in logic, in worldly common sense. He thinks that we are surrounded by real physical things with natures that are intellectually accessible. He also believes, in comparison to contemporary antirealists, that we have a firm grip on reality. Not an infallible grip, but a secure grip.

Aristotle is a naturalist, but not a positivist. His naturalism is a naturalism that explains physical events scientifically, of course, but it also opens up metaphysical space for God. Aristotle's cosmos has religious features that are irreducible and real in ways that cannot be dismissed or overlooked. His metaphysics is not the pedantic, doctrinaire, essentialist edifice it is sometimes made out to be. It is more like a hall of mirrors, each of those mirrors reflecting, however faintly, some aspect of a supreme, otherworldly god. This is not a fanciful gloss or a sentimental suggestion. Aristotle's god is the exalted archetype for everything inferior. Contrary to some suggestions, one does not have to surrender Aristotle's compelling account of reason, logic, natural philosophy, epistemology, and metaphysics to clear out a place for religious transcendence. On his encyclopedic account, transcendence is there, whether we choose to acknowledge it or not.

A certain type of modernist interpretation would have Aristotle looking like an Enlightenment positivist. Postmodernism, moving in from the opposite side, would have us believe in a straw-man Aristotelian essentialism that leaves no room for the mysterious aspects of being. Modernism wants to make Aristotle up-to-date and relevant;

---

196. *Nicomachean Ethics* (Rackman) X.7.1177b19–23.

postmodernism rejects the metaphysical tradition as an old-fashioned absolutist mistake. But these interpretations go wildly astray, at least when it comes to the original corpus. When we inspect carefully Aristotle's synoptic worldview, we find a cosmos replete with successive levels of divine imitation that include all sorts of transcendental possibilities. The whole cosmos is, again, an exercise in imitation piety. It would be a less than adequate metaphysics that ignores the spectacle of divine imitation that, according to Aristotle, surrounds us.

Chapter 4

Aristotle and Fate

> It appears, indeed, to me, [that] the ancient philosophers are divided into two parties on the doctrine of fate; some of whom maintain that fate works all in all, and that it exerts a necessary and compulsive force over all agents; of which opinion were Democritus, Heraclitus, Empedocles and Aristotle; while others asserted that fate had no influence whatsoever. […]
>
> Cicero, *On Fate* (Yonge)

> Aristotle thinks that those who become ecstatic or furious through some disease, especially melancholy persons, possess a divine gift of presentiment in their minds.
>
> Cicero, *On Divination*

> For Aristotle fate and luck are no longer supreme: they correspond to the imponderable element of becoming here below.
>
> Richard Bodéüs, *Aristotle and the Theology of the Living Immortals*

4.1. Terminology, Determinism

John Macfarlane, discussing the poetic technique of *anagnôrisis*, mentions a key passage in Aristotle: "A discovery [*anagnôrisis*] [...] is a change from ignorance to knowledge, [...] in those who are destined for good fortune or ill."[1] Macfarlane dismisses out of hand any religious interpretation of the passage because, he says (with a nod to Gerald Else), "the notion of destiny is foreign to both Aristotle's poetics and his metaphysics."[2]

I will not pursue his argument here.[3] What is so telling, however, is the summary way in which, with a wave of his hand, Macfarlane dismisses any interpretation of Aristotle that would take pagan Greek notions of destiny or fate seriously. This is remarkable, not simply because Aristotle seems to talk about fate in a serious tone, but because a belief in the mysterious workings of fate was a prominent theme in pagan Greek culture.

Yet, Macfarlane's attitude is shared by many, if not most commentators today. If the ancient Greeks generally believed that the gods used fate to reward or punish moral or immoral behaviour, contemporary philosophers tend to downplay Aristotle's engagement with such beliefs. In Chapter 2, I argued that while Aristotle is certainly not a Christian, there is evidence that he was a rather ordinary pagan believer with intellectualist reservations perhaps. In the previous In Chapter 3, I argued that there is a large place for God in his imitation metaphysics. In the present chapter, I argue, more specifically, that Aristotle is open to the possibility of the traditional pagan gods—or perhaps even the divine construed in a less mythological and more philosophical sense—intervening, for moral reasons, in the operation of the universe. Aristotle believes,

---

1. *Poetics* (Fyfe) 11.1452a30–32.
2. Macfarlane, "Aristotle's Definition of *Anagnôrisis*," 368; cf. Else, *Aristotle's Poetics*, 351.
3. I discuss contemporary positions at some length in Groarke, "Aristotle's Tyche."

in other words, that the divine, understood perhaps in some relatively ambiguous sense as a vaguely defined higher-order principle, may operate inside the moral economy that regulates the world. Aristotle does not believe that science refutes this religious possibility. Because religious or moral conceptions of fate operate through an accidental form of causality, they lie forever outside the realm of scientific investigation. I think Aristotle's views on this matter are largely correct and will consider his account from a critical, not merely an exegetical point of view.

There is a lot that needs unpacking here. Let us begin with the issue of terminology. Aristotle uses the Greek term τύχη in many contexts with different meanings. The word itself seems to combine ideas of fate, of necessity, and of accidental or particular occurrence. The root meaning of the original Greek term is "the good which man obtains (τυγχάνει) by the favor of the gods."[4] In various classical sources, it refers to fortune, to providence, to what an act of a god brings about (usually as moral reward or punishment). The idea seems to be that humans must cultivate good relations to the gods in order to benefit from those things that the gods control because they are a matter of fate.

A second meaning of the term—at least in Aristotle—has to do with the operation of nature according to the rules and principles of science. Aristotle believes that there is a natural necessity in the world that forces things to act in a certain way. If, for example, it is the nature of heavy things to fall down to earth, this happens independent of human influence. Such things are beyond human control and, in a second, broader sense, a matter of τύχη.

Finally, the term τύχη refers, in an overlapping way, to how particular circumstances clash and collide with one another for better or for worse according to no predictable pattern. Here again, the key idea is that such helter-skelter combinations are beyond human control. Τύχη, in this sense,

---

4. Cf. *Liddell and Scott*.

seems to equate to random luck or mere happenstance, but it leaves open the question of what is causing such conjunctions of events to happen. The gods? Natural necessity? Mere chance?

I will provide a more careful exegesis of the term below. Suffice it to say here that these overlapping shades of meaning pose exegetical obstacles. Especially as Aristotle refers to some notion of fate using a series of related words in various discussions. He speaks, for example, of:

- τύχη;
- εὐτυχία, meaning good luck or good fortune (the prefix ευ- meaning good);
- εὐτύχημα, instance(s) of good luck;
- δυστυχία, bad luck or ill fortune (the prefix δυσ- meaning bad, difficult);
- ἀτυχία, a mishap, when things fall out badly, a failure to obtain what was intended (the prefix α- meaning without, not possessing); and
- τυγχάνω (a verb), to just so happen, to hit upon success.

Loredana Cardullo has argued that the root "τύχη" for this family of words is best translated as "fate."[5] Carnes Lord in the *Politics*, J. H. Freese in the *Rhetoric*, and Stock in the *Magna Moralia* translate "τύχη" as "fortune," R. P. Hardie and R.K. Gaye and other translators of the *Physics* typically use "chance," and most commentators—too many to name here—use "luck" and/or "chance."

Most contemporary exegetes shy away from religious interpretations of τύχη. Monte Ransome Johnson, in discussing the role of τύχη in Aristotle's ethics and physics, proclaims unequivocally, "It cannot be due to being favoured by a god or a divine overseer."[6] But this self-confident assertion (and others like it) strips away essential layers of

---

5. Cardullo, "The Concept of Luck (τύχη and εὐτυχία) in Aristotle," 541–554.
6. Johnson, "Luck in Aristotle's Physics and Ethics," 259.

religious meaning associated with τύχη during Aristotle's time period. The modern secular notion of luck or chance as a meaningless, unmerited, random advantage (or disadvantage) that happens for no reason at all is largely foreign to the ancient Greek mindset.

Thomas Pangle writes, "The word for luck or chance (*tuchē*) also designates the goddess of that name and means primarily any act of a divinity."[7] In an older discussion, Francis Cornford points out the difference between ancient and modern notions of "chance." He comments:

> The word: "Chance" suggests to the modern educated intelligence something utterly impersonal; we think at once of the mathematical theory of probability, of the odds at a gambling table, and so on. But we must remember that the current name for "Chance" in Greek was the name of a mythical person τύχη, a spirit who was actually worshipped by the superstitious, and placated by magical means. The religious spoke of "the Fortune that comes from the Divine," and believed that God's will was manifest in the striking turns of chance, and in spite of appearances was working for the righteous.[8]

Cornford refers specifically to Aristotle's mention of the goddess Τύχη in *Physics* II.4, but the more general historical point is worth some emphasis.

The notion of τύχη understood in a religious sense was pervasive in ancient Greek culture. One encounters the goddess Fate (Τύχη) personified and depicted, in various guises, in, for example, the Homeric Hymn to Demeter, in Hesiod's *Theogony*, in Pindar's *Orphic Hymns*, in Herodotus' *Histories*, in Thucydides's *History of the Peloponnesian War*, and in the Greek tragedies.[9] The religious cult of Τύχη as Lady Fate or

---

7. Pangle, *Aristotle's Teaching in the "Politics,"* 314, n. 45.
8. Cornford, *Thucydides Mythistoricus*, 107.
9. See Greene, *Moira*.

Fortuna (later associated with her wheel of fortune) gains momentum towards the end of the Golden Age of Athens, but the red-figure vase of the Heimarmene painter (shown in Figure 4.1), dated to about 50 years before Aristotle's birth, depicts a personified figure of Τύχη as a separate goddess ready to punish Helen and the Trojans with the aftermath of the Trojan War. Nemesis (Retribution) has draped her arm around the shoulder of her sister Fate, pointing disapprovingly at Helen who is about to elope with Paris. This is a very bad act. It violates her previous marriage and is a sin against hospitality. Despite Aphrodite's involvement, the gods cannot allow such acts to go unpunished. On the vase, then, Nemesis seems to be alerting Fate (Τύχη) to the indiscretion so that through some bad turn of fortune, there will be just retribution, which produces the wholesale calamity of the Trojan War.

Figure 4.1. Nemesis (Indignation) and *Tuchē* (Fortune) from a depiction of the seduction of Helen: Red-figure ware (c. 430 BC).
Source: Museum Collection: Antikensammlung Berlin; Catalogue No. Berlin 30036; Beazley Archive No. 215552.

The religious background here has important ramifications for any adequate understanding of Aristotle's approach to the concept of τύχη. The pagan gods force their will upon the world through various agencies: the Fates (the Μοῖραι, Moirae), who decide the length of one's life; the Furies (or Erinyes, Ἐρινύες), who pursue and harass the wicked; Nemesis, the goddess of retribution, and Ἄτη (*Atē*), who wrecks mischief and ruin upon those guilty of hubris.[10] In *Works and Days*, Hesiod writes:

> They who give straight judgements to strangers and to the men of the land, and go not aside from what is just, their city flourishes, and the people prosper in it. [...] All-seeing Zeus never decrees cruel war against them. Neither famine nor disaster ever haunt men who do true justice. [...] But for those who practise violence and cruel deeds far-seeing Zeus, the son of Cronos, ordains a punishment. Often even a whole city suffers for a bad man who sins and devises presumptuous deeds, and the son of Cronos lays great trouble upon the people, famine and plague together, so that the men perish away, and their women do not bear children, and their houses become few, through the contriving of Olympian Zeus. And again, at another time, the son of Cronos either destroys their wide army, or their walls, or else makes an end of their ships on the sea. You princes, mark well this punishment you also; for the deathless gods are near among men and mark all those who oppress their fellows with crooked judgements, and reckon not the anger of the gods. Upon the bounteous earth Zeus has thrice ten thousand spirits, watchers of mortal men, and these keep watch on judgements and deeds of wrong as they roam, clothed in mist, all over the earth.[11]

In a very traditional text, Hesiod posits, then, a moral economy where the gods reward good and punish evil by intervening in the course of history. In this account, what happens to us in the details of our lives has a moral meaning. We need to understand in light of this bigger religious picture. This perspective is, however, very far from the random, mechanistic, secular notion of "luck" some commentators attribute to Aristotle. Of course, one might complain that

---

10. Cf. Duffy, "Homer's Conception of Fate," 477–485.
11. Hesiod, *Works and Days* (Evelyn-White), ll. 225–256, 264.

Aristotle is too sophisticated to be taken in by naïve religious notions, but in reading Aristotle thoroughly, one never encounters any radical anti-traditionalism in matters of politics or religion.

There is, in particular, a strand of fatalism in the Greek religious tradition that does not square with the modern sense of luck. The ancient phrase ἀναγκαία τύχη is noteworthy in Greek tragedy. Literally translated, it means "necessity fate" or "necessity luck"; the two words coming in immediate succession emphasize the inevitableness of whatever has transpired. (We could translate the phrase as something like fatal necessity or doomed fate.) Greek mythology associated fate, then, not only with Τύχη, Lady Chance or Fortuna, but also with the goddess Ἀνάγκη [*Ananke*] or Necessity and her daughters, the Fates.[12] There is a worry about a divine determinism here that is absent in the modern understanding.

Suppose you need an ace of spades to win your poker hand. If we say that your winning or losing is a matter of luck, we mean that any card is equally likely: Your fortune or misfortune has no inevitability; it is just random chance that unpredictably turns up one alternative or another. But when the ancient Greeks attribute your winning or losing to τύχη, they mean something different. They mean that your turning up an ace of spades is already decided and *must* happen, one way or the other. In fact, your winning or losing is *not* open to chance; it is going to happen one way or another and there is nothing you or anything else in the universe can do about it.

Whereas we moderns are worried about an ineradicable looseness in things; the ancients are worried about an ineradicable tightness in things. Whereas we think of chance as a product of what is not bound by necessity, the ancient Greeks instinctively think of chance as a product of what is bound by necessity. This also holds true for the more secular uses of the ancient Greek term. In both religious and secular cases, the primary concern of a Greek audience is about a

---

12. Cf. *Republic* 617c.

fatalism that forces some kind of necessity on us (with or without the gods). The worry is, for example, that someone like Oedipus or Priam was *necessitated* to experience his terrible fate and that no other alternative was even possible.[13]

If I argue that Aristotle leaves room for the operation of fate in the world, I am not arguing that Aristotle would have been open to any complete determinism, something the later Peripatetic Alexander of Aphrodisias (c. 200 AD) argues against in his book *On Fate*. Aristotle would have been leery of any belief system (including atomism and Stoicism) that interferes too drastically with human agency. He believes in free will: "The virtues [...] are voluntary. [...] The vices will also be voluntary."[14] As the much later Simplicus says in his commentary on Aristotle's *Physics*, Aristotle takes a middle position: There is some room for freedom; there is some room for necessity.[15] Some aspects of the world are, so to speak, set in stone; other aspects of the world are open to accidental change. In the latter case, there is room for free will.

In his famous discussion about the future sea battle in *De Interpretatione* 9, Aristotle is clearly worried about the implications of what is sometimes called "fatalism" (even "logical fatalism"). The specific argument relies on logical considerations, but it is clear that, as a general rule, Aristotle believes, like most of us, that the future is open and can be modified in important ways by human agency and random happenstance. He is not willing to accept any view that would result in a totally predetermined future.

Aristotle rejects the idea that determinism could result from religious, logical, or scientific considerations. In

---

13. Cf. *Nicomachean Ethics* I.9.1101a9.
14. *Nicomachean Ethics* (Irwin) III.5.23–25. There are inevitable arguments about this: cf. Hardie, "Aristotle and the Freewill Problem."
15. Sorabji reports, "In the section on luck and chance, Simplicus attacks both those who ascribe nothing to chance and those who ascribe too much." Sorabji, "Introduction," 4.

Metaphysics VI.3, he repudiates the notion that everything happens by *natural* necessity. We might compare the position he wants to refute with the Stoic account of fate (identified with the goddess Heimarmene) as a linking chain of cause-and-effect (like beads on a string).[16] On this sort of account, the cosmos must unfold according to necessary cause-and-effect, resulting in a future that is completely determined by what happened before. I discuss Aristotle's argument against such complete determinism below. For the moment, simply note that the natural world is not deterministic in this sense, at least not for Aristotle.

Suppose, for example, we were to think of chance or fate in terms of surprising coincidences caused by intersecting lines of natural causality. A human being walks across a path; a rock falls. If the line of causality that brings about the trajectory of the rock intersects with the line of causality that pushes the human being across the path, we may have a chance event: The human being is hit by the falling rock and dies. We wonder: Was this fate? Or mere happenstance? Is nature causing each line of causality to reach its own terminus and they just happen to intersect? That is, is nature blindly operating so that this intersection is mere meaningless coincidence? Or is there some divine power that is not only causing the lines of causality but intending their intersection as well? It would seem that any all-powerful god would have to intend (and have foreknowledge of) both the lines of causality and their intersection. But Aristotle never really approaches these problems from such a straightforwardly theological perspective. He wonders about these issues, but that is about it. He is open to possibilities; he has no definitive answer to such conundrums.

---

16. We already see this in the Atomists. Hence Leucippus (fifth century BC): "nothing happens in vain (*matēn*) but everything from *logos* and by necessity" (DK 67B2).

We can distinguish between two kinds of determinism: a determinism produced by the way nature operates (as discerned by science, metaphysics, or even logic), and a determinism produced by the divine will (akin to the problem of predestination Boethius grappled with). Aristotle does not subscribe to either view. He resists any complete determinism—scientific, metaphysical, religious, even logical—largely because he wants to preserve moral agency. In the *Nicomachean Ethics*, for example, he suggests that it is better to be happy through the practice of one's own virtue than by some lucky stroke of chance or fate.[17] "It is quite wrong," he reports, to judge an individual's ethical success "from his misfortunes. For his doing well or badly does not depend on them."[18] One can achieve moral greatness even in the most trying circumstances. "Nobility shines through, when a man endures repeated and severe misfortune with patience, [...] from generosity and greatness of soul."[19]

If, however, Aristotle rejects any overall determinism, in part, to preserve the free will necessary to moral agency, I will argue that pagan accounts of fate are not at odds with free will. As we shall see, Aristotle's metaphysics leaves plenty of room for the operation of free will and for the simultaneous operation of fate. On his account, divinity (of whatever sort) is able to rearrange physical events in the world to benefit or harm human agents in accordance with moral desert. Any other view seems to lead to moral nihilism, a perspective that would be distinctly unAristotelian.

4.2. Τύχη, Science, and the Particular

In the Aristotelian corpus, there are important passages commenting on fate, chance, and related issues in the *Physics*, the *Nicomachean Ethics*, the *Eudemian Ethics*, the *Magna Moralia*, the *Metaphysics*, the *Rhetoric*, and *De Interpretatione*. I am

---

17. *Nicomachean Ethics* I.9.1099b.20–27.
18. *Nicomachean Ethics* (Irwin) I.10. 1100b8–9.
19. *Nicomachean Ethics* (Rackham) I.10.1100b30–34.

going to consider his account (or, if one prefers, the edited account bequeathed to us by the larger Peripatetic school) as one logically consistent theory. I will aim to reconcile, to the extent that that is possible, various differing passages.

The starting point for Aristotle's investigations is not at all surprising. In the *Rhetoric*, Aristotle explains:

> Luck [or fate] is also the cause of good things that happen contrary to reasonable expectation: as when, for instance, all your brothers are ugly, but you are handsome yourself; or when you find a treasure that everybody else has overlooked; or when a missile hits the next man and misses you; or when you are the only man not to go to a place you have gone to regularly, while the others go there for the first time and are killed. All such things are reckoned pieces of good luck [or good fate, or good fortune].[20]

Elsewhere, Aristotle uses the example of a person who throws a six or a sequence of sixes playing dice.[21] And, in some famous *Physics* passages, he mentions the man who unexpectedly manages to collect money from someone when he goes to the market for an entirely different reason.[22] All these examples are, more or less, consistent with how we ourselves wonder about such things. The salient characteristic is that they involve something happening to the sharp advantage or disadvantage of someone through unexpected circumstances beyond their control.

Contemporary accounts of Aristotle's theory of luck give primacy to the passages in the *Physics*. Contemporary scholar Kent Johnson articulates a fairly typical account of τύχη, what he calls "luck," as mere epistemological ignorance. Johnson writes, "When we call the cause of something luck

---

20. *Rhetoric* (Freese) I.5.1362a6–12.
21. *Eudemian Ethics* VIII.2.1247a23–24; 1247b16–17.
22. *Physics* II.4.196a2; II.5.196b33–197a4.

[i.e., τύχη], we mean only to say that the true cause or causes are unknown to us."[23] So, τύχη is only a name for ignorance. To say something happened by chance is to say that we cannot figure out why it happened. When someone wins a lottery, for example, all the events leading up to that win scrupulously obey the laws of physics but there is too much information to compute and so we get a "random," unpredictable result that happens, we say, by chance. Meaning that it is impossible for us to know or calculate or predict who wins. What happens, happens in an epistemologically and scientifically opaque way.

On this standard account, Aristotle inquires in the *Physics* whether τύχη (understood as luck or chance) can be classified as a fifth cause and dismisses definitively any such suggestion. There are innumerable commentators who effectively wish away τύχη as a legitimate cause of anything. Daniel Schillinger contends that in Aristotle (as in Thucydides and Machiavelli) "the idea of luck [τύχη] is a piece of 'folk wisdom' that arises only because of the limitations of human agency: when agents prove incapable of foreseeing and controlling significant events, then luck is invoked in order to describe what has happened."[24] Schillinger sets out to demonstrate—following a line of argument that derives from Julia Annas and others—that "for Aristotle, the idea of luck [τύχη] refers to an explanation or an interpretation as opposed to a cause."[25] On this view, luck is something we ourselves add to what is really going on; it is something we project onto the event. It is, at best, an epistemological category; it has no ontological reality. When we say someone was lucky, this adds nothing real to the events that transpire; it adds an *interpretation* of the events that comes from us, not the events themselves. It

---

23. Johnson, "Luck and Good Fortune in the *Eudemian Ethics*," 91.
24. Schillinger, *Politics of Luck*, ii.
25. Schillinger, *Luck*, 43. Cf. Annas, "Inefficient Causes," 319.

is as if luck (or fate) is really a kind of make-believe; it exists inside our heads but not out in the world.

Commentators tend to view *Physics* II.4–8 as a dismissal of τύχη as a source of causal agency in the world. Robin Smith writes that chance and luck "are not causes or explanations for events, but rather denials of causality."[26] Pascal Massie reports, "The regularity of the Aristotelian cosmos," leads commentators "to consider that 'chance' is but a superficial 'name' (a 'manner of speaking' [...]) behind which there is, in fact, no reality." On this standard account, then, Aristotle "condemn[s] chance and luck as illusory."[27]

There are a minority of authors who argue that luck and chance play a causal role out in the world: Cynthia Freeland, Martha Nussbaum, Lindsay Judson, and John Dudley, for example.[28] But, mostly, the present-day discussion is about whether luck should be construed as something that is really "out there" in the world or as something inside our heads. I will side with the realists in this debate, but few authors seem to deal seriously with the possibility that Aristotle accepts that τύχη might be a result of divine intervention in accordance with the religious beliefs of the ancient Greeks.

I will argue, then, that Aristotle's account of τύχη, considered as fate or luck, is metaphysical, not merely epistemological. It is not a matter of adding another cause to the four causes of science. Science is complete in itself. On the other hand, there is an aspect of reality that causes

---

26. Smith, "Filling in Nature's Deficiencies," 300. Cf. Solmsen, *Aristotle's System of the Physical World*, 103–104.
27. Massie, "The Irony of Chance," 16. Massie articulates an artful presentation, but it amounts to the usual interpretation: chance is merely a figure of speech.
28. Cf. Freeland, "Accidental Causes," 68–71; Nussbaum, *Fragility of Goodness*, 334; Judson, "Chance and 'Always for the Most Part,'" 97–99; Dudley, *Aristotle's Concept of Chance*, 27–31; Mathews, "Accidental Unities," 223–240; Meyer, "Aristotle, Teleology, Reduction," 798–803; Allen, "Aristotle on Chance as an Accidental Cause," 45–65; Dworkin, "What Is Equality?" 293.

things to happen in the universe that cannot be explained by science because, as Aristotle sees it, science cannot explain the particular. It can describe the general case, but it cannot provide any full explanation of contingent, particular circumstances. Even in a deterministic world, Aristotelian science could not provide a complete explanation of everything because it focuses on the essences or natures of things. And, as John Dudly argues, no study of universal essences can provide a complete picture of a particular case.[29]

Given the modern enthusiasm for science, we moderns tend to overestimate its epistemic capacities. (With the exception of so-called postmodernists who understate its epistemic capacities, but that is another matter.) Many of us would like to believe, as Johnson claims, that science could explain every event if only we had enough data and an efficient enough calculating capacity. But *this is not Aristotle's view*. Aristotle clearly distinguishes between (1) a scientific causality that arises from the natures of things, and (2) a contingent causality that arises from particular circumstances. We must not conflate these two sources of causality. Particular causality, which belongs to the realm of fate (or luck) *exceeds* the limits of scientific explanation. It may not be a scientific category, but neither is it a purely made-up, mental concept.

Aristotelian science is a tool—like logic is an *organon*—that orders particulars in line with our knowledge of universal natures. But we need particulars to have a world and universal principles cannot supply the particulars. A plethora of particular possibilities (as in possible-world semantics) are consistent with the same set of universal rules and essences. Science cannot sort all this out by itself. Which is why, as neo-essentialist David Oderberg argues, possible-world semantics goes astray—because it tends to focus on

---

29. Cf. Dudley, *Chance*.

what must always be the same in each possible world whereas reality is inevitably particular.[30]

Aristotle makes a legitimate philosophical point. Even if we had all the universal knowledge of science, we would not provide the answer to a very important human question: Why did this particular thing happen to me yesterday on my way home from work? Why, for example, did George stop in at the convenience store and—"accidentally"—buy the last ticket on the counter, which turned out to be the winning ticket for the lottery? It is no good saying that no laws of physics were violated in the process. Fate has to do with George rather than Betty winning the lottery. Even if we could use the law of physics to calculate from a god's-eye point of view that George *had* to win the lottery that would not solve the problem. We could still ask: Why is the physical world organized in such a way that rich, conceited, arrogant George gets the prize instead of kind, benevolent, needy Betty? Even if physical science could show us why George had to win, we would be left with the question about fate, which is a moral and religious question.

When Aristotle discusses τύχη, fate, fortune, or luck, he is wondering about a moral possibility that science cannot explain. Consider two concrete examples. (I use the terms *luck* and *fate* interchangeably here.) Aristotle believes that science tells us how human teeth should be shaped: "the front teeth sharp, fitted for tearing, the molars broad and useful for grinding down the food."[31] Compare, then, two physical occurrences: (1) George's front and back teeth happen to be shaped in the *wrong* way and (2) George wins the lottery. We might think that the lottery win is a matter of luck and that George's badly shaped teeth are not. But this is the wrong way to think about it. George is unlucky to have such bad teeth and lucky to win the lottery. The first case is a matter of bad luck; the second is a matter of good luck. Both

---

30. Cf. Oderberg, *Real Essentialism*.
31. *Physics* (Hardie and Gaye) II.8.198b25–26; 198b34–37.

facts are a matter of luck, insomuch as they apply uniquely and unusually to his individual case.

Luck (or fate) happens when something good or bad happens in a way that strikes us as unusual. At least that seems to be Aristotle's sense of it. But we should not oversimplify. After all, someone winning the lottery is a regular occurrence. It happens every week. It is *George's* winning it this week with ticket No. 576300926731 that is a matter of luck because it is a contingent particular fact with possible moral and even religious implications. The same understanding applies to George's badly shaped teeth. The fact that teeth are usually shaped in a certain way is a matter of science, but the fact that *George's* teeth are *not* like this is a matter of bad luck. Poor George! But he is not alone in having badly shaped teeth. It is just that that is not the usual occurrence.

I have been using the word "luck," but note that both these incidents could be interpreted in terms of religious notions of fate. In the case of the lottery, we could ask: Are the gods rewarding George for good behaviour? Because he is an Athenian? Even because he will use some of the money to build a temple? George's bad teeth could be construed as a punishment rather than a reward. We could ask: Are they the result of some sort of a curse? Is he being punished for his sins? For his father's sins? This sounds strange to modern ears, but it was not so strange in ancient Greece. Of course, Aristotle is open to the possibility that luck is just purposeless accident. It is hard to know but whatever science tells us, it does not answer this question. This remains, at least, an open possibility.

I am not sure that Aristotle's account of luck or fate (τύχη) is entirely consistent. He is offering both a metaphysical interpretation and an account of how the word is used. This may muddy the waters. Aristotle writes, "now many events happen by chance," including "small pieces of good fortune or of its opposite."[32] Granted, he never says that *everything* happens by chance but, at least on the interpretation

---

32. *Nicomachean Ethics* (Ross) I.10.1100b23-24.

I am offering, that is because we tend to reserve the word (in Greek and in English) for special occasions when something unusually conspicuous occurs (even for the unusually conspicuous in small amounts). When something very bad or very good happens to someone, we notice the event and call it by a special name: good luck or bad luck. When something ordinary happens, we do not notice and do not give it a name (as Aristotle says about many character states). Because people in general have regularly shaped teeth, for example, we do not notice when this happens and do not think of it as luck (or fate). In effect, on a metaphysical level, we take it for granted.

Having regular teeth is not an unusual conspicuous event, so we do not use the term "lucky" to cover this type of case. We do not say that the person with regular teeth is lucky (in ancient Greek, εὐτυχές, well fated); we say rather that the person who won a million dollars in the lottery is lucky. Because winning a lottery is a conspicuously unusual event. Still, we should not make too much of these different usages. After all, having just left the orthodontist, we could say in regular conversation to someone who does not need to pay orthodontists: "You're so lucky to have good teeth." In ancient Greek parlance, we could say that you are fortunate the gods gave you good teeth. And, metaphysically, leaving open that possibility would be correct. After all, Aristotle attributes even the difference between being handsome or not being handsome to luck (or fate) but this difference, which might amount to little more than having a straight or a snub nose, is not categorically more serious than the difference between having straight or crooked teeth.

Aristotelian science is about general explanations about what causes what. We can scientifically explain, for example, my teeth having a specific shape through final cause, because they serve a certain purpose: through material cause, because they are made of a calcium; through efficient cause, because they were produced through human growth; or through formal cause, because they belong to the category "human teeth." But none of this explains why I happen to have regularly shaped teeth and my poor daughter—who was bullied because of it at school—has crooked teeth. (Just as Aristotle says, there is no scientific explanation when you turn out to be handsome when all your brothers are ugly.) Yes, we can come up with a scientific explanation for my daughter's crooked teeth—perhaps she was missing calcium as a child, perhaps she suffered an injury, perhaps it is genetics—but none of this explains why the particulars of the world were organized so that she ended up being the one with crooked teeth and I ended up being the one with regular teeth. This is, in Aristotle's mind, what questions of fate (or luck) are about. When commentators spin out a scientific explanation for particular facts so as to dismiss any possibility of fate, they royally miss the point. Of course, science can explain how things happen, but that is not the issue. The issue is why my daughter was chosen instead of me as the recipient of crooked teeth.

In the *Posterior Analytics*, Aristotle writes: "What is by chance is neither necessary nor for the most part, chance is what comes about from these."[33] Again, in the *Metaphysics*, Aristotle argues that there is no science of chance (i.e., no science of the accidental), "because all scientific knowledge is of that which is always or usually so."[34] As I explain below, Aristotelian science is in the business of composing demonstrations (syllogisms) that apply to entire classes of things that possess the same natures. When we speak of something happening by chance, luck, or fate, however, we are not formulating a general rule; we are pointing to a single case, which could have turned out differently. It is not that the general rules of science do not apply to individual cases; it is that there is room in contingent circumstances, when an "event follows from indefinite and undetermined

---

33. *Posterior Analytics* (Barnes) I.30.87b19–20.
34. *Metaphysics* (Tredennick) VI.2.1027a20–21. This is a repeated trope. Cf. *Eudemian Ethics* VII.14.1247a31–33.

antecedents," for alternate results (without exceptions to the rules of science).[35]

Aristotelian science explains the general rule about something that happens without exceptions or "for the most part" (*hos epi to polu*); i.e., with only a few exceptions.[36] Science is not in the business of explaining or accounting for the particulars instantiated in one single event. Tyler Huismann maintains that particular circumstances are, for Aristotle, "merely items that are accidentally conjoined to proper causes."[37] They are, he thinks, "causally inert." But this is a misunderstanding. The particular causes that gave rise to my daughter's crooked teeth, to you being handsome, or to you finding a treasure are not causally inert; they are operative in the world. What Aristotle means by the "accidental" (κατὰ συμβεβηκός) happens irregularly or only once, so there is no science of such things. We cannot predict accidentals, not merely because we lack the requisite knowledge, but because they exist outside any general scientific classification. I examine these issues in more detail below.

4.3. Τύχη in *Physics* II.4–6

Most commentators attempting to elucidate what Aristotle means by τύχη turn, first, to the famous passages in the *Physics* before proceeding further. They might come to rather different conclusions if they began, for example with the *Eudemian Ethics* VIII.2. The idea that Aristotle first got the science nailed down and only then proceeded to the moral aspects of the question presupposes a specific career chronology. But no one can know, definitively, the order in which Aristotle (or his followers) wrote various passages. (Hence, the eternal problems of developmentalism discussed above.) Again, I will treat Aristotle's account of τύχη

---

35. *Eudemian Ethics* VII.14.1247b11–13.
36. Cf., again, *Metaphysics* VI.2.1027a20-21; *Posterior Analytics* I.30.87b 19-22; *Nicomachean Ethics* I.2.1094b12-27.
37. Huismann, "Aristotle on Accidental Causation," 561.

as one consistent whole. We can use the terms "chance," "luck," "fate," or "fortune" as English equivalents, but with the understanding that the possibility of divine fate is always lurking in the background.

Let us consider, then, the famous passages in *Physics* II.4–6. We cannot know that all these passages were written at the same time by Aristotle himself and thus must pass over those imponderables. Aristotle begins, as is his wont, by summarizing sometimes overlapping opinions on the subject. Here is a list of his major points:

- There were the "early physicists" (the pre-Socratics including Empedocles), who "found no place for chance among the causes which they recognized." There are those who "say that nothing happens by chance," who subscribe to "the old argument that denied chance."[38]
- There are those who "speak of some things as happening by chance and others not."[39]
- There are those who believe that even the movement of the heavens is due to chance (an opinion Aristotle qualifies as surpassingly strange and absurd).[40]
- And there are the religious "who believe that chance is a cause, that is inscrutable human to intelligence, as being a divine thing and full of mystery."[41]

Aristotle's analysis of the concept begins in earnest in Chapter 5. The text overlaps and repeats itself at points. I am not going to follow the order of the text, verse by verse, and since I cannot solve all the exegetical puzzles here, I will set out the basics.

---

38. I will generally use the Hardie and Gaye translation. (There is an older and more recent version.) *Physics* II.4.196a17–18; II.4.196a16–17; II.4.196a15.
39. *Physics* (Hardie and Gaye) II.4.196a16.
40. *Physics* (Hardie and Gaye) II.4.196a25–26.
41. *Physics* (Hardie and Gaye) II.4.196b5–196b7.

First, it is clear that we have to distinguish chance from things that always or usually come about in the same way and, also, from things that happen by necessity. (This is why Aristotle finds it strange to attribute the movements of the heavens to chance, for stars and planets move in very regular and predictable ways.) Chance events are unexpected, unpredictable, and a matter of surprising circumstances. Chance is, then, in this precise sense, "a thing contrary to rule [...] for 'rule' applies to what is always true or true for the most part, whereas chance belongs to a third type of event."[42]

Second, Aristotle says that "the causes of what comes to pass by chance are indefinite."[43] There can be any number of causes for such events. I may win the lottery because I chose my mother's birthday for the number of the winning ticket; because my wife bought me a ticket as a joke; because the grocer gave me the second ticket in the pile instead of the top ticket; because the red ball fell the right way at a lucky instant in the lottery machine, and so on. There is no limit to the conjunction of particular circumstances that might result in a winning ticket. Unlike things that are deliberately planned, "in this sort of causation the number of possible causes is infinite."[44]

Third, Aristotle repeatedly says that chance is an accidental, incidental, coincidental, nonessential cause; it is "κατὰ συμβεβηκός" (from the verb συμβαίνω: to come to pass, to happen; hence, τὸ συμβεβηκός: a chance event, contingency).[45] I explain this below, but the main meaning Aristotle wants to communicate here is that a chance event depends upon an arrangement of *contingent* particulars. A number of events that do not have to happen together happen together on this

---

42. *Physics* (Hardie and Gaye) II.5.197a18–20. There are possibly philosophical problems here, but I will not take the time to investigate them.
43. *Physics* (Hardie and Gaye) II.5.197a8–9; II.5.197a20–22.
44. *Physics* (Hardie and Gaye) II.6.198a4. Or innumerable: II.5.196b28–29; II.197a15–7.
45. *Physics* (Hardie and Gaye) II.5.196b23–29; 5.197a5; 5.197a12–15; 5.197a24; 5.197a32–33; 6.198a6–11.

one occasion. To use a more contemporary example: Suppose you turn at the wrong corner because your neighbour gave you wrong directions and you hit a red light, arrive late at the train station and miss the train, which derails and kills all the passengers aboard. You escaped death by chance. All these things (and many others besides) had to happen together to produce this stroke of luck. Lucky or unlucky events depend on an array of accidental coincidences that line up together to produce the beneficial or harmful effect.

Fourth, Aristotle mentions that chance can be good or evil for humans; it can bring about good fortune, εὐτυχία, or bad fortune, δυστυχία.[46] This ability to enhance or mar our happiness is, of course, what makes τύχη a useful weapon for moral reward or punishment. On the religious view, the crafty Greeks gods knew how to align points of happenstance to ensure poetic justice when dealing with moral or immoral humans (or, sometimes, their partisan favourites).

Fifth, Aristotle claims that chance events belong among the things that come to be for the sake of something: "ἐν τοῖς ἕνεκά του γιγνομένοις."[47] Put another way, chance has a relation, somehow, with purposeful behaviour or human final cause. Except that it usually has to do with unexpected human purpose. Two examples: (1) A man goes to the market to buy food and meets someone who owes him money he is then able to collect; (2) a loose stone falls down a mountainside killing a man committing a serious crime (something the gods might have intended). In the first case, one human purpose produces an unexpected "purposeful" result; in the second case, a natural event without purpose produces a "purposeful" result.[48] When it comes to later commentators,

---

46. *Physics* (Hardie and Gaye) II.5.197a25–197a29.
47. *Physics* (Hardie and Gaye) II.5.196b17; II.5.196b29; cf. 196b18–23; cf. II.5.196b19–20; II.5.197a5–6; II.5.197a5–6; II.6.197b18–20, etc.
48. This is the meaning of Aristotle's odd phrase: "The stone that struck the man did not fall for the sake of striking him; therefore, it fell spontaneously, because it might have fallen by the action of an agent and for the sake of striking." *Physics* (Hardie and Gaye) II.6.197b29–31.

James Lennox attributes the first interpretation to Porphyry, the second to Simplicius.[49]

One can profitably compare Aristotle's concept of τύχη to the Greek concept of τέχνη, which is, in some sort, the opposite of τύχη. Τέχνη, which means skill or craft, has to do with what has been designed. Think of a clock. The parts of a clock have been deliberately shaped and assembled in one mechanism to keep track of time. If, however, one randomly threw the parts of an old clock into a garbage can in any which way and the pile of parts started to perfectly tell time—that would be a matter of τύχη, rather than τέχνη. In the case of τύχη, something that was not designed acts as if it were designed. Aristotle thinks that design can be produced by either intelligence (which is responsible for τέχνη) but also by nature. (It is of the nature of fish, for example, to have gills in order to breathe under water.[50] This can be thought of as a matter of τέχνη.) Both intelligence and nature are prior to τύχη in the cosmos in the sense that they produce what is to be expected.[51] Chance has to do with the accidental, with particulars that unexpectedly coalesce into something purposeful.

Sixth, Aristotle says that "Things do, in a way, occur by chance. […] but chance is not the cause without qualification of anything."[52] The first part of the claim insists on the reality of chance events (or events caused by fate). The second part points out that chance is an *indirect* cause; it operates through more direct immediate causes. If you happen to be more handsome than your brothers, we now know that this happens because of DNA chemical events that align themselves in a felicitous way. The fact that you were lucky enough to be rewarded with a handsome face only happens through the agency of these individual DNA reactions, which may be

---

49. Lennox, "Aristotle on Chance."
50. Cf. *Physics* (Hardie and Gaye) II.5.196b23.
51. *Physics* (Hardie and Gaye) II.6.198a5–13.
52. *Physics* (Hardie and Gaye) II.5.197a12–14.

considered, the direct or immediate cause of what happened. To speak of your fortunate face being caused by a lucky stroke of chance is to refer to the way these direct causes added together to produce your beauteous visage. Chance is, so to speak, always dependent on direct causes that are, in some scientific sense, the primary causes of the overall effect. Aristotle does not believe in miracles in the Humean sense of something contrary to the laws of nature. Chance is, in this sense, a secondary cause in that it is always supervenient on the workings of nature. It does not follow that it has no ontological reality. (I think Aristotle may conflate issues here; there is more to say but I will return to some of these issues below.)

Seventh, then, Aristotle distinguishes τύχη (chance) from αὐτόματον, which is usually translated as spontaneity. The spontaneous is what happens randomly by itself outside human control and without external agency. It is the mechanical, the automatic. As Aristotle explains, "spontaneity" is the wider term. Chance (luck, fate) is a more restricted category. Every result of chance is spontaneous, but not everything spontaneous is a matter of chance.[53] Aristotle makes a point of restricting τύχη to moral agents: "Chance or fate [τύχη] and what results from it are appropriate to agents that are capable of good fortune and of moral action generally. Therefore, necessarily, chance (or fate) is in the sphere of moral actions."[54] "The spontaneous, on the other hand, is found both in the lower animals and in many inanimate objects."[55]

Here Aristotle appears to be giving his own doctrine (as well as reporting on what people generally say). It is, after all, an important enough distinction for him to make it part of his philosophy of chance. The passage is important and worth

---

53. *Physics* (Hardie and Gaye) II.6.197a36–37.
54. *Physics* (Hardie and Gaye) II.6.197b1–3.
55. *Physics* (Hardie and Gaye) II.6.197b13–14.

quoting at length; I use the word "luck" here for *tuchē*, but one could just as easily use the term "fate." As Aristotle puts it:

> Necessarily, "luck" [τύχη] is in the sphere of moral actions. This is indicated by the fact that good fortune [εὐτυχία] is thought to be the same, or nearly the same, as happiness [εὐδαιμονία] and happiness is thought to be a kind of moral action, since it is well-doing. Hence what is not capable of moral action cannot do anything by "luck" [τύχη]. An inanimate thing or a lower animal or a child cannot do anything by "luck" [τύχη], because it is incapable of deliberate intention; nor can "good fortune" [εὐτυχία] or "ill fortune" [ἀτυχία] be ascribed to them, except metaphorically.[56]

In the modern dispensation, luck is not restricted to moral agents. Here is a genuine newspaper headline: "*Lucky* Stray Dog Escapes Animal Control 92 Times."[57] This sounds alright in English, but not in Aristotle's technical terminology. Aristotle does not think that stray dogs, babies, the senile, or inanimate objects can be lucky or unlucky. They cannot be truly lucky because they lack moral agency. This is an important point. Indeed, one might question why Aristotle would posit a moral agency criterion for τύχη unless he intends to link it to religious notions of fate as moral reward or moral punishment.

Contrary to the usual stereotype, even here in the *Physics*, Aristotle, given the historical period, intended to make room for religious accounts of fate. In a different text, he points out that Hippocrates was a silly person and yet was lucky and found success in business in spite of his silliness.[58] The

---

56. *Physics* (Hardie and Gaye) IVI.6.197b1–8. In emending the translation, I have substituted "fate" for "chance."
57. The article explains, "Animal Services in Fayetteville, Arkansas, have had a tough time trying to catch a stray dog, known as "Lucky Black Dog" or LBD, that has evaded capture 92 times since 2008." (www.treehugger.com.)
58. *Eudemian Ethics* VII.14.1247a16–20.

question he then poses is whether such a lucky individual "is loved by a god" or is lucky through some natural endowment.[59] The pseudo-Aristotle of the *On the Universe* piously quotes Plato: "God, then, as the old story has it, holding the beginning and the end and the middle of all things that exist, proceeding by a straight path in the course of nature brings them to accomplishment; and with him ever follows Justice, the avenger of all that falls short of the Divine Law."[60] One could not have, here, a more explicit appeal to something like moral karma. What precisely the authentic Aristotle thought of all this is hard to say. Note that I am not arguing that he takes a definite position here for or against the religious understanding of divinely inspired fate, only that he is leaving the door open for such a possibility.

I do not mean to overstate the case. If there is a moral dimension to chance (or luck) that makes it an apt tool for divine intervention, a religious person in ancient Greece (or elsewhere), presumably, need not attribute every chance event to divine fate. The Christian historian Herbert Butterfield remarks on an exaggerated religiosity that sees fate in everything. He reports:

> I remember taking part in a *viva voce* examination in Oxford over ten years ago when we were left completely and permanently baffled by a candidate who ascribed everything to the direct interposition of the Almighty and therefore felt himself excused from the discussion of any immediate agencies.[61]

This overenthusiastic theological occasionalism makes little sense. If bare chance supervenes on natural necessity, arising from the coincidental interaction of two or more particular causal lines, one might divide τύχη, into two kinds, one being

---

59. *Eudemian Ethics* (Solomon) VII.14.1247a22.
60. *On the Universe* (Forster) 7.401b24–8. Cf. *Laws* 715e, 730c.
61. Cited in Wilson, *Thinking with Concepts*, 87.

the product of entirely natural processes and the other being also motivated by supernatural designs. If, to use a modern example, someone walks down the hall to catch the elevator, and the elevator door opens just as he approaches, this surprising but trivial event seems to be little more than random happenstance. If, on the other hand, an evil person goes to the supermarket where he has been robbing people at gunpoint and a lightning bolt falls down from heaven and kills him before he can pull the trigger, this momentous coincidence seems to evince the workings of a god, depending on how the divine is conceived.

Aristotle would allow that the gods can intervene and be the cause of chance (or luck) in human affairs, but it need not follow from this that all cases of chance or luck have a divine cause. Presumably, the gods would have to care enough about a situation to actually intervene; there would have to be something momentous at stake. But there are inevitable ambiguities here as Greek paganism has no fixed orthodox doctrine; it is too early in the tradition for that. When it comes to some gods—for example, the Μοῖραι—they seem to control every aspect of a person's path in life. The practice of temple worship, on the other hand, seems more consistent with gods that listen to prayers and intervene on special occasions for special reasons.

Eighth, and in a similar spirit, note that Aristotle equates good τύχη, "εὐτυχία" with "εὐδαιμονία," his term for a successful moral life.[62] Aristotle would never say that we can, by sheer happenstance, achieve *eudaimonia*. We need external goods to be truly happy, which may derive from happenstance (divinely inspired or otherwise), but *eudaimonia* also requires "good conduct." What Aristotle seems to have in mind for *eudaimonia* is the coming together of virtuous behaviour and good external opportunities that mirrors, closely, the Greek religious conception of a good destiny or fate. (In these passages about good luck, Aristotle uses the same

---

62. *Physics* (Hardie and Gaye) II.6.197b1–197b5.

Greek terms [πρακτός, πρᾶξις] he uses to describe moral/practical endeavour in the *Nicomachean Ethics*.[63])

Note also Aristotle's choice of a term for supreme moral success: "εὐδαιμονία." This is a direct reference to Socrates's claim that he possessed a "good *daimon*" as a spiritual guide. Hence, Socrates's cheerful attitude at his trial. But Aristotle goes even further. If Socrates focuses on virtue, Aristotle emphasizes how happiness depends on external goods—goods outside our control *that only the gods can provide*. He writes, "happiness cannot exist apart from external goods, and these result from good fortune [i.e., from fate], [...] which will operate alongside with happiness."[64] It makes perfect sense, then, to assume that some account of fate, which may involve asking the gods for external goods, can play a meaningful role in human life. The fact that external goods are outside our control need not mean, as a contemporary commentator like Mayhew asserts, that the gods have no control over them. It means that *we humans* have no control over them, which is a very different thing. There is at least room here for speculations about whether there are divine forces behind the lucky or unlucky events that alter and shape our lives.

In Plato's dialogue of the same name, Phaedo reports that it was fate (τύχη) that provided an opportunity for Socrates's final discourses.[65] Socrates himself, in the *Crito* and in the *Apology*, interprets the last events of his life as a matter of good fortune or happy fate. He assures the jury that his guilty sentence must be, paradoxically, a *good* twist of fate. He lectures the court:

> You too, my judges, must face death with good hope, and remember this one truth, that a good man cannot suffer

---

63. *Nicomachean Ethics* I.1.1094a19; I.7.1097a22; I.7.1097a16; VI.4.1140a2.
64. *Magna Moralia* (Stock) II.8.1207b15.
65. *Phaedo*, 58A.

any evil either in life or after death, and that the gods do not neglect his fortunes. What has happened to me also is not mere [spontaneity] [ἀπὸ τοῦ αὐτομάτου], but I am sure that it was better for me to die now and be rid of my troubles.[66]

This is, however, an unequivocal invocation of fate (in Aristotelian terms, "ἡ τύχη" rather than "τό αὐτόματον") as something that restores moral order to the universe despite appearances to the contrary.

Aristotle is a very different sort of philosopher than Socrates. But the question is whether he takes seriously the idea that behind a wall of cold happenstance, there may be divine forces at work rewarding the good and punishing the bad. If, as Socrates believed, the world has to make moral sense, then, it cannot be—as some modern philosophers would have it—that the good and the bad are arbitrarily punished and rewarded. Aristotle is not an existentialist, a nihilist, a positivist, a postmodernist. A world in which the wicked go unpunished or the good go unrewarded seems *morally* absurd, which is the point of absurdist literature like Samuel Beckett's *Waiting for Godot*. Socrates and Plato, at least, would disagree. They adamantly believed that one cannot make sense of particular circumstances in one's life without a larger moral interpretation. (Hence Socrates's rejection of Anaxagoras's "materialist" philosophy in the *Phaedo*.[67]) I am arguing that Aristotle was—like other philosophers at the time—at least open to this moral possibility. To think that science explodes the religious concept of fate goes directly against the original spirit of Aristotelianism.

Aristotle concludes, "It is clear then that chance is an incidental [accidental, coincidental] cause in the sphere of those

---

66. *Apology* (Woodhead) 31e–d.
67. *Phaedo* 97c–98d.

actions for the sake of something which involve purpose."[68] There is nothing here that eliminates the religious concept of fate. If the gods are busy rewarding good behaviour or punishing bad behaviour, as on the Greek model, they do it indirectly, so that contingent circumstances turn out a certain way. On Aristotle's account, fate could never contradict science. The gods are behind-the-scene actors; they indirectly intervene, using nature to produce the morally just result. Their machinations would have to be technically classified as an *indirect* cause of what happens. They rearrange accidental happenstance, not the science of the universe.

Again, Aristotle does not subscribe to "miracles" in the Humean sense of something contradicting nature. When explaining what people ought to pray for, he advises that we should pray for conditions that meet our needs, "but not for conditions that are impossible."[69] Aristotle is a scientist. Even the gods cannot modify what nature is. But that leaves plenty of room for the operation of fate. Fate supervenes on the natural order; it rides piggyback on what happens naturally. It adds another level of explanation to happenstance that is beyond the reach of science. When a good man goes to the wrong place and gets his money, we can ask whether that happened by divine design. But nothing here breaks the rules of science.

4.4. Bechler: Accidental Causality, Contrary to Reason?

Before turning to further questions about the religious notions of fate, we need to clear up some misunderstandings about Aristotle's concept of τύχη as an accidental cause. Aristotle does, at times, seem to oppose good luck, good fortune, prosperity, a blessed fate, and a happy destiny (τύχη, εὐτυχία, εὐτυχέω) to reason. He writes that some people are lucky (or fortunate) "contrary to all the teachings of science

---

68. *Physics* (Hardie and Gaye) II.5.197a5–6: δῆλον ἄρα ὅτι ἡ τύχη αἰτία κατὰ συμβεβηκὸς ἐν τοῖς κατὰ προαίρεσιν τῶν ἕνεκά του.
69. *Politics* (Reeve) IVI.6.1265a16–17.

and correct calculation."[70] And again, that luck, chance, or fate "is the cause of things contrary to reason."[71] And yet, again, that "things due to luck [or fate] may actually be contrary to nature."[72]

The apparent dichotomy Aristotle posits between science and happenstance has led to some hostile, even alarming interpretations. Zev Bechler, for one, thinks that this is enough to show that Aristotelian science is futile and unable to explain anything.[73] In what can only be described as a hostile treatment, Bechler comments that "during the sixteenth and seventeenth centuries, Aristotle's definition of [physical] motion became the symbol of Aristotelian verbosity and vacuity."[74] Bechler, a self-professed modernist, is out to bolster and corroborate this negative evaluation of Aristotelian science. Mostly, his strategy boils down to a familiar argument, directed against pejorative caricatures of Aristotelian essentialism. What is more pertinent in the present context, however, is his derogatory account of what he sees as Aristotle's empty notion of particular or accidental causality. It must be the case, he thinks, on Aristotelian grounds, that chance (or fate) "is strictly not the cause of anything." But this makes Aristotelian science useless for determining particular events in the world.

I will use the terms "accidental," "coincidental" (Bechler's choice) and "particular," more or less, synonymously. Bechler, then, is at great pains to show that Aristotle accepts that there can be no causal explanation of particular/accidental/coincidental events. Remember Aristotle's comment in the *Metaphysics* that "there is no science, practical, productive, or speculative, of the accidental (κατὰ συμβεβηκὸς)."[75]

---

70. *Eudemian Ethics* (Rackman) VIII.2.1248a2–5.
71. *Eudemian Ethics* (Rackman) VIII.2.1248a9–10.
72. *Rhetoric* I.51362a3–4.
73. Bechler, *Aristotle's Theory of Actuality*, 61 ff.
74. Bechler, *Actuality*, 11.
75. *Metaphysics* (Ross) VI.2.1026b4–7.

In that discussion, Aristotle identifies the accidental with "that which admits variation from the usual."[76] There is, then, no science of the accidental "because all scientific knowledge is of that which is always or usually so."[77] Aristotelian science is, as Bechler insists, about rules, principles, essences, and laws that hold in all or most cases. It is about things like "all or most bileless animals are long-lived," or "old age causes death," or even "it usually snows in Northern climates in the winter." Accidents happen only once. (That is why they are called accidents.) For Aristotle, there is no science of such things; we cannot predict their peculiarities, not merely because we lack the requisite knowledge, but because they are dependent on contingent sequences of events that do not happen on a regular basis.

In the *Metaphysics*, Aristotle goes out of his way to argue, against determinism, that not everything that happens, happens necessarily.[78] Bechler explains:

> Analyzing the sense in which it is false that everything happens necessarily, Aristotle explains that there must be causal chains that lead back in time only to a finite limit, that is, to an origin which is itself not caused by any prior cause. Such an event is the coincident[al], and that is why not everything happens necessarily: "Clearly, then the process goes back to a certain starting point, but this no longer points to something further. This then will be the starting point for the coincidental, and will have nothing else as cause of its coming to be." (*Met* 1027b11-15). [...] The coincidental has no essence, contrary to things that belong to natural classes, for example. It serves here, therefore, to loosen the rigor of full determinism by being the noncaused event at the origin of the causal chain. So, even though the chain may be fully

---

76. *Metaphysics* (Tredennick) VI.2.1027a15–16.
77. *Metaphysics* (Tredennick) VI.2.1027a20–21.
78. *Metaphysics* VI.2.1206b26–32.

deterministic at each of its links, this is not true about its first member, the uncaused coincident. Uniqueness thus leads to being causeless, but it also leads to being effect-less, that is, being the cause of nothing, again, in the strict sense.[79]

There is much that needs explanation here, but first consider Bechler's calamitous conclusion. As he sees it, Aristotle believes that whatever is genuinely caused (in a scientific sense) begins in an accidental circumstance, but accidental circumstances—because they are unique and irregular events—have no place in any genuine chain of scientific cause-and-effect. As an account of the origins of things in the world sounds less than promising.

Bechler maintains, then, that Aristotle believes that causal chains begin in an accidental event, which must be, therefore, uncaused. But even worse, because accidental events are particular, they must exist outside any scientific chain of causality and cannot serve as proper causes for anything else in Aristotle's system. Bechler writes: "Given that coincidents have no causes, [...] it follows that the coincidental must be noncausative as well." In Bechler's reading, therefore, Aristotle believes that causal chains begin in an accidental event, which is both uncaused and non-causative. They were not caused by anything and no genuine effect can be attached to them. An alarming state of affairs. Bechler thinks that this is why Aristotelian science is uninformative and useless. Because events in the world are always particular, they escape, on his reading of Aristotle, any scientific analysis.

Bechler relentlessly drives home the point to its strangely antirealist conclusion. What results? He writes:

> [In Aristotle's system] coincidences are [...] not really facts at all. [...] To be statable "a fact must be defined by being so always or usually" (1027a23), [which] is also

---

79. Bechler, *Actuality*, 60–61.

> why an exception to a law, the once-only, and so the coincidental, cannot be explained. [...] The reverse holds as well: The unexplainable is also unstatable. [...] Luck [τύχη], therefore, being "opposed to the accountable," having "causes which are indeterminate" (*Phys* 197a19-21), is in fact also unstatable. This is why Aristotle says that the coincidental is, in a sense, not even existent, and actually is not much more than a mere word. [...] "a mere name (*onoma ti monon*)."[80]

On Bechler's reading, the only reality particular events possess in Aristotle's system derives from human interests and that is all the reality they have. All we have left, when dealing with particular causality, are the mental categories we project on the world. Bechler continues:

> Since the coincidental is defined as that which is once-only, it is thereby defined to be the nondefinable, and so its name does not carry any positive meaning and does not imply any positive information. It is practically a mere word. Not denoting any positive information, it denotes nothing definite, and so the coincidental is not a reality. [...] [Aristotle] would be ready to concede, I suggest, that just as it is strictly the cause of nothing, so it is, strictly, nothing.[81]

This is a very bold and eccentric interpretation of Aristotle. If, however, Bechler maintains that Aristotle's claims about the unscientific nature of particularity renders his science entirely vacuous, I want to counter that there is nothing wrong with Aristotle's theory because science is, as Aristotle *correctly* insists, uninformative on the issue of particular circumstances. This is not a fact about *Aristotelian* science; it is a general fact about science period. Science cannot tell us what

---

80. Bechler, *Actuality*, 64–66. Cf. *Metaphysics* 1026b14–18, 22.
81. Bechler, *Actuality*, 64–66.

we ought to believe about τύχη—chance, luck, fate, or fortune—because science is about identifying general patterns of causality. That does not mean that science cannot go about its business successfully. It only means that we should not ask from science something that science cannot give. If we want a deep explanation as to why the world is organized so that particular events unfold as they do, we need something more than science. For the ancient Greeks, religious notions of fate filled that void; perhaps contemporary thinkers could embrace alternative options instead.

There is more to say about Aristotle's meaning here, but, first, we must respond to Bechler's calamitous interpretation. Bechler is correct to point out (like many others) that Aristotle believes that science is not about the accidental, the contingent, the coincidental, or the particular. But what could it mean to say that the accidental causality is not real? At the very least, this does not sound Aristotelian.

It is common enough in the literature to restrict the metaphysical term "accidental" to non-essential or unnecessary properties like red hair colour on a human being. But accidental *causality* is not limited to the production of those alternative features. Accidental causality, at least in this context, is the efficient causality that produces a particular effect. It is not opposed to any account of causality that involves essential, necessary, or universal properties. If we claim that dogs give birth to dogs, we are discussing how essential traits are passed on to an entire class of things, but this does not exclude accidental causality. When we say that this particular dog Rover gave birth to this particular pup Spot, we are discussing accidental causality. Of course, Rover transmits to Spot the universal, necessary, and essential traits she shares with all other dogs. When we claim that dogs give birth to dogs and not to cats, we are making a claim about universal, essential, or non-accidental causality.

Aristotle writes: "Some causes are general or accidental; the cause of a statue is in one way a sculptor and in another

Polyclitus."[82] To say that sculptors carve statues is to make a claim about essential, necessary, and universal causality. But to say that Polyclitus carved the statue of the discus thrower in the Greek National Museum is to make a claim about particular causality. Aristotle gives other examples: To claim that this man with a pale complexion or that man who plays the flute carved the statue is to make other claims about accidental causality referring to one particular case. [83] And Aristotle mentions a particular father causing a particular child as another example of accidental causality.[84]

Aristotle did not fully understand human reproduction, but he would have agreed with the acknowledged complications of the modern account. Even modern biological science cannot tell us why that particular combination of DNA that makes you you came into existence instead of some other equally possible combination. There are too many contingent factors at play. As one popular science site explains: "[human] fertilization produces random combinations of genetically diverse sperm and eggs, creating virtually unlimited possibilities for variation."[85] As a human being, you possess essential and necessary human properties that apply to all human beings. Still, it is *your* appearance on Earth that is a matter of τύχη or accidental causality. Your birth was not miraculous; it followed all the rules of biology. You are not a mere collection of accidental properties. Indeed, in the best Aristotelian sense, you are a substance. Nonetheless, why you were born instead of someone else being born remains a matter of τύχη.

Contrary to what Bechler (and Huismann) contend, Aristotle accepts that particular events do, in a qualified sense, act as causes. He says so explicitly: "It is clear then that

---

82. *Physics* II.3.195a28–34.
83. *Physics* II.3.195b1–3. Cf. Physics II.5.197a14–15.
84. *Physics* II.3.195a35–36.
85. Kratz, "How Sexual Reproduction Creates Genetic Variation."

chance [τύχη] is an accidental cause."⁸⁶ And again, "Things do, in a way, occur by chance, for they occur accidentally and chance is an accidental cause. Although it is not the cause *without qualification* of anything."⁸⁷ As the Greek makes clear, Aristotle accepts that accidental causality is a fact in the world. If Polyclitus carves a block of marble, he really is the (efficient) cause of the statue. Or, to devise an example inspired by an amusing incident in Wittgenstein's biography, suppose I hit you with a hot poker in the midst of a philosophical argument and burn you terribly; if I am found guilty in a court of law of *causing* your burns, no one would dispute this on scientific grounds. Aristotle's distinction between the voluntary and the involuntary in his ethics presupposes all this.⁸⁸ If science is about identifying universal (or almost-universal) patterns of causality, Aristotle does not deny the reality of particular causality in the world. But this is accidental causality, not because it is random or uncaused, but because it is about the individual instance rather than the general case.

Aristotle is a scientist who privileges the observation of concrete particulars as the road to knowledge. In focusing on material cause as the carrier of individuality, he pays respect to individual material particulars in a way, perhaps, that Plato does not. If this is true, then Bechler must be misreading Aristotle. Why? Because, it seems, he is committed to the Enlightenment trope that the modern age corrects the scientific errors of the ancient and medieval world. He believes that Aristotelian essentialism involves a *petitio principii* and is merely descriptive rather than explanatory: the familiar *virtus dormitiva* criticism. While Bechler is thinking that every particular event in the history of the world is an accidental/coincidental circumstance (in a technical sense)

---

86. *Physics* (Hardie and Gaye) II.5.197a6–7.
87. *Physics* (Hardie and Gaye) II.5.197a13–15.
88. Cf., for example, *Eudemian Ethics* II.6–9; *Nicomachean Ethics* III.1, III.5, V.8.

and that any conception of science that leaves no room for the particular seems to leave out the whole of reality altogether, the texts of Aristotle are open to a wholly different interpretation. If the cluster of notes we call the Aristotelian corpus insufficiently highlight Aristotle's belief in particular causality (which seem to me a fair criticism), one can understand Bechler's alarm at a looming gap in Aristotelian science. Except that Bechler does not only misconstrue Aristotle; he misconstrues the nature of science. What Aristotle means still holds true today. This can be seen from the following contemporary example.

Suppose you pick up a physics textbook filled with mathematical formulas (Aristotle's view of science is not primarily mathematical but that does not matter here). You turn to the page with Newton's Second Law of Motion: you read "force = mass × acceleration." The textbook (which represents theoretical science) gives us the general formula for all instances but note: We have to insert specifics into the formula to get an answer about a specific event in the world. Using the formula, we can calculate how much force it takes to make my 1,600 kg car accelerate from 0 km/h to 60 km/h in 7.5 seconds. But the formula only gives us the general rule. It tells us what mathematical protocol gives us the right answer. This is how science operates. It tells us what we can expect (or predict) when confronted with this *particular* set of circumstances. But we get those particulars (the weight of my car, etc.) from our observation (or measurement) of the world, not from theoretical science. So, the formulas of contemporary physics—which are universals—do not by themselves give us what we need to understand particular events in the world. They only tell us how one contingent series of events must be related to other contingent events. They tell us: *If* your car weights this much and *if* you want to accelerate from this speed to this speed and *if* you want to do it in this amount of time, this is the amount of force you need. But this is a conditional. Observation and, in this case, human purpose, fill in the details. Even modern science is uninformative about accidental circumstance in just the way Aristotle suggests.

Whatever Bechler's own view of contemporary science, there is nothing wrong with Aristotle's analysis because science today and yesterday is, indeed, uninformative on the issue of particular causality. Bechler seems to ignore or overlook a real issue that Aristotle confronts. There are two things that need to be taken into account: generalities and particulars. Science (at least the theoretical science Aristotle denotes by *epistêmê*) gives us the general principles according to which nature operates; observation gives us the particulars—the accidental circumstances—that science renders intelligible. It is a fundamental mistake to think, as Bechler assumes, that the universals (of whatever type) can do all the work by themselves. No one opens up their physics textbook to find out what will happen to them at one o'clock the next afternoon. This is because—despite a certain bravado among science enthusiasts—a complete explanation of everything is *in principle* impossible. Can science tell me whether I will have a tomato, a baloney sandwich, rice, or a smoothie for lunch? Or perhaps I will miss lunch altogether. Science cannot tell us these things because they depend on innumerable particular factors, which exist in addition to the general rules of gravitation, space-time, electromagnetic radiation, digestion, and so on.

"Believers" in science might say that this is just a matter of information overload. There is too much information for us to cope with but if we could analyze all the data from a god's-eye point of view, we could use science to predict and know, exactly what I will have for lunch tomorrow. This is, of course, completely unverifiable. No one in the history of the world has come close to showing how this could be possible. To believe that science could explain all particularities is a matter of faith: If only we had all the information—which we will never have—science would give us all the answers. At the very least, Aristotle does not seem to believe this. We have universals that structure the form of reality but unpredictable particulars fill up that structure with content.

What will happen to me at one o'clock tomorrow seems to be dependent on accidental/particular/contingent/incidental circumstances that need to be inserted into the science from the outside. Science can tell us some things: We know, for example, that I will not float up to the ceiling if I choose to eat a ham sandwich. But it cannot come close to telling us the entire concatenation of events and properties that will produce my one o'clock lunch (if I decide to have one). Once we have a number of particulars, we might (to some extent) calculate, predict, or explain what will happen, but we do not get these particulars from the general principles of science. This is what Aristotle means when he says there is no science (i.e., no general, theoretical science) of the particular. Put in Aristotelian terms, theoretical science gives us essences and necessary natures; reality gives us the accidental properties.

Consider of the way events happen in the world using a sporting analogy. Imagine a perfect football game. And imagine perfect referees that ensure that the rules of football are perfectly followed. No violation ever occurs. Even if this were the case and you were to learn all the (universal) rules that regulate football, this would not tell you who will win a particular football game. Who wins a particular game depends on a lot of accidental properties that are not universally given. It is a question of τύχη, of happenstance, of chance, even of fate. Knowing the science of football, knowing all the rules, will not give us the score of every game beforehand. Knowing every rule, we can still ask: Which team will win? And, if we were an ancient Greek, we could ask religious questions. Do the gods intervene to help the morally good players and stymie morally bad players? Do pious teams always win in the end? Whatever one believes about such things, science cannot provide any answer, one way or the other.

Viewed from an Aristotelian perspective, the post-Enlightenment debates pitting science against religion (or religion against science) are beside the point. Partisans engaged in this debate have made a category mistake. Science tells you the rules of the game; religion asks a different question: Did the gods intervene to produce this contingent detail? Did the gods come to the winning teams' aid? Is victory or defeat punishment or reward for immoral or moral behaviour? At least that is the sort of questions the ancient Greeks, including Aristotle, asked. (We could make a distinction here between applied and theoretical science where applied science would apply the universal rules to the particulars of a team, a player, or wind conditions, although what Aristotle means by science, strictly considered, involves thinking about universals, not particulars.)

Here is another way of construing things. Divide metaphysics into formal and material cause. Science deals with formal cause, which is fixed and eternal. Material cause is the carrier of individuality. It separates each particular individual from another. When we try to explain the occurrence of particular events in the world through science, it is as if we are trying to explain the changing nature of matter through form. Of course, matter is structured according to form, but matter is not only form. Material cause is dynamic; form is static. Form can be reified into an eternal conceptual framework that is fixed in our mind forever. To a Greek way of thinking, this is the apogee of rationality. But material particularity is not like this. It is embodied in a landscape of potentialities moving (successfully or not) towards actuality. The landscape of these particulars is ever-changing. Science can read time backwards insomuch as all particular change has gone out of it. As Aristotle acknowledges, past events are static, fixed forever.[89] If, however, science can in principle read time backwards, it cannot read time forwards, at least when it comes to particular events, because happenstance, τύχη, gets in the way.

Aristotle is a scientific pluralist. There is a plurality of possible particular outcomes that conform to the rules of science. Polyclitus, Pheidias, Myron, or Praxiteles may carve

---

89. Cf. *On the Heavens* I.12.283b12–13; *On the Universe* 7.401b19-20; *Nicomachean Ethics* VI.2.1139b7–9.

the statue but whoever does it will have to chisel away at the hardness of marble because marble is, by nature, hard. That is a matter for science. But whether it is Polyclitus, Pheidias, Myron, or Praxiteles who is awarded the commission to carve the statue is not a matter for science; that is a matter of contingent human history and of particular or accidental causality. Although Polyclitus, Pheidias, Myron, or Praxiteles possess the same human form, each one has an individual physical body, which has to do, metaphysically speaking, with accidental causality. We should not confuse formal difference (which science studies) and material difference. What makes Polyclitus be Polyclitus is, in the terminology of some later philosophers, "haecceity": There is an individuality, a specific thisness, a particularity that makes Polyclitus himself, which cannot be captured solely in terms of formal cause. If Polyclitus was a triplet with two other identical body doubles, he would still be Polyclitus with a different material cause. These particular differences can be attributed to accidental causality; they are subject to the realm of τύχη or happenstance. At least in Aristotle, they escape scientific explanation.

There is more to say about accidental causality but let us turn back, for a moment, to the issue of fate. On Aristotle's account, fate can never contradict science; it adds another level of explanation that is beyond the reach of science. But we should not misunderstand. When we are doing science, we can dismiss fate entirely; viewed from a scientific perspective, fate "belongs to the class of the indefinite and is inscrutable to man," and this is "why it might be thought that [when it comes to science] nothing occurs by fate."[90] And this is why Aristotle mentions that there are those who believe that τύχη "is inscrutable to human intelligence, as being a divine thing and full of mystery."[91] Being inscrutable to human intelligence means being inaccessible to science.

---

90. *Physics* (Hardie and Gaye) II.5.197a8–12. Again "fate" for their "chance."
91. *Physics* (Hardie and Gaye) II.5.196b5.

In some much-misunderstood passages in the *Physics*, Aristotle uses the example of a man collecting money, who goes to a place for a different reason and, through sheer "luck," gets the money. Here is the passage (using "fate" rather than "chance" for τύχη):

> A man is engaged in collecting subscriptions for a feast. He would have gone to such and such a place for the purpose of getting the money, if he had known. He actually went there for another purpose, and it was only accidentally that he got his money by going there; and this was not due to the fact that he went there as a rule or necessarily, nor is the end effected (getting the money) the cause. [...] It is when these conditions are satisfied that the man is said to have gone there [on that occasion] by fate. If he had chosen and gone for the sake of this—if he always or normally went there when he was collecting payments—he would not be said to have [gotten his money] by fate.[92]

For fate to be the cause of something, it cannot be a matter of deliberate human purpose, because fate is in the power of the gods. It is beyond human capacity. When the man goes to the wrong place and gets his money, we can ask whether that happened by divine design. Maybe, maybe not. Whether one attributes this result to the gods or to random chance, Aristotle leaves open the possibility that the gods play a role. He is not asserting that they must play a role, but he is leaving that possibility open to the pious.

Laplace, the eminent French mathematician, once argued that a giant intellect who knew "all forces that set nature in motion, and all positions of all items of which nature is composed," could perfectly predict the future: "nothing would be uncertain" for such an intellect "and the

---

92. *Physics* II.5.196b33–197a5. Hardie and Gaye except for the emendation.

future just like the past would be present before its eyes."[93] But even a perfectly predictable, deterministic, Laplacean universe would not answer questions about fate. Questions about fate ask *why* the items in the universe were organized so that particular events happen? What is the reason behind this arrangement? One could respond that there is no reason, which is to say that no answer is possible. In a sense, this is just what Aristotle says; no *scientific* answer is possible. Science cannot answer questions about particulars. If we want to wonder about these things, we must turn to religion and morality and perhaps to literature (mythology), not as something opposed to science, but as something different and self-sufficient on its own account.

An infinite number of worlds can comply with the same set of universal equations and principles. So why did this particular world materialize? It is not enough to say: "There is a universal pattern of regularities that obtains in the world." That is an entirely ambiguous answer. Aristotle realizes this, which is why, naturally enough, many people through the ages did not find science metaphysically satisfying. Because it is unable to answer questions about why things specifically happen as they do. Why did the bullet kill the person I was with and barely miss me? That is a question for religion, not science. And that is why the ancient Greeks turned to religion and to wondering about how the gods intervene in the events of the world. Of course, one can reject religion but that is tantamount to conceding that there is no right or wrong answer to such questions—indeed, no answer at all. And that results in the predicament Bechler attributes to Aristotelian science: It turns out that there is no explanation of particular causality after all.

Interestingly enough, the apparent unintelligibility of the particular may help explain why Aristotle, in line with the philosophical tradition, would have been reluctant to give specific advice about petitionary prayer. Aristotle

---

93. Laplace, *Philosophical Essay on Probabilities*, 4.

explains, "what is good absolutely is more desirable than what is good for a particular person, e.g. recovery of health than a surgical operation; for the former is good absolutely, the latter only for a particular person, viz. the man who needs an operation."[94] If, then, one wants to ask the gods for good things, one should presumably ask for the highest, the best, the most absolute goods; that is, one should ask for general things like knowledge, friends, health, civil peace, enough prosperity to lead a good life. One should pray, for example, that one gain wisdom, but one should not pray that one be admitted to graduate school X to work with famous Professor X to get a PhD in X. The idea that we could know enough about where contingent events will lead is to assume that we can rationally *know* the contingent particular. But this is something Aristotle does not countenance as Bechler correctly points out in his confused argument. It would be epistemological overreach—indeed, hubris—to insist that the particulars of our lives ought to turn out according to our whims and fancies. It would seem better, on Aristotle's model, to leave particularity to the gods as something beyond our ken.

4.5. Four Levels of Accidental Causality

I am going to argue that, systematically construed, there are four levels of accidental causality or contingent reality that metaphysics has to take into consideration. The Aristotelian texts are underdetermined in that it is not always clear which level is being referred to. Still, one can make sense of his theory conceptually by means of this fourfold distinction.

I am going to use the word "happenstance." By that I mean all the particulars in the world taken together in the way they impinge and relate to one another. The accidental events in Aristotle's universe are not disordered, unlawlike, random, happening in any which way. They obey general rules and conform to necessary (or almost necessary)

---

94. *Topics* (Pickard-Cambridge) III.1.116b7–10.

patterns, but they are composed of particulars, which are, in the proper epistemological sense, beyond science.

Call, then, the most general level of accidental causality: happenstance. This is the largest category, what Aristotle calls αὐτόματον: the automatic, spontaneity, or broadly, chance.[95] It includes everything whatsoever understood in terms of a particular configuration of particulars. A rock tumbles down a mountainside. That is happenstance. Why this rock? Why at this time? Why did it hit this boulder and split in two? Who knows? How all these things are related to one another is happenstance.

The second level we can call human happenstance: This is when happenstance impinges on human destiny. It may produce good or evil, but happenstance may also be neutral; the fact that you hand me a stack of papers with a red paperclip instead of an orange paperclip is happenstance. The colour of the paperclip will not change my life much, yet the fact that a paperclip of this colour comes into contact (so to speak) with my personal life is an aligning of accidental properties that impinge (trivially) on a human situation in the world.

Aristotle does not seem to realize that *everything* that happens to a particular human being must be happenstance (in this wide sense) in that it depends on factors that are individual to that particular person. He tends to focus on conspicuous cases where something surprising or out-of-the-ordinary happens. Naturally, these are the occasions when we tend to take notice of the arrangement of particular circumstances and their influence on a particular person. But *everything* that happens to one particular human being—because it deals with particular events—must be a matter of happenstance in this wider sense.

The third level of happenstance, we could call beneficial or harmful human happenstance. This is the benefit or harm considered without metaphysical implications. This

---

95. *Physics* II.6.197a36.

is the realm of random secular luck. In the case of benefit, we say the person is lucky; in the case of harm, we say that the person is unlucky. This is what τύχη means when it is shed of moral or religious undertones and when someone significantly benefits or is disadvantaged.

The fourth level, we could call divinely appointed happenstance. More simply, fate. This is what τύχη means when it takes on moral and religious connotations. In the ancient Greek tradition, it was part of the job description of the gods to reward good behaviour and punish bad behaviour. The *eudaemôn* is blessed by the gods with external goods. All this has to do with τύχη understood, not merely as secular, meaningless luck, but as something with a deeper metaphysical foundation in moral karma. Somehow or other, the universe rewards virtue and makes you pay for bad deeds.

I am arguing that Aristotle is open to all these possibilities, including the religious option of fate. There is nothing in his epistemology that rules it out; as it has to do with accidental properties and events, it is beyond the reach of science. One could argue for different versions of fate (or providence) but that is not my aim here. I only want to make the point that Aristotle is fully aware of the religious option and takes it seriously, in line with ancient Greek religious belief and practice. The modernist trope (seen in the polemical literature, for example) that science and religion are competing systems gains strength with the Enlightenment. Religion and science are, for someone like Aristotle, two different things. The best scientist in the world cannot explain the vagaries of fate; that domain of explanation belongs to religion or to moralism or even to nihilism (understood as the doctrine that happenstance has no higher meaning). It seems extreme to suggest that anything approaching metaphysical nihilism could be an option for a stern moralist like Aristotle.

4.6. Mayhew: Prayer, Τύχη, and Politics

According to the familiar caricature, the whole point of Greek piety is to importune the gods to give us good things. In his

Politics, Aristotle talks of "ἡ κατ' εὐχὴν πολιτεία," "the city of one's prayers," usually translated as the ideal state, the state for which one should wish. Such a city would be blessed with the "external" goods (thought to be beyond human control and given by the gods) such as a good location, a healthy climate, the right size of population, a willing citizenry, an ideal class structure, and so on.[96] The technical phrase that Aristotle uses literally means the kind of city that would be the answer to wise prayers.[97]

Mayhew, in particular, has recently argued that "Aristotle's use of prayer-language in the *Politics* is only metaphorically religious."[98] According to Mayhew (and others), Aristotle uses terms like "pray" and "prayer" "to refer to wishes or hopes [...] but with the understanding that it is not a genuine request of the gods."[99] All Aristotle means by such language is the city "according to our highest hope."

Mayhew writes that "it is easy to translate 'κατ' ευχήν' without reference to prayer."[100] He backs up his assertion by pointing out that Aristotle believes that the things people pray for involve external factors and are wholly dependent on τύχη, which he translates as "luck." Aristotle writes, for example, (1) that "We pray that our city state will be ideally equipped with the [external] goods that *luck* [τύχη] controls (for we assume that *luck* does control them)."[101]

---

96. Cf. *Politics* II.1.1260b28–30, IV.1.1288b22–23, IV.11.1295a29–30, IV.11.1295b32–34, VII.4.1325b35–40, VII.11.1330a25–28, VII.11.1330a35–38, VII.13 1332a30–32.
97. Cf. Aristotle, *Politics* (Carnes), 25 n. 1. Carnes is one of the few scholars to provide a more literal translation of this language.
98. Cf. Mayhew, "Prayer," 301–302. This is the thesis he supports.
99. Mayhew, "Prayer," 301–302.
100. Mayhew, "Prayer," 300.
101. *Politics* (Miller) VIVI.13.1332a29–30 (my emphasis). Cf. Miller, "Aristotelian Statecraft and Modern Politics," 18. Mayhew ("Prayer," 303–304) translates it: "We pray (εὐχόμεθα) that the composition of the city be according to prayer, regarding things over which luck is authoritative (ἡ τύχη κυρία)."

And again, Aristotle explains (2): "Giving a precise account and discussing such things is pointless. For it is not difficult to think about such things, but rather to do [what is necessary to have] them. For speaking [about them] is a function of prayer, while their happening is [a function] of *luck* [τύχη]."[102]

Mayhew believes that such passages give "strong support for the non-religious reading of the references to prayer in the *Politics*." He comments:

> If Aristotle means by εὐχῆς here not merely a wish but an actual prayer, then [such statements are] an expression of the complete inefficacy of prayer: prayer is a matter of speech, but whether a prayer is "answered" is a function of luck. But if εὐχῆς here simply refers to a wish or hope, then we have good reason to believe that that is true for all of the prayer-language in the *Politics*. [...] According to Aristotle, [then,] the city that is according to prayer [...] possesses all sorts of external conditions that are often largely beyond human control and thus a matter of luck. [...] For example: the right location with respect to the sea; sufficient land for agriculture; the right number of citizens; the right kind of citizen body (for instance, well-educated, with virtuous habits, not slavish).[103]

But Mayhew's self-confident argument misses the point. If it is easy to translate "κατ' ευχήν" without reference to prayer, it is even easier (and more in line with ancient times) to translate as a reference, however distant, to prayer. Here are the key Aristotle passages Mayhew references that translate "τύχη" as fate (its primary meaning) rather than luck:

---

102. The Greek is: τὸ μὲν γὰρ λέγειν εὐχῆς ἔργον ἐστί, τὸ δὲ συμβῆναι τύχης. Mayhew, "Prayer," 303–304 (my emphasis); *Politics* VI.1331b18–22.
103. Mayhew, "Prayer," 303–304.

1. "We pray that our city state will be ideally equipped with the [external] goods that *fate* [τύχη] controls (for we assume that fate does control them)."
2. "Giving a precise account and discussing such things is pointless. For it is not difficult to think about such things, but rather to do [what is necessary to have] them. For speaking [about them] is a function of prayer, while their happening is [a function] of *fate* [τύχη]."

Translating them with "fate" instead of "luck" makes perfect sense. Indeed, it seems less anachronistic and more in keeping with the time period.

In the *Politics*, Aristotle is discussing the politics of his era (and earlier). But, unquestionably, the ancient Greeks believed that the gods rewarded or punished cities according to whether or not they were pious enough. There were temples in every town providing a suitable location where prayers for the city and its inhabitants could be offered up to the local gods. Praying for rain, for fertile fields, for good crops and calm seas, for wise rulers, for victory in war, etc.— these would have been common practices. In describing the ideal city-state as "the city we should pray for" Aristotle is surely echoing this tradition.

As we have already seen, Aristotle's *Last Will and Testament* leaves instructions for the erection of ex-voto statues for several dead relatives to be dedicated to "Zeus Saviour and Athena Saviouress" and to the goddess Demeter. It is not difficult to translate this sort of petitionary piety into some sort of civic aspiration. Plato, Aristotle's teacher, maintains that God (with Fate and Time) controls all human affairs and that the wise lawgiver should *pray* for a young, intelligent ruler who is noble-minded and temperate.[104] He also maintains that states should sometimes select political offices by lot (a common ancient practice), "calling upon

---

104. *Laws* IV.709b–e.

God and Good Fortune [θεὸν καὶ ἀγαθὴν τύχην] to guide for them the lottery aright towards the highest justice."[105]

Mayhew argues that Aristotle had a hidden agenda (as per the esoteric thesis). There are several problems here. First, Mayhew alleges that when Aristotle uses prayer language in the *Politics,* he intends to demonstrate "the complete inefficacy of prayer" because "whether a prayer is answered is a function of luck."[106] But, for the ancient Greeks, whether a prayer is answered is "a function of fate," not just luck. Second, Mayhew argues that the city we would pray for includes "all sorts of external conditions that are often largely beyond human control and thus a matter of luck."[107] But, on the Greek pagan model, things that exist beyond human control are precisely what we are supposed to pray for. Things within our control we can do for ourselves; we do not need the gods for that. What we need to importune the gods for are external goods, which only the gods can supply. Third, some of the external goods Mayhew mentions—the right location with respect to the sea, sufficient land for agriculture—are not, strictly speaking, a matter of luck. They are a matter of history or perhaps of military might. But, even so, the Greeks believed that their history and the success of their imperial adventures were very much dependent on the will and even the caprices of the gods, which they prayed to and venerated. There is nothing here that definitely discounts a higher religious level of intervention and divine favour.

I am not claiming here that Aristotle is intent on making any momentous claims about religion in the *Politics*. That is not the point of his exercise in political theory, which is mostly about history and about what we can do to govern well. Still, there is nothing here that conflicts with the general Greek trope that the gods reward or punish, not just individuals, but entire cities for their good or ill behaviour. Which is

---

105. *Laws* (Bury) VI.757e.
106. Mayhew, "Prayer," 303.
107. Mayhew, "Prayer," 304.

why we must be pious and pray to them. Aristotle's references to the city for which we ought to pray is, thus, in keeping with the religious beliefs of the era.

4.7. Inspiration and Supernatural Agency

The second place that contains a sustained discussion of τύχη—I will translate it as "fate"—in the Aristotelica is at the end of the *Eudemian Ethics*. I do not think Aristotle adequately solves the problem of what we should think about fate here or elsewhere; he is not a specialized theologian like Plotinus or the later Scholastics. But he wrestles with the idea and its logical ramifications. Granted, he is exploring *aporiai* and surveying diverse opinions; his style is scattered and heads off in various directions (as usual) but he also seems, occasionally, to answer pertinent questions in a forthright manner.

Aristotle and his students have much more to say about fate or fortune in some difficult passages that, looked at in isolation, might be misinterpreted. Anyone who subscribes to religious notions of fate will be faced with an age-old conundrum: How can bad things happen to good people? Or, put a little differently, how can such good things happen to bad people? Without really offering an answer to the question, the Aristotelian author of the *Magna Moralia* (using τύχη and εὐτυχία variants throughout) poses the question:

> Can it be, then, that good fortune is a sort of care of the gods? Surely it will not be thought to be this! For we suppose that, if God is the disposer of such things, he assigns both good and evil in accordance with desert, whereas chance and the things of chance do really occur as it may chance. But if we assign such a dispensation to God, we shall be making him a bad judge or else unjust. And this is not befitting to God.[108]

---

108. *Magna Moralia* (Stock) II.8.1207a5–11.

In this and other passages, the Aristotelian author sets up an *aporia*, a puzzle for philosophers to solve. He says that fate (or luck, or fortune) cannot be nature because it is not regular enough, that fate cannot be a matter of mind or intelligence because it involves unpredictable chance, and that fate cannot be the care of the gods because fate sometimes seems to reward evil and punish good. What is fate, then, since none of the answers work?

The *Magna Moralia* text (which is largely consistent with the *Eudemian Ethics* passages) concludes that "Good fortune is nature without reason."[109] Which may make it sound as if the Aristotelian author is giving up on any idea of fate as a religious phenomenon and acquiescing to some purely secular notion of random luck, but this may not be what he has in mind. For he immediately turns around and claims that "good luck" is the same as or at least similar to a sort of *religious* inspiration found in the soul. The entire passage (also cited above) reads:

> Good fortune, then, is nature without reason. For the fortunate man is he who apart from reason has an impulse to good things and obtains these, and this comes from nature. For there is in the soul by nature something of this sort whereby we move, not under the guidance of reason, towards things for which we are well fitted. And if one were to ask a man in this state, "Why does it please you to do so?" — he would say, I don't know, except that it does please me, being in the same condition as [or in a condition similar to] those who are inspired by religious frenzy; for they also have an impulse to do something apart from reason.[110]

The Aristotelian author relies here on an innovative notion of providence (discussed at the end of the *Eudemian Ethics*)

---

109. *Magna Moralia* (Stock) II.8.1207a35.
110. *Magna Moralia* (Stock) II.8.1207a35–1207b5. The Greek ὅμοιον could mean "merely similar to" or "the same as."

that operates, not so much by changing the course of particular events in the universe, but by filling individuals with an uncanny mental ability of making the right decision at the right time. In such cases, fate operates by inspiration, by a direct divine intervention which *breathes into* (to borrow the Biblical phrase) individual agents the uncanny ability of unthinkingly making the right decision.

The primary source differentiates between two types of εὐτυχία or "good fate." There is exterior good fate that "seems to result from the way in which things fall out," which "appears to arise from the vicissitudes of fortune."[111] This is good fate "accidentally" or "indirectly." And there is interior (inspired) good fate "wherein the principle of impulse towards the attainment of goods is in the man himself."[112] This interior type of good fate has, he says "surely more right to the name."[113] It involves an interior ability to make good decisions without reason. Whatever precisely we take this to mean in the final analysis, this is not the same as overlooking or eliminating the religious concept of divinely dispensed fate.

When Aristotle (or his editors) rework these themes in the *Eudemian Ethics*, we meet with a another distinction made between the two kinds of "good luck," "good fortune," or good fate (εὐτυχία). The relevant passage runs:

> It is clear, then, that there are two kinds of good fate/luck—one divine, owing to which the fortunate man's success is thought to be due to the aid of God, and this is the man who is successful in accordance with his impulse, while the other is he who succeeds against his impulse. Both persons are irrational. The former kind is more continuous good fortune, the latter is not continuous.[114]

---

111. *Magna Moralia* (Stock) II.8.1207b12–13; the second apt translation is from Armstrong.
112. *Magna Moralia* (Stock) II.8.1207b16.
113. *Magna Moralia* (Armstrong) II.8.1207b15.
114. *Eudemian Ethics* (Rackman) VII.14.1248b3–6.

Aristotle distinguishes here between secular random chance—good luck—where one's spontaneous impulse just happens to be correct, and a good fate understood as something that comes about because one has been favoured by the divine. Aristotle comments that the good fortune that derives from divine favour is continuous, whereas the good fortune that comes from mere luck is inevitably short-lived. In the first case, some interior inspiration with a divine origin continually pushes one to make the right decisions. Luck, on the other hand, is a matter of pure random happenstance, when thoughtless decisions, because of surprising circumstances, turn out unexpectedly well. This distinction (however inadequate) allows us to distinguish between religious fate and mere luck.

As I have already mentioned, (Monte) Johnson writes that Aristotelian "luck" (τύχη) "cannot be due to being favored by a god or a divine overseer." Johnson continues, "Although Aristotle in *Eudemian Ethics* VI.VI. raised the possibility 'of being overseen by some spirit' [...] as a possible cause of success, Aristotle argues in *EE* 7.14 that it would be absurd if the lucky succeeded 'because of something external and being loved, so to speak, by a god.'"[115] But this is a misreading of the passage. Aristotle is commenting, here, on the *utterly foolish* person who succeeds out of luck; he is not talking about human beings in general. He adds, by way of explanation, "It is absurd that a god or a divinity should love such a man who is not the best or wisest of men."[116] (This is a consistent theme in Aristotle.[117]) The passage is not, as Johnson suggests, a comment on the implausibility of divine

---

115. (Monte) Johnson, "Luck in Aristotle's *Physics* and *Ethics*," 59. The passage is from *E.E.* VII.14.1247a23.
116. *Eudemian Ethics* (Solomon) VII.14.1247a27–28.
117. Cf. *On Divination (or Prophesying) in Sleep* (Beare) 1.462b20–22. "For, in addition to its further unreasonableness, it is absurd to combine the idea that the sender of such dreams should be God with the fact that those to whom he sends them are not the best and wisest, but merely commonplace persons."

intervention but a comment on the more puzzling case of fools or ignorant people who enjoy good luck without deserving it. As Kent Johnson observes, "divinely inspired persons form an important kind of fortunate person" in Aristotle's system, "because they are needed to explain the fact that there are fortunate persons who, without having a λόγος [reason], are successful for the most part."[118]

Aristotle seems to reemphasize the point that some unreasoning people do well at the end of the *Nicomachean Ethics* when he links virtue (understood here as good character) to some sort of divine intervention. Aristotle reflects:

> Now some thinkers hold that virtue is a gift of nature; others think we become good by habit, others that we can be taught to be good. Natural ability is obviously not under our control; but by some divine dispensation [διά τινας θείας αἰτίας] it is bestowed on those who are truly fortunate [τοῖς ὡς ἀληθῶς εὐτυχέσιν ὑπάρχει].[119]

Literally, it is through a divine cause that we become genuinely "lucky," so as to be blessed with the capacity for virtue. This is, then, a kind of "good luck" that the gods bestow on mortals. Seen from a religious point of view, we cannot be held responsible for our innate abilities—they are outside our control—so Aristotle seems to be saying, at face value, that they must come from the gods. It is not a big mental step to go from this ancient trope to the idea that we can pray meaningfully for such things for our children, our leaders, and our fellow citizens.[120] If the gods can inspire someone so they are an intelligent success at something, they can also arrange the external circumstances of our lives for the better.

---

118. Johnson, "Luck and Good Fortune," 102.
119. *Nicomachean Ethics* X.9.1179b20–23.
120. Some overly enthusiastic suggestions pervade the "moral luck" literature associated with authors such as Nagel, Williams, and Nussbaum.

This is a basic Greek belief, which Aristotle himself seems to endorse in praying for Nicanor.

As discussed above, Greek paganism left plenty of room for the operation of inspiration in poetry, in theatre, in the religious cults, in oracles, and in the practice of divinations. Acting under the influence of something divine could have a good or a bad effect (for example, in Greek tragedy when the goddess Ἄτη [*Átē*] intervenes to ruin the protagonist, divine intervention has a bad effect). Aristotle and/or his students cleverly appeal to inspiration as a more subtle way of understanding religious fate. I am not at all sure this is a settled Aristotelian stance, but one can see why it might be an attractive option. If we want a worldview that is open to religious notions of fate but without *deus ex machina* interventions that violate natural causes and produce something akin to miracles, this handy arrangement solves the problem. Those who win the favour of the gods can enjoy a good fate, not because some invisible hand reaches down from Mount Olympus, but because they make good decisions through something akin to inspiration. The gods can influence agents from the inside—inside their invisible souls—while leaving the outside physical world untouched. Science can reign supreme over the physical world, and the gods can help moral agents navigate through an ordered world of necessary physical essences.

Aristotle is an empiricist. He observes that some people are able to make intelligent decisions while lacking intelligence. He asks the pertinent question:

> We see there are fortunate men [i.e., individuals with a good fate], who though silly are often successful in matters controlled by fate, some also in matters involving art but into which chance largely enters, e. g. strategy and navigation. Does their success, then, arise from some acquired mental condition, or do they effect fortunate results not because of their own acquired qualities at all [...] [or] does nature, rather, make men with different

qualities, [...] so that some are lucky and others unlucky from birth? That they do not succeed through prudence is clear, for prudence is not irrational. [...] It is clear that they succeed though imprudent.[121]

What, then, to make of this paradox of successful imprudence? Aristotle does not pass this off as sheer secular luck (in Mayhew's sense); he attributes it to a divine agency that operates not on external circumstances, but on the mind of the agent. At least that is what the text suggests, if we take it seriously.

If there are individuals continually favoured by the gods so that their impulses are right even when they do not rely on reasoning, whom might Aristotle have in mind? The obvious candidate is Socrates. Xenophon tells us:

> [Socrates] offered sacrifices constantly, and made no secret of it, now in his home, now at the altars of the state temples, and he made use of divination with as little secrecy. Indeed it had become notorious that Socrates claimed to be guided by "the deity." [...] He was no [different] than are other believers in divination, who rely on augury, oracles, coincidences, and sacrifices. For these men's belief is not that the birds or the folk met by accident know what profits the inquirer, but that they are the instruments by which the gods make this known; and that was Socrates' belief too. [...] [He] said that the deity gave him a sign. Many of his companions were counselled by him to do this or not to do that in accordance with the warnings of the deity: and those who followed his advice prospered, and those who rejected it had cause for regret.[122]

Socrates's ironic confession of his own ignorance (something Aristotle lightly criticizes), his reliance on his good *daimôn*,

---

121. *Eudemian Ethics* (Solomon) VIII.2.1247a1–22.
122. Xenophon, *Memorabilia Oeconomicus Symposium Apology* (Marchant and Todd) I.1.2–5.

which made him the poster boy for εὐδαιμονία, his firm conviction that he is a servant of the god on a divine mission, even (according to Xenophon) his almost oracular ability to act as a go-between between the gods and other citizens in the matter of practical advice—all this makes him a very likely candidate for someone who, in following his impulses, always did the right thing.[123] Xenophon says that those of Socrates's friends who followed his advice were blessed with a good fate—good τύχη—not through any reasoning process but because they paid heed to his religiously oriented inspiration. Compared to Socrates, Aristotle is more muted, more reserved, more aloof. But neither is he in the business of dismissing Socrates as a religious crank. One could make the argument that even Aristotle remains hopeful, along with Socrates, that "nothing can harm a good man, either in life or death: nor are his fortunes neglected by the gods."[124]

---

123. Cf. *Nicomachean Ethics* IV.7.1127b26–27.
124. *Apology* 41d1–3. Cf. *Gorgias* 523a–527a; *Republic* 614b–621d.

Chapter 5

Oedipus and Aristotle

> The most painful figure of the Greek stage, the unlucky Oedipus, is understood by Sophocles as the noble man who is destined for error and misery in spite of his wisdom. […] The noble man does not sin—that's what the profound poet wishes to tell us.
>
> Friedrich Nietzsche, *Birth of Tragedy*

> ὕβρις φυτεύει τύραννον. [Hubris begets a tyrant.]
>
> Sophocles, *Oedipus Tyrannos*

5.1. Reasoning from Examples

I have been arguing for a somewhat religious Aristotle, one who takes seriously at least the framework of Greek pagan religion. In this chapter, I argue that we need to situate Aristotle's *Poetics* within this historical context. If we hope to grasp Aristotle's own understanding of Greek theatre, we must make an effort to understand the tradition of Greek tragedy as he did. As we shall see, this larger perspective challenges much of the received wisdom in present-day commentary.

I will not offer a point-by-point analysis of Aristotle's *Poetics* here. Many fine translations and detailed summaries are readily available.[1] I use instead Sophocles's *Oedipus Tyrannos*, a pre-eminent example of Greek tragedy, to explore the ramifications of Aristotle's theorizing.

In Aristotle's logic, reasoning from examples is epistemologically prior to reasoning from abstract principles. Particular examples are "more knowable to us"; universal concepts are "more knowable in themselves."[2] Examples are a good way to get knowledge started. After moving from examples to universal principles using induction, we can reason from these universal principles in a deductive manner. As the present discussion is focused on establishing the first principles underlying Aristotle's account of Greek tragedy, it will be helpful to consider what he says about tragedy in light of an important play that he himself discusses.

5.2. The Story of *Oedipus Tyrannos*

Sophocles's *Oedipus Tyrannos* (henceforth, *Oedipus*) and Aristotle's *Poetics* are, so to speak, joined at the hip.[3] Aristotle's scattered comments on the play have made for

---

1. Multiple English translations of the *Poetics* are available in print and online, with introductory and explanatory material, including those by Thomas Twining, 1789; Mitchell Carroll, 1895; Samuel Henry Butcher, 1902; Ingram Bywater, 1909; W. H. Fyfe, 1926; L. J. Potts, 1953; G. M. A. Grube, 1958; Gerald F. Else, 1967; Leon Golden and O. B. Hardison, 1968; James Hutton, 1982; Richard Janko, 1987; Stephen Halliwell, 1987; Hippocrates G. Apostle, 1990; Stephen Halliwell, 1995; Malcolm Heath, 1996; Kenneth McLeish, 1999; Seth Benardete and Michael Davis, 2002; Joe Sachs, 2006; Anthony Kenny, 2013; Rune Myrland, 2018. My argument here does not rely on any controversial issues of philology or translation.
2. *Posterior Analytics* I.2.72a1–6; cf. *Posterior Analytics* II.19.
3. Many serviceable English translations are available. There is more latitude for differing interpretations when it comes to more poetic passages. English translations consulted include: *Ajax; Electra; Oedipus Tyrannis* (Lloyd-Jones), *Oedipus Tyrannus* (Meineck and Woodruff), *Oidipous* (Blondell), *Sophocles 1* (Grene), *Oedipus* (Kitto), *Oedipus* (Jebb).

heated exegetical debate. Similar debates have raged about Sophocles's precise intentions. I will try to navigate through these disagreements without losing sight of the larger picture. All too often, arguments about the precise meaning of a Greek term or an isolated passage override a more balanced, overall interpretation of the text.

The point here is, then, to provide an Aristotelian reading of Sophocles's *Oedipus*, with a sensitivity to religious and moral issues that is missing in familiar commentary. Of course, it is always possible, as some commentators forcefully suggest, that Aristotle himself misunderstood *Oedipus*, but I do not believe that this is the case. Mostly, I treat Aristotle's interpretation of tragedy and Sophocles's literary project as two expressions of a sophisticated Greek pagan mindset. I will use, then, the general framework outlined in the *Poetics* as a way into *Oedipus* and a close examination of *Oedipus* as a way into the *Poetics*. If we can get Aristotle right, then we have a better chance of getting Sophocles right, and if we can get Sophocles right, we have a better chance of getting Aristotle right. Still, it is possible to agree with Aristotle's overall method while disputing an allegedly Aristotelian interpretation of any particular play. Obviously, even devout Aristotelians can disagree about literary matters.

The basic plot of Sophocles's play is taken, of course, from Greek mythology and would have been well-known to ancient audiences. There is no indication that a sophisticated Greek such as Aristotle would have believed that the story of Oedipus had any literal basis in actual fact. What Aristotle seems to believe is that the story raises serious issues about the human condition, about the gods, about fate, about morality. It explores themes relevant to our understanding of the cosmos, but it is not a true, factual story that is to be taken literally. In terms of theatre, the sensational legend of *Oedipus*, the tyrant of Thebes, provides raw material for a gripping and disturbing spectacle. *Oedipus* is, in some sort, an ancient *Macbeth*.

The plot is straightforward. A great and very clever king has, through his wits, saved the people of Thebes from being preyed upon by a cunning monster, the Sphinx. He is acclaimed king by popular assent. But all is not well. Plague and famine have fixed themselves on Thebes. Believing that the gods have cursed the city for some internal moral outrage, the good king sets out to investigate the crime and punish the culprit in order to reconcile the city with the gods. He discovers, much to his chagrin, that he himself is the culprit and a perpetrator of the worst crimes imaginable: He has murdered his father and slept with his mother (who has already borne him children). Despite strenuous efforts to avoid this terrible fate, once foretold by the oracle, he is the one who has turned the wrath of the gods against the city. To cleanse the kingdom of moral pollution, he must punish himself and go into exile.

Sophocles's rendition of *Oedipus* is not a sensationalized, action-filled representation of the man's violent or sexual sins, but a detective-story-turned-psychological-thriller. It is mostly about the protagonist's increasingly desperate (and obsessive) pursuit of the truth and the suspense-filled steps by which he comes to a woeful realization of the grotesque fact that he himself is the evil one. Towards the end of the play, the chorus comments:

> Oh, what a wretched breed
> We mortals are:
> Our lives add up to nothing.
> Does anyone, anyone, harvest more of happiness than [an empty] image,
> And from that [mere] image fall away?
> [...] You, Oedipus, your misery teaches us
> To call no mortal blessed.
> You aimed your arrow high, and struck happiness,
> You self-made lord of joy.
> [...] I call you, King,
> Our king of highest glory
> Lord of mighty Thebes.
> Now is there a sadder story to be heard?

Madness so cruel? Pain so deep?
You have shared your home with catastrophe.[4]

Oedipus is tragedy through and through. A great man is utterly destroyed, through a terrible mistake but also through rashness and hubris, in spite of some good intentions.

In the *Poetics*, Aristotle refers to *Oedipus* ten different times. In a discussion of the best subject matter for a tragedy, he twice points to Oedipus as a fitting protagonist given his noble lineage and disastrous fate.[5] In a discussion of plot reversal, he mentions "the incident when the messenger from Corinth, who has come intending to make Oedipus happy, [...] does the opposite."[6] In a discussion of *anagnôrisis*, a negative sort of introspection in which the tragic protagonist suddenly realizes his mistake, Aristotle claims that the "most beautiful" kind of self-discovery "happens simultaneously with reversal [of fortune], as [...] in *Oedipus*,"[7] and that "the best self-discovery of all" derives from plausible, believable events "as in the *Oedipus* of Sophocles."[8] Aristotle also notes that there are tragic plots in which the moment of self-discovery happens after the terrible deed "as with Sophocles' *Oedipus*."[9]

In a discussion of plot, Aristotle goes on to explain that "the story ought to be organized in such a way that, even [without seeing a performance on stage], someone who hears [about the events] shudders and feels pity from the way they turn out, the very things one would experience while hearing the story of *Oedipus*."[10] He also mentions, in two different passages, that there ought "to be nothing unaccountable [ἄλογον, illogical]" in the plot sequence and that if one is forced to include fantastical elements, they should

---

4. *Oedipus* (Meineck and Woodruff) 1186–1205.
5. *Poetics* (Sachs) 13.453a11, 20.
6. *Poetics* (Sachs) 11.1452a24.
7. *Poetics* (Sachs) 11.1452a33.
8. *Poetics* (Sachs) 16.1455a17–18.
9. *Poetics* (Sachs) 14.1453b30.
10. *Poetics* (Sachs) 14.1453b7.

be placed outside the story as is the case "in the *Oedipus* of Sophocles."[11] Sophocles did well, then, according to Aristotle, to quickly pass over the highly implausible incident where Laius, Oedipus's father, was killed.[12]

Finally, in a comparison of the relative merits of epic poetry and tragedy, Aristotle maintains that tragedy "is more powerful [than epic poetry because] it has all the things that epic poetry does [...] and [because it includes] the music and the spectacle, by means of which its pleasures are organized most vividly [...] [and because it fulfills its goals] in a shorter length."[13] He then suggests that if one were to write out the plot of *Oedipus* in as many lines as the *Iliad*, it would lose its evocative power. The intense emotional impact of Sophocles's play is due to its tighter composition and shorter duration.

5.3. Aristotle's Opinion of Oedipus

Given the renown of Sophocles's play, it is hardly surprising that Aristotle should mention it by name as a model of proper Greek tragedy. His repeated references to *Oedipus* seem to indicate how highly he esteemed the play. Still, a few commentators balk at any such conclusion. Christopher Morrissey, for one, has complained that literary criticism has "made Sophocles' *Oedipus* into a sacred cow, by propagating (on the authority of a hasty reading of Aristotle) the idea that the *Oedipus Tyrannos* is Aristotle's favorite tragedy."[14] Morrissey dismisses this idea as a "popular prejudice," criticizing "the notion that Aristotle gives preeminent esthetic rank to the *Oedipus Tyrannos*" and rejecting the conventional view that it functions as "Aristotle's gold standard for tragedy."[15]

---

11. *Poetics* (Sachs) 15.1454b8.
12. *Poetics* (Sachs) 24.1460a30.
13. *Poetics* (Sachs) 26.1462b2.
14. Morrissey, "Oedipus the Cliché," *Anthropoetics*.
15. Morrissey describes the play as "a compendium of exemplary tragic clichés."

Morrissey is driven to his conclusion by an apparent contradiction in the original text. In chapter 13 of the *Poetics*, Aristotle suggests that a beautiful tragedy ends with the horrible deed already done and a resultant self-discovery as is the case in *Oedipus*.[16] In chapter 14, however, he gives a startlingly different ranking of tragic plots, identifying a story in which the tragic hero "makes the discovery in time to draw back" as the best plot of all.[17] Aristotle gives three contemporaneous examples of this latter type of plot: "in *Cresphontes*, where Merope, on the point of slaying her son, recognizes him in time; in *Iphigenia*, where the sister [recognizes her] brother [in time]; and in *Helle*, where the son recognizes his mother on the point of giving her up to her enemy."[18] Paradoxically, then, it seems that Aristotle recommends both the plot where the tragic deed happens and the plot where the looming disaster is averted as the best tragic plot. Which, then, is Aristotle's true opinion? As is often the case with Aristotle, there is no sure-fire way to decide this question. (As we have seen, the Aristotelian corpus is filled with passages that seem at odds with one another.)

Whether Aristotle views *Oedipus* as an example of the best or only the "second-best" kind of tragic plot is largely immaterial for our purposes, but I should point out that Morrissey argues, in line with the remarks in chapter 14, that Aristotle prefers a "tragedy" with a happy ending.[19]

---

16. Aristotle observes, "the prefect plot, accordingly, must have a single, not [...] a double issue. [...] In these days the finest tragedies are always on the story of some few houses, on that of Alcmeon, Oedipus, Orestes, [...] or any others that may have been involved, as either agents or sufferers, in some deed of horror. The theoretically best tragedy, then, has a plot of this description." *Poetics* (Bywater) 13.1453a12–22. Note that Aristotle states that a beautiful *(kalōs)* tragedy, not the most beautiful *(kallista)* tragedy, has a single ending.
17. *Poetics* (Bywater) 14.1453b34–36.
18. *Poetics* (Bywater) 14.1454b4–8. I have used Bywater as Sachs (with good reason) changes slightly the standard translation to deal with this problem.
19. Morrissey is arguing, in part, against Elizabeth Belfiore, *Tragic Pleasures: Aristotle on Plot and Emotion*.

Morrissey seems to believe that happy endings are morally superior to unhappy endings. Although this makes some sense, he inexplicably goes out of his way to rest his case on Eric Gans's distinctly post-Nietzschean account of literature as an interplay of form and content that results in the deferral or sublimation of "resentment" understood as "our emotional state with regard to those ways in which we are powerless to change our station in life."[20] On this oddly Nietzschean reading, we who "inhabit the social periphery" feel resentment towards more successful individuals "who inhabit the social limelight." *Oedipus* is, then, an immoral play in that it allows us, the readers, to resentfully enjoy the downfall of a great personage we secretly envy. As Morrissey explains, "The content of an unhappy *metabasis* [change in fortune] is consumptively enjoyed as I resentfully delight in the fearful downfall of a great man who had previously occupied the center inaccessible to us, dwellers on the periphery." It follows from all this that morally inferior tragedy allows us to wallow in resentment. Morissey thinks that Aristotle preferred a happy ending because resentment is deferred and sublimated rather than indulged in. A "happy tragedy" sublimates the power of resentment "by having us identify with characters as being 'like us' [instead of] having us resent them as being 'better than us.'"

Morrissey's psychoanalytic explanation seems more modern than Greek. But whatever we think of his proposed solution, Aristotle's contradictory preferences for both a happy and an unhappy tragedy remains a puzzle for many exegetes. Joe Sachs translates the text so as to reduce the possible tension, distinguishing the "most beautiful tragedy"[21] from "the most powerful story."[22] Certainly, there is room for pause here. The idea that a story with a happy ending is a better *tragedy* seems remarkably at odds with Aristotle's

---

20. Gans, *Signs of Paradox*.
21. *Poetics* (Sachs) 13.1453a19–23.
22. *Poetics* (Sachs) 14.1454a5, cf. n. 30.

own advice that a beautifully shaped tragedy must involve a change "not from bad fortune into good fortune but the opposite way, from good fortune to bad."[23] Aristotle goes so far as to argue that:

> those who blame Euripides because he does this in his tragedies (and many of his do end in misfortune) are missing the very point. For [...] this is the right thing to do. The greatest sign of this is that, on stage and in competition, such plays have shown themselves as the most tragic, if they are rightly put on, and Euripides, even if he does not manage other things well, still shows himself to be the most tragic of poets.[24]

As always in Aristotelian exegesis, the overall philosophical sense must take precedence over any isolated passage. Because the Aristotelian corpus is composed of snippets of text collected and stitched together by later editors, even adjacent passages sometimes address different problems. If we are to consider tragedy *qua* tragedy, it seems that *Oedipus*, with its stark ending, represents a very fine example. Perhaps the paragraph about "happy tragedies" was written at a different time, or by a later student, when Aristotle was intent on a comparison of plot possibilities seen in a larger moral light. Aristotle (and his followers) were clearly concerned about salvaging the moral rightness of tragedy as an art form as I discuss below.

In the secondary literature, Paul Schollmeier presents what may be the best solution to this exegetical puzzle.[25] If Aristotle uses the term "catharsis" to describe the purging of pity and fear that results from a tragedy, Schollmeier suggests, astutely, that instead of interpreting catharsis in purely psychological terms, we can also view it as a "mythological

---

23. *Poetics* (Sachs) 13.1453a13–15.
24. *Poetics* (Sachs) 13.1453a22–30.
25. Schollmeier, "Purgation of Pity and Fearfulness."

process." The best kind of myth has a happy ending that eventually purges the storyline of all the morally noxious elements.

Schollmeier divides possible plot lines into four different kinds of narrative. From worst to best: (1) stories in which the protagonist intends to harm a family member but does not carry through with the intention; (2) stories in which the protagonist knowingly harms a family member; (3) stories in which protagonists unknowingly harm a family member and then realizes what they have done; (4) stories in which protagonists unknowingly begin to harm a family member and then realize what they are doing in time enough to stop themselves. Stories in the fourth and last category "[do] not end in bad fortune."[26] These "happy tragedies" are, then, the best of all because the story retains its tragic power only to be cleansed, in the final instances, of any moral impurity. This produces a "mythological catharsis" of pitiableness and fearfulness.

Schollmeier presents a cogent explanation for a discussion in the Aristotelian school that would have pointed to a happy tragedy as the best possible tragedy, both morally and even aesthetically. Still, happy tragedies, even if they are more beautiful, are clearly less tragic. As such, they represent a less perfect example of the artistic single-mindedness that Aristotle champions in his complaints about overly long plots (which cannot hold our proper attention), about "episodic" or rambling plots (which lack unity), and about double endings (where different characters come to opposite fates). The idea that untragic tragedies should be preferred also seems to go against the grain of Aristotle's genre account of literature, which stipulates that all the parts of the text must work together to achieve the goal of that literary kind. But Schollmeier presents a useful account of how and why a certain Aristotelian contingent could have held up the

---

26. Schollmeier, "Purgation," 298.

happy tragedy, where the evil is never done and misfortune avoided, as the best raw material for a tragic plot.

5.4. Esoteric and Exoteric Interpretations

Whatever the nuances of his position, *pace* Morrissey, Aristotle seems to have held *Oedipus* in high regard. Legions of commentators have focused instead on a different sort of textual issue. Most contemporary commentators believe that the old idea that Oedipus is somehow punished in the play for his immorality, presumably because he displayed hubris against the gods, is fundamentally mistaken. According to this new orthodoxy, Oedipus's awful misfortune is unmerited; it results from an understandable intellectual mistake that produces entirely gratuitous suffering. In a 1966 paper entitled "On Misunderstanding the *Oedipus Rex*," E. R. Dodds thunders:

> The theory that the tragic hero must have a grave moral flaw, and its mistaken ascription to Aristotle, has had a long and disastrous history. It was gratifying to Victorian critics, since it appeared to fit certain plays of Shakespeare. But it goes back much further, to the seventeenth-century French critic Dacier, who influenced the practice of the French classical dramatists, especially Corneille, and was himself influenced by the still older nonsense about "poetic justice"—the notion that the poet has a moral duty to represent the world as a place where the good are always rewarded and the bad are always punished. I need not say that this puerile idea is completely foreign to Aristotle and to the practice of the Greek dramatists; I only mention it because [...] it would appear that it still lingers on in some youthful minds like a cobweb in an unswept room.[27]

Suffice it to say that the feisty Dodds traces any moralistic reading of *Oedipus* to a preposterous historical

---

27. Dodds, "On Misunderstanding the *Oedipus Rex*," 37.

misunderstanding that has its roots in an infantile optimism about human destiny—the (Socratic) belief that the bad are invariably punished; the good, inevitably rewarded.

Dodds, for all his huffing-and-puffing, is hardly alone. His view has become the received position on the issue, more moderately expressed in other quarters. R. D. Dawe assures us: "The question whether *hamartia* [the tragic flaw] may or may not mean a flaw of character is one no longer open to discussion; for this interpretation, which had already been challenged. [...] [has been] killed stone dead."[28] T.C.W. Stinton notes, in milder tones: "It is now generally agreed that [...] the moralizing interpretation [of Greek tragedy] favoured by our Victorian forebears and their continental counterparts was one of the many misunderstandings fostered by their moralistic society, and in our own enlightened era is revealed as an aberration."[29] Many others could be cited to the same effect. I will argue, however, that this new amoral approach to Aristotle and to Greek tragedy is guilty of anachronism; it avoids Victorian prudishness perhaps, but it reads modern attitudes into a moralizing ancient author. There is a religious dimension to the play—the gods punish the wicked—and Aristotle thinks that such moralistic aspects are an important part of tragedy.

If commentators like Dodds and company attribute moral interpretations of tragic flaws to Puritan Victorian sensibilities, the present-day convention seems to originate in a train of thought that can be traced back to someone like Nietzsche. Nietzsche's training was, after all, in philology. His groundbreaking account of Greek literature (expressed in *The Birth of Tragedy* and elsewhere) was an exercise in *creative* philology but it had a serious cultural impact. The general anti-moralism of his incisive approach and his extreme hostility to moralistic religion seems to have gripped the contemporary classicist imagination. In the technical

---

28. Dawe, "Some Reflections on *Ate* and *Hamartia*," 90.
29. Stinton, "*Hamartia* in Aristotle," 221.

literature, we find an aversion to ethical/religious readings of *Oedipus*, fuelled, in part, by a meticulous philological analysis of the Greek vocabulary used in ancient texts but also by some unexamined modernist attitudes towards literary criticism. Along with Thomas Gould (a rare authority who disputes the conventional reading), I will, however, "champion the judgment of the naïve reader" over the critic.[30] *Oedipus* is not a simple morality tale. Nonetheless, as Aristotle would maintain, it does make a moral point. But let us begin by summarizing the conventional amoral interpretation.

Modern classicists trace what they see as the misguided moralistic reading of *Oedipus* to a mistranslation of the Greek ἁμαρτία (*hamartia*), which Aristotle makes use of in a key passage in the *Poetics*. Ruby Blondell, somewhat typically, lays the blame on Aristotle. He explains:

> Some modern readers have mistakenly assumed that Oedipus' [has] a "fatal flaw" of character for which he is being punished by the gods. This familiar but misleading [notion] derives ultimately from Aristotle, who declares in the *Poetics*, that the central character of a tragedy falls because of a *megalē hamartia* [ἁμαρτία μεγάλη] or "great error" (1453a 15-16). But *hamartia* does not mean "character flaw." In its original context, the phrase is more accurately described as "huge mistake." In Oedipus' case, the mistake is quite obviously his ignorance of who his parents really are. And this is not, by any standard, a crime or flaw of character.[31]

Sachs reiterates the received view in more pointed terms, placing moralistic interpretations of Greek tragedy on the level of bad undergraduate essay-writing. He scornfully observes:

---

30. Gould, "Innocence of Oedipus," 479.
31. Blondell, "Essay" in *Oidipous*, 116.

> There is something of a cottage industry that produces term papers for literature classes by hunting up tragic flaws. Among those who take this approach to tragedy, there are some who would contend that the moral of any tragedy is, if you have a flaw, you will be destroyed. Among those who see that the shallowness of this view makes a travesty of any tragedy, there are some who are convinced that Aristotle is the source of the shallowness. There are three problems with that conclusion. (a) Aristotle never said that the tragic figure has a flaw. (b) Aristotle did say what it is that causes the tragic figure's downfall, and it is something other than a flaw. (c) Aristotle's explanation of why certain kinds of stories suit tragedies makes it plain that those in which a flawed character suffers on account of his flaw are not tragic.[32]

Sachs concludes with a sardonic attempt at humour: "The fatal flaw here is in the misinterpretation of Aristotle, not in any tragedy or in anything Aristotle said about them."[33]

If, however, commentators such as Sachs and Dodds dismiss moralistic interpretations of *Oedipus* out of hand, they miss out on a deeper point. Supposing, to start with, that "the majority of present-day undergraduates," most general readers, and a wide range of historical authorities (that Dodds maligns with the prudish epithet "Victorian") insist on reading a moral meaning into *Oedipus.* This might be an indication of something momentous.[34] Ordinary *human nature*, it seems, wants to read the play this way. Most of us would like to believe, it turns out, that the good will be rewarded and the evil, punished. Call this *karma*; call this poetic justice; call this fate; even call this Socratic metaphysical optimism. Whatever we call it, it seems to be a perennial

---

32. *Poetics* (Sachs), "Introduction," 7.
33. *Poetics* (Sachs), "Introduction," 7.
34. Dodds, "Misunderstanding," 38. Also: "as many undergraduates still think."

feature of how human beings make moral sense of things. Sophocles knew this and Aristotle himself says as much when viewing happiness—"good fate" or *eudaimonia*—as something associated with good moral behaviour. Is, then, the present-day intellectualist purging of moral content practised by contemporary commentators warranted? Or is it a kind of "catharsis" gone wrong? I will argue that adherents of the new orthodoxy end up producing another stock interpretation of the Sophocles's play to replace the stock interpretation which they, with some justification, reject.

Before I examine these issues in more detail below, simply note that it is not clear that either Sophocles or Aristotle was averse to a moralistic reading of Greek tragedy. Sophocles wrote three separate plays involving Oedipus's family: *Antigone, Oedipus Tyrannos*, and *Oedipus at Colonus* (listed in the order in which the plays were likely written).[35] Leaving aside the obvious ethical ramifications of *Antigone* and saving discussion of *Oedipus Tyrannos* for later, it is important to note that Sophocles provides an explicitly ethical treatment of the Oedipus story in *Oedipus at Colonus,* performed in 405 BC, the year after Sophocles's death. Darice Birge comments, "The crux of Sophocles' *Oedipus at Colonus* is the transformation of Oedipus from blind outcast to superhumanly powerful hero."[36] Sophocles presents the old man Oedipus in the last play, not merely as a hero, but as a *moral* hero who has won over the blessings of the gods by this patient repentance for his earlier sins.

It may seem contradictory to suggest that Oedipus is a villain in *Oedipus Tyrannos* and a moral saint in *Oedipus at Colonus*, but the later play hinges on just this sort of

---

35. As Hall, explains, "[these] three surviving plays [...] were not designed to be performed together sequentially [but] were independently conceived." Hall, "Introduction," *Oedipus* (Kitto), xi. Hall correctly debunks "the misleading latter-day myth of a Theban 'trilogy' or 'cycle,'" in the sense that these are distinctly individual plays on a related theme, not parts of some overarching attempt at artistic unity.
36. Birge, "Grove of the Eumenides," 11.

transformation. The earlier play is about "bad" Oedipus being cursed; the later play is about the same Oedipus being redeemed. It depicts, in effect, the fulfillment of a prophecy that Oedipus would be favoured in death and that his secret tomb would bring blessings upon the city that accepts his body. So, what is cursed, paradoxically, turns into what is blessed. But this movement from villain to hero would be impossible if the earlier play was, as many specialists suggest, bereft of moral ramifications.

Oedipus at Colonus is, to use theological language, a play about repentance, expiation, and redemption. Oedipus, now a blind old man, has accepted his punishment (despite persistent character flaws) for a crime he never intended to commit. He has paid for his sins, which redeems his memory and restores, to the full extent possible, his virtue. As David Grene explains:

> Sophocles is declaring that the sin of Oedipus is real; that the consequences in the form of loneliness, neglect, and suffering of the years of wandering are inevitable; but that the will and the consciousness are also some measure of man's sin—and when the sinner sinned necessarily and unwittingly, his suffering can be compensation enough for his guilt. He may at the end be blessed and a blessing. [...] [Here] at last, he [Oedipus] is, in a measure, vindicated.[37]

This is, however, Sophocles preaching a moral/religious lesson: we can make reparation for our own immorality by sincere repentance and thus be redeemed by the gods, especially under such extenuating circumstances.

It is hard to imagine that the earlier Sophocles, who wrote *Oedipus Tyrannos,* differed drastically in moral temperament

---

37. Grene, "Introduction," *Oedipus* (Grene), 5 (original italics). A nicely qualified judgment.

and aesthetic outlook from the later Sophocles, who wrote *Oedipus at Colonus*. Dawe observes:

> It is a commonplace of criticism that *Oed. Col.* is not to be used as a commentary on *Oed. Rex*. But Sophocles must have mulled over these problems, and is unlikely to have changed his mind drastically, for his religious thinking appears not to have undergone any profound changes in the course of his career—at any rate none that I can trace. [...] No one has yet [conclusively] established the dating of Sophocles' plays, but a large study [...] suggests that *O.T.* and *O.C.* may have been written only about ten years apart.[38]

The chronological details are interesting but what matters most of all is that the same moral attitudes would have motivated Sophocles on both occasions.

Sophocles seems guilty, then, of the "Victorian," "puerile," "undergraduate" sentiment scholars such as Dodds and Sachs hastily dismiss. Sophocles—with all the necessary qualifications in place—feels compelled, in his last play, to give the Oedipus myth a more-or-less happy ending. Why? Because he finds it unsettling to think that a repentant man who has faced up to his guilt in the light of extenuating circumstances should continue to be cursed by the gods. Oedipus has accepted self-punishment for his sins and suffered the total loss of worldly happiness. That is enough. It would be unjust for the gods to persecute him further. In turning the last episode of his life into a blessing, Sophocles obeys the requirements of "poetic justice." Even if Oedipus's goodness amounts to nothing more than his submission to a reparatory punishment for an objective evil he has committed, his patience has to be rewarded or the world could not make moral sense.

---

38. Dawe, "Some Reflections," 117, n. 44. The internal reference is to Walter Jens, *Statt einer Literaturgeschichte* (5th ed., 1962), 321.

So, it seems that Sophocles embraces poetic justice. In the context of ancient Greek paganism, this would hardly be novel. Witness Socrates's dogged insistence that pious behaviour has to be rewarded in this world or the next (and to just the right amount). As he puts it in the *Apology*: "nothing can harm a good man, either in life or death: nor are his fortunes neglected by the gods."[39] Socrates (rather artlessly) sets up an afterlife of reward or punishment to ensure that poetic justice (*karma*) is salvaged in spite of the appearance of injustice in the world (in his mythological account of the judgment of souls in the *Gorgias* and his retelling of the "Myth of Er" at the end of the *Republic*).[40]

For his part, Aristotle seems to think that playwrights must take moral feelings into consideration. Consider his discussion of the best type of plot for a tragedy. Aristotle advises:

> There are three forms of Plot to be avoided. (1) A good man must not be seen as passing from happiness to misery, or (2) a bad man from misery to happiness. The first situation is not fear-inspiring or piteous but simply odious to us. The second [...] does not appeal either to the human feeling in us, or to our pity, or to our fears. Neither on the other hand, should (3) an extremely bad man be seen falling from happiness to misery. Although such a story may arouse the human feeling in us, it will not move us to either pity or fear for pity is occasioned by undeserved misfortune and fear by the misfortune of one like ourselves; so that in the case of an extremely bad man [who is extremely unlike us and fully deserves to suffer] there will be nothing either piteous or fear-inspiring in the situation.[41]

---

39. *Defense of Socrates* (Gallop) 41d1–3.
40. *Gorgias* 523a–527a; *Republic* 614b–621d.
41. *Poetics* (Bywater) 13.1452b33–1453a6.

Although some might think that the third claim that the tragic protagonist should not be "extremely bad" exonerates Oedipus, it only follows from this that the protagonist of a tragedy must not be an immoral monster—a sociopath, if you will. (Because we do not feel empathy for a sociopath.) But it does not follow that the protagonist must be a properly moral person. Consider carefully what Aristotle is saying here.

Aristotle begins by telling us that a tragedy must not present (1) a good man who moves from happiness to unhappiness because this "is simply odious to us." Fyfe translates the same passage: "[because this] shocks our feelings"; Sachs renders it: "[because] this is [...] repellent." But does this not sound like the "puerile" theory of "poetic justice" Dodds lambasts? Bad things should not happen to good people. Aristotle—a subtle thinker, after all—does not say that good people never meet with a bad fate; he says, more carefully, that this kind of thing offends our moral sensibilities. It is, unfortunately, a grotesque possibility, but *it is not a fit moral subject for theatre*. So, we should avoid plots where this happens.

Aristotle next claims that the playwright must not depict (2) a bad man moving from misery to happiness. Why? Because, again, this sort of fate does not conform to "poetic justice" and violates human feeling. Fyfe translates the relevant passage: "That [situation] is the most untragic of all [...] since it does not satisfy our feelings" and adds a footnote: "i.e., our preference for 'poetic justice.'"[42] There are two sides to the poetic-justice medal: bad things should not happen to good people and good things should not happen to bad people. Again, Aristotle is not suggesting that bad men are never rewarded or that good men never suffer misfortune; of course, this sometimes happens. He is suggesting this is morally repugnant—it offends our feelings—and is, therefore, inappropriate subject matter for theatre. Because it fails

---

42. *Poetics* (Fyfe) 13.1452b36–1453a1n. 6.

the "poetic justice" test, it distracts our sensibilities and is not worthy of tragic representation.

Thirdly, Aristotle claims that tragedy should not depict an *extremely* bad man moving from happiness to unhappiness. If, then, Oedipus is a bad man, he is not an extremely bad man; he is not a psychopath, a serial killer, a Hitler, a Pol Pot, a Stalin. He is not Jack the Ripper. Aristotle maintains that a tragedy about a sociopath or a mass murderer is impossible because such people do not deserve and cannot elicit our sympathy. But why not? Because our *moral feelings* get in the way of any association with the main character. This third possibility conforms to the concept of poetic justice—the very bad get punished—but it does not make for effective theatre because it would be *morally* repulsive to even feel sorry for them. In this case, then, our moral feelings, once again, get in the way of good storytelling.

It follows from this single passage that *Oedipus Tyrannos* cannot be the story of an undeservedly unfortunate good man, an undeservedly fortunate bad man, or a depraved person, for Aristotle considers it an excellent example of tragedy. What kind of tragic protagonist does Aristotle favour then? He explains (in Bywater's translation):

> There remains then, the intermediate kind of personage, a man not pre-eminently virtuous and just, whose misfortune, however, is brought upon him not by vice or depravity but by some error of judgment [ἁμαρτία], of the number of those in the enjoyment of great reputation and prosperity: e.g. Oedipus, Thyestes, and noteworthy men of similar families.[43]

Oedipus fits the description. He is not a brute or a sociopath—filled with "vice or depravity"—but neither is he a perfectly good man. He exists somewhere between the two extremes: He is not be truly virtuous, but he cannot be

---

43. *Poetics* (Bywater) 13.1453a6–1453a11.

utterly evil either. His ignorance of whom his parents were makes him a somewhat more sympathetic character—surely, these are mitigating circumstances—but it does not follow that he is a moral role model. I will investigate the serious moral faults that led to his destruction below. But whatever we think about Oedipus, it is tendentious to suggest that Aristotle's discussion of tragedy is not couched in moral terms. Morality is about all degrees of goodness and badness; as such, moral considerations (including notions of karma or poetic justice) play a pivotal role in determining which plots and characters are suitable for effective tragedy.

5.5. *Hamartia*

A plethora of papers and books discuss Aristotle's use of the term *hamartia* in the *Poetics*. Once we have grasped the essential point, it seems a bit much.[44] Still, as this vein of reflection represents a major focus of critical commentary, we need to thoroughly investigate the issue here. Leon Golden summarizes the general consensus when he writes that, on the usual reading of the term, we are forced to conclude that:

> Aristotle's prescription for the ideal tragic hero in the *Poetics* requires an intellectual rather than a moral failing. Furthermore, the best criticism we have of the *Oedipus Tyrannos* agrees with assigning an intellectual and not a moral error to the hero of the play that serves as an Aristotelian model for excellence in tragedy.[45]

Those who champion this intellectualist as opposed to a moralist interpretation of tragedy argue that earlier generations of readers have misunderstood Sophocles's intentions because of a mistranslation of Aristotle's comment that a tragic plot results from a ἁμαρτία μεγάλη (*hamartia megale*),

---

44. There is vast commentary on this particular issue. Most repeat familiar tropes. I cite from some of the more influential sources.
45. Golden, "Hamartia, Ate, and Oedipus," 5.

a great error or flaw. The key passage in the *Poetics* reads: "The perfect plot, accordingly, must have a single [...] issue; the change in the subject's fortune must be [...] from good to bad; and the cause of it must lie not in any depravity, but in *some great fault* on his part."[46] Fyfe translates the passage: "the change must be [...] from good to bad fortune, and it must not be due to villainy but to *some great flaw* in such a man." Or, as Sachs renders it, the tragic disaster must involve the "changing [...] from good fortune to bad, not through badness of character but on account of *a great missing of the mark*."

As Sachs explains, "The word *hamartia* is used in many ways, but its root sense, and the illustration that is never absent from its metaphorical extensions, is that of missing a mark with a spear or an arrow." Hence the verb ἁμαρτάνω, the root meaning of which is to miss a target. [47] Sachs, however, seems a little zealous here. He overstates the case about etymological origins. When someone says to a spouse (in anger), "you drive me up a wall," they are hardly thinking about the origins of the phrase (literally, imagining being driven up a wall). When one is told to "keep a stiff upper lip," it is questionable how much we are really thinking about keeping one's superior labium rigid. When you think of an "automobile," you probably are not thinking of a vehicle that is a self (auto-)moving. Such etymological origins are easily accessible, but perhaps as an atavism we mostly leave behind.

All this makes it sound as if the question is good and settled, but further investigation shows that philological debate about the precise interpretation of these lines is rather more inconclusive. Aristotle maintains here that the change (the

---

46. Note that the best plot should focus on the misfortune of one person; it should not present the fortune and misfortune of say two opponents; presumably the good being rewarded with good fortune and the bad being punished with bad fortune. *Poetics* (Bywater) 13.1453a14–15.
47. Sachs, "Introduction," 8.

"turning around") should not be into good fortune (good luck, success, prosperity) from bad fortune (bad luck) but the opposite, from good fortune into bad fortune, not through wickedness (badness, depravity) but *through a great failure*.[48] Taken on its own, the key word *hamartia* is distinctly ambiguous. It could mean fault, mistake, sin, or guilt. As Stinton explains, "the sense of ἁμαρτία can be grouped under three main headings: to miss the mark (literally), to fail in some object or make a mistake; and to offend morally, to do wrong."[49]

I do not want to wander too far into philological debates here, but some acknowledgment of the scholarship is required. O. Hey, P. W. Harsh, Jan Bremer, and others concede that the ancient Greek term *hamartia* can have a moral sense, though they think that Aristotle usually employs the word in an *amoral* sense to designate a factual mistake.[50] Bremer insists that only 5 out of 139 instances in Aristotle refer to some kind of moral failure, concluding that it is "extremely probable" that Aristotle is using the term *hamartia* in an amoral sense in the *Poetics*.[51] Except that, as Stinton politely suggests, Bremer's line of reasoning (even if it were entirely trustworthy) is inconclusive.[52] If we were to randomly select an instance of the term *hamartia* from Aristotle's far-flung writings, it might be overwhelmingly probable that we will come across an amoral use of the term. But moral and amoral usages of the term in Aristotle's writings are not randomly distributed throughout his work. They are context-specific. Greek tragedians generally used this term with severe moral overtones, so it could be the case that Aristotle is using the term *hamartia* in a moral sense

---

48. The Greek: "καὶ μεταβάλλειν οὐκ εἰς εὐτυχίαν ἐκ δυστυχίας ἀλλὰ τοὐναντίον ἐξ εὐτυχίας εἰς δυστυχίαν μὴ διὰ μοχθηρίαν ἀλλὰ δι' ἁμαρτίαν μεγάλην." *Poetics* (Kassel) 13.1453a14–15.
49. Stinton, "Hamartia," 222.
50. Hey, "Hamartia"; Harsh, "Hamartia Again."
51. Bremer, *Hamartia*.
52. He uses the word "dubious." Stinton, "Hamartia," 222.

when it comes to discussions of Greek tragedy, even if that specific context does not happen very often in the corpus.

And, in fact, as it turns out, Aristotle uses the *hamartia* group of words in distinctly different ways elsewhere. Sometimes he uses the term and its derivatives to identify less serious moral errors as in the *Nicomachean Ethics* when he says that small-souled and vain men—i.e., men that lack virtue—are not thought to be vicious but merely in error (literally, they are those that are "mistaken," ἡμαρτημένοι) because they do no serious harm.[53] This might be interpreted as support for an amoral interpretation of the word (although it does suggest, *pace* Sachs, a close connection between *hamartia* and bad character).

But Aristotle does not restrict his use of the term *hamartia* to minor moral issues; he also uses the term to refer moral ignorance. A relevant passage reads:

> Every wicked person is in error about what one should do and what one should abstain from, and it is because they go wrong through that kind of flaw [literally, through such a *hamartia*] that they become unjust and generally bad.[54]

Yet moral ignorance is, in Aristotle's moral system, the *worst* possible vice. Unlike incontinence, it is incurable. It turns us into brutes.[55] So here is Aristotle using the term in a highly charged moral context.

As Stinton astutely notes, Aristotle also uses *hamartia*, in a discussion of moral deliberation, to refer to mistakes made in either the minor or major premises of a moral

---

53. Sachs renders it, "Now even these do not seem to be people with vices (since they do not do harm), but people who are in error." *Nicomachean Ethics* IV.3.1125a18–20.
54. That is, "διὰ τὴν τοιαύτην ἁμαρτίαν." *Nicomachean Ethics* (Taylor) III.1.1110b29. There are niceties about the differing translations, none of which negates the main point here.
55. Cf. *Nicomachean Ethics* VII.5.

syllogism.[56] Aristotle writes: "Error [literally, *hamartia*: ἡ ἁμαρτία] in deliberating concerns either the universal or the particular."[57] If, however, both failures have moral implications, ignorance of universal moral principles is, again, for Aristotle, a kind of moral ignorance, the worst possible moral fault, which turns us into beasts or brutes. Someone guilty of this sort of "missing the mark" or *hamartia* would be, in modern terms, something close to a sociopath.[58] I am not suggesting, of course, that the Oedipus character is a vicious, depraved moral monster (although he suffers from great moral faults just the same). The important point here is that Aristotle sometimes uses the term *hamartia* to describe very serious moral failings. There is no indication that he only used it in an amoral sense.

5.6. Oedipus and *Hamartia*: Adkins

In an influential treatment, A. W. H. Adkins attempts to establish the amoral meaning of Aristotle's use of the term *hamartia* in *Poetics* 13. Adkins concludes:

> It seems unlikely that, in using ἁμαρτία [*hamartia*] here, Aristotle had moral error in mind at all. [In Aristotle's view,] the best kind of tragedy portrays a man who is ἐπιεικής [gentle, fair, reasonable, moderate], but not extremely [who is] making a mistake of fact.[59]

If, however, Adkins' argument has been widely cited, his position is also open to dispute. I cannot examine all the details of his carefully crafted account here but let us take a brief look at his argument.

---

56. Stinton, "Hamartia," 223.
57. *Nicomachean Ethics* (Sachs) VI.8.1142a21.
58. It carries the risk of slipping into brutishness. Cf. *Nicomachean Ethics* VII.5. Cf. Groarke, *Moral Reasoning,* chapter 5, "Aristotle," 147–201, for more detail than is possible to fit in here.
59. Adkins, "Aristotle and the Best Kind of Tragedy," 90.

Most importantly, Adkins claims that Aristotle uses the term *hamartia* to refer to a blameless error in intellectual judgment. He claims that although the misfortune of a very good man is not the best tragic plot, it is a workable possibility. A very good man could make a mistake of fact, a *hamartia*, and still be a very good man and be the protagonist in a successful tragedy.[60] There are, however, some serious problems with this notion. Adkins takes some liberties with the Greek (slipping a word into the text at 1452b34 and changing the usual meaning of another word).[61] But textual ambiguities aside, this line of reasoning misconstrues the spirit of Aristotle's take on tragedy.

In order to explain why Aristotle dismisses the misfortune of a very good man as a fit subject for tragedy, Adkins has to maintain that Aristotle would be "shocked" "by the portrayal of a very virtuous man making a mistake of fact." But why would it be shocking if a virtuous person made a mere mistake of fact? Morality does not protect us from human fallibility. As Aristotle himself recognizes, many people in past ages made mistakes of fact and remained virtuous people. The only reason anyone could be shocked by a virtuous person making a factual mistake is if they believed that good people never make factual mistakes, which is wildly implausible. Who could be so intolerably naïve as to accept the idea that good people never make mistakes of fact that lead to sorrowful consequences? It makes more sense to argue that Aristotle dismisses the misfortune of a very good person as a good plot for tragedy because very good people cannot be guilty of a *hamartia* understood as a *moral* error or flaw. Very moral people cannot make serious moral errors (or they would not be "very moral").

Aristotle thinks that a tragedy must involve something more than a curious accident of happenstance. The fact that

---

60. Adkins writes, "Beyond a certain degree of excellence in ἐπιείκεια [a quality of moral goodness], the portrayal of the tragic character making a moral ἁμαρτία is [...] impossible." Adkins, "Best Kind," 90.
61. He does this for philosophical rather than textual reasons.

something sad unexpectedly happens to an innocent person is not truly tragic; it is merely, as Aristotle himself says, "shocking" or upsetting (μιαρός).[62] If such incidents make for attention-grabbing headlines in tabloid newspapers, we need something more substantial and profound for serious tragedy. As we shall see, in proper tragedy there must be some connection between the character of the protagonist and the precise nature of the catastrophe that befalls him.

5.7. Oedipus and *Hamartia*: Stinton

Stinton, who rejects, out of hand, Aristotle's understanding of Greek tragedy, provides an exhaustive and scholarly treatment of the *hamartia* problem. After all is said and done, he comes out in favour of a compromise. He concludes that although the term *hamartia* retains an inalienable moral residue that cannot be explained away, it denotes a "mistake of fact" in the *Poetics*' passage.

Stinton is convinced that the suffering of the protagonist in an effective tragedy must be undeserved. He separates, then, the question of Oedipus's (somewhat) bad character from the question of his downfall. On this bifurcated account, Oedipus's bad character is one thing; his ruinous fate is something altogether different. There is no causal link between the two. Oedipus is *guilty* insomuch as he is a flawed human being, but his disastrous fate is *underserved*. It is, then, this (odd) conjunction of *guilty* character and *undeserved* fate that Stinton views as necessary to successful tragedy.

Stinton points out that Aristotle uses the term *hamartia* in the *Nicomachean Ethics* to cover cases where the moral culpability of an immoral agent is diminished by various factors. Aristotle's list of such mitigated bad acts includes: acts done through factual ignorance (δι'ἄγνοιαν), passionate acts fuelled by drunkenness or anger (ἀγνοῶν διὰ πάθος), acts done through unbridled appetite (ἀκρασία), and wrong

---

62. *Poetics* 13.1452b36.

acts knowingly done for the sake of a greater good (μικταὶ πράξεις).[63] Stinton concludes, "What is common to all these is that the agent has some excuse for his act, ranging from a complete defense (when his act is pitiable in itself) to various degrees of extenuating circumstance permitting a plea of mitigation."[64]

Stinton insists, then, that Oedipus must be *somewhat* immoral but that he does not deserve such a calamitous fate. If his downfall can be traced to a factual mistake (not a moral flaw), he still must be an unsavoury enough character to make his downfall morally acceptable. His great misfortune must make poetic sense somehow because we will not be pleased by the sight of bad things happening to a person we like and admire. Stinton comments: "If the agent is ἐπιεικής [*epieikēs*: decent, morally good], [then] his fall is morally repulsive."[65] And again, "The point of diminishing the agent's ἐπιείκεια [*epieikeia*: goodness] is to avoid the sense of moral outrage which impedes the tragic pleasure."[66] If, however, Stinton tries to disentangle Oedipus's admittedly worrisome character traits from the mechanism of his downfall, and if he recognizes the importance of poetic justice to Aristotle, his bifurcated model of tragedy is out of keeping with the basic gist of Aristotle's account.

Aristotle emphasizes the importance of tragic unity. He observes: "the plot, an imitation of action, must represent one action, a complete whole, with its several incidents so closely connected that the transposal or withdrawal of any

---

63. Stinton, "Hamartia," 254. Cf. *Nicomachean Ethics* V.8.1135b12ff. This latter case, what Aristotle refers to as "mixed acts."
64. Stinton, "Hamartia," 254.
65. Stinton, "Hamartia," 229. The term is taken, of course, from the *Poetics*. The *Liddell and Scott*: ἐπιείκεια: reasonableness, fairness, equity, clemency, goodness; ἐπιεικής: reasonable, fair, kind, gentle, good: there are varying translations: co-operative excellences (Adkins), decency (Sachs); equity (Schütrumpf); moral goodness, morally excellence (Stinton).
66. Stinton, "Hamartia," 239.

one of them will disjoin and dislocate the whole."[67] Aristotle also claims that in a good play the events and the characters have to be tied together in some nexus of cause-and-effect: "whenever such-and-such a personage says or does such-and-such a thing, it must be the necessary or probable outcome of his character."[68] We cannot separate, then, Oedipus's angry, lordly, obsessive character from the tragic chain of cause-and-effect that constitutes the play. The events have to arise out of his character—probably or necessarily—so that everything makes sense as a perfect unity. The bifurcated scheme Stinton recommends cuts the play in two, making this ideal of total unity impossible.

Stinton maintains that every tragedy must depict (1) a flawed character and (2) a mistake of fact—*and that these cannot be linked.* "The point" of the flawed character is not to precipitate the catastrophe but "to alienate our sympathies from the agent."[69] The agent must be morally flawed—although only in some diluted sense—and this diluted moral failing cannot be the mistake that leads to his downfall. But how could this result in a plot where everything works together to produce one utterly unified effect?

Suppose we were to write a modern "tragedy" about a flawed person that gets accidentally killed by a car while crossing the street. And suppose this person's character flaws have nothing to do with the accident. He just happens to get run over and it also happens that he is a (moderately) bad person. This is how Stinton conceives of Aristotelian tragedy. But this is not, in any Aristotelian sense, a tragedy. It is just a report on random happenstance (in the third sense described in the previous chapter). To transform this modern incident into the kind of portrayal Aristotle has in mind, we would have to somehow connect the car accident and the person's flawed character. Perhaps the protagonist could be a careless

---

67. *Poetics* (Bywater) 8.1451a16–19; 30–36.
68. *Poetics* (Bywater) 15.1454a32–38.
69. Stinton, "Hamartia," 254.

car driver who has killed someone in a hit-and-run accident without being detected and later meets his own death in another hit-and-run accident. If one careless driver dies because of someone else's careless driving, this consequence arises in a thought-provoking and morally relevant way. It also raises interesting religious questions.

Stinton drives a wedge between the protagonist's character and the plot, which must, inevitably, fracture the play into adjacent but unrelated factors. It is not just that the main character in an Aristotelian tragedy is "somewhat wicked"; this "somewhat wicked" character must give rise to the incidents portrayed so that they become a poetic unity. It is not even enough (as Van Bramm suggests) that there is a causal link between the two.[70] The moral taint of the main character has to link up with all other aspects of the tragic catastrophe: Everything has to work together to produce one, undivided, sublime, moral, and religious effect.

In an interestingly twist, Stinton lambasts Aristotle's understanding of Greek tragedy, claiming that Aristotle very much misunderstands what Sophocles is trying to do. Stinton tells us:

> A serious critique of Greek tragedy can never be achieved by a piecemeal adjustment of Aristotelian insights. It should start by a complete rejection of his terms of reference: by realizing that his psychology of tragic effect is distorted by overreaction to Plato, that his insistence on the moral content of tragedy and its inherent logic merely represents his own philosophical preoccupations, and misrepresents the aims of the tragedian no less than it distorts their values.[71]

Stinton's criticism of Aristotle is extreme. There is something to what he is saying, except that he largely overstates the case.

---

70. Van Braam, "Aristotle's Use of *Hamartia*."
71. Stinton, "Hamartia," 242.

Ancient audiences did not divorce tragedy from moralistic considerations the way some modern commentators tend to do. In a book about Sophocles, historian Robert Murray explains:

> A Greek of the fifth century [...] would not have objected at all to the presence of morality, didacticism, even messages in poetry, and especially the drama. Indeed, he felt that moral instruction was a vital and valuable function of tragic drama, in particular, and that the voice of the poet was the voice of morality and wisdom as well as of beauty. Indeed, it was the habitual tendency of the Greek mind to identify beauty and the good, or rather to accept this identification without any question (in any dictionary of ancient Greek, the adjective *kalos* will be translated as "beautiful, good, genuine, virtuous, noble, honorable"; its opposite *kakos*, as "ugly, cowardly, base, evil"). This attitude is clearly reflected in the fifth-century view toward any form of art; that which is beautiful must be morally good, and that which is evil must of necessity be ugly. Aesthetic pleasure and moral instruction are truly one and inseparable, a unity soon to be recognized by Aristotle. [...] To sum up, the Greeks of the fifth century and *well into the fourth* were convinced that poetry, especially tragedy, is essentially moral; that there is meaning in the drama, and that meaning is closely related to the aesthetic impact of the whole. Thus, to the contemporaries of Sophocles, a poet was expected to express a view of life, even a "message." Had he not done so, he would have failed his audiences. Had they thought he had not done so, he would not have won prizes in the Theatre of Dionysius.[72]

If, then, Aristotle views tragedy in explicitly moral terms, this is not, *pace* Stinton, far removed from what his contemporaries believed. This dovetails with his time period and the aspirations of the Greek tragedians.

---

72. Murray, "Thought and Structure in Sophoclean Tragedy," 23–24.

Murray distinguishes between two exaggerations in historical accounts of Greek tragedy. Moralists (such as Bowra) insist rather too urgently on the moral message in the plays, whereas formalists (such as Waldock) go to another extreme and deny the aesthetic importance of any moral content whatsoever.[73] Murray himself considers the possibility that Sophocles himself was not seriously interested in the moral ramifications of his subject matter but only made a pretense of being interested in order to meet with audience expectations. He maintains, nonetheless, that a thorough comparison of *Oedipus Tyrannos* and *Oedipus at Colonus* reveals "a deep rethinking of serious ethical, even metaphysical attitudes" and concludes that although "we may not share those attitudes, [...] think them shallow, [and] find them to be not much more than commonplaces of the Athenian tradition. [...] we have no license to dismiss [this moral aspect of Sophocles's work] as unintended or inconsequential to the emotive effect of his theatre."[74]

To depict *Oedipus* as an existential, Nietzschean tragedy of meaningless fate without moral overtones is a modernist invention. At the very least, one should not attribute such nihilistic views to Sophocles or Aristotle. As far as we can tell, Greek playwrights and their audiences viewed the world in distinctly moral and religious terms that linked together fate and morality. What Greek tragedy is about is happenstance in the fourth, religious sense described in the previous chapter. It is not just about sad events—it is about the moral/religious implications of those events. Which is to say, it is an exploration, from a moral and a religious point of view, of the dark side of humanity. It is not simplistically didactic or theologically dogmatic, but it involves a moral/religious consideration of evil.

---

73. Cf. Bowra, *Sophoclean Tragedy*; Waldock, *Sophocles the Dramatist*.
74. Murray, "Tragedy," 28. He continues, "Structure and thought are inseparable in the seven [extant] plays; to stress one element and disregard the other is a decision of Solomon, a dismemberment of the living work of art."

5.8. *Hamartia* as a Term with Moral Colour

Not every authority agrees with amoral interpretations of Aristotle's use of the word *hamartia*. Thorough philological investigations by Bremer and others show that the *hamartia* family of words was used, in various contexts, to mean "to miss" (originally, "to miss the mark,") "to err," or "to morally or criminally offend." As G.M. Kirkwood observes, "statistics show that [the meaning of] 'offend' is much commoner in tragedy […] than 'err,' and that [the term] *hamartia* itself is […] invested with a moral connotation in tragedy."[75] It is not hard to imagine, then, that Aristotle would mean the term in a moral sense when speaking of tragedy.

In his review of Bremer's book-long defence of the amoral interpretation, Kirkwood comments:

> I began Mr. Bremer's book without a preconception about the meaning of *hamartia* in chapter 13 of the *Poetics*; though Bremer is satisfied that it means "error," and that it is wrong to suppose that there is any notion of fault or moral defect involved, I have ended up with the conviction that no single, sharply defined meaning can be assigned to it. Neither Bremer's conclusion nor my scepticism is startling: "error" is an interpretation enjoying favor currently, but the point is notoriously controversial. I suspect that the meaning of *hamartia* is one of those problems which become the more insoluble the more fully they are examined. The evidence is both abundant and inconclusive; the very thoroughness with which it is here presented is fated to induce the scepticism that the study is intended to allay.[76]

Kirkwood concludes, even more ominously, that "Aristotle does not" in the passages Stinton refers to, "make a *clear* distinction between moral and non-moral mistake." It follows,

---

75. Kirkwood, "Review," 712.
76. Kirkwood, "Review," 711.

he thinks, that "the two occurrences in the *Poetics* are, obviously, ambiguous" and that there are "no sure grounds" for attaching either a moral or an amoral meaning to the word.[77] We simply cannot know what Aristotle intended, one way or the other.

Some authorities take an even harder line. Cedric Whitman insists:

> It is clear beyond doubt that Aristotle did not use the word [*hamartia*] without moral implications. The moral interpretation of the tragic *hamartia* is the only one that is consistent with Aristotle's thinking and that preserves the universal validity of poetry which Aristotle himself said made it more philosophic than history—a view which the particular "error of judgment" theory would seriously violate.[78]

Aristotle does claim that tragedy (like philosophy) deals with universal truths. When an agent with a rash character acts rashly to produce the inevitably tragic consequences of rashness, this provides a universal moral template. This seems to what Aristotle has in mind. A play about the disappointingly negative consequences that stem from someone making a factual mistake might pique our curiosity, but it is not how Aristotle or the ancient Greeks understood tragedy.

If, however, Whitman thinks that Aristotle is a moralist when it comes to tragedy, he also believes, like Stinton, that Aristotle got Greek tragedy wrong. He begins by pointing out the difference between what he views as Aristotle's narrow, technical use of the word *hamartia* and the looser use of the term in the actual plays. Whitman reports:

> In tragedy the word [*hamartia*] is used with the completest freedom, in contrast to its strict significance in

---

77. Kirkwood, "Review," 712 (my emphasis).
78. Whitman, *Sophocles*, 34.

Aristotle, to cover a multitude of errors, sins, crimes, petty mistakes, and transgressions of authority, whether for moral or immoral reasons. There is no English equivalent which can embrace all its internal and external aspects, its moral or merely technical constituents of guilt. [...] It remains to question Aristotle's [moral] use of it, and therewith the whole moral scheme which he imposed on the drama of the proceeding era.[79]

Whitman disputes Aristotle's interpretation of tragedy *because Aristotle is too moralistic*. Because it substitutes, he thinks, didactic for aesthetic aspirations. Whitman's subtle criticism of Aristotle is worth quoting at some length. He comments:

It is indeed surprising that Aristotle [...] should have been so bound by his own moral beliefs as to think that a play that represented the fall of a just man would be "disgusting." [...] Plato's original complaint against poetry was just this—that it was not moral enough, that the good man did not receive his just deserts. [...] His complaint was a real one. [...] The failure of [Aristotle's] attempt to fit poetry into the political scheme of even a good state lies [...] simply in the fact that poetry does not, and cannot, exist to fulfill a political function [...] Its function is personal and universal. [...] Poetry may proclaim the law, [...] or it may deny the law. [...] But poetry will not obey the law. And this seems to be the chief trouble with the *Poetics*. Aristotle tried, experimentally, to see tragedy within the moral law as recognized by the Academy and his own efforts; his recommendations for the best kind of tragedy are a curious mixture derived partly from what he found so effective in the works themselves, and partly from what he felt must be there in order to satisfy moral necessity. [...] And these suggestions, or statements of

---

79. Whitman, *Sophocles*, 34–35.

preference perhaps, innocent and tentative as they no doubt were in Aristotle's original lectures, have become rules of thumb, in spite of the fact that the steady search for *hamartiae* has all but taken the life out of Sophocles' vital works. [...] It is a choice between Aristotle's theory or Sophocles' plays.[80]

A hopeless predicament, it would seem. As Whitman sees things, one must choose between Aristotle and Sophocles. One can have moralistic tragedy with Aristotle. Or realistic and often unedifying tragedy with Sophocles. But one cannot have both. Ironically enough, Whitman agrees with Dodds that moralistic interpretations of *Oedipus* grossly misrepresent what is going on in *Oedipus*, but he traces these Victorian interpretations back to Aristotle himself. He wants to pin the "tragic flaw" interpretation of Greek tragedy onto the tail of the Aristotelian donkey. It is Aristotle bringing naïve morality and poetic justice to the game of theatre and art that is at the origin of all these misunderstandings.

Philosophers like Dodds and Sachs both dismiss Whitman's claim that Aristotle could be behind such moralistic nonsense with evident irritation. But, as we shall see, Whitman's assertion that Aristotle was trying to rescue tragedy from the moral criticisms of Plato and his school is not far off the mark. Where Whitman goes wrong is in his over-enthusiastic insistence that ancient Greek drama is without moral content. Any careful student of literature understands that a commitment to truth must, at times, disturb the tranquil sleep of the dogmatic moralist. It is a serious error, however, to go to the opposite extreme and to interpret *Greek tragedy* in completely amoral terms. I will argue that we cannot properly understand or appreciate what Sophocles intends without coming to grips with the deliberate moral content of *Oedipus*. I do not mean to suggest that Greek tragedy is, in any simplistic sense, didactic. If overly pious

---

80. Whitman, *Sophocles*, 35–36.

schoolboy and schoolgirl readings of the "tragic flaw" interpretation are implausible, more sophisticated ideas about poetic justice make a great deal more sense than commentators such as Whitman make it sound.

5.9. Missing the Mark: The Aristotelian Mean

It seems unfortunate that the general debate about Aristotle's *Poetics* has been sidetracked into a philological focus on Aristotle's use of the term *hamartia*. Whatever one makes of the various arguments, this academic approach relies on a technical perspective that is too narrow to settle the deeper questions. Gould nicely captures what we can take away from the debate:

> That the word *hamartia* in Poetics 13 means an unavoidable mistake in the facts is confidently believed by the majority of critics today. [...] Now there is no doubt that the word taken in isolation, might mean "mistake in fact," that *hamartema* does mean that, both in key passages in Aristotle's own writing and also in interesting passages in the tragedies themselves. But it is also true that the word can mean a catastrophic error for which one can blame oneself morally and this use, too can be found in Aristotle (e.g. *Nic. Eth.* 3.110b28ff) and in a tragedy (e.g. *Antigone* 126ff). It is simply not possible to find a conclusive answer to the puzzle of the *Poetics* 13 by studying the various uses of the word *hamartia* and adding to that only our own understanding of what in fact does happen in the tragedies.[81]

In all this debate, a much larger point goes unnoticed. Although Aristotle may use the *hamartia* family of words sparingly in his work, the concept is, we could even say, the linchpin of his ethics for Aristotle's virtue ethics revolve around the key idea that morality is a matter of hitting the mark and immorality is a matter of "missing the mark" (the

---

81. Gould, "Innocence," 514.

original meaning of *hamartia*). Aristotle argues that the virtuous individual needs to *aim* at the golden mean, a middle spot on a vertical line that extends between opposite vices. Agents who succeed at morality must hit the mark; agents who *miss the mark*, fail at morality.

Roger Crisp translates a key passage from the *Nicomachean Ethics*:

> Virtue is concerned with feelings and actions, in which excess and deficiency constitute misses of the mark [ἁμαρτάνεται], while the mean is praised and on target, both of which are characteristics of virtue. Virtue then is a kind of mean, at least in the sense that it is the sort of thing that is able to hit a mean.[82]

Leave aside *Oedipus* and Aristotle's conception of tragedy for a moment. It is important to note how the concept of "missing the mark" is omnipresent in Aristotle's ethics. Consider the virtue of courage, for example. Aristotle comments: "One kind of missing the mark [ἁμαρτιῶν] is to fear the wrong things, another to fear in the wrong way, another to fear at the wrong time, and so on. [...] and the same goes for what inspires confidence."[83] When we fear the wrong things, *we miss the mark*; when we are overly confident, *we miss the mark*. In neither case, do we act morally. When it comes to virtue and vice in general, Aristotle advises that "one can miss the mark [ἁμαρτάνειν] in many ways [...] but one can get things right in only one way for which reason [...] missing the target is easy, hitting it difficult."[84]

Consider more examples. Aristotle writes, for instance, that "the wasteful person misses the mark [διαμαρτάνει: a

---

82. *Nicomachean Ethics* (Crisp) II.6.1106b24–27.
83. *Nicomachean Ethics* (Crisp) III.7.1115b14–17.
84. I have emended "unlimited" for "infinite." *Nicomachean Ethics* (Crisp) II.6.1106b29–34.

strengthened form of ἁμαρτάνω]."[85] That "the number of people who miss the mark [ἁμαρτάνουσι] in the case of natural appetites is low, and they do so only in the direction of excess."[86] Again, in a reference to behaviours that are always wrong—"spite, shamelessness, envy, [...] adultery, theft, homicide"—he comments that those guilty of such behaviours "can never hit the mark, but always miss [ἁμαρτάνειν]."[87] This also explains Aristotle's famous use of the archer metaphor. As he expresses the thought, "if we, like archers, have a target [the mean], are we not more likely to hit the right mark [τυγχάνοιμεν]?"[88]

Aristotle is using the *hamartia* vocabulary in his ethics and, more importantly, the general idea it represents, when discussing the golden mean. When do we act morally? When we hit the mark. And when do we act immorally? When we miss the mark. Surely, Aristotle would have had this understanding in the back of his mind when discussing tragedy.

Of course, Oedipus's parricide and, indeed, his murders are not ordinary matters of misjudging or missing the mean. To talk like that trivializes what he did. Oedipus's acts are (in a technical sense) brutish acts (except that his ignorance of the facts complicates the situation). In any case, the mean is only indirectly about acts; it is, more precisely, about character states. Where Oedipus misses the mean is that he aims at *megalopsychia*, at greatness of soul, as I explain below. But he fails to be a great-souled person—he misses the mark—in that he overshoots and ends up possessing hubris rather than proper pride.

Aristotle tells us that the protagonists in really good tragedies "miss the mark" in a conspicuously calamitous but not thoroughly evil way. Given the central role this metaphor plays in his virtue ethics, how could any such suggestion be entirely without moral colour? We compartmentalize our thoughts on

---

85. *Nicomachean Ethics* (Crisp) IV.2.1121a8.
86. *Nicomachean Ethics* (Crisp) III.11.1118b15.
87. *Nicomachean Ethics* (Crisp) II.6.1107a9–17 ff.
88. *Nicomachean Ethics* (Crisp) I.2.1094a25.

different topics; there is always some overlap, something from other subject matters and discussions that bleeds through. But we will return to the question of *hamartia* again below. For the moment, let us shift our focus to other relevant issues. As I suggest next, carefully examining Sophocles's play brings to light Oedipus's unambiguous moral faults.

5.10. Oedipus's Passion for Truth?

In commentary on Oedipus, one discovers a great deal of special pleading intended to exonerate Oedipus from any wrongdoing. One of the strategies used to demonstrate Oedipus's innocence begins with an acknowledgment of some of the morally questionable aspects of Oedipus's character— his anger issues, his pride, his reckless haste, his obsessive behaviour, his irreverence, his refusal to heed advice—but then quickly excuses them in light of the strained circumstances or, turning morality upside down, portrays them as a noble example of what the Greeks conceived of as a manly, princely character in a bygone age. This approach effectively scuttles moral interpretations of Aristotle that would see Oedipus punished for any vice, any fault of character, or any crime. But even if it were the case, as Kirkwood overconfidently asserts, "scarcely anyone doubts that Oedipus is morally innocent,"[89] no one can overlook disagreeable traits of character in the Theban king.

The notion of Oedipus as selfless truth-seeker is a staple trope in the exoneration literature. Dawe writes, for example, that "the tragic element in Sophocles' treatment of the story must lie in Oedipus' insistence on finding out the truth," and that "Oedipus' *hamartia* consists in his repeated resolve" to discover the truth.[90] Bernard Knox, for his part, tells us that Oedipus:

---

89. Kirkwood, *A Study of Sophoclean Drama*, 276.
90. Dawe, 117–118.

represents all that is intelligent, vigorous, courageous, and creative in man. In his relentless pursuit of the truth he shows his true greatness; all the powers of intellect and energy which make him a hero are exhibited in his lonely, stubborn progress to knowledge. [...] No man [...] can look on Oedipus, even when he is most ignorant and blind, without sympathy. For Oedipus represents man's greatness.[91]

Sachs too takes up the refrain, in his turn, telling us that "it makes no sense to say that Oedipus' *passion for truth* is a flaw," adding as a needless rejoinder that "tragedy is never about flaws, and it is only the silliest of mistranslations that puts that claim in Aristotle's mouth."[92]

But a sensitive reader of the play must wonder. Oedipus's relentless pursuit of the truth is less reasoned inquiry and more irrational obsession. Even if we could say that furiously digging out whatever truth at whatever the cost is always a good thing—obviously, it is not—Oedipus's heedless, self-absorbed, headstrong pursuit of what he wants to know (despite religious advice to cease and desist) is heavily tainted by his feverish pride. Oedipus wants to be the saviour of Thebes for a second time. He has decided this on his own, without consulting the gods. As he insultingly remarks to the blind oracle (the gods' representative): "It was I, Oedipus [...] who stopped the Sphinx, who triumphed through my own intelligence, not [through] the help of gods or birds [omens]."[93] This is, for the pagan Greeks, irreverent hubris. Oedipus is a headstrong man. Oracles, religion, tradition, good sense, other people's opinions—or anything else that stands in his way, be damned! He will save the city, on his

---

91. Knox, *Oedipus at Thebes*, 50–51.
92. Sachs, "Aristotle: Poetics."
93. *Oedipus* (Fainlight and Littman), 396–398. A very readable recent translation. The line numbers are the same as for the Greek text, with a few exceptions for the chorus.

own, through his own cleverness and detective powers, a second time. He will be the saviour of Thebes raised to a power of two. It is not difficult to imagine ancient Greek audiences viewing this not merely as hubris but as insane hubris.

Oedipus's obsession with solving the dark riddle of his crime whatever the consequences could be construed as another instance of ἄτη [atê], the spirit of ruin and destruction that the Greek gods visited on those who displeased them. As the *New Companion to Greek Tragedy* explains, ἄτη is "punishment for crime, sometimes for hubris. [...] Such destruction may [...] be brought about by some fatal infatuation or mental blindness. [...] When the gods wish to punish a person for a crime, [...] they may visit him with infatuation so that he brings destruction on himself."[94] This seems to be precisely what happens to Oedipus. He is "infatuated" with his own kingly role as detective, judge, and jury; he aims to take care of moral business on his own, without the gods interfering. A serious miscalculation as it turns out.

At the beginning of the play, the impetuous Oedipus scoffs at dark rumours and holy warnings: "Learn then that I will not be named a murderer."[95] As the plot progresses and the worrisome evidence piles up, he will not relent. He works himself up to a frenzy, unwittingly pursuing his own destruction. Once he—as the great king—has decided what he is going to do, nothing can stop him. He ignores the oracle; he will not listen to his wife's or the shepherd's pleas. In the play, Sophocles himself explicitly attributes ἄτη to Oedipus at the moment when, having discovered his own guilt, he blinds himself in a furious frenzy. Different translations variously render the Greek term as "ruin," "madness," "woe," "destruction," "bewilderment, mischief, ruin."[96] But the concept of

---

94. Brown, *New Companion to Greek Tragedy*, s.v. *ātē*, 46–47.
95. *Oedipus* (Fainlight and Littman), 576.
96. *Oedipus* 1284. Translators such as Fainlight, Littman, Richard Jebb, E. H. Plumptre, David Grene, Geoffrey Steadman, Ian Johnston.

ἄτη explains what is going on throughout the play, not just in the final instances where ἄτη, we could say, climaxes.

If, of course, Oedipus is afflicted by ἄτη, modern defenders of Oedipus may think this lets him off the hook. Since the gods are devising his destruction, he cannot be held responsible for whatever grandiose exaggerations or delusions they visit on him. Except that this is not how the ancient Greeks understood things. As one reference work observes:

> 'Atê' is explained by the agency of the gods [...] like anything else which 'comes over' a man from outside his conscious personality. This does not mean, however, that a man is not accountable for reckless or criminal acts committed under the influence of such infatuation; in a famous passage of Homer (*Iliad* 19. 78-144) Agamemnon accepts blame for the quarrel with Achilles precisely because Zeus sent '*atê*' to take away his wits.[97]

In the Greek mind, ἄτη is fundamentally about justice. The gods rightfully punish those who break the moral laws of religion and the cosmos by inflicting them with such bouts of self-possessed ruin. If, then, we are to interpret Sophocles's *Oedipus* the way it was intended to be interpreted at the time, we must hold Oedipus responsible for the spirit of reckless impulse and self-pride that eventually pulls him down the path to his spectacular ruin.

We must not misunderstand. If the goddess Ἄτη, personified as the eldest daughter of Zeus, spends her time fomenting troubles and cultivating folly and mischief among humans, this is not a *deus ex machina* explanation in the sense of something that *only* comes from the outside to rearrange the playing pieces on the tragic chessboard. Ἄτη happens *in*

This is interestingly ironic, because in blinding himself physically, he finally sees with his mind what he has done. His "madness" is rationality, and his "confusion" is correct insight.

97. Brown, s.v. "ātē, 47.

accordance with nature. When the gods intervene, the natural propensities of individuals are pushed further, in natural directions. It is like a snowball rolling downhill. The gods give an extra push—so that snowball rolls even faster. But it was already headed in that direction.

As I discuss below, Oedipus is not a mere puppet of the gods. Sophocles portrays him as formidable, proud, angry, aristocratic; he is used to being in charge of his own and others' destinies. He is a spirited (*thymoeidic*) man, a born leader, a noble presence with a sense of authority and a regal bearing. Still, he is too sure of himself; he is human, not divine. He pushes himself too far both in his early and later life and, throughout the play, refuses to heed multiple warnings from the gods (another feature of ἄτη). Oedipus himself complains, in retrospect, that it was the gods that made him do it (specifically Apollo).[98] But this is another instance of impiety. In setting himself up as the "saviour" of Thebes raised to the power of two, independent from and even equal to the gods, Oedipus is guilty of the archetypical Greek fault of hubris.

5.11. Human Agency in Oedipus and Ancient Greek Culture

There is a caricature that surfaces, with surprising frequency, in academic literature, according to which the ancient Greeks lacked any developed sense of self. In a recent paper on ethics. David Richards explains:

> It was [...] the common sense of ancient Greece, which Plato and Aristotle understandably shared, that humans do not, in general, have what contemporary ego psychology denominates a developed ego (i.e., the executive capacity to formulate an integrated plan of life and pursue it as an

---

98. "Apollo, my friends, it was Apollo who made me do these acts which caused such suffering." *Oedipus* (Fainlight and Littman), strophe B, 1329–1330.

independent person). The general view of personal competence of the ancient Greeks suggests [a] fragmented ego, [a] 'divided self'—generally passive, with appetites, emotions, and intellect [, each] isolated [...] [and] unintegrated by any coherent higher-order planner within the self. Rather than integration from within, the Greeks supposed that each person, internally divided and vulnerable, depended for the order of his life on his *agathos*, the noble man, on whom the *kakos* [the ill-born, mean, ignoble man] depended to provide the order of his life that the *kakos* was constitutionally unable to [derive] from internal resources of the self. Certain exceptional people might achieve something close to the contemporary concept of developed ego strength [...] but they were rare, exceptional, god-like, the natural rulers of society. Correlatively, Greek political theory understandably focuses on rule by the best. The fundamental Greek vision is that of Plato's *Republic*: the ruler, a benevolent physician who alone understands the health of the balanced human organism, has unlimited power to realize the desirable health which [individual] humans cannot realize on their own. Such a benevolent physician may quite completely control the life of the disabled patient, as in chattel slavery and the institutionalized subjection of woman, both of which Aristotle justifies.[99]

Sophocles's Oedipus is just the sort of "benevolent physician" ruler Richards has in mind. His play is about healing physical ailments—the plague and pestilence that has settled on the city—by a moral remedy put in place by the great ruler, the local *agathos*. The paradoxical plot unfolds according to the strict demands of retributive justice: A serious evil needs to be met with an equally serious punishment (at the very end of the play) to set things right again. Kant would approve. If, however, one cannot make decent sense of what is happening here except in moral terms, Richards goes too far.

---

99. Richards, "Rights and Autonomy," 8–9.

The audience at the play was fully capable of understanding the requirements for moral agency and identifying with the moral predicament of a bigger-than-life character like Oedipus.

Richards's account of ancient Greek attitudes relies on a familiar stereotype that eliminates what we now call "autonomy." As if external, foreign factors determine how we individually act. But ancient philosophers attribute autonomy to those of moderate ability and to citizens generally. Athens was, after all, a direct-participation democracy that enabled a degree of civic participation unknown in modern mega-states. Socrates walks around Athens, trying to make people think for themselves. Like other ancient philosophers, he views the naïve conformism of the masses as a moral failure, as something to be resisted, not as a metaphysical reality that must be.

If the condition of women and slaves in ancient Greece is not to be envied, they were not as two-dimensional or as passive as Richards seems to suggest. Sophocles presents Antigone as a very strong-willed and independent character. Even slaves in ancient Greece were capable of some semblance of autonomy. As the *Life of Aesop* or *The Book of Xanthus the Philosopher and Aesop His Slave* (fourth century BC?) demonstrates, peasants and slaves were not passive, colourless, unintelligent beings without higher-order plans.[100] In the Aesop story, the illiterate peasant outwits the princely academic philosopher. Diogenes the Cynic, the philosopher-qua-homeless-man, is another example of non-aristocratic intellectualism in Athens; the presence of courtesans in Epicurus's circle, though scandalous, demonstrates a more egalitarian view of the female sex. Socrates's reliance on Diotima in the *Symposium* (a mythical figure but, nonetheless, a female) and his unapologetic identification

---

100. The *Vita* depicts a resourceful, independent, sharp-witted peasant slave who continually outwits his noble, academic-philosopher master to shrewdly achieve his own self-interested ends.

with his midwife mother Phaenarete (*not* his father) also demonstrate a more respectful series of gender relations. Finally, Aristotle's acknowledgment that some slaves are *not* slaves by nature and his own personal initiative of freeing his slaves in his *Last Will and Testament* as well as his insistence that man and wife must be friends (i.e., share in some kind of equality) points to a more complicated situation than Richards suggests.[101]

What Sophocles's Oedipus, the *agathos*, the great ruler of Thebes, lacks is not autonomy. If anything, Oedipus possesses too much autonomy. His actions betray, to use Richards's clinical-sounding language, a highly developed sense of self and a conspicuous capacity for pursuing self-chosen goals. Oedipus possesses "the executive capacity to formulate an integrated plan of life and pursue it as an independent person." He is brimming over with agency and busies himself with securing the welfare and liberation of Thebes, first, by defeating the Sphinx and, second, by his investigation into the murder.[102] Sophocles presents him, not quite as everyman, but as "every-king" or, better, the "every-tyrant," who is too sure of himself, too self-confident, too filled with self-absorbed agency to avoid secular disaster.

In Sophocles's play at least, we do not witness a human being acted on by purely external forces; the gods may play an implacable, moralistic role in the background but all the characters, as Aristotle would have required, act according to their character type. They do not control all that happens, but they are a potent source of their own agency and, in Oedipus's case, their own self-destruction. The fact that the Pythian oracle had "made terrible forecasts" that Oedipus was

---

101. One could amass more evidence but leave that for other times and places.
102. It is a mistake to think that only aristocrats were capable of such displays. The whole point of the *Vita* of Aesop, who repeatedly comes up with the shrewd solution to riddles and puzzles, is to show that natural intelligence—from an ugly slave and a mere peasant no less—defeats effete, academic, aristocratic learning almost every time.

doomed to sleep with his mother and murder his father does not eliminate free will.[103] Contrary to a common assumption, fate (in the religious sense of τύχη) is not incompatible with free will. The gods know everything (or just about everything) even before it happens. But the fact that they communicate to the oracle how Oedipus will behave does not eliminate his free exercise of choice. It does not follow that Oedipus's bad behaviour is forced on him by truthful prophecy but only that his self-made behaviour confirms the truthful prophecy. Suppose I know, for example, that a colleague is an inveterate liar. I have seen him tell lies many times in that past; I know how he operates. The fact that I can successfully predict that he will tell a lie tomorrow does not make me responsible for his dishonesty.

Ruth Scodel writes, "The nature of Oedipus is a necessary component of his fate. […] [His] character is necessary for the disaster, and he acts freely both within the drama and in the events he recounts. He is no puppet."[104] Alister Cameron abounds in the same sense:

> It is a commonplace to speak of Oedipus' fate as being given. But […] the implication [in the play] is that whenever Oedipus' fate occurs, […] Oedipus is characteristically active in it. We cannot then speak of a given fate without also speaking of a given character. In fact, the implication [is] that it is nonsense to speak of Oedipus' fate […] without his being active and alive in it.[105]

Cameron resists claims about Oedipus's moral innocence because,

> Such a reading of Oedipus simply removes him from the action, takes him out of the play. […] Oedipus is not a

---

103. *Oedipus* (Fainlight and Littman) 790–793.
104. Scodel, *Sophocles*, 67–68.
105. Cameron, *The Identity of Oedipus the King*, 131.

> man who is assailed by fate or waits until it comes upon him; on the contrary, he seizes his fate and throws the whole force of his personality into it. [...] In the fullest sense Oedipus' fate belongs to him. [...] [We cannot] fail to see what we should call a fitness in him or even an aptitude for what happens.[106]

Aristotle writes, "All who are not maimed as regards their potentiality for excellence [virtue] may win excellence by a certain kind of study and care. [...] To entrust to chance [fate, τύχη] what is greatest and most noble would be a very defective arrangement."[107] Human success or failure is not a matter of passively acquiescing to what one is given without individual effort.[108] It follows that Oedipus has to shoulder at least some responsibility for his impulsive character and the unnatural behaviours that result. If Oedipus is an arrogant, hasty, politically ambitious agent, these character traits are what he has chosen for himself as a way of life. There are no grounds for seeing Sophocles's Oedipus as someone forced into the unfortunate behaviour that seals his fate.

Aristotle does accept that there are external factors outside our control that may, in unusual circumstances, thwart any reasonable possibility of personal success. He uses Priam, defeated king of Troy and father of slain Hector, as an example of someone so beset by misfortunes that he cannot be happy. He observes, "many changes occur in life [...] and the most prosperous may fall into great misfortunes in old age, as is told of Priam in the Trojan Cycle; and no one calls someone happy who has experienced such happenstance and has ended wretchedly."[109] Could Aristotle, then, have

---

106. Cameron, *Identity*, 132–133.
107. *Nicomachean Ethics* (Ross) I.9.1099b18–20.
108. For example, he quips, "men fancy that external goods are the cause of happiness, yet we might as well say that a brilliant performance on the lyre was to be attributed to the instrument and not the skill of the performer." *Politics* (Jowett) VII.13.1332a25–27.
109. *Nicomachean Ethics* (Ross) I.9.1099b32–1100a9.

thought of *Oedipus* as a tragedy due to circumstances beyond the protagonist's control? Could Oedipus be another Priam?

Priam tells Achilles, "I have endured what no one on earth has ever done before."[110] Surely, one could say something similar about Oedipus. But then the comparison stalls. Priam suffers because of what happens to him, Oedipus suffers because of what he has done (as I explain below). In the Greek mindset at least, Oedipus's unnatural actions (whatever their origin) are so unsavoury as to be almost incomprehensible. He is like a circus freak. Whoever is at fault, what he has done is abominable. Priam is a good father, a good king; he is not guilty of the unnatural crimes. He gets caught up in events much bigger than himself. Paris, his impetuous, sinful son provides a much better parallel to Oedipus. Oedipus is not another Priam; these are not equivalent cases.

5.12. Oedipus the Tyrant

Sophocles's play, Οἰδίπους Τύραννος [*Oedipus the Tyrant*], has long been referred to as *Oedipus Rex* or *Oedipus the King*. This is a bit of a misnomer. Sophocles's Oedipus is not merely a king [βασιλεύς] but a tyrant [τύραννος]. At least in Athenian discourse, the term tyrant can have pejorative or neutral associations. Vincent Rosivach explains:

> On the non-political level, the tyrant was seen, for example, as wealthy, immoral, or self-indulgent. Here the emphasis is on what tyranny allows its possessor to become, and not on tyranny itself as a political institution, i.e. as one form of government as opposed to another. At other times, however, the emphasis is on the tyrant, not as ogre, but simply as sole ruler, especially as one who can do as he chooses free from external restraints. In contexts such as these the words *tyrannos* and *tyrannis* sometimes appear with no pejorative overtones, as e.g. in the fragments of Gorgias and in Isocrates' pieces addressed to the

---

110. *Iliad* (Fagles) XXIV.590.

> Cyprian ruler Evagoras and his son. These neutral uses of *tyrannos* suggest that, at least originally, the word meant simply "monarch", and that if one found monarchic rule distasteful the word was accordingly pejorative, while if, like Isocrates and Evagoras, one had no objections to such rule, the word itself was not.[111]

In original Greek usage, the king–tyrant distinction does not hinge so much on a good ruler vs. bad ruler comparison. It is more that the tyrant is a self-made ruler; he is someone from outside the traditional power structure who shrewdly (and, usually, forcefully) manages to insert himself into a governing role. The tyrant is, likely, a Machiavellian character. He rules through decree, not through proper law. Through clever scheming and the use of force, he is able to take over a city-state and appoint himself as ruler with all power concentrated in himself. He is not there because of royal lineage (appointed by the local gods) or because of constitutional protocol. He has assumed power—not necessarily, though often, by nefarious means—through some irregular, shrewd, bold strategy of his own ambitious devising. Of course, once he has total control, this often (if not usually) leads to moral excess.

As for Oedipus, he appears to come to power as a foreigner in Thebes. Unbeknownst to anyone at the beginning of the play or to Oedipus himself, he is a rightful heir to power. But this is not the role he plays. Oedipus appears in the play as someone who comes from outside the community; he is a foreigner who takes control over another city. This is momentous. Modern readers (like Freud) sometimes focus on the lurid sexual content of the play and overlook the political sense of what is happening. But Sophocles and his intended audience were probably focused on the political implications. When Oedipus is acclaimed king and marries his mother, Jocasta, this is, first and foremost, a political move. It is a power alliance. What better way to win or at

---

111. Rosivach, "Tyrant in Athenian Democracy," 44–45.

least reinforce his legitimate right to kingship after Laius's death than to marry the queen. The marriage brings him into the royal family and makes him, *ipso facto*, the king of Thebes.

In the Greek mind, tyrants are not necessarily evil but power-hungry and ambitious. Sophocles's Oedipus is certainly power-hungry. After he wins the right to rule by defeating the Sphinx and marrying the queen, he has no intention of giving up that role. At the beginning of Sophocles's play, the suspicious Oedipus confronts his brother-in-law Creon (another hothead), whom he imagines is secretly plotting to overthrow his power. The passage reveals the mind of a tyrant, as a Greek audience would have immediately understood. Oedipus yells at Creon:

> You—wretch—how dare you show your face?
> are you so shameless that you come to my house
> openly, [...] [you] who schemes to rob me of my kingdom?
> By the gods—do you regard me
> as such a fool and coward that you can do these things,
> or think that I would not guess your most secret
> plans and then protect myself?
> What a stupid plan—without
> the backing of party and fortune and friends —
> to think you could track and seize the crown.[112]

It is not just that Oedipus is factually mistaken. Creon is not plotting to overthrow him. It is that tyrants being self-made men, without the support of the usual political process, were worried about holding on to power. They often resorted to manipulative schemes to preserve their precarious perch on the top of the political ladder (something Plato mentions).[113] Aristotle mentions the well-known strategy of asking for a bodyguard, which could then be turned against the

---

112. *Oedipus* (Fainlight and Littman) 532–542.
113. Cf. Book IX of the *Republic*.

populace.[114] Oedipus is a good tyrant; he has, it seems, the welfare of the city uppermost in his mind. Yet, at the same time, he is clearly a political animal. He knows how to get and maintain power and mocks Creon because he thinks his rival is not crafty enough to achieve his own political goals.

In further dialogue with Creon, the political relationship between Oedipus and the queen comes to the fore:

> Creon: Yet, did you not take my sister for wife?
> Oedipus: How can I deny it?
> Creon: And rule with equal power, you and she, over this land?
> Oedipus: She has an equal share in everything.
> Creon: And therefore am I not also equal to you both, one third of three?
> Oedipus: Now you show your true thoughts—treacherous fiend![115]

Note that the equality between male and female portrayed here hardly conforms to the inherited stereotype frequently invoked about male-female relations in Greek antiquity. But, politically, what is going on here? Oedipus suspects that Creon, brother of the queen, wants an equal share in the ruling power. But successful tyrants keep competitors as far away from the throne as possible. Oedipus accepts to rule with the queen, a strategic source of political legitimacy, but not with Creon. He insults Creon, calling him a "treacherous fiend" (κακὸς φίλος, an evil [false] friend), but that is not enough. The dialogue continues:

> Creon: What do you want? To banish me?
> Oedipus: Exile is not enough. I want your death. […]
> Creon: That's what envy leads to.[116]

---

114. *Rhetoric* (Roberts) I.2.1357b25-36.
115. *Oedipus* (Fainlight and Littman) 577-582.
116. *Oedipus* (Fainlight and Littman) 622-625. (There is a line missing from the text.)

Keep in mind that, for an ancient Greek, even exile is an extremely harsh penalty. Socrates, for example, prefers a death sentence to exile at his trial. If, however, Creon was sent into exile, he could eventually return and contest Oedipus's power anew. So, Oedipus, on the basis of very hasty suspicions, without any formal inquiry or judicial process, demands his rival's immediate death. (So much for Oedipus the truth seeker.) He only relents at the request of the queen. He tells her:

> It is *not* his words [Creon's] that move me but yours.
> Wherever he is, I shall always hate him.[117]

Oedipus has set himself up as the absolute sovereign (with the queen's connivance) of Thebes and is jealously guarding his power. He and Creon continue their heated exchange:

> Creon: And you understand nothing.
> Oedipus: Except that I am king and rule.
> Creon: –Rule badly.
> Oedipus: O city! My City!
> Creon: My city also, not only yours![118]

This is successful tyranny. Oedipus, the usurper, has assumed total control of Thebes. He says it is "My City!" when he has been accepted as a foreigner (a big deal in the Greek scheme of things). The queen's brother, Creon, who has a legitimate family claim to power, has been pushed to the outside. If he is upset by such political machinations, he can only complain from the sidelines.

To Sophocles's audience, this tyrannical consolidation of political power would be intrinsically worrisome. Contrary to the caricature Richards relies on above, the Athenian citizens vigorously prized ἐλευθερία, liberty. They saw themselves as

---

117. *Oedipus* (Fainlight and Littman) 672 (my italics).
118. *Oedipus* (Fainlight and Littman) 628–630.

free men and jealously guarded their individual autonomy. (Hence, their traditional use of formal ostracism.) Tyrants were known for wanting full control; they aimed to wrest political power from the established structures. To make matters worse, Oedipus is depicted as a *Theban* tyrant, which means that he was, for Athenian audiences, a semi-barbarian; recognizably Greek but provincial, half-wild, unsavoury, and a quasi-enemy, all at the same time. After all, Thebes had aided Xerxes in the Persian wars and was an ally of the enemy Sparta in the contemporaneous Peloponnesian conflict.

Tyrants have always had a reputation for being more concerned about their own political careers than the common good. Plato treats a tyrant-ruled city [τυραννουμένη πόλις] and a king-ruled city [βασιλευομένην] as "direct contraries."[119] If the king-ruled city is the best form of government (because the king takes care of the whole community), the tyrant-ruled city is the worst (because the tyrant takes care of himself). Aristotle theorizes in the same direction, defining tyranny [τυραννίς] as "a kind of monarchy [μοναρχία] [...] which has in view the interest of the monarch only."[120]

Oedipus's attitudes reinforce these negative views. Worried that, in the course of his investigations, he may eventually discover that he is born to "three generations of slaves," Oedipus decides that he will not be intimidated by any such finding.[121] As he tells the chorus:

> As for myself,
> no matter how base born my family,
> I wish to know the seed from where I came.
> Perhaps my queen is now ashamed of me
> and of my insignificant origin—

---

119. *Republic* 576d.
120. *Politics* (Jowett) III.7.1279b6–8.
121. Oedipus tells the queen, "Be brave woman! Even if I am proved three times a slave, from three generations a slave, that will not make you base-born." *Oedipus* (Fainlight and Littman) 1062–1063.

> she likes to play the noble lady.
> But I will never feel myself dishonoured.
> I see myself as a child of fortune [Τύχης], —
> and she is generous, that mother of mine
> from whom I spring, and the months, my siblings,
> have seen me by turns both small and great.
> That's how I was born. I cannot change
> to someone else, nor can I ever cease
> from seeking out the facts of my own birth.[122]

We need to look at the passage with ancient eyes. Grene adds a footnote: "Since Fortune, or good luck, saved him from death, Oedipus refuses to feel shame at being illegitimate or of humble origins."[123] Whether Τύχη here is a sincere reference to the goddess or mere random luck (which would be impious), this is the mindset of a tyrant; it does not matter if I was born a slave—even if I am descended from slaves all the way back. In Oedipus's mind, as long as a slave has personal talent, political boldness, and cunning—he has the right to rule. Although we moderns might look kindly on such meritocratic notions, this would have seemed, to an ordinary ancient citizen of Athens, like lunacy. Oedipus is doubly impious, because he mocks religious belief and practice and because—like Callicles, Thrasymachus, Critias, and Alcibiades—he seems more than ready to ignore the institutions and customs blessed by the local gods and reconfigure political power in line with his own human plans and desires.

There is a political dimension to Oedipus's killing of his own father that is often overlooked. Leaving aside the issue of intention for the moment, the guilty act is not mere murder; it is also regicide. Although Oedipus does not know that the man was his father, he would have known that he was a king,

---

122. *Oedipus the King* (Ian Johnston) 1294–1305.
123. *Oedipus* (Grene) n. 62. But Fortune, of course, did much more than save him from death; it brought him to Thebes where propitious circumstances set his political career in motion.

for Sophocles tells us that, when Laius was killed, he was surrounded by a courtly procession and preceded by a herald who would have announced who he was. But the killing of a foreign king is a heinous act and a matter of abject political subversion. Although one may try to diminish the added complication of patricide by tracing it to ignorance of the facts, the political ramifications of Oedipus's killing spree are not so easily dismissed. However rude the royal entourage, Oedipus's rebellious attitude and disrespect for authority is blatant and obvious. It is a matter of proper political etiquette to allow a king to pass first. In ancient history, power-hungry tyrants regularly killed kings to usurp their power and seize political control. The mere fact that Oedipus is unwilling to give way to a courtly parade (in a foreign country) illustrates his obstreperousness.

The ancient world emphasized piety as the ultimate virtue. It is not merely that tyrants plot and assassinate to undermine local authority (which they do). One cannot disconnect the link, in the ancient mind, between tyranny and abject immorality. In Plato especially, the tyrant's drive to power originates in ungoverned appetites. (Plato's tyrant is, paradoxically, an ungoverned governor.) What this means for Plato is that the tyrant has allowed his animal appetites to enslave his rationality. He is driven by sensuality and greed for power. Whereas Sophocles presents Oedipus as a sexually cold tyrant, Plato associates the Oedipus of legend with unleashed carnal appetites. In an obvious reference, he describes how the human soul "can bring itself to do absolutely anything" in dreams when reason has gone to sleep. Without a rational guide, "it has no hesitation in attempting sexual intercourse with its mother," and "there is no murder it will not commit."[124] Later in the same text, Socrates points out that the tyrannical man is in a sleeping, irrational state "in his waking hours."[125]

---

124. *Republic* (Griffith) IX.571c–d.
125. *Republic* IX. 576b.

Sophocles downplays this sexualized aspect of the story. In the play, Queen Jocasta shrugs off Oedipus's worries about the unsettling prophecy that he will sleep with his mother. "Many a man has slept with his mother in his dreams," she tells him. "He who dismisses such thoughts lives easiest."[126] This is, on another level, a dig at the gods—to ignore divination and embrace a commonplace naturalism to explain disturbing dreams would have seemed impious to ancient audiences. Sophocles presents Jocasta's lazy indifference, not as a model of morality, but as another aspect of self-destructive impiety.

Doubtless, the best literature does not reduce the complexities of human life to a moralistic caricature. It explores them with dispassionate, even scientific detachment. Sophocles's literary genius lies, in part, in the way he is able to strip away the Platonic caricature and present Oedipus as someone who is not revelling in flagrant immorality, at least not knowingly. If, however, Sophocles presents a more morally ambiguous case of tyranny than the stark depiction of Plato, Thebes is in a most wretched state. Why? The gods are visiting evil on Thebes because Oedipus slept with his mother and slew his father the way men do in irrational, libertine dreams. Of course, the literary twist is that he did not know he was doing this. Still, Oedipus's unnatural offences are an objective fact. So, in a strange way, the city is, indeed, suffering because of the evil tyranny.

5.13. Oedipus Killing Laius

I have already discussed some of the scholarly debate surrounding Aristotle's ascription of a *hamartia* or fatal flaw to the protagonist in a tragedy. Dodds writes, "The ἀμαρτία of Oedipus [...] lay quite simply in parricide and incest, a μεγάλη ἀμαρτία [big mistake] indeed, the greatest a man can commit."[127] Stinton concurs: "The ἀμαρτία of Oedipus, as is now generally agreed, consists in killing his father and

---

126. *Oedipus* (Fainlight and Littman) 982–983.
127. Dodds, "Misunderstanding," 40.

marrying his mother, a mistake of fact."[128] Neither Dodds nor Stinton believe that this mistake is a moral failing—after all, Oedipus *unknowingly* killed his father and *unknowingly* slept with his mother; what transpires is simply a case of mistaken identity. Perhaps the gods tricked Oedipus, perhaps he was unlucky but, according to this modern bit of wisdom, he cannot be viewed as someone whose moral failures led to a downfall, particularly as he went out of his way to flee from his foster parents in Corinth whom he mistakenly thought were his mother and father. But this is not how the ancient Greeks would have viewed things. Even if Oedipus's fate can be traced to ignorance of who he is and who his parents are (among other things), I will argue that Oedipus is a seriously immoral protagonist. Not a sociopath—not wickedness personified—but most significantly immoral. Considered by the standards of the time, Athenian audiences would have seriously disapproved of Oedipus's character and his conduct.

Consider, then, Oedipus's original crime of parricide. Here is his own description of what happened:

> As I came near to where the three roads join
> I met a herald and a horse-drawn carriage [...]
> and the herald, and the man in the carriage,
> forced me off the road.
> It was the driver, as he tried to turn me aside,
> I struck at first in my anger.
> Then, as I pushed past, the old man
> jabbed from above at my head with his double goad.
> But he paid for this—for now,
> with the staff in my hand, I tumbled him out of the cart
> and onto his back in the road
> and slaughtered them all.[129]

---

128. Stinton, "Hamartia," 238.
129. *Oedipus* (Fainlight and Littman) 801–813.

As Jocasta makes clear: "there were five of them, including a herald, and Laius rode in the carriage."[130] One lucky survivor, it seems, fled, so the final tally was bold Oedipus triumphant with four dead and one in retreat. A stunning physical feat for a lone combatant, outnumbered and seemingly without weapons. Indeed, with a weapon he steals from his enemy.

Despite familiar attempts to sanitize the event, Oedipus's multiple homicide is not a case of virile macho Greek pagan culture expressing itself. This is not a case of ancient cowboys will be ancient cowboys. What he did would have been seen as an abhorrent crime throughout ancient Greece. This is not proper warfare on a battlefield, where there are rules of engagement, where love of country is foremost, where friend and foe are armed for battle, where both sides are on an equal footing, where killing can be fairly described as patriotic duty or even as a matter of courage. This is road rage at an intersection, with arrogant strangers bumping into one another, each too proud to give way, and losing their tempers as a result. This is a case of criminal overreaction, of "overkill" about a trivial matter. Any suggestion that the ancient Greeks would have thought that this was a courageous or even legal is historically inaccurate. What Sophocles shows us is Oedipus lashing out as a haughty, impatient man. He is, no doubt, an immensely powerful warrior-youth, but he is losing his temper over a trifle. The ultimate result—four dead—is ridiculously out of proportion with what was at stake. If Sophocles wanted to portray Oedipus as a glorious Greek warrior, he would have chosen heroic circumstances. This gory set of four murders over a case of something akin to rush-hour traffic is a parody of heroism, not the real thing.

Sophocles gives us a description, then, of road rage, ancient Greek style. He intends this as a case of murderous fury: Oedipus strikes *first* and takes the time to slay everyone—servants and slaves included. Oedipus is technically

---

130. *Oedipus* (Fainlight and Littman) 752.

guilty, not of manslaughter, but of *premeditated* murder. As one internet legal site puts it, "The time you thought on your decision to kill does not have to be long to establish premeditation. And the amount of time between when you formed your intent to kill and the actual killing may be very short."[131] For Oedipus to kill that many people would require multiple intentions. He went about his business mercilessly. He shows no remorse. It is obvious from the description of the event that he wanted to kill them; he did this with deliberation, with full intent—as they say in the courts, "with malice." He planned to use the cudgel to assault his victim and kill all the others after the initial skirmish. This is, by modern standards, at least second-degree murder but maybe even first-degree.

In a paper on the intricacies of ancient Athenian social life, Michael Gagarin points to a possible argument from self-defence actually employed in the ancient Athenian law courts. He explains:

> We know that one possible defense against a charge of homicide in Athens was a plea of simple self-defense. Demosthenes refers to the case of Euaion, who killed a certain Boiotos at a dinner party in retaliation for a single blow and was later convicted (presumably of homicide) by one vote. As further evidence we have in Antiphon's *Third Tetralogy* a hypothetical case in which a man defends himself against a charge of homicide in part by arguing that the victim struck the first blow. We must assume that although the first case resulted in conviction and the second would likely have ended in conviction had the case actually been tried, nonetheless the possibility existed that a plea of self-defense could lead to the killer's acquittal.[132]

---

131. Feldman-Royle, "Homicide: First Degree Murder."
132. Gagarin, "Self-Defense in Athenian Homicide Law," 111.

Sophocles is careful to point out that Oedipus *struck first*, not in retaliation; he initiated the violent conflict, so an argument from self-defence is not available in this case. Viewed from this ancient legal perspective, Oedipus is guilty of murder. Although he was roughly treated, there is no indication that the herald, driver, or even the king tried to kill him. They pushed him off the road—as a police officer might push someone off the road if a procession with the King of England or President of the United States was coming down the street. Oedipus responded to this rough treatment by killing most of them. One escaped in terror. We are left with a picture of a haughty, powerful Oedipus, who takes the initiative and acts lawlessly, without any adequate legal defence in Athenian law.

Apologists may try to pass Oedipus off as a bold warrior; with a little too much θυμός (spiritedness), but an admirable, manly Greek specimen, nonetheless. This is the Nietzschean route. But it is an adolescent male fantasy to think of Athens as a cowboy town, where spear slingers and sword fighters duelled with one another in the streets without moral limits. The ancient city had strict regulations governing homicide.

Aristotle includes murder (ἀνδροφονία: the slaying of men) among those passions and behaviours that are *always* bad: "It is not possible ever to be right with regard to such actions; one must always be wrong. [...] However they are done they are wrong."[133] In the *Athenian Constitution*, he (or his editors) refer to cases of lawful killing—catching an adulterer, mistaken killing in war, accidentally killing a competitor in the Olympic games—but none of these qualifications can apply to Oedipus.[134] Indeed, Oedipus's case is more serious than most, for it did not involve a person of low degree; given the carriage and the herald, Oedipus knew he was killing royalty. This is a much bigger crime in ancient Greece; it has political implications. One is not merely killing the individual; one is "killing" the state.

---

133. *Nicomachean Ethics* (Ross) II.6.1107a11–25.
134. *Athenian Constitution*, 57.iii–iv.

Historian James McGregor explains the legal and social situation in ancient Athens with respect to crime of murder:

> Murder was the most troubling crime to Athenians. [...] Taking a human life was as grave a matter for the Athenians as it is for us, but [...] murder [also] created pollution in the religious sense of the word. This pollution, which was brought on by the private act of spilling blood, ultimately involved the whole community. [...] Every Athenian murderer committed a double crime: one against the victim and his or her family, and another against the gods. It was the community's responsibility to identify the murderer and to expel him or her in order to annul the pollution that spilled blood had created. A case of murder required extreme diligence and also extreme seriousness of purpose. The venerable Council of the Areopagus [...] remained the high court that prosecuted murderers.[135]

I discuss the issue of moral pollution below. For the moment, note that, in the ancient world, there are disastrous religious, moral, and legal ramifications attached to any community connected to the shedding of human blood. Yet, Oedipus intentionally killed four men. He tried to kill five. And, again, he would have known he was killing a king. He spilled blood, in an uncontrolled rage, in a private affair, against a person of high degree, an old man, without knowing who he was killing. This is an obvious instance of hubris; Oedipus did this, not because he had been jabbed at by a stick, but, more fundamentally, because his pride was hurt. He wanted to pass first so he struck first. Ancient communities would have considered this insolence, in the highest degree.

To get a sense of how outrageous Oedipus's behaviour is in ancient eyes, consider an anti-Oedipus figure, Plato's Euthyphro, who knowingly brings a murder charge against

---

135. McGregor, *Athens*, 91.

his father. Viewed from the perspective of the ancient world, Euthyphro is a ludicrous character. One does not initiate court proceedings that might lead to a death sentence against your father. But leave aside the impious nature of what this religious fanatic was trying to do. This is how Euthyphro describes the victim of his father's murder:

> The man who is dead was a poor dependent of mine who worked for us as a field labourer on our farm in Naxos, and one day in a fit of drunken passion he got into a quarrel with one of our domestic servants and slew him. My father bound him hand and foot and threw him into a ditch, and then sent to Athens to ask of a diviner what he should do with him. Meanwhile he never attended to him and took no care about him, for he regarded him as a murderer; and thought that no great harm would be done even if he did die. Now this was just what happened. For such was the effect of cold and hunger and chains upon him, that before the messenger returned from the diviner, he was dead.[136]

There are many mitigating factors here: The man who died was an admitted murderer, a drunkard and troublemaker; he was low-bred and not a citizen; the father did not kill him directly but accidentally; if anything, the father is guilty of negligence, a lesser crime than murder; he was in the process of consulting religious authorities; one could even argue that by his death the gods saw to it that justice was done. And yet, Euthyphro can still bring a charge of murder, which could lead to capital punishment, against his own father.

If, however, Euthyphro's scrupulous standards are far too high, the standards of those who push an amoral interpretation onto Sophocles's Oedipus are far too low. They focus on a single mitigating factor: the fact that Oedipus did not know that the man he was killing was his father. As if killing people other than one's father was excusable. This is to

---

136. *Euthyphro* (Jowett) 4c–d.

seriously underestimate the moral seriousness of homicide in ancient Greece. This is, in part, why Aristotle mentions how unbelievable ἄλογον (inexplicable, absurd) the crime is.[137] It is unbelievable because ancient peoples would have broadcast the shocking news, investigated the incident, hunted down the perpetrator, made temple sacrifices to alleviate the moral pollution, and so on.

Oedipus is a fearfully angry man, which still counts as an instance of conspicuous vice. On Aristotle's account, the protagonist in a tragedy must have serious moral faults but be less than completely evil. Oedipus, as the Theban king, is devoted to the common good (unlike mass murderers or paid assassins), but he is also a rash, arrogant person who disrespects the gods, pushes other people around, and gives vent to violent anger thoughtlessly. He is not pure evil, but he is far from being a moral exemplar or an innocent third party.

Sophocles, who is not always an Aristotelian, walks a careful line. If Oedipus had knowingly killed his father, this would have turned him into a moral monster in Greek eyes. As Aristotle maintains, an audience could not have felt any empathy for him. Still, Oedipus is a prince by birth, an *agathos*, with very serious moral flaws. As we shall see, these princely moral flaws ultimately derive from his own corrupt father. (The Greeks, along with other ancient cultures believed that the sins of the fathers *are* passed onto the sons.) The murder at the intersection is, indeed, poetic justice doubled over, as both father and son, who share the same incontinent, arrogant streak, are involved on opposite ends of a terrible crime.

5.14. Oedipus's Excusable Crimes? Aristotle's Ethical Exceptions

In the *Poetics*, Aristotle puts plot first and character second when it comes to what we observe on the stage.[138] As the plot

---

137. *Poetics* 15.1454b6–8.
138. Plot must come first, for a tragedy is composed "in a dramatic, not in a narrative form." *Poetics* (Bywater) 6.1149b27.

develops, we come to understand who the characters are. In terms of cause-and-effect, however, character comes first, and plot second, for character is the deeper cause of human behaviour. Plot is in the foreground—it is what we see—character, in the background—it is the agency that moulds and shapes what happens.[139] In Greek tragedy generally, the characters are able to respond according to their own temperament or moral personality to the gods' implacable schemes. This certainly seems to be the case with Sophocles's *Oedipus*.

Oedipus kills his father in an outburst of anger. He marries (and sleeps) with his mother for largely political motives. The main issue with Oedipus's worrisome character is his impetuous politically ambitious nature, prone to outbursts of rash temper, hasty judgments, and suspicious pride. Those who favour the amoral interpretation of *Oedipus* will argue that the main character's precipitous actions, even if they could be construed as immoral, can be excused for reasons of duress. Sachs insists on this point.[140] He (and others) point out that Aristotle does allow for forgiveness in agents that spontaneously lose their temper. But this line of interpretation is rather misleading.

In a discussion of unintended harm in the *Nicomachean Ethics*, Aristotle uses the *hamatia* group of words several times, in both a wide and a narrower sense.[141] The passage is rather garbled, but Aristotle is mostly intent on distinguishing between different levels of moral and legal culpability, listing four different situations, to which he attaches varying degrees of moral and legal guilt. Commentators on Oedipus like to focus on the third case,

---

139. Cf. Aquinas's distinction between the order of intention and the order of execution.
140. Sachs, "Introduction," 9.
141. Aristotle writes, for example, that harms due to ignorance "are mistaken" ("ἁμαρτήματά ἐστιν": *hamartēmata*, the plural of *hamartēma*: ἁμάρτημα). *Nicomachean Ethics*, V.7.1135b12ff.

in which someone acts in ignorance without knowing the identity of the person with whom they are acting. Because Oedipus did not know he was interacting with his father, they think this excuses his murderous actions. But consider what Aristotle says more closely.

Aristotle is discussing here marginal cases where people are carried away by *natural* passion. Sometimes normal people (with good characters) do bad things that injure others. These acts are *always* wrong but, in exceptional circumstances, they may not be a sign of a depraved character. Why? Because they are done under duress. Because they derive from human feelings or dispositions that are ἀναγκαῖος: "inevitable," "unavoidable," or "necessary."[142] To use a modern example of this mitigating emotional excuse, suppose someone makes an uncouth joke about your daughter or your wife to your face; you lose your temper, you beat him up. Losing one's temper and beating people up, we might say, is always wrong. Nonetheless, this act was not premeditated; it was an understandable, "honourable" response under duress. We might say, as Aristotle does, that "it is the man who gave the provocation that began things, not the one who responded in a fit of passion."[143] If, however, Aristotle accepts that circumstances leading to righteous anger can be a mitigating factor, we cannot apply this reasoning to Oedipus for the bar Aristotle posits for unavoidable or necessary passion is extremely high.

Elsewhere in the *Nicomachean Ethics*, Aristotle does deal with "matters that surpass human nature and could be endured by no one."[144] He uses two examples: (1) obeying an unlawful request of a tyrant who will otherwise kill your children and (2) casting other people's possessions overboard

---

142. Translations by Rackham, Broadie, Rowe, Sachs. Three different translations for the same word.
143. *Nicomachean Ethics* (Rackman) V.8.1135b26–28.
144. *Nicomachean Ethics* (Bartlett and Collins) III.1.1110a24–26.

in a storm to avoid shipwreck.[145] Here, then, we really do have extenuating circumstances. There is no other way out of the predicament. You are not responsible for getting yourself into these impossible circumstances. We will forgive you if you obey the tyrant and murder someone to save your children or if, in a sea storm, you throw overboard the cargo and deprive others of their possessions. But the case of Oedipus is not the same.

Oedipus's road rage was not necessary or unavoidable. It is simply not true that there was no other way out his predicament. He could have simply stepped aside at the approach of the herald. He could have walked away. He could have let Laius and his entourage pass. He could even have argued, remonstrated, complained—without killing. Again, he struck first. And he persisted in the violent engagement long enough to slaughter four people. He was alone. He had no duties to protect anyone else in the situation. He was not on the battlefield. He was not doing his honourable patriotic duty. (Just the reverse.) This is not the kind of forgivable act that Aristotle has in mind.

Aristotle writes, "when a man acts [wrongly] from choice, he is an unjust man and a vicious man."[146] But Oedipus makes a choice and must be judged accordingly. If Oedipus was a kindly, just, moderate, prudent, god-fearing man who, for some excusable reason, lost his temper—to protect his country, to prevent sacrilege against the gods, to defend his family—that would be one thing. But this does not fit with Sophocles's story. Oedipus's road-rage incident is in keeping with his character: an ambitious man of violent angry outbursts and hasty judgments who loses his temper

---

145. *Nicomachean Ethics* (Bartlett and Collins) III.1.1110a 5–10. Aristotle's examples: "if a tyrant should order someone to do something shameful while the tyrant has control over his parents and offspring, and if he should do it, they would be saved, but if not, they would be killed…Something comparable occurs also when it comes to casting off cargo in a storm."

146. *Nicomachean Ethics* (Ross) V.8.1135b24–25.

at some perceived slight. A bit of an overreaction, to say the least.

Aristotle further distinguishes between spontaneous and premeditated acts with the usual suggestion that the former is morally less serious. It may seem, at first glance, that Oedipus did not act with premeditation but, as I have already explained, premeditation—more cumbersomely, "acting with foresight"—can involve a split-second decision. Imagine someone picks up a knife, glares at his adversary, screams, "I'll show you," and plunges the blade into his chest. This happens in an instant, but this is enough for premeditation in all jurisdictions. Oedipus did not wrest the cudgel from the king and then throw it away. He was not under a spell, in a stupor, mentally insane, drugged, or poisoned by something that befuddled his mind. No god or goddess forced his hand. He took away the club and deliberately used it to kill four people. He tried to kill five. This would be impossible without the element of legal intention.

It strains credulity to think that any juridical analysis, ancient or modern, would absolve Oedipus of all charges of criminal intent. To borrow a refrain from Aristotle:

> It is laughable to attribute to external things the cause of one's being easily snared by such things, rather than to attribute the cause to oneself. […] That which is forced [and, therefore, innocent] appears to be something whose origin is external, while he who is forced contributes nothing thereto.[147]

But this notion—that what is forced comes from the outside so that the agent contributes nothing—is entirely against the spirit of Sophocles's play. As I have already argued, Oedipus is an autonomous agent. How could one say that Oedipus did not contribute anything to violent episode that led to Laius's death? Aristotle ridicules the idea that actions done

---

147. *Nicomachean Ethics* (Bartlett and Collins) III.1.1110b12–17.

out of passion or spiritedness (διὰ θυμὸν) are never voluntary. He shrewdly suggests that when we do noble things out of spiritedness, we take credit for them and that when we do shameful things out of spiritedness, we excuse ourselves by insisting that they are not our fault.[148] A very convenient but self-indulgent strategy.

Even if Oedipus could somehow be excused for his behaviour—even if he had suffered from some unavoidable passion no human could endure—it would not follow, as the amoralists argue, that Oedipus's *hamartia* was only a factual mistake. Aristotle's point is that although we can perhaps forgive someone who does something *morally wrong* under great duress, but this is not the same as saying that the act was a good act. The act remains an evil act, even if we can forgive and commiserate with the agent.

5.15. Oedipus Furious

There is a second passage, which ancient editors have surely misplaced in the text of the *Nicomachean Ethics*, that deals with exceptional cases where a wrongdoer should not be considered a bad person even though they do a bad act. Aristotle's point seems to be that when someone does something once—not out of habit or settled inclinations—he or she is acting out of character and, in this sense, is not a bad person, although the act is still wrong. Rather uncharacteristically, Aristotle writes:

> I must ask what sort of unjust acts imply that the doer is unjust with respect to each type of injustice, e.g. a thief, an adulterer, or a brigand. [...] A man might even lie with

---

148. "Do we do nothing stemming from desire and spiritedness voluntarily, or do we do noble things voluntarily and only the shameful ones involuntarily? Or is this laughable, since they both arise from the same, one cause." *Nicomachean Ethics* (Bartlett and Collins) III.1.1111a27–30. Aristotle also points out that animals and children—who do things out of spiritedness despite lacking rationality—act voluntarily (1111a26–27).

a woman knowing who she was, but the origin of this act might not be choice but passion. He acts unjustly, then, but is not unjust; e.g. a man is not a thief, yet he stole, nor an adulterer, yet he committed adultery; and similarly in all other cases.[149]

The adultery example (which is intended to be extreme) is decidedly very odd—it effectively contradicts Aristotle's general attitude towards sensual excess, but we can explain the passage in terms of ancient Greek ideas about sexual hubris. The idea seems to be that immoral sexual relations that occur unthinkingly in the heat of genuine passion are less evil than more deliberate, planned sexual relations that are intended to produce a feeling of shame or humiliation in their victims and therefore unjust as well as intemperate. David Cohen explains the thinking of the ancients:

> If the sexual relation arises from an act of power, rather than passion, then it necessarily merely expresses a relation of domination where the boy or girl submits to hubris and the disgrace it entails. [...] In the *Politics* (1311b19) [Aristotle] describes a man who regards himself as an object of hubris because he comes to believe that he submitted to someone who was not motivated by passion.[150]

Cohen then continues, "The same point arises in other contexts, and helps to explain what it is about passion that eliminates the hubristic quality of the conduct, namely the absence of the intent to assert oneself through the infliction of harm, humiliation, or disgrace."[151]

Leaving aside sexual cases, one can come up with a multitude of unproblematic examples that better make the same basic point. Suppose someone were, on a single occasion, to

---

149. *Nicomachean Ethics* (Bywater) V.6.1134a16–24.
150. Cohen, *Law, Violence, and Community,* 146.
151. Cohen, n. 11. He is referring to *Politics* V.10.1311b2 and V.11.1315a24.

steal food because he is desperately hungry. Aristotle reasons that it is not fair to call this man a thief—he is not someone who habitually steals, he does not possess the ἕξις (*hexis*), the active disposition of a thief—he is someone who stole something once without being a thief. In extraordinary situations, then, people can give into bad acts, on a one-time only basis, and be less immoral than someone who is a regular at such things. And, of course, be much less immoral than someone who deliberately plans to hurt others and bring them into disgrace.

Aristotle's main point seems to be that vice is not a single act; vice happens when repeated acts form a regular pattern. To be immoral, in his virtue ethics sense, is to have bad habits; it is to possess a bad inclination to repeat the same sorts of immoral acts over and over again. A very good man, under great stress and strain or in a fit of unthinking passion, may succumb to temptation once in his life whereas the vicious person regularly has a developed propensity that continually pushes him in an immoral direction. Aristotle is not saying that bad acts that happen only once are innocent; they are clearly wrong. He is merely saying—whether his own specific examples are convincing or not—that unjust individual acts and a vicious character do not always coincide.

But how can we apply such reasoning to Oedipus? Oedipus is not like this. At least, not the Oedipus that Sophocles depicts. His Oedipus is a character-type, who keeps on acting in the same way. It is not that he does one isolated act that is out of character. The way Sophocles sets up the action, Oedipus is, again and again, angry, self-interested, impatient, stubborn, irreverent, arrogant, immoderate, impetuous, presumptuous, authoritarian, and violent. Think of how Oedipus repeatedly acts: In the original roadside incident, in his murderous exchange with Creon (a member of the royal family), in his bitter denunciation of the oracle Tiresias, in the threats of torture directed against the shepherd, in his later attempt to kill the queen (who has already committed suicide), and in his final self-destructive act of ripping out his own eyes, we see here his character-type clearly.

A messenger describes Oedipus seeking to slay the queen and desperately blinding himself:

> Oedipus roaring with grief,
> burst into the hall and I could only watch him,
> raging around the walls, begging one after another
> to give him a sword—and tell him where
> to find it, that double-ploughed field:
> his wife, not a wife, his mother the mother to his children
> [...]
> Shouting in frenzy, he threw himself
> at the great double doors,
> tore the hinges from their sockets, and fell into her room—
> and we saw, O horrid spectacle, the woman hanging,
> her neck entangled in a noose of coiled rope.
> Then with a ghastly roar he leapt
> to loosen the cord and lay her gently on the ground.
> Poor suffering man—and the horror,
> to watch him tear away the beaten golden brooches
> from each shoulder of her robe, lift them high
> and plunge them into the sockets of his eyes,
> crying aloud that they should never see again [...]
> but only darkness, forever.
> Like a dirge, over and over he chanted,
> lifting the pins, striking his eyelids
> until bloody matter spurted out down his cheeks and beard—
> not drops, but a gush like black rain
> or hail drenching him.[152]

These are not the acts of a serene, temperate, restrained man. These are ferocious, savage reactions—triggered, no doubt, by extreme emotional distress—but Sophocles means them as a

---

152. *Oedipus* (Fainlight and Littman) 1252–1279.

continuation of the character-type he has assigned to Oedipus. Oedipus is someone who takes everything to the extreme. Leave aside the frenzied way he finishes up the play by repeatedly stabbing his own eyes. He is already *blind* with rage and despair. It is not simply that Oedipus acts cruelly towards Creon, Tiresias, and the shepherd. Adding to parricide, an act like killing your own mother, the queen, which Oedipus fully intended to do, would be another blasphemy and another pollution, even in such appalling circumstances. Oedipus is, then, rashness and fury personified. Imagine his blind rage at the first fatal meeting with his father (from whom he inherited his personality type) at the crossroads. With father and son sharing in the same savage nature, it would have been a harrowing event.

Could the amoralist critic interpret Oedipus's final rampage in Sophocles's play as an unavoidable human reaction to tragedy? It seems far too extreme for that. And, in any case, the playwright's intentions are rather different. Sophocles's Oedipus is a larger-than-life figure, physically intimidating, lordly, utterly self-confident, swashbuckling, wilful, dangerous: just the kind of *agathos* that would have appealed to machismo sensibilities of warrior Greek males. As Thomas Webster reports, Sophocles's "chief object in writing tragedy [was] to create and display great personalities."[153] Sophocles is as much a virtue ethicist as Aristotle. His play is psychological drama, with an emphasis on the "psychological." There is an unbroken thread of naturalistic development that makes Oedipus into a plausible personality who is inclined to do extreme deeds. He is never a puppet, a plaything of the gods, but a fearsome, towering, and fallibly human presence. His tempestuous nature leads him astray and is the ultimate cause of his precipitous downfall.

5.16. Oedipus and *Akrasia*
Attempts to absolve Sophocles's Oedipus of all moral guilt "miss the mark" in yet another way. Oedipus is a very angry

---

153. Webster, *An Introduction*, 82.

man. But Aristotle says that anger is a form of ἀκρασία (*akrasia*), of weakness of will. He distinguishes between two kinds of *akrasia*.[154] One sort of *akrasia* is driven towards sensual gratification: These people yield to bodily appetites "concerned with food and our sexual needs."[155] The other sort of *akrasia* is driven by ambition for worthy things such as "victory, honour, and wealth."[156] Aristotle calls the former condition simple or unqualified *akrasia*; he calls the latter condition, *akrasia* with respect to some particular good. As he puts it, "when people, contrary to the correct reason in them [...] go to excess in relation to the intrinsically choice-worthy goods, we do not say that they unconditionally lack self-control but add that they lack self-control regarding wealth, profit, honour, or spirit."[157] Aristotle thinks that this second form of spirited or ambitious incontinence is a more elevated condition for, at the very least, it aims at something higher than the satisfaction of brute appetites. It is a sign of a spirited, noble condition to aim at higher goods such as honour, victory, and even wealth. It is just that the weak-willed agent is carried away by the spirited element in his soul that goes too far and cannot restrain itself.[158]

Sophocles's Oedipus is afflicted by this higher sort of *akrasia*. He is, precisely, someone who lacks self-control with respect to higher things like honour, power, spirit, and ambition. He is aiming high, very high; except he aims too high and overshoots the mark. This makes him a more appealing if still immoral character. In a sense, he rivals the gods and loses his competition with them. Sophocles's play is a more sophisticated treatment of the Oedipus legend because it is about something more than Freudian self-indulgence. Still, spirited *akrasia* is a very serious moral failing.

---

154. Cf., *Nicomachean Ethics* VII.4.
155. *Nicomachean Ethics* (Reeve) VII.4.1146b26–27.
156. *Nicomachean Ethics* (Reeve) VII.4.1147b29–31.
157. *Nicomachean Ethics* (Reeve) VII.4.1148a30–33.
158. Cf. *Nicomachean Ethics* (Irwin) VII.6. 11491–94; cf. Groarke, *Moral Reasoning*, 177–180.

Aristotle distinguishes between general and special injustice in *Nicomachean Ethics* V. One might think of Oedipus's specific moral failing as a form of special injustice, "which is manifested in distributions of honour or money or the other things that fall to be divided among those who have a share in the constitution."[159] Oedipus is hungry for honour; indeed, he is ravenous for power and glory. His crimes are unjust in the most general sense; he disrespects the gods, murders the king, commits parricide and incest—these are all unjust (i.e., in the sense of being unlawful) behaviours. But it seems to be, more specifically, this spirited sort of *akrasia* that fuels his crimes. He demands the largest portion of honour for himself, which leads to his downfall.

Akrasia is, for Aristotle, a temporary sort of moral ignorance. How are incontinent agents able to do something they know is wrong? Aristotle's answer is that they are like those "sleeping, mad, or tipsy."[160] When someone is asleep, insane, or drunk, the moral knowledge in them goes to sleep. They temporarily "forget" who they are and what they ought to do. When they wake up, sober up, recover their wits, they recover the moral knowledge inside them and feel guilty.[161] Aristotle thinks that something similar happens with overly ambitious people. Under the influence of extreme desire or passion, these agents lose sense of who they are and what morality requires. "Spirited feelings," the pursuit of political power, the desire for a glorious reputation, in effect, makes us drunk and disordered. Pushed to an extreme, such things intoxicate us. Agents who suffer from *akrasia* are capable of

---

159. *Nicomachean Ethics* (Ross) V.2.1130b31–32.
160. *Nicomachean Ethics* (Reeve) VII.3.1147a13.
161. Aristotle is building here on Socrates's doctrine that all immorality stems from moral ignorance of the true good. Cf. *Protagoras* (Lamb) 345d–e. Socrates says: "I am fairly sure of this—that none of the wise men considers that anybody ever willingly errs or willingly does base and evil deeds; they are well aware that all who do base and evil things do them unwillingly."

criminal and monstrous things, which, upon later reflection, they deeply regret.[162] This pattern fits Oedipus fairly well.

First, in the play, Oedipus seems to be in some respects, a good ruler, caring for the city. After all, he is trying to save Thebes from divine punishment. He exhibits his anger, mostly, in his parricide, in his attempted matricide, in his impatience, in his disrespect of the gods and the oracle, in his arrogance. His has bouts of unreasonable emotional intensity. At the end of the play, he comes to his senses and punishes himself as an embodiment of ghastly criminality. He is not thoroughly vicious because, then, as Aristotle argues, we could feel no sympathy for him.

There is something undeniably magnificent in Oedipus's forceful personality. He is like one of the "young lions" Callicles enthusiastically praises.[163] But he is missing the most important Attic virtue: σωφροσύνη. F. E. Peters supplies the following philosophical definition of *sôphrosunê*:

> Self-control, moderation. [...] rooted in the Pythagorean notion of *harmonia* [...] is closely linked with Plato's tripartite division of the soul: [a] harmonious subjection of the two lower parts [appetites and spirit] to the ruling, the rational part. [...] For Aristotle *sophrosyne* is the mean (*meson*) between the extremes.[164]

Commentators note a narrowing of the meaning of the term in the later Plato and in Aristotle, where *sôphrosunê* is primarily seen as a sort of temperance that provides a bulwark against oversized appetites, particularly against *akolasia*, self-indulgence or licentiousness.[165] (Perhaps there is a latent

---

162. Aristotle tells us that such things alter the body physically and "in some people even produce states of madness." *Nicomachean Ethics* (Reeve) VII.3.1147a15–16.
163. Plato, *Gorgias* 483e ff.
164. Peters, *Greek Philosophical Terms*, s.v. "*sophrosyne*."
165. Cf. *Nicomachean Ethics* III.10.1117b28–1118a2. Suffice it to say here that these issues need further elaboration.

Puritanism at work here or a mechanical insistence on a more precise but more restricted philosophical categorization.) Aristotle does provide a spurious etymology of the term *sôphrosunê* which he interprets as "preserving prudence."[166] In any case, *sôphrosunê* or "temperance" puts a brake on the sensual desires that get in the way of sound, balanced thinking "about what must be done."[167] And a lack of temperance may destroy our conception of the good altogether.

Oedipus's irascible, violent temper denotes a lack of *sôphrosunê* in the original, richer, more popular sense of a bad relationship to the gods and fate. Anger pushes the agent into an irrational condition that obscures pious reverence for the gods and encourages extreme, unbalanced behaviour. An Athenian audience, at least, would have understood things in this way. As Jerome Pollitt explains:

> All Greeks were subject to and respected the maxims of the Delphic oracle: "know thyself" (i.e., "know thy limitations") and "nothing in excess." These pleas for restraint and measure, which were summed up in the virtue of *sophrosyne* ("discretion, temperance, self-control"), were not, it should be emphasized, a purely negative prescription. From Hesiod through Solon to the Classical dramatists and philosophers, such virtues were presented as the key to right living, to a happiness which was keeping with man's nature and was divinely sanctioned.[168]

Oedipus is the king of Thebes and is also associated with Corinth, but both city-states were on the wrong side of conflicts with Athens and tainted by historical associations with Persia and the hated Persian emperor Xerxes. Pollitt observes,

---

166. *Nicomachean Ethics* (Rackman) VI.5.1140b12–13.
167. *Nicomachean Ethics* (Ross and Urmson) VI.5.1140b16.
168. Pollitt, *Art and Experience in Classical Greece*, 11.

The meaning for Greek culture of the victory over the Persians and its outcome is brought into sharpest focus in the portraits of Xerxes drawn by Aeschylus (a veteran of the war) in the *Persians* and by Herodotus, nearly half a century later, in his history of the war. Xerxes is the anti-Greek, the man of unlimited power who is subject to no restraint, no limit to desire, the man who does whatever he wants, when a whim demands it. One day he augments the already large fortune of one of his subjects; the next day he has the same man's son cut in half. He flogs and enchains the Hellespont because it dares to be rough when he wants to cross it. The greater part of his army, moreover, consists of slaves from all parts of the Orient who go into battle under the lash. By contrast the Greeks, or at least most of them, fight for their freedom, their homes, their personal honour, their localistic way of life, and their ideal, often violated, of *sophrosyne*. Victory in such a conflict was interpreted as something more than a successful, heroic act of self-preservation; it was triumph of order over irrationality, a divinely sanctioned justification of Greek culture.[169]

Sophocles's wild Oedipus embodies, then, the barbarian disregard of *sôphrosunê*. He is presented as an obvious foil to the virtuous, *sôphrosunê*-filled, pious Greek. He is still a Greek but a tainted Greek, tainted by his association with Persia, by his tyranny, by his lack of *sôphrosunê*, by his hubris, and by his unsavoury family connections. Oedipus does not properly acknowledge his limitations. He does everything in excess; he is puffed up with self-importance. His actions, his words, his emotions, his thirst for power: It is all too much. It is not merely that Oedipus makes a factual mistake about who his real parents were; he does not "know himself" in the proper pious Greek sense. He is merely human, not divine; it

---

169. Pollitt, *Art*, 14.

is an affront to the gods and to pagan morality that he takes it upon himself to master fate.

Oedipus is, obviously, a hale warrior and a very intimidating fellow. Not someone one would want to meet in a back alley. One of the virtues associated with the Greek male ideal is, of course, courage (ἀνδρεία, literally, "manliness"). But fearlessness is not enough, on Aristotle's account, for the virtue of courage.[170] Aristotle says, among other things, that we are not truly brave when we are driven by passion for "lust makes adulterers do many daring things" and even donkeys, urged forward by hunger, withstand physical blows to get to their food.[171] He observes that experienced and temperamentally overconfident soldiers are not brave "for they are confident in danger only because they have conquered often and against many foes."[172] Drunk people become brave, but, again, this is false courage. Aristotelian courage requires moral behaviour, done in an intelligent way, for the right reason. One has to experience fearlessness "at the right time, toward the right objects, toward the right people, for the right reason, and in the right manner […] this is the mark of virtue."[173] This is not Oedipus.

In a proper Aristotelian scheme, every virtuous agent has to have *phronêsis*, practical wisdom. The term applies equally to smart statesmanship as well as to moral decision-making. Sophocles's Oedipus is a doer, not a thinker. Temperamentally, he is one of Plato's silver class, an auxiliary. Although he does display a cunning intelligence (μῆτις, *mêtis*) in answering the Sphinx's original riddle, it is a flash in the pan. Sophocles's Oedipus signally lacks *phronêsis* or practical wisdom. He has perhaps a young man's mental acuity, which, with repentance, can grow into wisdom, but he displays, at moments in the play, a remarkable lack of insight into what is really going on.

---

170. Cf. *Nicomachean Ethics* III.8.
171. *Nicomachean Ethics* (Ross) III.8.1117a1-2.
172. *Nicomachean Ethics* (Ross) III.8.1117a10-12.
173. *Nicomachean Ethics* (Rackman and Ostwald) II.6.1106b21-23.

5.17. Was Oedipus Guilty of Parricide?

Harold Bloom, in a recent collection of essays, refers to the "guiltless Oedipus."[174] This is another riff on Dodd's attack on poetic justice. Bloom seems to blithely overlook the deeply troubling nature of Oedipus's brooding, hubristic, tyrannical disposition. I am arguing, in contrast, that Oedipus is deeply immoral. If, however, Oedipus is an immoral character, can we hold him responsible for the death of his father, namely can we hold him responsible for the crime of parricide? This is, admittedly, a perplexing question. The fact that Oedipus does not knowingly kill his own father would seem to mitigate the villainy of his crime. Still, careful consideration of whether any court, ancient or modern, should find Oedipus guilty of *parricide* brings to the fore a number of vexing moral and legal issues. Consider the matter, first, in the light of what Aristotle says on this subject and, second, in the light of some rather helpful comments on the nature of parricide by Thomas Aquinas. Medieval, neo-Aristotelian ways of thinking about such issues are, it seems to me, much closer to the original Greek mindset.

Rackham notes that Aristotle distinguishes between three types of mistakes that result in social harm.[175] There are harms resulting from accidents [ἀτύχημα], which are morally neutral; harms resulting from instances of oversight, negligence, or carelessness [ἁμάρτημα: *hamartema*], which are unjust but do not denote a vicious character; and, finally, unjust harms [ἀδίκημα], which are committed from passion or from a vicious character. In these particular discussions, Aristotle explicitly identifies the *hamartia* group of terms with a middle range of morally culpable error.[176] Errors of fact due to such negligence are not vicious but neither are they morally blameless. One has a duty, after all, not to be

---

174. *Sophocles' Oedipus* Rex (Bloom) 1.
175. *Nicomachean Ethics* (Rackham) n.2 to V.8.1135b12.
176. *Nicomachean Ethics* V.8.1135b17–19. The discussion here uses the *hamatia* terms in several places.

negligent and to properly understand what one is doing and the consequences of one's actions.

In a discussion of involuntary acts, Aristotle himself seems to suggest that someone who unknowingly beats his father should not be held responsible for the specific act of father-assault. (For the ancient Greeks, father-assault was a worse crime than ordinary assault.) The passage is not entirely clear except to suggest that sometimes, we do bad things we do not mean to do. You may hit someone "but you do not know he is your father."[177] In which case, you presumably are not someone guilty of father-assault. Aristotle does not consider the specific case of Oedipus, which is complicated by a number of conflicting factors.

Let us turn, then, to Thomas Aquinas, who surely had the Oedipus myth in mind, when he discusses these issues in the *Summa Theologiae*. Aquinas (like Aristotle) thinks of stranger-assault and father-assault as two separate crimes. The second is more serious than the first. Suppose, then, someone assaults his father without knowing that it is his father; is he guilty of stranger assault or father-assault? Aquinas claims that crucial factor is whether he would have struck the man even if he had known it was his father. Would knowledge that he was his father have been sufficient to restrain him? If he would have stopped upon recognizing that the man was his father, he is only guilty of stranger-assault, not father-assault. The fact that he struck his father would be an unfortunate coincidence, not a contributing factor to his crime.

In a discussion of the sin of pride, Aquinas comments, "he who, in ignorance, slays his father, is a parricide effectively, but not affectively, since he did not intend it."[178] Again, in a discussion of involuntary acts, he writes: "Ignorance

---

177. *Nicomachean Ethics* (Irwin) V.8.1135a27–30. Cf. Rackman, n.4 to V.8.1135a30.
178. *Summa Theologiae* II.II.Q162.A2. "Whether Pride is a Special Sin?" Reply to Objection 2.

[sometimes] excuses from sin. [...] For instance, [in the case when] a man strike someone, knowing that it is a man (which suffices for it to be sinful) and yet [is] ignorant of the fact that it is his father, (which is a circumstance constituting another species of sin)."[179] Aquinas's point is that the person who does not know he is hitting his father may be guilty of the sin of assault but not the sin of family insubordination or parricide (if he kills him).

In parsing out the moral logic of such situations, Aquinas distinguishes between mistakes in particular and universal reasoning. He reasons:

> A man is restrained from an act of parricide, by the knowledge that it is wrong to kill one's father, and that this man is his father. Hence ignorance about either of these two propositions, viz., of the universal principle [that patricide is immoral], or of the particular circumstance [that this person in front of him is his father], could cause an act of parricide. [...] Consequently if a man's will be so disposed that he would not be restrained, even though he recognized his father, his ignorance about his father is not the cause of his committing the sin, but is concomitant with the sin [it accompanies the sin]: wherefore such a man sins [i.e., commits patricide], not "through ignorance" but "in ignorance."[180]

On this account, someone who does not acknowledge the universal interdiction against father-killing deserves to be regarded as a father-killer even if it so happens that he does not realize that the man he is killing is his father. To the contrary, someone who knows that all father-killing is wrong and who would have restrained himself if he knew—"this is

---

179. *Summa Theologiae* I.II.Q76.A3. "Whether Ignorance Excuses from Sin Altogether?"
180. *Summa Theologiae* I.II.Q76.A1. "Whether Ignorance can be a Cause of Sin?"

my father!"—is not a father-killer, even if he literally kills his father. Such are the niceties of careful moral reasoning. (The old discipline of casuistry.)

What then are we to make of Oedipus? Is he guilty of patricide? Would he have restrained himself if he realized that Laius was his father? Or would he have beat him (and his servants to death) anyways? There can be no definitive answer to this sort of a question. Oedipus did everything he could to flee Corinth and those he believed were his parents. He did this to avoid the possibility that he might kill his father. In some sense, he went out of his way to respect the moral injunction "Thou shalt not kill thy father." But this does not suffice to settle the question.

Oedipus killed Laius in a rage. The overlooked question is not whether Oedipus would have killed his father in a calm, rational state of mind. Both Aristotle and Aquinas think that excessive passion blocks access to the moral universals stored in one's mind. If Oedipus knew that parricide was morally wrong, would he have remembered or heeded that moral restriction when enraged? That is a much harder question to answer. Given the fact that Oedipus regularly suffered from *akrasía* (of the second sort), he might have lost his temper with his father in some inevitable power struggle. This is not what happens in the play, but an angry man is a dangerous quantity. Incontinent agents like Oedipus do things under the influence of anger that they would not normally do. Aquinas would argue that if Oedipus was capable of working himself up into such a blind rage that he could have killed anybody who disrespected him, including his father, he can be considered guilty of parricide. Was he capable of that degree of anger? He did want to kill Creon, his brother-in-law, as well as his mother and wife. So, it seems he could have killed even his father in a rage.

Commentators interpret the prophecy about Oedipus killing his father and sleeping with his mother in literal terms. Perhaps the oracle was, mostly, a warning to Oedipus about his tempestuous character. Telling an ancient Greek male that he would commit such crimes is the equivalent of warning him that he is going to commit the greatest evil. Perhaps the warning was about what inevitably happens to those who lack the key Greek virtue of *sôphrosunê* or moderation. This moralistic, even didactic reading of the Oracle's message is more in line with ancient thought. It makes entire sense from an Aristotelian perspective.

One could imagine someone cut from uncouth cloth saying colloquially something like: "Oedipus messed up. That is what happens when you keep losing your temper. You can't always get your own way. So much for lack of self-control!" I discuss the precise explanation for Oedipus's downfall below. What is important here is that any attempt to uncouple Oedipus's bad character from his eventual downfall destroys the unity necessary, in Aristotle's eyes, for a successful play. One cannot properly understand Oedipus's story without drawing some link between the serious defects in his character and his tragic situation.

It is easy enough to romanticize about make-believe violence, but I should add that criminal law, in many jurisdictions, would find Oedipus guilty of parricide. Many courts (for example, California) have a category of what is sometimes called "felony murder." According to this line of reasoning, any third-party death caused by those involved in a criminal offence qualifies as murder. The rationale is relatively straightforward. If you decide to engage in felony criminal activity, you will be held criminally responsible for all the bad consequences of such activity. If you accidentally kill someone when robbing a bank, you will be charged with murder as well as robbery. (This is sometimes called "concomitant" crime.) If, however, we apply this line of reasoning to Oedipus, we will have to hold him responsible for the unintended death of his father, for his father's death occurred when he was engaged in the felony crimes of grievous bodily assault and multiple murder. Because Oedipus freely decided to indulge in the serious crime of road rage, he must be held responsible for all the bad consequences therewith, including the more grievous ancient crime of patricide. This is, admittedly, a legalistic way of looking at things, but it is rooted in a deep intuition about moral responsibility.

5.18. Purity and Pollution (*Miasma*)

Perhaps we could argue that because Oedipus did not consciously intend to kill his father, he was not guilty of father-killing but only of stranger-killing. And yet, this interpretation seems like another modern gloss on a very old play. I will argue that, according to the ancient way of looking at things Oedipus is clearly guilty of parricide. It is not what he intended but what he objectively did that matters.

Ancient views of morality do not correspond to "softer" modern views. From an ancient point of view, the blood on Oedipus's hands was his father's blood. We can excuse, we can psychoanalyze, we can quibble, but the objective fact is that Oedipus deliberately killed his father. How this came to pass is a different issue. To view him as anything other than a father-killer is, according to ancient standards, to misconstrue human agency. At no point in the play was Oedipus forced to do anything. Even if one wants to think of the gods as tricking Oedipus, it is Oedipus himself who made all the decisions that led to his downfall. The most one can say is that the gods, being smarter, outwitted a mere mortal. This is hardly surprising. We should not compete with the gods for we will lose every time. Not because they force our actions, but because they are crafty enough to exploit all our weaknesses.

If ancient audiences would be more willing than contemporary audiences to find Oedipus guilty of parricide, two salient issues account for the difference between ancient and contemporary opinions: the first has to do with the moral value of purity, the second has to do with the communitarian political views of the ancient Greeks. Consider these issues, in turn.

Purity was an important virtue for all ancient civilizations. Prominent psychologists Jonathan Haidt and Joseph

Craig, in identifying six different moral intuitions that lie at the origin of moral judgment, point to an opposition between clean and unclean (what they call "sanctity and degradation") as an important moral focal point in earlier cultures.[181] Using the expected Darwinian model of social science explanation, they trace this particular moral criterion to the "adaptive challenges of life in a world full of dangerous microbes and parasites" and a naturally selected aversion to unhealthy "things like rotting corpses, excrement, and scavenger animals."[182] But whatever the remote anthropological origins of the moral importance of purity, the ancient mind sharply distinguished between clean and unclean acts in ways that our modern, more permissive culture has pushed to the margins. However, vestiges remain. As Haidt and Craig point out, even we feel shame and embarrassment at acts that seem dirty or repugnant, although we may find it very hard to justify those moral emotions. In their words:

> [We moderns find it difficult to appreciate] the profound moralization of the body and bodily activities, such as menstruation, eating, bathing, sex, and the handling of corpses. A great deal of the moral law of Judaism, Hinduism, Islam, and many traditional societies is explicitly concerned with regulating purity and pollution. […] Purity and pollution were important ideas in Europe from antiquity through the Victorian age, but they began to fade as the twentieth century replaced them with an increasingly medical and utilitarian understanding of hygiene and an increasing emphasis on personal liberty and privacy in regard to bodily matters. However, even contemporary American college students, when we interview them […] will confess to feeling flashes of disgust and disapproval when asked about violations of purity taboos.

---

181. In fact, these intuitions overlap considerably. Cf. Haidt and Craig, "Intuitive Ethic"; Haidt, *The Righteous Mind*.
182. Haidt and Craig, "Intuitive Ethics," 60.

> Stories about eating one's dead pet dog, about harmless cases of cannibalism, or even about homosexuality may elicit feelings of disgust, which the students attempt, often comically, to justify afterward. [...] Culture does not support a purity-based morality anymore (at least for liberal college students), so the students are left to struggle to explain a judgment produced by [this] intuitive system.[183]

Indeed, if one looks at contemporary social media with cancel culture and the various attempts to shame, bully, and ostracize the political opposition with unsavoury gossip and misleading calumny, one can perhaps find, hidden under a modern libertinism, a puritan reflex that operates according to purity standards that are ever-present and morally influential even today.

The ancient Greeks took the task of differentiating between clean and unclean acts very seriously. This is, in part, what is going on in *Oedipus*. The mere thought of killing one's father and sleeping with one's mother would have elicited a visceral reaction of disgust in an ancient audience. It is not merely that these are immoral acts—they are unclean acts. It is like someone with bowel problems soiling himself in public. The issue is not merely: Who is at fault? The issue is: Ugh! So disgusting! It may not be their fault but, nonetheless, people feel revulsion—even if biology unfairly conspired against them. If you soil yourself unknowingly, and other people discover it, see it, smell it, they point it out and say "it is on your clothes." You saying in turn, "it is not my fault" will hardly eliminate the shock and embarrassment. When someone soils themselves, everyone is disgusted—including the person themselves—it does not matter how it happened.

The same mentality holds, in the ancient Greek mind, when it comes to crimes like parricide and incest. To suggest that Oedipus's parricide and incest are merely factual errors sanitizes the way the ancients conceived of these things.

---

183. Haidt and Craig, "Intuitive," 60–61.

This is not how the ancient Greeks would have reacted to Oedipus's crimes. They would have thought that Oedipus was a filthy, disgusting individual because of the filthy disgusting things he did, excuses notwithstanding.

We moderns put the priority on consent. But, as Haidt and Craig suggest, that is a very restricted notion of moral values. We can ask two questions when considering Oedipus's behaviour. (1) "Was he pure or polluted?" (2) And, from a modern liberal perspective: "Did he consent?" "Did he do this deliberately?" The answer to the second question is perhaps "no"—or better, "maybe." But the answer to the first question is an unequivocal "yes." One can do things deliberately or un-deliberately and still be unclean or polluted.

For an ancient Greek, the answer to the first question is, indeed, unambiguous. The moral filth associated with Oedipus is so obvious and extreme that any suggestion that his flaws had no moral colour would have seemed incredible to an ancient Greek. It would be like suggesting that the person who soiled themselves has no reason to feel embarrassment. They would feel embarrassment even if we can somehow clinically insist that it was not their fault. Oedipus's crimes cannot be separated from their disgustingly moral content, at least not in the ancient Greek mind.

And, yes, the answer to the second, liberal question is more complex. One could argue that Oedipus deliberately left his presumed home so as to avoid the fulfillment of the dire prophecy. It may seem that the gods tricked him and forced his hand. But Aristotle's ethics focus on issues of character. The question is not: Did Oedipus do one bad act? The question is: Did he master his bad temper? Did he cultivate moderation? Was he pious? Was he rational? And the answer is clearly: no. The gods did not force Oedipus to do anything; he had plenty of autonomy; he engineers his own self-destruction. The goddess Ἄτη may have intervened but in line with Oedipus's prior inclinations.

Think about what is going on. Oedipus is sure he can outwit the gods and ignore their dire warnings by simply changing location. But this is hubris again. The real problem is not where Oedipus lives. Instead of changing what has to be changed—his tempestuous character—Oedipus takes a trip on the bus to the next town. It may seem a clever gambit, but the gods are not to be fooled. This is what foolish, naïve human beings do; they take the easy way out and adjust the external circumstances of their lives rather than addressing the internal source of the real problem. Eliminating prideful wrath would be an arduous moral task. Much harder than moving to the next town. Travelling to another location is not enough to ward off the disastrous consequences of an intemperate character.

And there is a further complication. Oedipus is not only a source of monstrous impurity. The ancient Greeks also believed that uncleanliness or impurity was contagious. It cannot be limited to a particular individual. It quickly spreads to the whole community. The liberal idea is that society does not have the right to restrict private behaviour. If individuals wish to indulge in prurient behaviour, to watch horror movies, read slasher novels, indulge in smut and pornography, that is for the individual to decide. Society has no right to enforce its values on them, and, in any case, individual purity is not that big a deal. We do not believe that moral pollution will call down a divine curse upon us. Impure actions, particularly those undertaken by private individuals, have no determinate effect on society as a whole, at least this is what we like to suppose. We often conceive of shame as something produced by a society forcing public standards on interestingly eccentric individuals from the outside. But the ancient Greeks thought quite differently.

Greek philosophers such as Plato and his school thought that moral impurity was something like an invisible dirty stain that spreads out over anything it touches. Gould points to Aristotle's rare use of the word *miaron* [τὸ μιαρόν] in the *Poetics*.[184] One standard lexicon defines the

---

184. Gould observes, "The word *miaron* and the verbs and nouns related to it are, as I have said, not found in Aristotle. There are in fact only

word μιαρός (*miaros*) as: "stained with blood," "defiled with blood," "polluted," "unclean," "abominable," "foul," "brutal," "coarse," "disgusting," "ugly."[185] Gould himself makes a convincing case that Aristotle borrowed the term from Plato (and the Academy) who conceived of immorality as a contagious uncleanliness that derives, mostly, from unruly appetites. As he explains the root sense of the word:

> Applied to an act, [*miaron*] nearly always means (in the fourth and fifth centuries, anyhow) that the event brings *miasma* or pollution. Applied to a person, it means that he has done, or is the kind of man that might do, something that makes him a carrier of pollution and therefore one who will pollute everyone who comes into contact with him.[186]

It is a worry about moral pollution or defilement that is at the very heart of Plato's complaints about theatre. Of course, ancient tragedies deal with human behaviour at its most bloodthirsty, brutal, disgusting, vile, ugly, and extreme; they depict—with the flair and sensationalism—bizarrely repugnant events like murdering one's parents, killing and cannibalizing one's children, or sleeping with one's own daughters. Seen with an ancient mindset, however, this is morally dangerous. In the case of Sophocles's *Oedipus*, the playwright is sensitive enough to place the filthy acts offstage beyond the reach of the audience. Nonetheless, he deals with unclean things that carry a high risk of moral contamination. As Gould explains:

> To Plato it seemed clear that Oedipus was *miaros* [a polluted person], and that anyone who allowed himself to

---

five exceptions, the three appearances of *miaron* in the *Poetics* and two appearances of *miaiphonos*, a rare compound meaning 'guilty of committing a *miasma*-causing murder' [one in the *Nicomachean Ethics* and one in the *Rhetoric*]." Gould, "Innocence," 521.

185. *Liddell and Scott*.
186. Gould, "Innocence," 516.

get sympathetically excited by his crimes was risking that most dangerous of *miasmata* [sources of infection], the surrender of that part of his psyche that is just as *miaros* [polluted] as Oedipus.[187]

Plato believes that there is a bestial part inside us that has to be reined in and kept under lock and key. When we watch a play about Oedipus committing filthy crimes like parricide and incest, we are titillating ourselves with filthy things. The filthiness gets inside us and it spreads to other people. If large numbers of Athenian citizens watch a filthy play, the filthiness leaves the stage and rubs off on them, and when they rub up against other citizens in the marketplace, the rest of Athens—and, indeed, the whole marketplace; then, the whole city—becomes smeared with filth. It is like the spreading of a viral infection. This is impious to the highest degree. The gods will notice. They may withdraw their divine favour from the filthy city or even actively persecute it just as they cursed the city of Thebes for Oedipus's filthy parricide and incest. Just as, to stray further afield, the god of a different tradition had to wipe the earth clean in Noah's time or send fire and brimstone on Sodom and Gomorrah.

In Sophocles's play, Oedipus declares: "It is wrong to talk of wrongful acts."[188] This is what he means. It is not only bad to commit parricide and incest; it is also bad to linger over, to focus attention on, and to be titillated by such events. Morbid, lurid behaviours are shameful and should be hidden away, far from prying eyes, in dark corners where no one sees them. Displaying them prominently on stage in the city square—gawking at them—revelling in vile dirtiness and giving in to dirty ideas is to invite moral and political disaster. Those who touch filthy, decaying things spread the contamination on themselves; this happens on a physical level, but in the mind of the ancient peoples, on a moral, religious,

---

187. Gould, "Innocence," 522.
188. *Oedipus* (Fainlight and Littman) 1410.

political level as well. How then is someone like Aristotle, a proponent of theatre and tragedy, a fan of *Oedipus*, to prove that such plays do *not* involve moral pollution or religious defilement of the people and city?

Gould insightfully presents Aristotle's *Poetics* as a philosophical defence of literature from the criticisms of Plato and his school. The challenge was to counter Plato's negative interpretation of the plays:

> [Aristotle] concluded that Plato had read the plays incorrectly. If tragedies did indeed imply that a man who had achieved the necessary and sufficient conditions for happiness could nevertheless be forced or tricked by the gods to do what no good man would want to do, […] then watching and enjoying these tragedies would clearly be a dangerously misleading experience in the eyes of Socrates, Plato or Aristotle. But the best tragedies, Aristotle argued, do not really imply any such thing for they have protagonists who do what they want to do, in part at least, because they are not perfectly good men.[189]

Gould points to two circumstances that move a tragic plot in a polluting or impure direction: (1) To the extent that the protagonist is deliberately wicked, this makes the evil greater and the act is even more taboo; (2) If, in contrast, the perpetrator is a good human being punished for being unwittingly evil, this detracts from poetic justice and spoils the pious belief that goodness and happiness should coincide. Gould expands on the point in reference to *Oedipus*:

> There are two different things, therefore, that would have made the story of Oedipus *miaron* [morally polluting]—if Oedipus had known what he was doing, or if he had been a thoroughly excellent man instead of one of the intermediate kind. His act had to have two qualities that are by

---

189. Gould, "Innocence," 519–520.

no means easy to reconcile with one another: it had to be done in ignorance, and it had nonetheless to stem from an imperfection in his character. The failure to have either one would have heightened the *miara* to an intolerable degree, Aristotle insists.[190]

On Gould's reading, the *hamartia* or failure that produces the bad act in a Greek tragedy is traceable to a moral fault in the main character. Otherwise, we would witness a virtuous man doing evil, which would turn the moral world upside-down. So, the "naïve" theory that Greek tragedy hinges on a morally culpable fault in the main character is not so far off the mark.

Viewed from a hostile perspective, *Oedipus* may appear to present a universe *without* poetic justice. If, however, the melodramatic complications that make up the plot of the Oedipus story may offend, Gould thinks that Aristotle's response is to insert a moralism into the Oedipus tale. The unknowing nature of Oedipus's crime attenuates his guilt—so we can tolerate, at least, his appearance on stage. But because he does very bad things—in part, because of a bad character—he must be punished by fate to rescue the story from sensationalist immorality. A prince with seriously bad character traits is punished. What could have produced moral contamination becomes a source of moral edification. Poetic justice is salvaged, morality is reinforced, and literature becomes a positive moral influence after all.

5.19. Guilt and Shame
The Oedipus story depends on an ironic twist of fate. As James McGregor explains, "[Oedipus] as king of Thebes, must do everything in his power to rid the city of a spiritual pollution brought on by the murder of the city's former king. Every Athenian […] would have understood that obligation."[191] Of course, the person who is charged with cleansing the city and

---

190. Gould, "Innocence," 518.
191. McGregor, *Athens*, 110.

restoring justice is the very person that is polluting it. It is as if Typhoid Mary were the doctor battling a typhoid epidemic. This is what is happening with Oedipus. He is both physician and also the infection, the doctor and the disease that must be purged. He correctly diagnoses the symptoms and, in the end, excises the nub of infection by casting himself, the diseased canker, out of the ailing body-politic.

When Oedipus finally understands what has happened, he calls himself a "murderer," "the defiler of the mother who bore me," "an unholy child rejected by the gods," an incarnation of "evil," a "sinner," "a miserable creature," "the impious one," the "sinful" one.[192] He declares to onlookers that his crimes deserve "worse than hanging."[193] That he "should never have slain his father and his entourage."[194] He asks to be killed:

> Everything cries out [...]
> that I, the parricide and sinner must die.[195]
> He then demands to be banished. He asks Creon:
> Expel me from this land, as soon as you can, to some place far from the sight of man, where I cannot hear another human voice.[196]

This exile will serve a dual purpose. Oedipus will not have to put his shameful state on embarrassing display and the citizens of Thebes will not have to put up with the disgusting (and polluting) sight of Oedipus. Again, Oedipus himself insists:

> Quickly, for the gods' sake, hide me somewhere
> far from this land; kill me or throw me

---

192. *Oedipus* (Fainlight and Littman) 1357, 1356–1357, 1360, 1397, 1441, 1444, 1382, 1384.
193. *Oedipus* (Fainlight and Littman) 1373–1374.
194. *Oedipus* (Fainlight and Littman) 1185.
195. *Oedipus* (Fainlight and Littman) 1440–1441.
196. *Oedipus* (Fainlight and Littman) 1436–1437.

into the sea so that you will never have to look at me again.[197]

For the Greeks, even for Oedipus himself, ridding Thebes of the soiled Oedipus is a necessary solution; the only way to deflect the ire of the gods from Thebes.

In modern moral psychology, it has become commonplace to distinguish between shame and moral guilt. According to usual opinion, guilt happens when we violate our own internal conscience; shame is about the social disapproval we experience when we are ridiculed or scorned by others. As one textbook puts it, "all shame episodes involve a real or imagined audience that expresses […] unwelcome opinions about us."[198] But this bifurcation is exacerbated by the liberal alienation of the individual from society. The identification of the individual with society is much greater in communitarian ancient Greece; so that shame and guilt come together. Oedipus feels both guilty and ashamed at the very same time and for the very same reasons. Although Oedipus is surrounded by a universal chorus of abject condemnation, there is no gap between his view of himself and the view of onlookers. His own acceptance of his tragic plight leads to his redemption in Sophocles's later sequel.

Alessandra Fussi argues that Aristotle links guilt and shame together in overlapping categories. As she observes:

> Aristotle conceives of shame from two different but inter-related perspectives. From the point of view of self-evaluation, shame allows an agent to perceive and acknowledge his or her responsibility with respect to bad actions, omissions, and character flaws. […] From the point of view of […] social interactions, shame contributes to the awareness that certain situations are diminishing or humiliating.[199]

---

197. *Oedipus* (Fainlight and Littman) 1411–1413.
198. Deonna, Rodogno, and Teroni, *In Defense of Shame*, 24. These authors aim to re-establish shame as a positive moral emotion.
199. Fussi, "Shame," 113–114.

On Fussi's account, Aristotle identifies two kinds of shame, one that is more or less equivalent to moral guilt, and another that is tantamount to the social stigma we moderns associate with shame. Her suggestion, however, does not go far enough.

Fussi sharply separates anger from shame. At the end of Sophocles's play, however, Oedipus experiences anger, guilt, and shame all together, in one single cumulative experience. He discovers his moral guilt. He feels shame at what he has done, and immediately loses his temper: He tears down locked doors with a roar and tries to kill the queen and, deprived of that possibility, turns his anger towards himself and rips out his own eyes. We should not misunderstand. Oedipus is not angry at society—as in the modernist trope of the persecuted figure made to feel shame by others. Oedipus agrees with society that he is a vile individual. He is not angry at the gods or his judgmental peers—he is anguished; he feels the full burden of his repulsive destiny—and, mostly, he is angry at himself. Angry because he is plainly guilty; angry because he is a monster in his own eyes. Fussi says that anger is about revenge—but Oedipus takes out his "revenge" on himself: ripping out his eyes and sending himself into exile—if that can be properly called "revenge." At the end of Sophocles's play, shame, guilt, and anger—these three moral emotions—swell up together, united in one great wave of despair.

5.20. Bloodguilt and Oedipus

As I have already mentioned, Gould is an insightful exegete who insists, nonetheless, that Aristotle misunderstood the aims of Greek tragedians. He maintains that the playwrights put an implacable amoral world on display in their plays. They had little use for poetic justice and intended to show innocent people tricked and maimed by deceitful goods for no fault of their own. Their mission was transgressive; they were out to undermine traditional morality and religion. Greek tragedy was, to use an overused term, a subversive art form that Aristotle rehabilitates through a mistaken moralism.

I must limit my comments here to *Oedipus*. Although I do not believe that Aristotle quite captures what Sophocles is about in this particular play, I will argue that his general account of tragedy closely corresponds to the aesthetic sensibilities of authors like Sophocles. It is not merely that Sophocles saddles Oedipus with serious character faults. It is that the concern for moral pollution that preoccupies Plato and even Aristotle is a generalized feature of ancient Greek culture outside of philosophical circles. Sophocles, along with other authors, is not unusual in sharing those same concerns.

In a useful essay on "The Concept of Purity in Greek Sacred Laws," Noel Robertson turns his attention to ancient Greek stone inscriptions and their religious and legal meaning.[200] These archaic monuments are a window into ancient Greek attitudes in a way that bypasses some of the obfuscatory details of later literature and philosophy. As Robertson explains, Greek civilization, from a very early period, had two separate ways of dealing with the issue of moral pollution. In a comment on the archeological evidence, he observes:

> [Purity] inscriptions on stone begin to appear widely [in Greece] in the 6th century BC. [...] [These] καθαρός [purity] inscriptions [...] continuing for long ages and occurring throughout the Greek world, [...] set forth the means of purifying a homicide or lesser assailant who is not after all driven out of the community. Such persons need to be cleansed—often by literal washing, scouring, absorbing—so as not to sully others. [...] An opposite procedure is [also] widely known. [...] A community that feels itself somehow sullied offloads the dirt on a wretched scapegoat and expels him. Beyond a doubt these drastic and expressive procedures were handed down in Greece from very early times. [...] At Cleonae in the Argolid [...]

---

200. Robertson, "Concept of Purity in Greek Sacred Laws."

one of the earliest inscriptions [early 6th Century BC] of any kind sets forth an elaborate procedure for purifying a homicide, referred to repeatedly as μιαρός [again, polluted].[201]

There are, then, two ways to get rid of the moral pollution (*miaron*) produced by a homicide in ancient Greece. First, one can expel the perpetrator (or a scapegoat who represents the perpetrator) from the city. Second, one can wash the perpetrator down with pure water at the temple, a sort of ablution that is connected to Aristotle's notion of catharsis (from καθαρός: purity) as I discuss further below. In Oedipus's case, exile is the chosen solution—presumably because no amount of washing could be enough to get him clean again. He is too dirty.

Sophocles could not have escaped the weight of such a generalized, established Greek tradition. The religious rule is that the community is to expel any homicide. But witness what happened in Thebes. The city (unknowingly) welcomes a homicide—even worse, a parricide—and makes Oedipus a king, who proceeds to sleep with his mother. That he did not mean to do it is irrelevant for he still did it. Thebes is a filthy place and must be cleaned or the heavens will curse it forever.[202]

Because Sophocles is a sophisticated storyteller, he inserts more than one ironic twist into the proceedings, but none of this negates the need for the traditional remedy of exile for moral pollution. It only makes the reality of what transpires more complex—less stereotypical. Oedipus is a

---

201. Robertson, "Purity," 198, 200.
202. Sophocles employs a similar device in *Antigone* where Creon does the exact opposite of what morality requires, leaving the dead body of Polynices above the ground and burying Antigone, a living person, under the ground. The dead unburied and the living buried: the decaying exposed and the living covered up—this is morality turned upside down again. Catastrophe had to ensue—a divine reestablishment of moral order was necessary.

hero insomuch as he heals the city. But he is also the cancer that needed to be excised, the infection that needed to be removed. Oedipus is the magistrate who passes sentence on the criminal, but he is also the criminal who needs to be punished. He is the problem and the solution. He is the saviour of Athens twice: He defeats the Sphinx and exiles himself. But he is also the enemy who defeats the city twice, by killing his father and marrying his mother (and, thus, bringing the curse of the gods on the city). At the beginning of the story, he can physically see but is morally blind; at the end, he is physically blind but morally sighted. Sophocles breaks down the usual categories, which is how great literature operates. But any suggestion that one can make sense of all this without focusing, fairly and squarely, on moral issues at the centre of all this commotion seems incredible.

I have already pointed out that Sophocles presents Oedipus as a tyrant, not merely as a king. But here is another masterful stroke of irony. In actual fact, Oedipus is a rightful heir to the throne. By birthright, he should take over the rule from his father and mother. But he does not know this. No one knows this at the beginning of the play. He comes to Thebes as a tyrant; he acts like a (power-hungry) tyrant. Everyone thinks of him as a tyrant; he himself thinks he is a (benevolent) tyrant. This taints his claims to power. But the moment he discovers that he is not the child of a slave but the rightful king of Thebes is the precise moment of his downfall. Good news is bad news; political "correctness" is political incorrectness. In discovering his legitimacy, he discovers his illegitimacy. Just when Oedipus finds out that he has the right to reign over Thebes, he finds out that he must exile himself from the city forever. He proves and disproves his illegitimacy at the same instant in time. It is his vicious, hasty, hubristic character—his immorality—that transforms the rightful heir into political monster.

And there is a second issue that needs airing. We moderns tend to restrict guilt and moral responsibility to the guilty individual. For better or worse, this is not the ancient way. In the ancient world, the sins of the fathers are passed on to the sons and continue to work their evil ways in the world, long after the guilty deed is done. The disease engendered by moral contagion continues to spread through succeeding generations. As Ruth Fainlight and Robert Littman explain:

> Pollution and its cure played a major role in Athenian society. In the mid fifth century BC Pericles could still be charged with being under the curse of the Alcmaeonidae for a pollution committed by his ancestor, Megacles, in the seventh century, almost two hundred years before he was born. The idea of a family curse and collective guilt would have seemed justified to a Greek audience, as well as to other ancient Mediterranean cultures. God says in the Hebrew bible (*Deuteronomy* 5:9), […] "I the Lord your God am an impassioned God, visiting the guilt of the parents upon the children, upon the third and the fourth generation." […] A descendant several generations removed would feel himself equally guilty of a family curse as the person who had caused the pollution. Sophocles would not have seen Oedipus' inheritance of the curse of Laius [the father of Oedipus] as particularly unusual or tragic. Group guilt was taken for granted. […] Bloodguilt, pollution, and expiation became major themes of Aeschylus' works. For Sophocles, these were secondary themes, but still an integral part of the myth of Oedipus and his portrayal.[203]

Oedipus, then, is polluted and morally defiled in a second way we moderns overlook. There is karma at work in the world. Oedipus comes from tainted blood. There are at least three generations of sins, miscues, and tragedies in his family. It turns out that his father does something wrong; he does something wrong, and his sons do something wrong. His daughter Antigone is sentenced to death and commits

---

203. Fainlight and Littman, *Oedipus* ("Introduction"), xxx–xxxi.

suicide (as Sophocles himself relates). And his other daughter Ismene is, according to one story, murdered.

What did Oedipus's father Laius do that was so morally offensive? He kidnapped and raped Chrysippus, the son of King Pelos of Pisa (Greece), a particularly egregious crime because the king had provided him with a safe refuge from political troubles. Laius also disobeys the gods who had warned him to remain childless. In a drunken—i.e., an incontinent—state, he sleeps with his wife and sires Oedipus, whom he unsuccessfully tries to kill. Under the influence of the curse, Oedipus suffers a woeful fate, and, later on in the Sophoclean narrative, curses his own sons Eteocles and Polynices in several episodes of rage (incontinence) because, ironically enough, they disrespect their father. Once Oedipus is expelled from Thebes, his overly ambitious—i.e., tyrannical—sons kill one another in a struggle over control of the city. Antigone is sentenced to death by Creon and hangs herself, inciting Creon's son to fall on his sword in despair. Creon is slain by Lycus. This harvest of ill fortune—homicide, parricide, regicide, suicide, incest, abdication, political machination, rebellion, termination of a royal dynasty—this is, in the ancient mind, how evil spreads. It is not merely that one reaps what one sows. Future generations reap what one sows. Evil begets evil begets evil to produce a bitter harvest for a long time to come. In the ancient mind, Oedipus is from a poisoned seed; he is hardly a moral exemplar. The gods of ancient Greece reinforce this religious/moral cosmology; they see to it that the children of evil parents get their comeuppance in turn.

For the ancient Greeks, Oedipus is guilty both because of what he does and because of what his father did. The individual is connected to his family—family members are one blood; they are, so to speak, in it together. Evil is not subjective but objective; evil is a dirty reality. It has to be gotten rid of or it will have disastrous consequences. Moral responsibility is as much a matter of family obligation as anything else. When you participate in evil, you condemn your whole family to punishment. (Tribal law took the same approach the world over.) One needs to ward off the brunt of divine retribution for the sake of the entire family, not merely for the sake of one's own individual well-being and future prosperity.

Current interpretations that Sophocles's play is about the subversion of the traditional moral order, that it shows the capricious gods dealing unjustly and randomly with the world, turns Sophocles on his head. The play is, rather, a grim illustration of how an objective moral order is implacably enforced unless sins are properly and promptly dealt with through religious ceremony, piety, absolution, proper regret, reparation, humility, and penance. Sophocles leans heavily on the traditional, moralistic, religious reading of the Oedipus story, despite his genius for irony and complication and his ability to make old stories come alive in compelling, naturalistic, psychological detail. But let us return, now, to Aristotle's theory of tragedy.

5.21. Plato, Aristotle, and Catharsis

Aristotle is as concerned as Plato about the possible polluting effects of tragedy. He approaches the problem in a more scientific spirit, advancing a solution to philosophical worries about the immorality of drama. Gould sensibly suggests that Aristotle eventually came to see the "happy endings" mentioned in *Poetics* 14 as better than the unhappy endings favoured in Chapter 13 because, in cases where the "tragic" protagonist discovers the truth early enough to refrain from doing the terrible deed, the audience feels the suffering (*pathos*) without the moral pollution (*marion*) that comes from witnessing the terrible deed. But the crux of Aristotle's case for tragedy lies elsewhere.

Plato famously argues for the censorship of poetry and drama in his *Republic*. This involved a personal renunciation. According to the story, after a youthful career as a poet he burnt his own creative work and turned to philosophy. Plato is worried about literature because Homer, Hesiod, and the poets depict the gods and heroes in an unedifying light. He thinks that poetry, which rouses unhealthy, irrational emotions, may lead ordinary citizens into depravity. He recommends the censorship of immoral poetry as a means of safeguarding the moral fabric of society. Bad ideas and salacious subject matter infect—pollute—good souls. Citizens may imitate immoral aspects of what they see on stage. (*Mimēsis* in reverse.) Plato's heavy-handed solution is strict state control over the arts. As Socrates tells Adeimantus:

> We must supervise the makers of tales; and if they make a fine tale, it must be approved, but if it's not, it must be rejected. We'll persuade nurses and mothers to tell the approved tales to their children to shape their souls with tales more than they shape their bodies with their hands. Most of the tales they now tell must be thrown out. [...] The ones Hesiod and Homer told us, and the other poets too.[204]

Some commentators view Plato's complaint in epistemological terms. But, for Plato, the problem with drama is not the fact that theatre is literally untruthful. Plato himself recommends using *noble lies* for propaganda purposes. The problem with poets and playwrights is the immoral content of the traditional tales they tell. These authors are brazen enough to show gods, heroes, and ordinary men profiting from immorality or the innocent being punished for moral behaviour. Their stories sever the connection between happiness and virtue. As Socrates tells Adeimantus: "What both poets and prose writers say concerning the most important things about human beings is bad—that many happy men are unjust, and many miserable ones just, and that doing injustice is profitable if one gets away with it."[205] In other words, the problem with poetry is that it does not deal in poetic justice.

---

204. *Republic* (Bloom) II.377b–d.
205. *Republic* (Bloom) III.392b.

And there is a second problem. The poets, in striving after sensational effects—something theatre naturally depends on—unleash dangerous emotions. Plato tells us that the good man "laments last and bears it most gently when some such misfortune overtakes him."[206] Tragedy, in sharp contrast, is filled with sensational displays of extreme emotion: In the midst of the most horrific events, blood-splattered people wail and moan and lament. And the audience joins in enthusiastically as Socrates explicitly mentions, for example, in the *Ion*.[207]

But this is, for Plato, a very unhealthy practice. In the *Republic*, where Socrates devises his philosopher-king utopia, he suggests, somewhat crossly, the appointment of a censorship board that, in placing strict controls on the production of literature, will "eliminate the laments and wailing of famous men."[208] Pushing his suggestion even further, he borrows from the ancient stereotype of overly emotional womankind and goes so far as to insist: "we'd be right in eliminating the wailings of renowned men and we'd give them to women—and not to serious ones at that—and to all the bad men."[209]

It is the emotional efficacy of poetry that Plato fears. Theatre titillates. It distracts, interferes with reason, makes us lose control; it gets in the way of clear thinking and moral rectitude. Eloquent, powerful turns of phrase deeply affect us. They stir us in our guts. But that makes them exceedingly dangerous. Like sophistry. Take this Platonic line as a proverb: "The more poetic such things are [i.e., the more effective they are at affecting us], the less they should be heard."[210] Add emotional punch to lurid tales that feature immorality and ordinary citizens are bound to be negatively affected and permanently harmed. When emotion is mixed with filthiness (*miasma*), it acts like glue; it sticks to us. The

---

206. *Republic* (Bloom) III.387e.
207. *Ion* 535d.
208. *Republic* (Bloom) III.387c.
209. *Republic* (Bloom) III.387e–388a.
210. *Republic* (Bloom) II.387b.

chattering classes (locked in the cave looking at the shadows on the walls) add their clever commentary and the pollution spreads. We cannot stop talking about the play we saw that featured Oedipus the moral monster; we tell others about it, and they tell other people as well, and the unholy and the unnatural perversity takes over people's imaginations and the public consciousness.

Perhaps there is a sliver of hope. Despite his hostile criticism of poetry and drama, Socrates does seem to leave a place for an argument in favour of poetry. In the *Republic*, he expresses the wish that some future poet or philosopher might be adequate to the task of providing a logical defence of literature. As he put it:

> If poetry directed to pleasure and imitation have any argument to give showing that they should be in a city with good laws, we should be delighted to receive them back from exile, since we are aware that we ourselves are charmed by them. [...] We would also give its protectors, those who aren't poets but lovers of poetry occasion to speak an argument without meter on its behalf, showing that it's not only pleasant but also beneficial to regimes and human life. And we shall listen benevolently. For surely we shall gain if poetry turns out to be not only pleasant but beneficial.[211]

The wished-for argument in favour of literature never materializes in Plato except perhaps, to some inadequate extent, in the *Ion* where Socrates proposes a religious theory of inspiration. But this is not enough to rescue poetry from censure.

If we want to find the argument in favour of literature Plato hoped for, we need to turn to Aristotle's *Poetics*, which can be thought of as a later attempt by Aristotle, one of Plato's students, to supply just the sort of argument Socrates asked for. Aristotle responds to both of Plato's concerns.

---

211. *Republic* (Bloom) X.607c–d.

First, he argues that good tragedy has moral content. The downfall of the protagonist is inevitably linked (with the necessary aesthetic distance) to some character flaw. In a play like Sophocles's *Oedipus*, we have an incontinent agent who brings ruin on himself. Oedipus "unknowingly" killed his father. But, on closer inspection, he is not an innocent victim savaged by devious, crafty gods. He is someone who receives just deserts. Oedipus comes to a terrible end because of his hasty, precipitous, unruly character and a tyrannical thirst for power. Morality is saved. Poetic justice upheld.

In a mostly overlooked passage, Aristotle explicitly proposes a moralistic turn of events as the very best plot for tragedy. He writes:

> Tragedy represents not only a complete action but also incidents that cause fear and pity, and this happens most of all when the incidents are unexpected and yet one is a consequence of the other. For in that way the incidents will cause more amazement than if they happened mechanically and accidentally, since the most amazing accidental occurrences are those which seem to have been providential [i.e., a fulfillment of fate], for instance when the statue of Mitys at Argos killed the man who caused Mitys's death by falling on him at a festival. Such events do not seem to be mere accidents. So such plots as these must necessarily be the best.[212]

Aristotle recommends, here, as the *best* sort of plot for a tragedy a story that is an unequivocal instance of poetic justice. A murderer had killed Mitys, an Olympic charioteer. When the murderer visits the statue commemorating his Olympic victory, the statue falls on him and kills him. How befitting! (Almost like Dante's use of *contrapasso*.) The murderer is killed by τύχη, by an arrangement of individual circumstances that seem to be orchestrated by the gods in

---

212. *Poetics* (Fyfe) 9.1452a2–10.

retribution for his own evil deeds. You kill someone; you will be killed in turn. As Aristotle says, "such events do not seem to be mere accidents." In this ideal plot, the invisible gods, those shadowy supernatural forces, seem to intervene and impose a strict moral order in the cosmos. This is moral retribution, not random, secular happenstance.

Aristotle argues that Mitys's story is also a good plot for tragedy because it fills us with wonder. We move from naturalism to supernaturalism, to the transcendental edges of things. We might ask, however: Where is the *hamartia* in this proposed "best plot"? The only flaw in the Mitys story *is not a factual error*; the great flaw is a *moral flaw*—murder—not a mere mistake of fact. Dodds and other amoralists, in eviscerating tragedy of all moral content, not only seem to overlook Aristotle's own advice; they also unwittingly deprive him of any adequate response to Plato's worries about the immoral content of literature. In the Mitys case, Aristotle comes close to proposing a didactic account of the best sort of tragedy.

Plato's second argument against the poets focuses on the alarming emotional intensity of drama. Aristotle responds to this criticism by turning the emotional efficacy of tragedy in a positive direction. Hence his doctrine of catharsis, which he mentions, very briefly, in advancing a definition of tragedy:

> Tragedy is a representation of an action that is heroic and complete and of a certain magnitude—by means of language enriched with all kinds of ornament. [...] It represents men in action and does not use narrative, and through pity and fear it effects relief [κάθαρσις, catharsis] to these and similar emotions.[213]

Aristotle does not expand on this point any further and perhaps too much ink has been spilled on this issue. The Liddell and Scott lists the following meanings for the term κάθαρσις: cleansing from guilt or defilement, purification,

---

213. *Poetics* (Fyfe) 4.1449b21–28.

clarification, clearing of morbid humours, evacuation, the pruning of trees (in Theophrastus, Aristotle's successor), the winnowing of grain, the clearing of land. Commentators usually maintain that Aristotelian catharsis in tragedy refers to (1) a cleansing or purification, (2) a purgation as in a medical context, or (3) some sort of mental clarification.[214] But these ideas overlap and need not be viewed as mutually exclusive alternatives.

Given the historical context, the basic idea seems clear. If Plato and the philosophers are concerned about the polluting effects of tragedy, Aristotle neatly turns the accusation on its head and presents tragedy as a ritual cleansing of worrisome, bad emotions in line with the καθαρός (i.e., purity) temple inscriptions already mentioned. This therapeutic effect can be understood as involving the removal of these emotions completely or as their purification so that we still have these emotions but in a more refined manner. I will not resolve this debate in the commentary here. Suffice it to say that—however we understand the cleansing action of catharsis—this account of audience response is a clever jujitsu move, turning Plato's line reasoning on his head. Defilement becomes absolution, watching filth becomes a method of purification, an alleged source of religious pollution becomes a source of religious cleansing. If Oedipus washed the city clean by banishing himself into exile, Greek tragedy washes the audience clean of emotional filth; it makes us confront the dread possibilities of human nature, lancing the boil, drawing off the pus (the expression is not too strong), and restoring health and holiness. And this is, again, why we have to interpret Aristotle's theory in moral and religious terms, because this is the way his invocation of catharsis is intended to be read. Without the religious element—remember the catharsis temples—we miss the clever inversion, the way Aristotle turns Platonic criticism of tragedy upside down and restores literature's moral

---

214. Cf. *Poetics* (Lucas translation), Appendix II, "Pity, Fear, and Katharsis," 273–290.

credibility. Whatever the details of Aristotle's thought, the catharsis of pity and fear is clearly intended to wash over the audience in some morally commendable way, making us cleaner, purer, holier, better.

Aristotle discusses catharsis elsewhere in the corpus. In the *Politics*, he mentions it in relation to music, another dangerously emotional art associated with theatre.[215] Aristotle explains:

> Feelings such as pity and fear, or again, enthusiasm, exist very strongly in some souls, and have more or less influence over everyone. Some persons fall into a religious frenzy, and we see them restored as a result of sacred melodies—when they have used the melodies that excite the soul to a mystic frenzy—as though they had found healing and purgation. Those who are influenced by pity or fear, and every emotional nature, must have a similar experience and others insofar as they are susceptible to such emotions, and all are in a manner purged and their souls lightened and delighted.[216]

According to Aristotle, then, sacred music can be used to siphon off excess feeling (frenzy); it can cure the overexcitement of a mystical soul. But it does not take much to transfer this account of catharsis to tragedy.

Plato and his fellow critics viewed tragedy like an exhibitionist spectacle: In Greek theatre, an audience of peeping Toms, morbidly titillated, soaks in the bloody, thrilling mixture. Filth is exposed, gore indulged in, unregulated emotion unleashed, moral infection spreads through the populace. But Aristotle corrects the Platonic suggestion that all emotion is bad. Tragedy pushes monstrous events up close. We feel

---

215. *Politics*, VIII.7.1341b36 ff. This discussion includes a direct reference to the *Poetics*. Cf. Belfiore, "Pleasure, Tragedy, and Aristotelian Psychology," 272–288.
216. *Politics* (Jowett) VIII.7.1342a5–14.

Oedipus and Aristotle 351

disaster "so near as to be imminent."[217] But this closeness of feeling can result in the discharge of something excessive that allows the soul to return to a more tranquil, rational state. It can wash clean the sore and *purify* the restless heart.

When Aristotle specifically mentions the two negative emotions "pity and fear," he is using a general formula that refers to extremely negative feelings focused on ourselves and on others. He proposes a simple enough dichotomy. As Schollmeier points out, we fear for ourselves; we pity others.[218] In Aristotle's lexicon, fear is a self-regarding emotion; it visits us when we are upset about evil that threatens us. Pity is, on the other hand, the sympathetic fear we feel for other people. We experience pity when we feel sorry for others threatened by evil. Aristotle remarks in his *Rhetoric* "anything that causes us to feel fear (on our own account) causes us to feel pity when it happens to or threatens others."[219] To maintain that tragedy unleashes pity and fear in an audience is, in effect, to say that it makes us experience the negative emotions we feel for ourselves and others.

Surely, there are religious overtones here. One could get another Calvary out of these emotions without much difficulty. (In the New Testament, the term *hamartia* is, in fact, translated as sin.) In Athenian drama, the tragic protagonist is not without fault like the Christian Jesus, but there is a striving to devise an awesome spectacle that points to the numinous, to some *mysterium tremendum* that elicits a searing religious and moral response in the audience. The catharsis of pity and fear drains us of feelings for ourselves and others.

Aristotle points out that we more readily feel pity for those that resemble ourselves.[220] The male Greek audience for Sophocles's plays would have identified with Oedipus as the

---

217. *Rhetoric* (Roberts) II.5.1382a24–25.
218. Schollmeier, "Ancient Tragedy," 185.
219. *Rhetoric* (Roberts) II.5.1382b24–26
220. In age, character, habits, rank, or birth. *Rhetoric* II.8.1386a24–26.

embodiment of so many masculine virtues: courage, physical strength, initiative, authority, shrewdness, perseverance, self-confidence, assertiveness. We feel pity for Oedipus on the stage because he suffers a ghastly fate, whatever his moral faults. But Aristotle thinks that the play should also make us wonder about our own situation. Could some equivalent destiny—on a much smaller but more personally intrusive scale—befall us as well? Are we filled with hubris? Do we thoughtlessly assume that we can control fate? Will the gods pay us back with just retribution for our own moral lapses?

The play *Oedipus* encapsulates pity and fear in two different ways. First, the characters in the story experience pity and fear as they succumb to the events portrayed on stage. Second, the audience members, as onlookers, experience pity and fear. Call these "pity and fear," or call them something else. The important point is that the spectacle of what happened to Oedipus pushes us to a more universal reckoning with the unsavoury aspects of our shared human condition while wondering about the necessity of divine retribution.

How, then, can negative emotions like fear and pity bring us pleasure? After all, Aristotle understands that theatre is entertaining—in an elevated sense perhaps—but entertaining, nonetheless. Tragedy brings with it a special sort of pleasure. Aristotle advises, "Not every kind of pleasure should be required of a tragedy, but only its own proper pleasure. The tragic pleasure is that of pity and fear, the poet has to produce it by a work of imitation; [so] the causes of pity and fear should be included in [...] his story-line."[221]

We can think of tragic pleasure as a kind of release. If violent or unsavoury emotions are locked up within us, releasing these emotions in a theatre may have a therapeutic role. Think of anger. We lose our temper but after the outburst—however right or wrong—we calm down.[222] We feel better.

---

221. *Poetics* (Bywater) 14.1453b10–13.
222. I should note that Aristotle does believe that there are cases where anger is justified.

Aristotle claims that tragedy releases some pressure on the human soul; it calms the nerves, introduces a steadiness of purpose, and stabilizes dangerously unstable human beings. Perhaps it promotes the *ataraxia* valued by later Hellenistic philosophers. And yet, there is more to his notion of "tragic pleasure" than this.

In fact, Aristotle only hints at a proper theory. At the beginning of the *Poetics*, he argues that theatre is pleasurable because human nature loves art understood as imitation and that imitation teaches us the meanings behind things.[223] He also suggests we take pleasure in viewing things that are skillfully made and in the sensual experience of what is beautiful, colourful, melodious, rhythmical, textured, symmetrical, and so on.

5.22. Sophocles's *Oedipus*: A Tragedy Without *Hamartia*?

Although much scholarly commentary focuses on Aristotle's use of the term *hamartia* in his theory of tragedy, Sophocles's *Oedipus* is not really an investigation of the mistakes of the protagonist, which set the scene for the psychological drama that then transpires, but are not the focal point of attention.

Aristotle praises Sophocles for pushing the road rage scene to the margins of the plot. He explains: "Stories should not be made up of inexplicable details; so far as possible there should be nothing inexplicable, or, if there is, it should lie outside the story—as, for instance, Oedipus not knowing how Laius died."[224] Aristotle is commenting here on the implausibility of the incident described in the play. One does not kill four people including a royal personage, have one of them run away, leave the bodies lying there, wash the blood off one's hands and calmly disappear, as if nothing had happened, as if no one would notice, as if there would be no investigation, no aftermath, as if Oedipus would not be hunted down or confronted. This is all absurd.

---

223. *Poetics* 1448b19.
224. *Poetics* (Fyfe) 24.1460a27–30.

Alexander Rubel notes that, in ancient Athens, "there were regulations excluding from public life anyone suspected of a murder, a murderer, or anyone who killed another in self-defence, until they were cleansed."[225] The idea that Oedipus could become king without some ritual cleansing (a catharsis) is a non-starter. If there were plague and pestilence sent to Thebes by the gods, he would have been immediately suspect. When Oedipus causally refers to the quadruple homicide in a conversation with Jocasta, his only concern seems to be whether he killed his father or not. This sort of thing could only confirm Oedipus as half-barbarian, a magnificent half-barbarian perhaps, but hardly a model of civic responsibility for an Athenian audience. In any case, this is only marginal to what the play is about.

Oedipus is mostly a play about ἀναγνώρισις (*anagnôrisis*), Aristotle's term for the discovery or recognition that precipitates a tragic hero's awareness of his downfall. The *hamartiai*—the previous acts of parricide and incest—set the scene for the awful moment of self-realization at the end of the play but they are done and gone. As Aristotle explains the concept of *anagnôrisis*:

> A discovery [ἀναγνώρισις] is, as the very word implies, a change from ignorance to knowledge, and thus to either love or hate, in the personages marked for good or evil fortune. The finest form of discovery is one attended by reversal of fortune [περιπέτεια], like that which accompanies the discovery in *Oedipus*.[226]

This is what Sophocles's suspense-filled psychological drama is all about. We know what is going to happen, but we are pulled along to the dreadful conclusion where an individual is forced to discover an enormous evil inside himself.

A Greek audience, familiar with the myths would know how the play ends before it starts. What we watch with dread

---

225. Rubel, *Fear and Loathing in Ancient Athens,* Chap. 2, n. 224.
226. *Poetics* (Bywater) 11.1452a30–33.

anticipation is the inexorable, step-by-step process of disastrous self-realization that draws ever closer. Sophocles, a Greek Dostoevsky, chronicles the psychology of the protagonist as he comes to grips with the awful reality. His play depicts a mental journey; we move through stages of self-confidence, self-denial, anger, stubbornness, discovery, rage, resignation, and grief as Oedipus is inexorably led to acknowledge his immense guilt.

Sophocles writes an Aristotelian play, not because of any fatal flaw but because it is a play about character, and he too is a virtue ethicist. What dooms Oedipus is his diseased hubristic character that pushes him to do these evil deeds. The moral meaning is not that men who kill their father and sleep with their mothers are doomed. That would be easy to shrug off; presumably no one in the audience is capable of such monstrous acts. The moral meaning is: Beware! Hubris is a moral error, but the bigger issue is perhaps the poisoned fruit hubris produces. If you are power-hungry, insolent, intemperate, who knows what you might end up doing? You might be responsible for something really horrible. And the gods will know. And they will punish you given enough time. There is moral karma at work inside the cosmos.

5.23. Oedipus and Hubris

Sophocles is more interested in character analysis than in any forensic exploration of Oedipus's terrible crimes. Oedipus is a vicious individual. His specific crimes—a sort of moral ugliness objectified—are the inevitable effect of his skewed moral personality. If we are to capture in a word what is wrong with Oedipus, it would be the traditional sin of hubris (ὕβρις). This is the archetypical ancient fault of misplaced pride. But this is at odds with much present-day commentary.

Nancy Sorkin Rabinowitz provides some rather typical advice on how to interpret Aristotle's account of tragedy. She informs us:

> [Aristotle] uses *hamatia*, which comes from a word that also means missing the mark in archery; thus, it is an

> error, not a character flaw and certainly not pride. Some small mistake that you make unleashes catastrophic consequences. [...] Modern students and critics writing in the wake of Shakespearean drama often see pride as the error, and they look for evidence in Greek tragedy; people also mistakenly assume that the Greek concept of hubris against the gods is the ancient equivalent for a modern (and Christian) notion of pride. For the Greeks hubris was problematic, but it was typically externalized in an arrogant and violent action and not simply an attitude. Pride within bonds, not humility, was appropriate for an aristocratic Greek male in the heroic age [which] was the subject of tragedy; therefore, we have to be wary of importing Christian values into pagan times.[227]

We can all agree that one has to be wary about importing specifically Christian values into Aristotle. But Oedipus's road-rage incident where he killed a foreign king and almost all his retinue could hardly be considered a "small mistake"—even if he did not know he was killing his father. This display of bravado does not seem to be that "pride within bounds" of a proper aristocratic Greek male; it seems more like blind, bestial, unleashed fury—what Aristotle calls "incontinence." It seems odd, furthermore, not to consider hubris as a character flaw when Aristotle himself views morality, chiefly, from a virtue-ethics perspective. But this is a familiar enough strategy in the exegetical literature.

Peter Meineck and Paul Woodruff move in the same direction. They puzzle over the manuscript line 873, "ὕβρις φυτεύει τύραννον: Hubris begets a tyrant," and favour amending it to "Hubris grows from tyranny" (following Blayde, Dawe, and others). Here is their explanation for the "correction":

> The correction is justified by noting that it makes no sense to say that Oedipus became a tyrant because of hubris;

---

227. Rabinowitz, *Greek Tragedy*, 15.

> he never asked to be a tyrant. But it does make sense to claim that his extraordinary power led to hubris, and this is a very Athenian thought. Most recent editors, however, have followed the manuscripts, which have "Hubris begets a tyrant." On this reading the line cannot refer to Oedipus, because hubris did not make him a tyrant, though his father's hubris may have caused him to be born. But the line ought to refer to Oedipus, not to Laius.[228]

There are several problems here. First, it ignores the very Greek problem of bloodguilt. Yes, Laius was guilty of hubris, but he passed that character trait on to his son. The guilt of Laius is not entirely distinct from the guilt of Oedipus. Second, both Sophocles and Aristotle are mostly interested in character types. It is not one hubristic crime that makes one a hubristic character; it is an overall, persistent attitude that puts on display hubristic habits. Third, the act which makes Oedipus king is, on closer analysis, twofold; yes, he defeats the Sphinx (and even here there is a self-conscious show of bravado), but, more importantly, he killed the king in a blatant act of hubris before outwitting the Sphinx.[229] (Remember, he struck first.) As the chorus sings: Hubris begets a tyrant. It is not that tyranny is the cause and hubris is the effect. No, it is the other way around; hubris is the cause and tyranny is the effect. The new translation "hubris grows from tyranny" interchanges cause and effect. It is the kind of person who Oedipus is which causes him to become a tyrant, in the negative sense of the word.

Fourth, remember that tyrant means *self-made* ruler; it conjures up images of a Machiavellian character who uses the

---

228. Meineck and Woodruff, *Oedipus Tyrannos*, 64.
229. It is never very clear why the Sphinx has been inflicted as a punishment on Thebes. Is it because the king has been killed by his son (a monstrous event)? This would make Oedipus responsible for the Sphinx's presence in Thebes. His defeat of her would, then, be mere appearances. He does not solve the problem (he caused) of which the Sphinx is only a symptom. But the incident plays no role in Sophocles and this is speculation.

opportunities provided by Madame Fortuna to his own advantage. This is precisely what happened with Oedipus. After a shrewd battle of wits with the Sphinx, he rode the resulting wave of popularity to secure a kingly power, which, from that point forward, he shrewdly and jealously guarded. Plato tells us that this is what tyrants do—they make themselves champions of the populace. ("Aren't the people always in the habit of setting up one man as their special champion, nurturing him and making him great."[230]) But once they get power, they begin to act—not as servants of the gods (which they should be)—but as a law and an authority onto themselves.

There are, of course, many facets to Oedipus's moral personality. He is filled with absolute, blustering self-confidence as if he were a god. He is not a thinker except in a flashy superficial sense; he is clever rather than wise. He is stubborn, inflexible, and obsessively single-minded. He is short-tempered, given over to emotion and hasty conclusions. He is violent. He is incontinent; he craves honour, power, wealth, and distinction. But at the epicentre of this maelstrom of impetuous character traits is hubris, the vice the ancient Greeks considered to be the opposite of *sôphrosunê*. *Sôphrosunê* exists at the midpoint of Aristotle's golden mean; it is what characterizes the *phronimos*, Aristotle's morally wise person. There is no midpoint of hubris. It is always offensive, always a mistake, always a vice. It can never be anything but a dangerous exaggeration. At the end of *Oedipus*, Creon tells the deflated protagonist:

> You cannot control everything.
> All your former power is ended.[231]

Oedipus is put in his place. There is something higher than him; his glory has turned to shame. Aiming too high, he has been brought down low.

---

230. *Republic* (Grube) III.565c ff.
231. *Oedipus* (Fainlight and Littman) 1522.

The term "hubris" denotes a very specific sort of moral offence in ancient Greece, where it had political, legal, moral, and religious overtones. As David Castriota explains:

> The religious connotation and dimension of *hubris*, particularly as it was depicted in Greek tragedy and epic, probably constitutes the most familiar usage of this theme. But the issue of *hubris* was hardly a special preserve of the poets; it was a human flaw whose effects translated readily into the fabric of daily life among the ancient Greeks. In its broadest sense, *hubris* connoted insolent and wilful acts of outrage, a form of behaviour arising from a lack of restraint or a lack of respect for lawful limits of various kinds. Such acts included far more than arrogance or impiety against the gods; they could be directed at one's superiors, at one's equals, and against inferiors as well. Men might commit *hubris* against acknowledged civic or religious authority, or toward one another. [...] Acts of *hubris*—physical violence and sexual or verbal abuse that dishonoured other citizens, women, children, and even slaves—could be prosecuted under a severe indictment. Demosthenes warns his countrymen that an act of *hubris* wrongs not only the victim, but the state as well: "Nothing, men of Athens, nothing is more intolerable than *hubris*, or more deserving of your anger." Isokrates advances a similar argument as a basic principle of statecraft: "You [, the king,] will lead the people wisely if you allow the masses neither to commit nor to endure *hubris*."[232]

As Castriota points out, the dramatic representation of the hubris trope takes place within this larger legal and political context. Although legal issues will not detain us here, it is important to keep in mind that crimes involving hubris ranged from physical or even verbal abuse to improper sexual

---

232. Castriota, *Myth, Ethos, and Actuality*, 17–18. The Isocrates's passage is in *To Nikokles* [II], 16.

relations (even with inferiors) that were forced or homosexual.[233] Oedipus's principal crime is the usurping of his father's kingly power. This is what young male lions do to old male lions; they kill them and take over the pride. Oedipus unwittingly abuses both his father and his mother; both count as crimes of hubris, not merely because dishonouring your parents is insolent, but because it rejects the established order, an order that was enshrined in tradition and nature and, ultimately, enforced by the gods.

Oedipus is not hungry for sex; he is hungry for political power, for glory, for distinction. He will not suffer any perceived slight, insult, or challenge to his power. But this is hubris directed against the gods because they are the guardians of the established moral order and demand that human aspirations be held within reasonable bounds. When Oedipus refuses to yield to a royal personage and slaughters his entourage, this is hubris. When he belittles the oracle, this is hubris. When he wants to kill Creon, this is hubris. When he tries to slay his wife (and mother!), this is hubris. When he threatens to torture the frightened shepherd, even this is hubris. And so on. Disrespecting established chains of authority, demanding more than one's due, having entire confidence in one's own abilities: These are all tell-tale signs of a hubristic (or insolent) character. Aristotle defines hubris while discussing anger in the *Rhetoric*:

> Hubris consists in doing and saying things that cause shame to the victim. [...] for the pleasure of it. The cause of the pleasure thus enjoyed by the insolent men [the *hubrizontes*] is that they think themselves greatly superior to others when ill-treating them. That is why youths and rich men are insolent; they think themselves superior. [...] One sort of insolence is to rob people of the honour due to them.[234]

---

233. Cf. Cohen, "Sexuality, Violence, and the Athenian Law of 'Hubris,'" 171–188.
234. *Rhetoric* (Roberts) II.2.1378b23–32.

Oedipus owes honour to his father, his mother, his wife, the king in a foreign land, the prince Creon, the oracle, the gods. Even when he withheld honour from them unwittingly, this disrespect is an objective fact. One does not honour one's father by murdering him.

More generally, Oedipus is a man who thinks himself greatly superior to others. He loves lording it over other people; he cannot brook disagreement or contrariety. There is a pleasure involved in becoming king, in wielding political power, in imposing one's will on others, in feeling superior, in being admired and held in high regard, in being seen as the saviour of Thebes, in being a self-made man. Pleasures that Oedipus hankers after and indulges in before his downfall. The road-rage incident was a matter of macho pride. He refused to give way to a king (and his father). One can imagine him savouring his victory over five men and thinking of himself "as greatly superior when ill-treating them."

Aristotle is not concerned with religion here; he is talking about the hubris (variously translated as "insult," "insolence," "affront") that manifests itself in human relations. But Oedipus's crimes are also against the gods. His queen (and mother) expresses scepticism about the power of the supernatural generally—"I pay no heed to prophecies,"[235] and Oedipus himself, upon learning that his foster father Polybus has died, disavows his earlier belief in prophecy. As he tells his queen:

> Ah, wife, why would anyone go
> to the shrine of the Pythian seer, or look for auguries
> from the screeching birds above, who prophesied
> that I would kill my father. Now he is dead,
> [...] and I am here, innocent, [...]
> Those useless oracles now rot in Hades.[236]

---

235. *Oedipus* (Fainlight and Littman) 857.
236. *Oedipus* (Fainlight and Littman) 964–972.

Jocasta replies "Isn't that just what I always said."[237]

Even if some Greek tragedians composed "plays of fate" to demonstrate the harsh reality of innocent people being tricked by the gods—one thinks of Euripides' *Bacchae*—this template does not apply, at the very least, to *Oedipus*. It is not that the gods tricked Oedipus; it is Oedipus that is trying to trick the gods. Think, again, about what Oedipus is doing. Singled out as a dangerously hubristic character destined to do the most terrible acts, the gods send him a warning through the oracle. How does he respond? He does not remedy his character flaws. He remains as hubristic, as short-tempered, as violent, as headstrong, as ambitious as before. Poor foolish mortal! He travels to a new location. He thinks he can defeat the prophecy by doing an end-run around his presumed birthplace. This is like a womanizer who moves from New York to Paris in order to disprove rumors about his philandering. He ends up womanizing in Paris instead of New York. How does this solve the underlying problem? Yet this is Oedipus's strategy. He thinks he can outmanoeuvre and outwit the gods by a simple change of location. The Greek gods, who are always filled with *mētis* or cunning (as Aristotle himself mentions), put him in his place. The seed of destruction is in the character, the *hexis* of Oedipus. As one of the messengers says: "The worst woes seem to be those we bring upon ourselves."[238] The point of Sophocles's play is not to expose a lack of human agency; the point is to show that there is a transcendental moral order that must be respected.

Aristotle prizes a virtue he calls μεγαλοψυχία (*megalopsychia*), literally "greatness of soul."[239] This supreme virtue has an element of rightful pride. (Which is why Aristotle needs to come up with an explanation for the great Socrates's

---

237. *Oedipus* (Fainlight and Littman) 973.
238. *Oedipus* (Fainlight and Littman) 1230–1231.
239. Aristotle starts his specific discussion at *Nicomachean Ethics* IV.3.1123a34 ff. But the previous discussion on μεγαλοπρέπεια (magnificence) has a bearing on all this, starting at IV.2.1122a17.

ironic self-denigration.[240]) Oedipus would have viewed himself as possessing "greatness of soul."

But Aristotle is at great pains to point that true *megalopsychia* is a species of moral conduct. He keeps repeating the same point over and over again:

- "It would seem characteristic of a great-souled person to be great in each virtue."[241]
- "Greatness of soul, then, seems to be like a sort of adornment of the virtues since it makes the virtues greater and does not come about without them."[242]
- "A great-souled person […] will be the best person."[243]
- "A great-souled person would appear completely ridiculous if he were not good."[244]
- "Nor would the great-souled be worthy of honour if he were base, since honour is a prize of virtue and is awarded to good people."[245]
- "A great-souled person seems, then, to be someone who thinks himself worthy of great things and *is* worthy of them."[246]

Oedipus does not fit the bill. For all his grandiose aspirations, he suffers from *akrasia* and immoderate pride. He is a violent man. He is not as smart as he thinks. He is self-absorbed and insolent; he lacks moral wisdom (*phronêsis*). He does not hit the mean. (Even *megalopsychia* is a midpoint between extremes.)[247] His hubris is pretense at being great-souled; it is not the real thing.

---

240. Cf. *Nicomachean Ethics* IV.7.1127bff.
241. *Nicomachean Ethics* (Reeve) IV.3.1123b29.
242. *Nicomachean Ethics* (Reeve) IV.3.1123b36–1124a2.
243. *Nicomachean Ethics* (Reeve) IV.3.1123b 26–27.
244. *Nicomachean Ethics* (Reeve) IV.3.1123b32–33.
245. *Nicomachean Ethics* (Reeve) IV.3.1123b34–35.
246. *Nicomachean Ethics* (Reeve) IV.3.1123b1–2 (my italics).
247. At the lower end, smallness of soul; at the upper end, vanity, presumption, folly. To wit: "Though therefore in regard to the greatness

Aristotle says that the μεγαλόψυχος most values honour, which is close to the gods and what the gods value most of all. Yet, such people are concerned with honour "in the way they should be."[248] Which means that they value virtue as more important than honour for, as he puts it, "no honour can match the worth of virtue that is complete in every way."[249] The truly great individual prizes all the virtues taken together; the honours he sometimes receives (if fate favours him) is of secondary importance. Aristotle does mention several men who could have aspired to great-souledness: Alcibiades, Achilles, Ajax, Lysander, and Socrates.[250] But we could also include Oedipus in the list: The tragic effect in Sophocles's play is heightened because he falls so far, from almost achieving the supreme virtue to being revealed as an evil monster.

At the end of Sophocles's play, the sightless Oedipus (like the blind Tiresias) can finally see! To save Thebes from the curse, he orders his own banishment from the city:

> I, wretched creature, have banished myself, I myself insisting
> that the impious one should be thrust out. Now, I am
> the one revealed by the gods as defiled—of Laius' lineage.
> My sinfulness exposed.[251]

Oedipus tells the others: "my sins are not contagious, / No mortal can bear them but me."[252] Oedipus becomes something like a scapegoat, a Christ-like figure—except, of course, that Christ is innocent whereas the calamity that Oedipus suffers is self-made. Still, Oedipus saves the city

---

of his claim the great-souled man is an extreme, by reason of its rightness he stands at the mean point, for he claims what he deserves; while the vain and the small-souled err by excess and defect respectively." *Nicomachean Ethics* (Rackman) IV.3.1223b13–14.

248. *Nicomachean Ethics* (Reeve) IV.3.1123b20–21.
249. *Nicomachean Ethics* (Reeve) IV.3.1124b7. Cf. 1124b5–11.
250. *Posterior Analytics* II.13.97b16–25.
251. *Oedipus* (Fainlight and Littman) 1381–1384.
252. *Oedipus* (Fainlight and Littman) 1413–1415.

by willingly accepting his own guilt and exiling himself as expiation for the harm he has caused. His behaviour, surely, marks a change in character. But this willingness to accept the necessary penalty—he banishes himself, this punishment is not forced on him by the gods—his readiness to sacrifice his own welfare for others is true magnanimity; perhaps, something close to greatness-of-soul.

Aristotle writes in the *Ethics*, "Nobility shines through when one bears with resignation many great misfortunes, not through insensibility to pain but through nobility and greatness of soul [μεγαλοψυχία]."[253] In Sophocles's complex plot, it is at the end, when Oedipus loses his political power that he becomes morally powerful. It is only when he is ashamed that he has any hope of glory. His self-inflicted punishment washes clean the city; Thebes is undergoing a catharsis, an absolution, that resembles the catharsis that Aristotle attributed to tragedy more generally. One cannot appreciate all this without situating the moral content of the play within a larger religious framework. In Aristotle's mind, tragedy is not about proving anything; it is about making us feel that the transcendental possibility of a higher moral order in the cosmos. (Of course, the idea that the gods punish and reward us necessitates an account of divine efficient causality that might be at odds with other claims in Aristotle's metaphysics, but that is matter for technical discussion.)

5.24. *Oedipus*, Theatre, and *Theôria*

We find ourselves returning to the age-old idea that a tragedy like *Oedipus* is about poetic justice—that shadowy divine forces will see to it that evildoers get the fate they deserve. Although Aristotle accepts that virtuous agents may be unhappy because of external factors beyond their control, he also believes that a vicious agent cannot achieve genuine happiness. Sophocles's play is about the second circumstance, not the first. *Oedipus* is *not* the story of the thoroughly

---

253. *Nicomachean Ethics* (Ross and Urmson) I.10.1100b30–33.

good man, someone like a Socrates or a Jesus who comes to a dreadful end through a harsh and fickle turn of fate. It is the story of a heroic temperament, a man who has a potential for *megalopsychia*, but who fails through his own hubris and is justly, if harshly, punished by the gods.

The most important aspect of tragedy, in Aristotle's mind, is the way it opens the mind up to cosmic possibilities. It is this aspect of literary epiphany—call it "catharsis" if you will—that is at the forefront of his admiration for Greek theatre. In Aristotle's mind, Greek tragedy does not teach simplistic platitudes; it triggers a negative sense of wonder that washes over the audience (the *catharsis*) purifying them of short-sighted human preoccupations. Tragedy makes the world bigger. Think of catharsis, not as mere washing, but as a sort of being shaken to the core: like being awakened brutally from a deep uncritical sleep to see a world soaked in cosmic significance. Pity and fear are the enzymes that instigate this intellectual epiphany.

Although Aristotle himself does not explicitly move in this direction, I suggest that the experience of theatre, from an Aristotelian perspective, is best seen as another sort of θεωρία (*theôria*). Of course, the word "theatre" is derived from the related Greek root θέατρον, meaning "a place for viewing," and from θεάομαι: to see, watch, witness, observe. But the more important point is that theatre has cognitive, aesthetic, and religious aspects that parallel Aristotle's philosophical notion of *theôria*.

I have already explained the historical background to Aristotle's technical use of the term *theôria*. In its root sense, the term was used to describe pilgrimages. It means, literally, "witnessing a spectacle."[254] Although one could do this privately, Greek city-states sent official delegations to "religious oracles or festivals." As Nightingale explains, the *theôros* (the pilgrim) was:

---

254. Nightingale, "*Theôria*," 23.

> Required to return to his city and give a complete and honest account of what he had witnessed and heard. The *theôros* [was] thus charged with the task of communicating to the city what the god ha[d] unveiled to him. [...] [This] transaction with divine as well with human beings [...] [was] a mission that must be done with religious correctness.[255]

But this parallels what happened when festival goers in ancient Greece watched Sophocles's *Oedipus*. In fact, there are two levels of *theôria* here. On the first level, Sophocles is the *theôros*. He communicates to the city what he has seen after journeying, in his imagination, to an event overflowing with moral and religious significance: the downfall of Oedipus. On the second level, the audience is the *theôroi* (plural: pilgrims); they are on a pilgrimage, transported to an exotic destination to see "firsthand" a momentous event in faraway Thebes. For poetry does not operate the way philosophy does. It operates, not by argument, but by direct re-enactment (with the help of imagination). The audience witnesses—through the magic of theatre—the same event that Sophocles witnesses; they go on the same journey.

Nightingale points out that *theôria* "involved a detachment from one's homeland, an act of seeing or spectating, and (in many cases) some sort of transformation of the viewer."[256] Aristotle believes that theatre viewers are transformed through catharsis. They are cleaned rather than made dirty (contrary to Plato's model). In Sophocles's case, the religious ritual of Greek theatre has been largely naturalized; the gods are in the background. The psychology of a flawed man follows its natural course. Nonetheless, the moral and religious dynamic of divine "poetic justice" is still at work. That is, despite protestations to the contrary, the subject matter of the play.

---

255. Nightingale, "*Theôria*," 29–30.
256. Nightingale, "*Theôria*," 29–30. Cf. Nightingale, *Spectacles*, 4, n. 3.

Aristotle identifies the theoretical life (*theôretikos bios*) with "perfect happiness."[257] He chiefly has in mind the life of the thinker or philosopher. As we have seen, however, Aristotle compares the experience of doing philosophy to the experience of going to a religious festival (which would have included theatre) and to the experience of watching the Olympic Games (which were permeated by religious overtones).[258] Could we not say, then, that theatre—like philosophy—provides an experience of contemplation of the kind Aristotle has in mind when discussing the intellectual activity of his self-thinking god?

Aristotle tells us, in the *Nicomachean Ethics*, that his philosophical god is doing *theôria*.[259] What this means is that God is not making deductive arguments; he is gazing on the truth in an immediate, intuitive, all-embracing apprehension. God's knowledge happens through a firsthand witnessing of the most fundamental principles of reality somehow working together inside his own nature. But our experience of theatre involves a sort of contemplation. At least according to the analysis advanced here, serious tragedy is an embodiment of the universal moral principles of poetic justice that govern the cosmos. A play like *Oedipus* is a firsthand demonstration of "poetic justice." Audience members do not think about poetic justice, they *see* it enacted in front of them; they apprehend it directly. They gaze upon it; they behold it. In effect, they witness the *entelechia* of poetic justice; they see a fearful illustration of how it operates in the world. This happens in a non-discursive, intuitive way. It is almost a religious, mystical experience. Just as catharsis cleans devotees who sing sacred hymns in the temples, it cleans those who watch theatre.

Aristotle believes that tragedy has a cognitive dimension. (Hence his comment that poetry is more philosophical than

---

257. *Nicomachean Ethics* (Ross) X.7.1177b18–25.
258. Iamblichus (Aristotle), *Protrepticus,* IX, 52.16–54.5.
259. Again, cf. *Nicomachean Ethics* X.8.1178b20–4; 1178b32; *Protrepticus*, B44.

history.) But theatre is not an argument. It is not science or logic; it is not about proving (or disproving) moral or religious dogma. Tragedy has important normative content but is not didactic, in any simplistic sense, as the Victorian authors mistakenly construed an ancient Greek author like Aesop. When the Mitys dies on stage in such a fitting manner, we are astonished—morality seems to be a cosmic force that takes prisoners and enforces an unalterable code. Hubris seems real; the punishment for hubris seems real. Tragedy makes us see these moral failures as momentous events. It magnifies them. It viscerally reminds us that evil is evil and good is good. The denominational details behind the tricks of fate are, for Aristotle, of secondary importance.

What a play like Sophocles's *Oedipus* does is provide a non-philosophical way of reaching a peak intellectual experience: the direct contemplation of poetic justice played out in all its dreadful magnificence. I have argued, in a previous chapter, that Aristotle is open to the possibility of fate intervening in human affairs. Greek tragedy takes that possibility for granted. The Greek pagan tradition insists, again and again, that the gods reward the good and punish the bad (and their children, and their subjects). All this would have been a familiar trope to Sophocles's audience and to ancient readers of Aristotle. Sophocles does not deny this reality but naturalizes it; he turns it into something "believable" on a psychological level with the gods in the background, so to speak. But the gods are still there, and the play still puts Oedipus's fate on display with all the moral cosmic machinery in the background.

On Aristotle's account, *theôria* is, as Nightingale points out, "a contemplative activity that is completely 'useless' in the world of human affairs."[260] According to someone like Aristotle, we do philosophy in order to do philosophy; philosophy is intrinsically valuable, god-like, leisurely, pleasurable, and self-sufficient. But we could say something similar about

---

260. Nightingale, "*Theôria*," 23.

theatre. We go to watch a play for entertainment; it may have been religious entertainment in the ancient world, but it was still entertainment. Theatre is something extra—something we do when we take a break from practical exigencies, something that we do for its own enjoyable sake. Aristotle discusses the *pleasure* proper to tragedy in Chapters 13 and 14 of the *Poetics*. Successful theatre is a form of leisure, which effortlessly captures our attention and turns us towards a contemplation of the world that is self-sufficient as an experience for its own sake.

Aristotle is no Nietzsche. If we rid Greek tragedy of religious content, we end up with tragedy as an expression of despair. Some might argue that the dubious intentions of cynical playwrights drain pagan morality of all its authority; I would disagree but, at the very least, that is not Aristotle's approach. Without the gods as the guardians of morality, we watch a human being suffer the worst calamity possible. How does that lead to anything but despair? This secularist interpretation reinforces the negative emotions rather than curing them. This is not what Aristotle, a rather severe moralist, has in mind. Aristotle thinks tragedy is supposed to heal us; to wash us clean of negative emotions. He also believes that the world has an objective moral structure, a rather tenuous proposition without the operation of some sort of cosmological karma.

One may, perhaps, disagree with Aristotle's moralistic worldview—just as one can disagree with Socrates's optimistic pronouncements that the gods will see to it that nothing bad happens to a good man. Aristotle, however, would never have accepted that literature (or life) could be summed up in any *amoral* understanding of things. He would have strenuously objected to any interpretation of his theory of tragedy that moves in a nihilistic direction. However fanciful the Greek gods may seem to us, the pagan world of ancient Greece was not a meaningless place without moral or religious direction. Aristotle entertains at least the possibility of a world illumined by moral wisdom. In the case of tragedy, this requires some sort of divine retribution. Otherwise, as Socrates always insisted, the world does not make moral sense.

Chapter 6

A Phenomenology of Discovery

> This kind of degenerate learning did chiefly reign amongst the schoolmen, who having sharp and strong wits, […] but their wits being shut up in the cells of a few authors (chiefly Aristotle their dictator) […] and knowing little history, either of nature or time, did out of no great quantity of matter and infinite agitation of wit spin out unto us those laborious webs of learning which are extant in their books.
>
> Francis Bacon, *The Advancement of Learning*

6.1. Aristotle and the New Testament

I have tried to present a religious perspective on Aristotle, one that is consistent with his works, but also one that is open to and takes seriously the cultural and religious values of his place and time. Aristotle, the cautious philosopher, is more aloof than Plato; his personal convictions remain a bit of an enigma. But he comes across as a proud pagan Greek, cautious and philosophically precise, a moderate conservative. He demonstrates an interest in religious, spiritual, and even mystical questions; he does not neglect intercessory prayer. He recognizes the role of state religion; he often begins his investigations by reverently repeating *endoxa*—the commonly held beliefs of his time and place. He does not contradict his public teachings in his esoteric texts; he does not reject all Plato. He devises a metaphysics of theological imitation that includes things like unmixed and immaterial souls, unmoved movers, and such like; he maintains that God is the final cause of the cosmos and even hints, at times, that God *might* act as an efficient cause in the world. He is open to the possibility of fate; he believes that scientific knowledge is severely limited when it comes to the worrisome, edifying, or awe-inspiring particulars that shape human lives. He leaves room for divine inspiration; he understands theory as a form of intuition, contemplation, and direct insight rather than deductive argument. He is open to literature as a distinctly moral endeavour; he does not limit *hamartia* to amoral mistakes of fact. He devises a response to Plato's critique of literature, and so on. This Aristotle is rather different than the highly secularized, modernized Aristotle, wiped clean of the atavisms of pagan belief and conviction, which we sometimes encounter in the secondary literature.

But, in this chapter, I want to move in a different direction. I want to show that Aristotle's account of cognition is surprisingly amenable to a religious worldview outside the Greek pagan tradition. If, in the Western world, a combination of Aristotelian metaphysics and Judeo-Christian revelation produced medieval scholasticism, one might think that these theological thinkers subverted Aristotle's highly secularized, scientific account of the origins of intelligence and turned it to their own religious ends. I think that is a mistake. Quite to the contrary, I want to argue that Aristotle's descriptions of the most fundamental mechanisms of knowing closely parallels what we find in religious texts such as the *Iliad* and the New Testament.

I will compare an Aphrodite story from the *Iliad* with the Emmaus story from the New Testament to show that the type of sudden enlightenment, discovery, or "quick-knowing" depicted in both "miracle stories" resembles the burst of intelligence Aristotle attributes to knowledge-producing states such as ἀναγνώρισις (*anagnôrisis*), νόησις (*noêsis*), ἐπαγωγή (*epagôgê*), εὐστοχία (*eustochia*), ἀγχίνοια (*agchinoia*), and δεινότης (*deinotês*), etc. This type of knowing is what Enlightenment authors (like Bacon) pejoratively referred to as the mysterious "agitation of wit." In the philosophy tradition, this mental operation is variously described, but it always involves an immediate "intuition," a non-discursive, non-argumentative burst of understanding. I will argue, then, that in Aristotle the mechanism of knowledge at the first levels of understanding is not so different than what is depicted in the ancient religious tradition (pagan or Christian). The denigration of this first-principle necessary step in learning has hampered the broad project of contemporary epistemology.

We will consider these religious stories from the viewpoint of the pagan or early Christian believer. I am interested in what things look like from the perspective that views the stories as deeply truthful, not from an aggressively secular outside perspective that is hostile to the religion. I will assume what I take to be a mainstream understanding of both religious traditions without taking a deep dive into details. Let us begin with the two stories.

6.2. Aphrodite and Emmaus

Let us turn, then, to the New Testament story of the supper at Emmaus (Luke 24:13–35) and a parallel incident from Homer's *Iliad*, involving Helen and the goddess Aphrodite (III.381–400). Needless to say, neither the New Testament nor Homer counts as philosophy. Nonetheless, I will suggest that both stories line up, not exactly, but to a large degree, with the first levels of Aristotle's basic epistemology. There is something shared in Aristotle, Homer, and Luke, even if Homer and Luke were not philosophers and had other things on their minds.

The Emmaus story hardly needs an introduction. After Jesus's death by crucifixion, two disciples, Cleophas and an unnamed companion, are sharing a meal with a stranger—who explains the Scriptures to them—when they suddenly realize that the stranger is Jesus. From Luke: "When he was at table with them, he took the bread and blessed, and broke it, and gave it to them. And their eyes were opened and they recognized him."[1] The Greek is "αὐτῶν δὲ διηνοίχθησαν οἱ ὀφθαλμοί, καὶ ἐπέγνωσαν αὐτόν": more literally, "of them were opened their eyes and they recognized him."[2] We have, then, an incident of recognition that precipitates a series of realizations: Jesus is risen! He is the Messiah! Etc. Presumably, something supernatural opens the disciples' eyes—not their physical eyes but the eyes of their minds—so that they not only recognize the risen Jesus but grasp what all this means theologically: This is the Son of God, risen from the dead, as he himself truthfully proclaimed!

One finds, perhaps surprisingly, a somewhat parallel case in Homer in his description of the encounter between Aphrodite and Helen in the *Iliad*. The tone of Homer's narrative is emotionally frustrated and even harsh; here, the intervention of the goddess is a matter of some rebuke. Still, the scene pivots around the same sort of sudden theological revelation. A goddess swoops down to Earth, whisks a wounded Paris away to safety, and goes to find Helen to wait in attendance on him. The important passage reads:

> Aphrodite snatched Paris up [from the battlefield] in a moment (as a god can do), [...] and conveyed him to his own bedchamber. Then she went to call Helen and found her on a high tower with the Trojan women crowding round her. The goddess took the form of an old woman who used to dress wool for Helen. [...] Thus disguised, she plucked Helene by the perfumed robe and said, "Come hither; Alexander [Paris] says you are to go to the house. [...]" With these words, she moved the heart of Helen to anger. [But] when Helen marked the beautiful neck of the goddess, her

---

1. Revised Standard Version Catholic Edition, Luke 24:30–31 (28–35).
2. "And their eyes were opened, and they recognized him." *Young's Literal Translation*.

> lovely bosom, and sparkling eyes, she marvelled at her and said, "Goddess, why do you thus beguile me? [...] You are come here to betray me. [...] I shall not go [...]" Aphrodite was very angry, and said, "Bold hussy, do not provoke me; [...] [otherwise] I will stir up fierce hatred between Trojans and Achaeans, and you shall come to a bad end." At this Helen was frightened. She wrapped her mantle about her and went in silence, following the goddess.[3]

I will not investigate the details of the plot here. What matters is that a goddess visits a particular mortal disguised as an old hag and is suddenly transformed—one could say she is "transfigured"—in a split instant. The old woman suddenly morphs into a divinely beautiful figure with graceful neck, lovely bosom, and sparkling eyes. Helen immediately realizes her mistake—this is not a hag but the goddess! Instead of the joy, however, the merely human confronts the fearfully divine.

6.3. *Anagnôrisis*: Discovery

As we have already discussed, Aristotle emphasizes the role of *anagnôrisis* (ἀναγνώρισις) in Greek tragedy. As J. Hutton translates the famous passage from the *Poetics*: "Recognition [*anagnôrisis*], as the word itself indicates, is a change from ignorance to knowledge, leading either to friendship or hostility on the part of those persons marked for good fortune or bad."[4] So, for example, in *Oedipus*, the moment of (dual) recognition happens when Oedipus discovers he has killed his father and slept with his mother. He finally realizes, not simply the fact of patricide and incest but that he is the criminal whose moral pollution has drawn down the gods' ire on the city. It is the element of discovery, of suddenly realizing something, that I want to focus on here. Whenever we have an instance of recognition, we have a sudden shift

---

3. *Iliad* (Butler) III.381–418.
4. *Poetics* (Hutton) 11.1452a30–32.

from unawareness to some momentous new instance of knowledge.

In both the Emmaus and the Aphrodite stories, then, we have an ideal example of *anagnôrisis*. Although neither episode quite fits into any theatre mode, the epistemological narrative is the same in both cases. In the Aphrodite story, an instantaneous change from ignorance to new knowledge produces a resigned submission to the goddess's biding. In the Emmaus story, an instantaneous change in understanding produces supreme joy; what could have been tragedy is suddenly transformed into redemption and triumph. Indeed, the Emmaus story resembles those untragic tragedies that Aristotle mentions where there is a happy ending.[5] We have a distinct *peripeteia*, a reversal of fortune, but it is an upward, not a downward change. Jesus's apparent failure—being punished like the worst criminal—turns out to be glorious success. Death has been conquered and redemption has come to the world; the two disciples rush back to Jerusalem to share the good news.

There is a wealth of scholarship touching on *anagnôrisis* both in Homer and Christian scripture (notably, Erich Auerbach with respect to the Abraham-Isaac story in the Old Testament and Kasper Bro Larsen with respect to the Doubting Thomas story in the New Testament).[6] Kurt von Fritz and Jakob Ziguras insightfully discuss the Helen and Aphrodite incident (in relation to Aristotle) but do not draw on the scriptural parallel I am going to make.[7] Take the present chapter in the spirit of a comment on broad themes, not on philological details.

We can understand narrative literature and scripture more generally in terms of the skillful use of the literary device of

---

5. The protagonists "may be about to do something deadly in ignorance [of one's relationship] but to recognize it before doing it." *Poetics* (Janko) 1453b29–30.
6. Auerbach, *Mimesis*, Chap. 1, "Odysseus' Scar," 3–23; Larsen, *Recognizing the Stranger*.
7. Cf. Ziguras, "Aristotle's Rational Empiricism," 154–166.

recognition. In a discussion of the *Odyssey*, Pierre Han writes: "At appropriate places in the narrative, Homer introduces the device of the recognition [*anagnôrisis*] scene. In fact, one might venture the observation that the *Odyssey* is stitched together by a series of continuous, unending recognitions on the part of characters."[8] One could say something similar about the *Iliad* but also about the Christian New Testament. Think of Simon Peter's confession: "You are the Messiah, the Son of the living God"[9]; think of what the centurion says: "Truly, this man was the Son of God"[10]; think of the transfiguration (what better recognition scene!), and so on. (Of course, the gospels and the *Iliad* also include many examples of failed recognitions, when a potential *anagnôrisis* is never realized and tragedy results. Think of the death of Patroclus who is mistaken for Achilles or the Good Samaritan story where religious authorities fail to recognize the injured traveller as a brother and fellow believer.) But let us turn now, to the epistemological side of the argument.

6.4. Aristotelian Induction

Although Aristotle generally does not use the term *anagnôrisis* in his logical or scientific work, he does use it in the *Prior Analytics* to describe the sudden realization that happens when someone discovers that some shape is, in fact, a triangle and, therefore, has interior angles equal to two right angles.[11] This is very different subject matter, of course, but the mechanism described here is not so different from the situation in which someone recognizes that someone is actually divine—a goddess or a messiah—so that all the consequences of that recognition are immediately apparent. But I am not so much interested in the content of a moment of intellectual discovery here; I am interested in

---

8. Han, "Recognition in the Odyssey," 51.
9. Mathew 16:16.
10. Mathew 27:54.
11. *Prior Analytics* II.21.67a 23–26.

how this dawning of understanding—and it is understanding not mere psychology—happens. I will argue then that Aristotelian *anagnôrisis* is only a more specific manifestation of an archetypical mental process by which the mind happens to hit—in a flash, in a twinkling—on what something is, on what its nature is, or on why it happens. As we shall see, the sudden intellectual discovery in the Emmaus and the Helen stories parallels Aristotle's model for cognition at the very first levels of knowing.

For Aristotle, knowledge begins in induction, not in logical or scientific demonstration (as a familiar stereotype would have it). I have treated the topic of Aristotelian induction at length elsewhere. For the moment, suffice it to say that Aristotle calls the most rigorous form of inductive thinking *epagôgê* (επαγωγή). This grasping of the nature of the thing operates via direct intelligence or νοῦς (*nous*). It supplies "an account which makes clear why a thing is."[12] A thing is the way it is because it possesses a certain nature. In *epagôgê*, there is a click of understanding, a leap of intelligent discernment that penetrates to the underlying essence. In understanding what a thing is, we understand the reason, the cause, and the explanation for what we observe.

In scattered passages, Aristotle gives diverse examples of scientific explanations discovered through induction. Why do deciduous trees lose their leaves in the fall? Because sap thickens (forms a sticky ball) in the stem.[13] Why are horse, mule, and man relatively long-lived? Because they are bileless (i.e., they have clean blood).[14] Why do storm-clouds thunder? Because fire is extinguished inside them (a noisy operation).[15] Why does an eclipse darken the moon? Because of the interposition of the earth.[16] Think of Watson and Crick's modern

---

12. *Posterior Analytics* (Barnes) II.9.93b38–40.
13. *Posterior Analytics* II.16.35–39.
14. *Prior Analytics* II.23.19–25.
15. *Posterior Analytics* II.8.93b8–14; 10.94a1–8.
16. *Metaphysics* VIII.4.1944b10–15; *Posterior Analytics* II.8.93a29–31ff.

account of the double-helix shape of DNA, which happened through a brilliant intuitive leap that resulted in the discovery—a scientific *anagnôrisis*: "A double helix! So, that's the reason why DNA replicates itself!" This is the kind of thing that Aristotle has in mind when he discusses *epagôgê*.

Aristotelian induction differs from Humean induction. It is not, fundamentally, an enumerative or statistical mode of thought. It is not about counting observations, adding up probabilities, or producing Bayesian calculations. If we moderns tend to view induction, primarily, as a matter of empirical confirmation, Aristotle views it, primarily, as a method of *discovery*. The stock analytical model of logical induction, "this crow is black, this crow is black, this crow is black; therefore, all crows are black," misses the point seen from an Aristotelian perspective. Blackness is an accidental, not an essential feature of crows. Knowing that all crows are black—even if that were true—does not tell us *why* crows are black. It only reports on a statistical regularity. It does not explain the underlying cause in the nature of the thing.

As the discussion at the end of the *Posterior Analytics* (II.19) suggests, Aristotelian induction often (or even usually) happens in an instant. Aristotle recognizes, of course, that repeated observations have a way of pushing us to the intuitive leap that gives us the reason why. But he also accepts that a flash of understanding can be produced by a single observation. He says, for example, that if someone had magnified vision and could see the light particles coming through the pores in the glass on a single occasion, they would immediately know why, in *every* case, light passes through glass.[17] They would know why glass is transparent from a single observation because, in every case, the nature of light and the nature of glass will be the same.

Aristotelian induction is not a matter of X-ray vision into a secret or occult essence as in the Humean (really, Lockean)

---

17. Note that Aristotle proposes a different theory of light; this is meant as an explanation of induction, not light. *Posterior Analytics* I.31.88a14–17.

empiricist caricature. For that would make induction a matter of magnified perception. Aristotelian induction is not a matter of perception but of cognition. Perception pushes us to the verge of a realization, but it is the moment of mental seeing, the cognitive click that makes us realize something—"oh! here is the underlying reason why!"—that is properly constitutive of an induction.

Induction, then, can be thought of as a kind of scientific *anagnôrisis*: There is "a change from ignorance to knowledge" that happens in a moment of recognition. Just as Oedipus suddenly realizes who he is and all the resulting implications, the scientist realizes what the nature of something is and all the relevant implications. As in the *Oedipus* play, piece after piece of evidence piles up until—bang!—the sudden realization breaks through the present ignorance and the agent finally understands what is the case. We could even say that there is a change from bad to good fortune in induction as the knower gains knowledge and wisdom. It is bad fortune to be ignorant and good fortune to know something. As we have seen, however, the same sort of instantaneous mental sequence applies in both the Aphrodite and the Emmaus case, something I expand upon below.

6.5. Other Kinds of Aristotelian Induction

But, along with *epagôgê*, Aristotle mentions many other kinds of knowing that fit into this mental illumination model of cognitive understanding. To begin with, Aristotle discusses weaker forms of induction that deal with merely contingent, probable, or plausible properties, including so-called arguments from analogy (τὸν ὅμοιον) and anecdotal reasoning (argument from παράδειγμα, i.e., from examples).[18] All such inductive arguments hinge on an *anagnôrisis*-like intellectual discovery: Technically put, the reasoner recognizes that the

---

18. Cf. *Topics* VIII.1.156b10–19; *Topics* I.XII.105a10–16; *Rhetoric* II.23. 139b10–16; *Rhetoric* I.2.8; *Rhetoric* I.3.1356b14–15; 1357b31–1358a1; also see, *Prior Analytics* II.24.

terms in a syllogism are convertible (ἀντιστρέφω, *antistrephō*) because they possess the same (or similar) natures. This happens non-discursively, not through any step-by-step logical process, but through a direct realization that this is the same as that.[19] In all such cases, there is an intuitive grasping that happens holistically and without logical steps.

Lambertus Marie de Rijk describes the intellectual act of discovery behind all forms of inductive reasoning as a "noetic, sudden, and instantaneous cognition," "an instantaneous effect of sudden grasping," and "a flash of insight into a universal point."[20] Ross mentions "the flash of insight by which we pass from knowledge of a particular fact to [...] the corresponding general principle."[21] And Ralph Eaton, in an old textbook, interestingly claims that an inductive syllogism is not a true syllogism because it includes this extra non-logical, non-discursive step.[22]

There is also a moral side to induction, which I can only mention in passing here. Aristotle's account of *phronêsis* (φρόνησῐς), or practical wisdom, seems to be a sanitized version of the ancient Greek concept of μῆτις (*mêtis*), the cunning intelligence associated with a trickster like Odysseus, who had a remarkable talent for quickly and decisively grasping what was the case in perplexing situations.[23] Aristotle also mentions ἀρετή (*aretê*), understood, not as the habit of virtue but, more specifically, as the mental engine of moral

---

19. Cf. Groarke, *Aristotelian Account of Induction*, "Convertibility," 129–131.
20. De Rijk, *Aristotle: Semantics and Ontology*, vol. 1, §2.55, 153; §2.56, 153 n. 222; §2.56, 155.
21. Ross, *Aristotle's Prior and Posterior Analytics*, 50.
22. Eaton, *General Logic,* 487.
23. Cf. *Nicomachean Ethics* VI.13.1144b10–16, 21–28, 30–32. Further, note in a similar vein: "Virtue ensures the aim is right." *Nicomachean Ethics* VI.12.1144a6–9; "Virtue points out the end," VI.13.1145a5–6. Cf. Guthrie, *History of Greek Philosophy*, vol. 4, 192–194; Vol. 6, 347; Groarke, "Moral Induction," 226–253; DeMoss, "Acquiring Ethical Ends," and "Aristotle, Connectionism."

judgment that must operate speedily and without verbal equivalent in unpredictable situations. Even the so-called practical syllogism, concluding in an action rather than a verbal proposition, might be said to rely on a very adaptable moment of intuitive reasoning that happens instantaneously in the midst of action.[24]

6.6. Other Aristotelian Kinds of Quick-Knowing

Along with *anagnôrisis* and all these different weaker and stronger forms of induction, Aristotle also mentions many other kinds of quick-knowing: εὐστοχία (*eustochia*, skill in conjecture), which "involves no reasoning and is speedy in its operation"[25]; ἀγχίνοια (*agchinoia*, acumen), "the talent for hitting on" the nature or essence "in an imperceptible amount of time"[26]; δεινότης (*deinotês*), meaning practical "cleverness" or "quickness of mind"[27]; and γνώμη (*gnômê*), a non-discursive sort of moral understanding older people can possess without argument.[28]

That Aristotle should think of the beginnings of intelligence as a speedy, non-discursive mental vision that happens without deductive inference is unsurprising. As Ziguras explains, non-philosophical Greeks did not situate the origins of knowledge in logic. They did not view understanding as "the result of any discursive process."[29] As Von Fritz reports, they tended to think of it as "a kind of mental

---

24. For a key passage, cf. *Movement of Animals* 7.701a7–701b1. Note that this placement in a work on animal behaviour has occasioned much debate. (Practical syllogism is implied elsewhere.) Aristotle writes: "So what we do without reflection [i.e., without having to rehearse it in our heads], we do quickly" (701a29). More needs to be said, but this must suffice here.
25. *Nicomachean Ethics* VI.9.1142b10.
26. Or, as Tredennick has it, "without a moment's hesitation." *Posterior Analytics* I.34.89b10–12; *Nicomachean Ethics* VI.9.1142b5–6.
27. *Nicomachean Ethics* VI.12.1144a23ff; VI.13.1144b1ff.
28. *Nicomachean Ethics* VI.11.1143b8–13.
29. Ziguras, "Aristotle's Rational Empiricism," 163.

perception."[30] Greek terms such as νοῦς (mind, thought, intellection), νοῖεν (to think, perceive, contrive, notice, suppose), and νόησις (understanding or intellection) all point to immediate intuition, not discursive reasoning, as the root source of human intellectual abilities.[31]

One sometimes has the impression that modern readers believe Aristotle introduced science and left behind the religiously encumbered belief system of his age. As if his works marks a clean break with what went before. But this is not what happened. In ancient culture generally, knowledge, even knowledge in myth and scripture, is a matter of grasping what is the case through a shrewd intellectual penetration. Aristotle develops this generalized understanding in highly specialized ways. He clarifies the intricacies of mental processes. But he always begins his epistemology at the same place with a form of mental illumination that is surprisingly close to what we encounter in the religious tradition.

Of course, Aristotle does elaborate a formal logic that moves in a scientific direction. But syllogistic logic was never intended as a replacement for immediate, intuitive understanding. Syllogisms do not replace the first flash of intelligence; they depend upon it for their logical operation. Syllogisms that tell us what we already know have their place in formal logic, but they are not really serving the epistemological purpose of logical reasoning. Some syllogisms seem like bald exercises in pattern recognition. The subject matter seems inconsequential. We already know what the conclusion will be. But when we come across what I will call a "heuristic syllogism," an argument that makes us realize something we did not know beforehand, the premises stimulate the mind so that it can make the noetic leap to a brand new understanding.

---

30. "Originally, and in Homer, νοῦς [mind, thought] never meant 'reason' and νοῖεν [thinking] never meant 'to reason,' whether deductively or inductively." Von Fritz, "ΝΟΟΣ and Noein," 90.
31. Ziguras, 4.13: "Kurt von Fritz on νοῦς in Homer and the Pre-Socratics," 154–166. Note, the verb νοῖεν = νοέω.

Think of the formal structure of an argument like a loaded gun. The way the premises are set up triggers an intellectual recognition or discovery; by the time we reach the conclusion, we are supposed to experience a burst of intelligence that makes us *see* something new.[32] So, syllogistic and logic generally are not at odds with the first levels of immediate knowing; indeed, logic presupposes direct-knowing and makes use of it to motivate inferences to a conclusion.

Formal logic is, of course, a systematic way of testing apparent instances of reasoning; it extends first principles in legitimate directions and provides a criterion that shows us where and how reasoning can go wrong. In other words, Aristotle uses syllogistic to demonstrate when inferences (really, pseudo-inferences) are incorrect and how they can be "checked" and validated with respect to a larger, rigorous system of simplified formal inference. Of course, logic as a discipline focuses on patterns of correct (or incorrect) inference and leaves the subject matter behind. But even logic itself requires first principles such as the principle of non-contradiction, which we access through direct insight, not logic. (I have discussed this at length elsewhere.)

Doubtless, Aristotle is not alone. One can find many other mainstream philosophers referring to non-discursive reasoning as the first and most basic level of intelligence. Authors as diverse as Plotinus, Alexander of Aphrodisias, Augustine, Boethius, Abu Nasr Al-Farabi, Ibn Sina (Avicenna), Maimonides, Thomas Aquinas, Thomas of Ghent, René Descartes, and Blaise Pascal point to some sort of immediate understanding or intuition as the very origin of knowledge.[33] I am not arguing that they agree with Aristotle

---

32. Robert Schmidt has nicely captured this aspect of demonstrative argument in an older treatment of Thomistic logic. Schmidt, *Domain of Logic*.
33. For some contemporary discussion, see diverse sources. Cf. Hacking, "Leibniz and Descartes"; Groarke, "Intelligibility Versus Proof"; Pasnau, "Divine Illumination"; Silva, "The Epistemology of Intuition."

in all the specifics, only that they begin knowledge in some sort of mental insight or illumination. A modern author such as Charles Sanders Peirce introduces the term "abduction" as a more scientific way of describing induction, but that process also depends on a "leap" to the best explanation, which operates as yet another form of mental intuition.

In recent times, Bernard Lonergan's account of so-called insight places a heavy emphasis on the flash of intelligence phenomenon I have been discussing.[34] Except that Aristotle maintains that this first intelligence is infallible *when used correctly*. On his account, "intuition" (or whatever word we want to use) is not a psychological but an epistemological reality. Lonergan thinks that non-discursive reasoning is fallible and must be backed up by evidence. We can experience an aha! moment—a seeming flash of understanding—and come to the wrong conclusion. That is not how Aristotle views things. He would maintain (as would the schoolmen, generally) that a flash of understanding that comes to the wrong conclusion was not really a flash of understanding but a misguided, *counterfeit* apprehension. Aristotle accepts that opinion and even logic admit of error but assures us, in the *Posterior Analytics*, that "scientific knowing and intuition" are "unfailingly true."[35] Aristotle believes that any true exercise of human intelligence must be entirely reliable at its origins (i.e., when it comes to induction and first principles) or we could never secure any reliable system of knowledge. Human agents are fallible and may be led astray by emotions and by misguided experience, but those types of pseudo-epiphany experiences are not truly epistemological however much we may be deceived.

6.7. Putting It All Together: Formalizing the Flash of Understanding

Let us formalize, in general terms, this quick-knowing or flash-of-intelligence phenomenon I have been discussing. The

---

34. Lonergan, *Insight*. Cf. Meynell, *Introduction to Bernard Lonergan*.
35. *Posterior Analytics* (Mure) II.19.100b6–9.

goal here is not to provide a detailed account of Aristotle's nuanced epistemology but to present a basic description, a phenomenology if you will, of how this non-discursive knowing operates at the beginning stages of knowing. I show, then, that the ancient religious tradition, both pagan and even Christian, makes use of a similar conceptual framework to describe the epistemological content of religious experience. The distance between Aristotle and the mythological-scriptural tradition is not nearly so great as is generally supposed.

The mental operation at the heart of all this may be termed "insight," but one could just as easily call it intuition, intellection, immediate intelligence, direct understanding, or some other apt epithet. Ross uses the word "psychological" in connection with his description of *epagôgê*, but the sort of rational process I am describing is cognitive, not merely psychological. Consider, then, how Aristotle conceives of a pure act of mental seeing in the best case scenario.

Here is how an insight, of the very best sort (as in scientific induction), happens:

1. There is an act (or many acts) of physical perception.
2. This precipitates a mental flash: an understanding in a twinkling.
3. Through this act of immediate understanding, the knower peers into the underlying nature of something. There is a sudden *understanding*.
4. This understanding lays bare the nature of something so that we can properly classify it; it makes things intelligible.
5. In the best cases, we identify necessary or essential properties.
6. This knowing does not happen piecemeal, stage-by-stage, but all of a sudden, in one fell swoop.
7. We gain universal knowledge about every instance of the same kind of thing.
8. We can extend this knowledge in arguments and demonstrations.

We can return, then, to our twin stories before moving on to some complications.

6.8. Rapid Insight in Homer and Luke

My point here is that this phenomenological process of first knowing that Aristotle outlines, in various ways, in his texts, is not so different from how knowing is presented in ancient religious traditions. In both the Aphrodite and the Emmaus stories, there is a recognition that happens through some rapid-fire stroke of intellect. In both stories the eyes of participants are opened and they *see*! A direct illumination, engineered by the divine and not by logic, precipitates a sudden moment of understanding. This is the goddess! This is Jesus! Although it is not exactly clear how all this happens, we can apply our eight criteria to each incident.

1. In both cases, there is a physical seeing. Even in the Aphrodite story, it is not a hallucination or a vision; the goddess comes to Earth and is physically present as an old hag. In the Emmaus story, the disciples see a physical man.[36] The risen Jesus is not a ghost, not a Platonic form of a man, not a collective hallucination; what they see is what an Aristotelian would call the hylo-morphic composite, the "primary substance" Jesus. In both stories, there is an act of perception that precipitates an understanding. Criterion No. 1, that knowing is preceded by observation, is satisfied.

2. In both cases, the protagonists suddenly, instantaneously, understand what they are confronting. They immediately *understand*: This is Aphrodite; this is Jesus! There is quick-knowing. This is the salient features of the two stories. Criterion No. 2, that some understanding quickly comes about, is satisfied.

3. In both cases, the knowers suddenly recognize a nature. They correct a mistaken impression: This is not a mere human being but a god! This requires a gigantic leap to a new reality. The protagonists "see" the divinity that

---

36. Cf. Luke 24:36–43.

underlies the human appearance and *understand* what kind of thing this is. It is a divine nature—that is what it is!

All this happens as in Aristotelian induction. Intelligence penetrates to the essence of something. The agents perceive the sensory image—which triggers a flash of discovery. This parallels Aristotle's twinkling-in-an-eye inductions. Technically: In both stories, the participants discover that the nature of a human person is "convertible" with a divinity. This is even more startling in the Jesus case, where a large point of the story is, surely, to confirm the resurrection.

We should not underestimate what is happening here. Aristotle mentions a very ordinary case when, as a white patch in the distance approaches, we suddenly realize—"Oh! That is Cleon's son dressed in a white toga!"[37] What happens in the *Iliad* and the New Testament stories is more momentous. Each encounter unveils a *hidden* supernatural nature: In an instant, there is a Gestalt switch—as the duck becomes the rabbit, the merely mortal becomes divine. Suffice it to say that Criterion No. 3, that an underlying nature is apprehended, is satisfied.

4. Once the participants in the stories see that "this is Aphrodite" or "this is Jesus," they can properly classify what they see. A flash of intelligence makes what is happening intelligible. In both stories, this piercing of the misleading appearances precipitates a universal understanding with wide metaphysical and theological implications. Criterion No. 4, that proper classification becomes possible, is satisfied.

5. Divinity—the status of being a god—is both a necessary and the essential nature of both Aphrodite and Jesus. The protagonists discover this nature. Criterion No. 5, that an essential or necessary nature is discovered, is satisfied.

6. This mental penetration to a divine nature does not happen piecemeal, stage-by-stage, but all of a sudden. In one fell swoop, the agents move from ignorance to knowledge.

---

37. *De Anima* III.I. 425a25–27. Cf. *De Anima* II.6.418a20–23 (about Diares's son). Cf. Keeler, "Aristotle on Error."

They know what they come to know instantaneously. No one makes an argument. No one performs a scientific experiment. No one adds up evidence statistically. No one comes up with a mathematical proof; and yet, in both stories, there is a sudden switch from ignorance to knowledge based on penetrating observation. Criterion No. 6, that enlightenment happens holus-bolus and instantaneously, is satisfied.

7. Is the knowledge gained universal? As best I can make out, in the Aphrodite story: maybe. In the Jesus story: definitely, yes. Consider each story in turn.

In the Aphrodite story, Helen does not just see a goddess. She gains an understanding of how closely the gods are intervening in the Trojan War. She discovers how vehemently Aphrodite supports Paris, her favourite. This is knowledge about a larger historical event, so it is not quite (in an Aristotelian sense) scientific (or universal) knowledge. Perhaps one could claim that the event vividly reveals how the Greek gods care about particular human beings like Paris—or something along these lines. This would be a universal claim.

The Emmaus story has definite metaphysical implications. Jesus had explained the Scriptures before they sat down to dinner. Presumably, he was explaining that he was the Messiah, the Son of God, the Son of Man, the anointed one, the Saviour of the World, and that everything he had said was true. The sudden recognition of Jesus in the breaking of the bread (the Eucharist) secures and triggers a cascade of realizations: His teaching is true! The prophecies have been revealed! Death has been defeated! He is the Messiah! *Everyone* who believes will be saved! And so on. The experience of seeing that this is Jesus makes a click that unleashes a cascade of realizations that can be drawn out from the nature of that experience.

Note that it makes no difference whether the Christian believer reads the story now, or a thousand years in the future, or in 300 AD. The truths revealed by the story apply forever and everywhere to all people, to everyone and everything—angels, devils, saints, prophets, sinners, historical figures, martyrs, alternate planets, alternate universes, and so on. So, universal knowledge of some sort is had. At least in the Emmaus case and perhaps in the Aphrodite case. Criterion No. 7, that universal truths are discovered, is satisfied.

8. Aristotle thinks of theology as a science (because it deals with the necessary and the eternal), but his theology is not based on revelation except perhaps in a very tenuous way.[38] Nonetheless, a devout pagan reader of Homer may well have argued: "Aphrodite saved Paris from death and threatened Helen with punishment if she did not tend to him. Therefore, the gods intervene for the sake of human beings under their care." That is, the believer could see the story as a verification of the pagan religious practice of χάρις (reciprocal goodwill) between patron gods and their followers.[39] One could widen the argument to make claims about how important it is to honour one's local god. As we have seen, Aristotle himself insists that we owe even the lesser gods honour and that those who do not honour the gods should be punished.[40]

But let us turn to the Emmaus story. Here is one of many arguments a Christian reader might make:

- Jesus rose from the dead (physical evidence from the story).
- People who rise from the dead should be believed. (What could be more compelling than defeating death?)
- Jesus said: "I and the Father are one" (John 10:30).
- Therefore, Jesus and God the Father are one.

Such theological inferences can be multiplied endlessly. Suffice it to say that Criterion No. 8, that the original knowledge can be extended and developed, is satisfied in both cases.

---

38. Cf. *Nicomachean Ethics* VI.3.1139b19–25; *Metaphysics* XII.1074b1–14.
39. Pulleyn, *Prayer*, 37.
40. *Topics* 1.11.105a1–10; *Nicomachean Ethics* V.3.1123b19–23; IX.2.1165a15–16; IX.2.1165a14–1165a36: Cf. *Eudemian Ethics* VII.10.1243b12–13; VII.11.1244a1–1244a19.

6.9. Complications

I have tried to show that neither the Aphrodite nor the Emmaus story is as far removed from the analytic tools found within Aristotelian epistemology as one might imagine. If, however, the phenomenological form or structure of these reported religious experiences resembles what Aristotle describes at the first levels of learning, the religious subject matter differs radically from Aristotle's technical preoccupations. If we want to propose a science–religion divide, Aristotle (at least in his esoteric philosophy) veers to the science side of things. Although no one believes in the Aphrodite story anymore, the New Testament narrative is still a living part of surviving religious tradition. I want to briefly consider, then, the subject matter of the Emmaus narrative. Could Aristotle or a member of the ancient Peripatetic school ever maintain:

1. That someone physically rose from the dead?
2. That knowledge can be directly attributed to a divine source?
3. That the divine visited the world for the benefit of particular people?

If we have examined some of these issues in previous chapters, let us revisit them briefly here in light of the reported Emmaus incident.

6.9.1. Physical Resurrection?

As we have seen, commentators generally reject any suggestion that Aristotle (or even a devoutly pagan Aristotelian) could give any credence to a belief in physical resurrection. Although there is a good bit of ancient mythological hinting at the possibility (given figures such as Asclepius, Achilles, Castor, Heracles, Persephone [etc.], and the various mystery cults), I will not investigate that here. Aristotle's teacher Plato obviously took the possibility of physical resurrection to heart as his inclusion of myths about the afterlife in the *Gorgias*,

Phaedo, Phaedrus, and *Republic* demonstrate. Aristotle, of course, is not given to this sort of literary production.

As I have already argued, there is more evidence for the possibility of Aristotelian religious belief than is generally acknowledged. McClymont, who maintains that Aristotle's popular works were more in line with Greek mythology, claims that the Stagirite accepted traditional pagan beliefs about the dead according to which souls journey to Hades and remain there forever. McClymont points to the Hermias hymn, which poetically implies that the latter had become a god (or like a god). Aristotle could not have believed that Hermias was *physically* resurrected but was likely insisting that his good deeds deserved an everlasting reputation (i.e., that his friend had achieved *eudaimonia*). Aristotle might have believed (as a good pagan) that Hermias's soul lived on in Hades, where it could rightfully continue to receive honour and praise. As we have already seen, the philosopher actively participated in the cult of the dead, commissioning ex-voto statues in his will. In the *Politics*, he does recommend that temples be built throughout the land so that we can continue to honour immortal gods and human heroes.[41] His attitude to religious practices such as petitionary prayer could be summed up as ambiguous.

But whatever Aristotle's degree of religious belief, he would have been astounded at the very notion of a physical resurrection. Except, of course, Jesus's disciples were also astounded. From the believer's perspective, the incident really happened. Had the non-Christian Aristotle actually seen a risen Jesus (or like Doubting Thomas put his hands in his side), that would make for a perplexing juxtaposition. If the story is true, the moment of intellection that the disciples experience is, in effect, an instance of Aristotelian induction: One observes something physical that triggers an insight into the nature of something. Eureka! One understands. One perceives something and this act of perception precipitates an

---

41. Cf. *Politics* VII.12.1331b16–19; VII.14.1332b16–21.

act of cognition. Of course, one can always contest the veracity of the account, but this would amount to a complaint about the content rather than a complaint about how cognition is structured.

6.9.2. Can We Have Knowledge Directly from the Divine?

In both of our stories, some supernatural intervention opens the eyes of human agents. Is there any room in Aristotle's metaphysics for such an eventuality? Again, it is not easy to come up with a definitive answer to such questions.

As we have seen, Aristotle repeatedly borrows from a very common ancient trope that intelligence is divine. Suffice it to say that Aristotle seems to believe that knowledge originates from some divine source in the rational soul. Although Alexander of Aphrodisias's identification of the active intellect with God seems extreme, Aristotle unquestionably models the nature of the active part of the mind on the pure actuality of God's nature.[42] We might venture to claim that, for Aristotle, all knowledge and perhaps even perception originates in some sort of divine capacity.[43] Some passages in the corpus raise the possibility of direct communication with the divine via mystical experience. Other passages do not entirely dismiss the paranormal.

Whatever all this means precisely, Aristotle seems to situate the ultimate origins of knowledge in some sort of close contact with a divine source. Assuming that the eyes of Helen in the *Iliad* or the disciples at Emmaus were "opened" by some divine power is not as far from Aristotle's naturalistic epistemology as we might first think. Aristotle's introspecting philosophical god would not be in the business of sending messages to people. That would seem to be the purview of the pagan mythological gods—who play almost

---

42. Cf. Clark, *Aristotle's Man*, 174ff; Guthrie, 309–327; Owens, "Aristotle's 'Definition of the Soul'"; Rist, *Mind,* 181–182; Frede, "*La théorie aristotelicienne,*" 383–390; Caston, "Aristotle's Two Intellects," 211–212.
43. Cf. *De Anima* (Smith) II.12.424a17–25.

no role in Aristotle's technical philosophy. Still, as we have seen, there are hints of pagan belief throughout the corpus.

In the Aphrodite incident and the Emmaus situation, it is as if something divine reaches into the mind from the outside and opens the eyes of the participants. There are pagan and Christian tropes that involve an interior presence of the divine, but let us leave that aside here. What a religiously inclined Aristotelian could have thought about the divine sending personalized messages to his faithful is difficult to access. That the communication of knowledge could arise from a specific supernatural revelation was a familiar theme in Greek pagan culture: hence, the reliance on oracles, on the interpretation of omens and dreams, on mystical cults, and so on. As we have seen, Aristotle is at best noncommittal on such issues (for example, in *On Divination*) but does not rule them out entirely.

6.9.3. Divine Visitation?

In both our stories, the divine enters the world and appears to carefully chosen mortals. Could an ancient adept of Aristotelian philosophy accept this sort of patronage and possibility?

On the interpretation advanced in this book, there is nothing in Aristotle's science that prevents the gods or God from intervening in history. Science does not tell us anything about fate, and as the Aphrodite story makes clear, intervention by the divine in human affairs was a common pagan theme. On the standard interpretation, Aristotle's god is the final, not the efficient cause of reality. Still, the temple oracle cult of ancient Greece was based on the idea that the divine itself (or a messenger) entered human history on a regular basis to communicate something of benefit to select human agents. A χάρις relationship of loyalty and care joined Greek gods and petitioners together in an almost familial bond.

The aristocratic Aristotle would have been highly perplexed by the Christian narrative of a god who so loved all humanity he sent his only son to redeem the *entire* world. The original Aristotle probably would not have believed in reports of the Aphrodite and the Emmaus stories, but it does not follow from this that the religious believer's faith in divine solicitude could not be accommodated into his overall worldview. Of course, Aristotle's thought-thinking-thought god, beloved by philosophers, could not (or would not) orchestrate any such event. He would be too busy thinking (of himself). If, then, we think of Aristotle as a single-minded philosopher strictly enforcing this conception of the divine to the exclusion of any other possibility, the idea of a personal visitation—by a contradictory god-made-man no less—in the New Testament narrative, in particular, becomes too much to handle.

To summarize this last chapter: I have argued that the kind of intellectual awakening depicted in the Aphrodite and Emmaus stories is not unlike an Aristotelian induction in that it meets the eight criteria outlined above. For Aristotle, all knowledge begins in a similar sort of acute penetration into the natures of things. One could argue, then, that Aristotle's epistemology does not pose any absolute barrier to religious belief.

Aristotle was by no means a Christian. In Christianity, the unfolding of history is the ultimate source of revelation; the divine enters into history, alters it, and uses it as a salvific tool. The basic thrust of religious Christian belief is, then, turned towards history. (We see some of this in the pagan tradition as well when, for example, the gods intervene in the Trojan War and affect the outcome to suit their own purposes.) Aristotle's metaphysics, on the other hand, attempts to draw up a time-independent map of the world. At least, this is mostly what his metaphysics is about. So, the Aristotelian metaphysical project is generally ahistorical and, in this sense, at odds with the Christian impetus. If Aristotle thought that tragedy (art) was more philosophical than history, the Christian sense of history as the primordial locus of truth, even metaphysical truth, requires something beyond what Aristotle leaves us with in his metaphysical work.

Suffice it to say that the phenomenology of religious experience is not entirely at odds with the scientific cast of Aristotle's turn of mind. Immediate learning, quick-knowing, knowing something in an instance, coming to a realization through a rapid stroke of insight without argument or logic: This is a phenomenological motif one often encounters in the religious tradition. A meeting with the divine, if it really happens, would be an almighty sort of *anagnôrisis*. But whatever one thinks about the religious content of such claims, the form of mental illumination depicted is not violently at odds with the phenomenology of the original Aristotle.

Chapter 7

Concluding Postscript

> It is true that Aristotle tries to explain dreams and inspiration from natural causes, but this does not imply that he did not take their divine character seriously. For natural causes are at the same time divine causes.
>
> W. J. Verdenius, "Traditional and Personal Elements in Aristotle's Religion"

> There is too much about the gods in the treatises to permit us to discount Aristotle's theologizing as empty word-play; and, on the other hand, Aristotle's gods are too abstract, remote and impersonal to be regarded as the objects of a religious man's worship.
>
> Jonathan Barnes, *Aristotle*

7.1. An Overall View

In this postscript, I would like to review and summarize the argument of the book. I began this research project because I believed that the religious element in Aristotle was not getting fair shrift in the contemporary interpretative literature. Without a doubt, every age "retrojects" to find views that harmonize with its own in earlier historical periods. In a scientific age, we correctly view Aristotle as a fierce champion of science. Add the scientific legacy of Aristotle to the old Enlightenment dichotomy of science versus religion and we end up with a picture of Aristotle as an adversary of religion. But this is deeply problematic. There is a religious side to Aristotle—not a Christian side, because Aristotle had no inkling of the Judeo-Christian tradition—but a religious, pagan, myth-loving, theological side, which we also need to take into account.

As I explain in the first chapter, the Aristotelian corpus is a group project, added to, rewritten, and edited over hundreds of years. The surviving manuscripts are, generally speaking, compilations stitched together by succeeding generations from irrecuperable primary source notes. Some passages and some books are more central to the project, some more subtly argued, and some, more revered in the tradition. Although expert philologists do good work, coming up with a *definitive* account that weeds out from the larger compendium what the original Aristotle did or did not write is a hopeless task. Any such project seems historically naïve, as if one could somehow isolate the exact words of Aristotle from the rest of the bulky narrative.

As any veteran reader of Aristotle soon realizes, there are passages in the corpus that seem paradoxically at odds with one another. Some inconsistencies can be resolved, but others seem to defy any satisfactory resolution. Given that the original sources are an amalgam from various editors and students as well as from the master, we should not be surprised to find different passages expressing differences of opinion on religious matters. And that is what we do find. Needless to say, that makes unearthing the original Aristotle's opinions a rather hazardous project.

As I argue in the second chapter, Aristotle comes across as a moderate, somewhat conservative, pagan Greek who respected the religious traditions and practices of his culture and era. His philosophy is mostly about other things. He did not view religion in a technical, philosophical light. Yet, at the same time, the philosopher who pointed to commonly shared opinions (*endoxa*) as a source of truth must have shared in some of the almost universal religious convictions that were central to his Greek pagan identity. Passages in diverse primary sources in the corpus, along with his *Last Will and Testament*, seem to recommend religious observance as a worthwhile endeavour.

The familiar view that Aristotle was a relentless agnostic and perhaps even a hidden atheist usually relies on three arguments: (1) that Aristotle's philosophical career follows a trajectory from Platonic religious enthusiast to secular scientist; (2) that Aristotle expresses entirely secular or even atheist sentiments in his esoteric works; and (3) that the famous passages from *De Anima* III.V leaves no room for an eternal individual soul because of the elimination of the passive *nous*. The first argument (from Jager and others) is based on historical speculation, but we cannot know, in any precise way, when Aristotle wrote specific texts. The second argument presupposes a radical disjunction between Aristotle's private and public teachings that does not withstand textual scrutiny. The third argument, which focuses on some very important but fragmentary passages, overlooks the basic fact that Aristotle is arguing here for a religious position: That a separate immaterial soul (the active *nous*) is immortal. If this is true, this seems to defeat any aggressive materialism. My own view is that the technical Aristotle (or whomever) wants to eliminate the passive *nous* so as to undermine any possibility of Platonic recollection. If each soul has to start afresh and learn the basic truths of the world on its own, this is an argument for Aristotelian induction (*epagôgê*) over Platonic *anamnêsis*.

In my investigation of Aristotle's religious stance, I also discuss ancient attitudes about petitionary prayer, Aristotle's view of the role of mythology as religious revelation, what he has to say about divine inspiration, and his interest in the paranormal and mystical. Aristotle does provide an account of human philosophical friendship with the gods, explaining what this entails, and what results from this.

In Chapter 3, I argue that an analytically rigorous reader will find theological intimations in Aristotle's metaphysical texts. I acknowledge that Aristotle does not present, in any finished way, an overall picture of the cosmos (including God). His metaphysics comes to us in jumbled up fragments. Although he emphasizes the importance of particularized being and material cause, he also posits God as the Final Cause of everything and describes the many different ways this divine purpose is echoed throughout existence. To what degree his philosophical god might be an efficient cause is not fully worked out in the texts, but there are at least some passages that move in that direction. The resulting *imago dei* we find in Aristotle's texts provides a template for systematizing Aristotelian metaphysics in a theological direction.

In Chapter 4, I consider whether Aristotle believed in a religious notion of fate. Most contemporary commentators maintain that the Aristotle of the *Physics* dismissed the ancient Greek pagan idea that gods rewarded moral agents and punished evildoers. According to this way of construing things, τύχη, understood as chance or fate, is not a real cause in the world. It is something we project onto particular events without ontological reality.

I argue against this familiar way of reading the relevant passages. Generally considered, Aristotle's view is that τύχη (or fate) is not a *scientific* cause; it cannot be included in his catalogue of four causes because it has no universal applicability. If, however, fate is not a scientific cause, it may play a rather mysterious causal role in the real world. Aristotle believes that individual events obey the general rules of natural causality, but he does not believe that those general principles can tell us what will happen at a particular moment in time. He is an indeterminist, so to speak. Fate has to do with incidental or accidental causality, the kind of causality that produces unique individual events for which there is no scientific explanation.

In Chapter 5, I apply Aristotelian principles to Sophocles's *Oedipus Rex*. I argue that highly secularized and amoral interpretations of the play misinterpret how Aristotle and Greek audiences in general understood tragedy. Most contemporary commentators claim that, in a tragedy based on Aristotelian principles, the *hamartia* or "error" that precipitates the downfall of the protagonist is an amoral mistake of fact. Relying on a detailed analysis, I show that this familiar argument ignores the more complicated use of that term in Aristotle's ethics and in ancient drama. If, in the *Poetics*, Aristotle is replying to Plato's harsh condemnation of theatre, he cannot provide an adequate riposte to his teacher without emphasizing the positive moral content of tragedy.

The nihilistic, Nietzschean account of Oedipus as the great Promethean Greek prince tricked by the nasty gods is a modern invention. Tragic plays like *Oedipus Rex* had a didactic role in Athenian society: Oedipus is a hubristic king who unsurprisingly suffers his downfall. On Aristotle's account, the main purpose of tragedy is not moral teaching; Aristotle believes that successful tragedy instills wonder, but a wonder tinged with a religious and moral tone.

In the final chapter of the book, I use an Aphrodite story from the *Iliad* and the Emmaus story from the New Testament to show how religious accounts of knowledge provide a model of intellectual insight that is similar in structure to the immediate kind of mental intuition that Aristotle places at the beginning of the learning process. When Aristotle discusses mental operations such as *anagnôrisis, eustochia, agchinoia, deinotês, gnômê*, and *nous*, he describes each use of intelligence as a speedy, non-discursive mental vision that happens without deductive inference. I set out the phenomenological features he highlights in a series of eight criteria and demonstrate how these same criteria can be applied to the inspirational accounts of knowing one finds in both Homer and the Gospel story. In finishing, I consider, without arriving at any firm conclusion, what Aristotle might have thought about a narrative like the Gospel story.

Aristotle (and his school) left such a broad record of metaphysical and moral speculation that diverse readings of his unfinished philosophical project are possible. Aristotle is, at heart, a naturalist in that he is always looking for naturalistic explanations of worldly phenomena. But he never takes a partisan position against all religious explanations or possibilities. That the world has an immaterial aspect, that the myths contain truths however metaphorical, that there is a living god, that destiny may shape events in the world, that purpose of some sort permeates all nature, that public life requires some religious supervision: These are all elements in Aristotelian thought.

Aristotle is not, in this sense, an Enlightenment thinker. The intellectual war between science and religion is a later development. There are certainly atheistic trends in early philosophy, but Aristotle is more moderate and more distant when it comes to pronouncing on religious questions. Unlike the great medieval schoolmen, he is not primarily a theologian; he does not provide us with any ultimate or explicit synthesis of religious dogma. Nonetheless, as an open-minded thinker, he inquires into all aspects of the realities and structures that shape our lives and orient human aspiration and striving. Science is not everything. Morality, politics, literature, art, and religion are equally deserving of serious intellectual consideration.

Whatever we make of Aristotle's position on precise metaphysical and epistemological questions, his philosophy has to be inserted into a pagan Greek context that is very different from the secularized liberalism we take for granted today. Perhaps every age reconfigures Aristotle in its own image. But we lose something decisive when we eliminate the divine from our exegesis of this great historical thinker. Aristotle did not intend his philosophy as a definitive, finished system of philosophy. His school carried on their research in the same systematic spirit long after he was dead. I think that a contemporary Aristotle would want more open-ended discussion on religion as well as other topics.

Bibliography*

Aristotle, Collected Works

Aristotle in 23 Volumes. Cambridge, MA: Harvard University Press; London: William Heinemann, various dates.

Complete Works of Aristotle: Revised Oxford Translation. Edited by Jonathan Barnes. 2 vols. Princeton, NJ: Princeton University Press, 1984.

Works of Aristotle. Edited by W. D. Ross and John Alexander Smith. 12 vols. Oxford: Clarendon Press, 1908–1952.

Aristotle, Other

Aristotelis Ethica Eudemia. Edited by R. R. Walzer and J. M. Mingay. Oxford: Oxford University Press, 1992.

Aristotle's Ethics: Writings from the Complete Works. Revised and edited with an introduction by Jonathan Barnes and Anthony Kenny. Princeton, NJ: Princeton University Press, 2014.

Aristotle on Comedy: Towards a Reconstruction of "Poetics" II. Edited and translated by Richard Janko. Berkeley, CA: University of California Press, 1984.

Aristotle: Poetics. Translated by D. W. Lucas. Oxford: Clarendon, 1972.

Aristotle Poetics: Editio Maior of the Greek Text with Historical Introductions and Philological Commentaries. Greek and Latin text edited by Leonardo Tarán. Arabic and Syriac text edited by Dimitri Gutas. Leiden: Brill, 2012.

---

* These bibliographical entries are restricted to works cited in the text, with some exceptions.

Aristotle's Prior and Posterior Analytics: Revised Text with Introduction and Commentary (Greek Text). Edited by W. D. Ross. Oxford: Clarendon, 1965.

Aristotle on the Constitution of Athens. [Athenaion Politeia]. Edited and translated by F. G. Kenyon. Oxford: Clarendon, 1892.

Athenian Constitution, Eudemian Ethics, On Virtues and Vices. Translated by H. Rackman. Cambridge, MA: Harvard University Press; London: William Heinemann, 1935.

Constitution of Athens and Related Texts. Translated and introduced by Kurt von Fritz and Ernest Kapp. New York: Hafner, 1974.

De Anima. Translated by J. A. Smith. Oxford: Clarendon, 1931.

Ethica Nicomachea (Greek text). Edited by I. Bywater. London: Oxford University Press, 1962.

Ethics of Aristotle. Edited and translated by J. Thompson. Harmondsworth: Penguin, 1956.

Eudemian Ethics. Translated by J. Solomon. Vol. 7 of *Complete Works of Aristotle. Eudemische Ethik (Aristotle's Works in German Translation)*, translated with commentary by Franz Dirlmeier. Darmstadt: Wissenschaftliche Buchgesellschaft, 1967.

Magna Moralia, Ethica Eudemia, De Virtutibus et Vitiis. Translated by J. Solomon. Oxford: Clarendon, 1915.

Metaphysics. Translated by W. D. Ross. 2 vols. Oxford: Clarendon, 1924.

Nicomachean Ethics. Translated by Robert Bartlett and Susan Collins. Chicago: University of Chicago Press, 2011.

Nicomachean Ethics. Revised ed. Edited and translated by Roger Crisp. Cambridge: Cambridge University Press, 2014.

Nicomachean Ethics. Translated with introduction and notes by Terrence Irwin. Indianapolis, IN: Hackett, 1999.

Nicomachean Ethics. Translated by Martin Ostwald. Indianapolis, IN: Bobbs-Merrill, 1962.

Nicomachean Ethics. Bilingual ed. Translated by H. Rackham. Cambridge, MA: Harvard University Press, 1934.

Nicomachean Ethics. Translated with introduction and notes by C. D. C. Reeve. Indianapolis, IN: Hackett, 2004.

Nicomachean Ethics. Translated with an introduction by W. D. Ross. Revised by J. Ackrill and J. Urmson. Oxford: Oxford University Press, 1998.

Nicomachean Ethics. Translated by Christopher Rowe with commentary by Sarah Broadie. Oxford: Oxford University Press, 2002.

Nicomachean Ethics. Translated with introduction by Joes Sachs. Newburyport, MA: Focus, 2002.

Nicomachean Ethics Books II–IV. Translated with commentary by C. Taylor. Oxford: Clarendon, 2006.

On Rhetoric – A Theory of Civic Discourse. 2nd ed. Translated by George Kennedy. New York: Oxford University Press, 2007.

Poetics. Edited and translated by Joe Sachs. New Bury, MA: Focus, 2006.

Poetics. Vol. 23 of *Aristotle in 23 Volumes*, translated by W. H. Fyfe. Cambridge, MA: Harvard University Press; London: William Heinemann, various dates.

Poetics I with "The Tractatus Coislinianus," A Hypothetical Reconstruction of "Poetics II," The Fragments of the "On Poets." Translated and reconstructed with notes by Richard Janko. Indianapolis: Hackett, 1987.

Politics. Translated with introduction by Carnes Lord. Chicago: University of Chicago Press, 2013.

Politics and the Constitution of Athens. Edited by Stephen Everson. Translated by B. Jowett. Cambridge, UK: Cambridge University Press, 1996.

Posterior Analytics. In *Complete Works of Aristotle: Revised Oxford Translation.* Edited and translated by Jonathan Barnes. 2 vols. Princeton, NJ: Princeton University Press, 1984.

Posterior Analytics; Topica. Translated by H. Tredennick and F. S. Forster. Cambridge, MA: Harvard University Press; London: William Heinemann, 1966.

Protrepticus. Translated and edited by D. S. Hutchinson and Monte Johnson. Accessed Jan. 20, 2010. www.protrepticus.info.

Rhetoric. Translated by W. Rhys Roberts. New York: Dover, 2004.

Topics I, VIII, and Selections. Translated with commentary by Robin Smith. Oxford: Clarendon, 1997.

Plato

Collected Dialogues of Plato Including the Letters. Edited by Edith Hamilton and Huntington Cairns. Princeton, NJ: Princeton University Press, 1961.

Defense of Socrates; Euthyphro; Crito. Edited and translated by David Gallop. Oxford: Oxford University Press, 1997.

Dialogues of Plato. Translated by Benjamin Jowett. New York: Random House, 1937. (Includes *Theaetetus.*)

Plato in Twelve Volumes. Cambridge, MA: Harvard University Press; London: William Heinemann, 1967–1977.

Protagoras. Vol. 3 in *Plato in Twelve Volumes*, translated by W. R. M. Lamb. Cambridge, MA: Harvard University Press; London, William Heinemann, 1967.

Republic. Edited by G. R. F. Ferrari. Translated by Tom Griffith. Cambridge, UK: Cambridge University Press, 2000.

Republic of Plato. Translated with notes and an interpretative essay by Allan Bloom. New York: Basic Books, 1991.

Sophocles

Ajax; Electra; Oedipus Tyrannos. Bilingual ed. Edited and translated by Hugh Lloyd-Jones. Cambridge, MA: Harvard University Press, 1994.

Antigone; Oedipus the King, Electra. Edited by Edith Hall. Translated by H. Kitto. Oxford: Oxford University Press, 1998.

Oedipus the King. Translated by Ian Johnston. 2014. http://johnstoi.web.viu.ca/sophocles/oedipustheking.htm.

Oedipus Tyrannos. Translated with introduction and notes by Peter Meineck and Paul Woodruff. Indianapolis: Hackett, 2000.

Oedipus Tyrannos of Sophocles. Bilingual ed. Edited and translated by Richard Jebb. Cambridge, UK: Cambridge University Press, 1887. https://www.perseus.tufts.edu/hopper/text?doc=Perseus:text:1999.01.0192.

Sophocles' Oedipus Rex: Updated Edition. Edited, translated, and introduced by Harold Bloom. New York: Chelsea House, 2007.

Sophocles' King Oidipous. Translated with essay and introduction by Ruby Blondell. Newburyport, MA: Focus, 2002.

Sophocles 1. (Including *Oedipus the King, Oedipus at Colonus, Antigone*). 2nd ed. Translated with introduction by David Grene. Chicago: University of Chicago Press, 1991.

Other Historical Primary Sources

Aquinas, Thomas. *Summa Theologica.* Translated by the Fathers of the English Dominican Province. New York: Benziger Brothers, 1948.

———. *Summa Theologiae.* Translated by Thomas Giby et al. 60 vols. London: Eyre & Spottiswoode; New York: McGraw-Hill, 1964–1973.

Aristophanes. *The Clouds*. Translated by John Claughton and Judith Affleck. Cambridge, UK: Cambridge University Press, 2012.

Augustine. *De utilitate credenda (On the Profit of Believing)*. Translated by C. L. Cornish. Vol. 3 in the first series of *Nicene and Post-Nicene Fathers*, edited by Philip Schaff. Buffalo, NY: Christian Literature, 1887.

Bible, *Young's Literal Translation of the Holy Bible*. Grand Rapids, MI: Baker Book House, 1956.

Cicero, Marcus Tullius. *De Natura Deorum*. Translated by H. Rackman. Cambridge, MA: Harvard University Press; London, William Heinemann, 1933, 1967.

———. *Treatises of M.T. Cicero: On the Nature of the Gods; On Divination; On Fate; On The Republic; On The Laws; and On Standing for The Consulship*. Translated by C. D. Yonge. Stamford Street and Charing Cross, UK: W. Clowes and Sons, 1878.

Dante Alighieri. *Divine Comedy*. Translated by Henry Cary. New York: P. F. Collier & Son, 1909–1914.

Diogenes Laërtius. *Lives of Eminent Philosophers*. Translated by R. D. Hicks. Cambridge, MA: Harvard University Press, 1925.

———. *The Lives and Opinions of Eminent Philosophers*. Translated by C. D. Yonge. London: Henry G. Bohn, 1853.

Epictetus. *The Discourses as Reported by Arrian, the Manual, and Fragments*. Translated by W. A. Oldfather. 2 vols. Cambridge, MA: Harvard University Press, 1925.

Hesiod. *The Homeric Hymns and Homerica*. Translated by Hugh G. Evelyn-White. Cambridge, MA: Harvard University Press; London: William Heinemann, 1914.

———. *Works and Days*. Translated by Gregory Nagy. Centre for Hellenic Studies, 2020. https://chs.harvard.edu/primary-source/hesiod-works-and-days-sb/.

Homer. *Iliad*. Translated by Robert Fagles. New York: Penguin, 1998.

Homer. *Iliad of Homer and the Odyssey*. Translated by Samuel Butler. Chicago: Encyclopaedia Britannica, 1989.

Laplace, Pierre Simon. *A Philosophical Essay on Probabilities*. Translated by F. W. Truscott and F. L. Emory. New York: Dover, 1951.

Nietzsche, Friedrich. *The Birth of Tragedy or Hellenism and Pessimism*. Translated by Ian Johnston. Opensource, 2003. https://archive.org/details/BirthOfTragedy/page/n1/mode/2up.

Origen. *Contra Celsum*. Translated by H. Chadwick. New York: Cambridge University Press, 1980.
Tatian. *Tatian: Oratio ad Graecos and Fragments*. Edited and translated by M. Whittaker. Oxford: Clarendon, 1982.
Xenophon. *Memorabilia, Oeconomicus, Symposium, Apology*. Translated by E. C. Marchant and O. J. Todd. Cambridge, MA: Harvard University Press; London: William Heinemann, 1923.
———. *Symposium*. Translated by O. J. Todd. Cambridge, MA: Harvard University Press; London: William Heinemann, 1979.
Xenophanes. *Xenophanes of Colophon: Fragments: A Text and Translation with Commentary*. Translated with a commentary by J. Lesher. Toronto: University of Toronto Press, 2001.

Modern and Contemporary Sources
Adkins, A. W. H. "Aristotle and the Best Kind of Tragedy." *Classical Quarterly* 16, no. 1 (1966): 78–102.
Allen, James. "Aristotle on Chance as an Accidental Cause." In *Aristotle's Physics: A Critical Guide*, edited by Mariska Leunissen, 45–65. Cambridge, UK: Cambridge University Press, 2015.
Altman, W. H. F. "Why Plato Wrote *Epinomis*: Leonardo Tarán and the Thirteenth Book of Plato's Laws." *Polis* 29, no. 1 (2012): 83–107.
Annas, Julia. "Aristotle on Inefficient Causes." *Philosophical Quarterly* 32, no. 129 (1982): 311–326.
Auerbach, Erich. *Mimesis: Representation of Reality in Western Literature*. Translated by Edward Said. Princeton, NJ: Princeton University Press, 1953, 2003.
Bacon, Francis. *Advancement of Learning*. New York: R. Worthington, 1884.
Baggini, Julian. *Atheism: A Very Short Introduction*. Oxford: Oxford University Press, 2003.
Barbera, André. Review of *Education and Culture in the Political Thought of Aristotle* by Carnes Lord, "On Music in Aristotle's Politics," *Review of Politics* 45, no. 4 (October 1983): 616–620.
Barnes, Jonathan. *Aristotle*. Oxford: Oxford University Press, 1982.
———. "Metaphysics." In *The Cambridge Companion to Aristotle*, edited by Jonathan Barnes, 66–108. Cambridge: Cambridge University Press, 1995.

Bechler, Zev. *Aristotle's Theory of Actuality*. Albany, NY: SUNY Press, 1995.

Belfiore, Elizabeth. "Pleasure, Tragedy, and Aristotelian Psychology." In *Aristotle: Critical Assessments*, edited by Lloyd Gerson. Vol. 4. Oxon, OX; New York: Routledge, 1999.

———. *Tragic Pleasures: Aristotle on Plot and Emotion*. Princeton, NJ: Princeton University Press, 1992.

Bernabé, Alberto. "Aristotle and the Mysteries." In *Greek Philosophy and Mystery Cults*, edited by María José García Blanco and María José Martín-Velasco, 27–42. Newcastle upon Tyne: Cambridge Scholars, 2016.

Biondi, Paolo. *Aristotle: Posterior Analytics II.19 Introduction, Greek Text, Translation and Commentary Accompanied by a Critical Analysis*. Québec: Les Presses de l'Université Laval, 2004.

Birge, Darice. "The Grove of the Eumenides: Refuge and Hero Shrine in Oedipus at Colonus." *Classical Journal* 80, no. 1 (October–November 1984): 11–17.

Bodéüs, Richard. *Aristotle and the Theology of the Living Immortals*. Albany, NY: SUNY Press, 2000.

Bowra, C. M. *Sophoclean Tragedy*. London: Oxford University Press, 1944.

Brady, Ryan. "A Defense of Aquinas's Reading of Aristotle Regarding God's Efficient Causality." *Angelicum* 93, no. 1 (2016): 1–20.

Bremer, Jan Maarten. *Hamartia: Tragic Error in the Poetics of Aristotle and in Greek Tragedy*. Amsterdam: Adolf M. Hakkert, 1969.

Broadie, Sarah. "Aristotelian Piety." *Phronesis* 48, no.1 (2003): 54–70.

Buckels, Christopher. "A Platonic Trope Bundle Theory." *Ancient Philosophy Today: Dialogoi* 2, no. 2 (2020): 91–112.

Bush, Stephen S. "Divine and Human Happiness in 'Nicomachean Ethics.'" *The Philosophical Review* 117, no. 1 (2008): 49–75.

Butterfield, Herbert. *The Whig Interpretation of History*. London: G. Bell and Sons, 1931.

Brown, Andrew. *A New Companion to Greek Tragedy*. Oxon, OX; New York: Routledge, 2014.

Burkert, Walter. *Greek Religion*. Translated by J. Raffan. Cambridge, MA: Harvard University Press, 1985.

Cameron, Alister. *The Identity of Oedipus the King: Five Essays on the Oedipus Tyrannos.* New York: New York University Press; London: University of London Press, 1968.

Cardullo, Loredana. "The Concept of Luck (τύχη and εὐτυχία) in Aristotle." *SpazioFilosofico* 12 (October 2014): 541–554.

Carrier, L. S. "Aristotelian Materialism." *Philosophia* 34, no. 3 (2006): 253–266.

Caston, Victor. "Aristotle's Two Intellects: A Modest Proposal." *Phronesis* 44, no. 2 (1999): 199–227.

Castriota, David. *Myth, Ethos, and Actuality: Official Art in Fifth-Century B.C. Athens.* Madison, WI: University of Wisconsin Press, 1992.

Chroust, Anton-Hermann. *Aristotle: New Light on His Life and Some of His Lost Works,* vol. I. London: Routledge and Kegan Paul, 1973.

———. "Comments on Aristotle's 'On Prayer.'" *New Scholasticism* 46, no. 3 (1972): 308–330.

———. "Eudemus or on the Soul: A Lost Dialogue of Aristotle on the Immortality of the Soul," *Mnemosyne,* 1966, Fourth Series, vol. 19, Fasc. 1 (1966): 17–30.

Cingalia, Valeria. "Aristotle and Meander on the Ethics of Understanding." PhD diss., University of Exeter, 2011.

Clark, S. R. L. *Aristotle's Man: Speculations Upon Aristotelian Anthropology.* Oxford: Clarendon, 1975.

Cleary, John. *Aristotle and Mathematics: Aporetic Method in Cosmology and Metaphysics.* Leiden: Brill, 1995.

———. "On the Terminology of 'Abstraction' in Aristotle." *Phronesis,* vol. 32 (1985): 13–45.

Cohen, David. *Law, Violence, and Community in Classical Athens.* Cambridge, UK: Cambridge University, 1995.

———. "Sexuality, Violence, and the Athenian Law of 'Hubris.'" *Greece & Rome* 38, no. 2 (October 1991): 171–188.

Cohen, Marc. "Alteration and Persistence: Form and Matter in the *Physics* and *De Generatione et Corruptione.*" In *The Oxford Handbook of Aristotle,* edited by Christopher Shields, 205–226. Oxford: Oxford University Press, 2012.

Cornelli, Gabriele, Richard McKirahan, and Constantinos Macris, eds. *On Pythagoreanism.* Berlin: De Gruyter, 2013.

Cornford, Francis. *From Religion to Philosophy.* New York: Cosimo Inc., 2009.

———. *Thucydides Mythistoricus*. London: Edward Arnold, 1907.

Crombie, I. M. *An Examination of Plato's Doctrines: I. Plato on Man and Society*. Vol. 6. London and New York: Routledge, 2013.

Crowley, Timothy. "*De Generatione et Corruptione* 2.3: Does Aristotle Identify the Contraries as Elements?" *Classical Quarterly* 63, no. 1 (2013): 161–182. https://doi.org/10.1017/S0009838812000584.

Dawe, R. D. "Some Reflections on Ate and Hamartia." *Harvard Studies in Classical Philology* 72 (1968): 89–123.

De Rijk, Lambertus Marie. *Aristotle: Semantics and Ontology*. 2 vols. Leiden: Brill, 2002.

DeMoss, David. "Acquiring Ethical Ends." *Ancient Philosophy* 10, no. 1 (1990): 63–69.

———. "Aristotle, Connectionism and the Morally Excellent Brain." The Paideia Project On-Line: Proceedings of the Twentieth World Congress of Philosophy (August 1998). https://www.bu.edu/wcp/Papers/Cogn/CognDemo.htm.

Deonna, Julien, Raffaele Rodogno, Fabrice Teroni. *In Defense of Shame: The Faces of an Emotion*. Oxford: Oxford University Press, 2012.

Dodds, E. R. "On Misunderstanding the Oedipus Rex." *Greece and Rome* 13, no. 1 (April 1966): 37–49.

Drehe, Iovan, "The Aristotelian Dialectical Topos." *Argumentum. Journal of the Seminar of Discursive Logic, Argumentation Theory and Rhetoric* 9, no. 2 (2011): 129–139.

Dudley, John. *Aristotle's Concept of Chance: Accidents, Cause, Necessity, and Determinism*. Albany, NY: SUNY Press, 2012.

Duffy, James. "Homer's Conception of Fate." *Classical Journal* 42, no. 8 (May 1947): 477–485.

Dworkin, Ronald. "What Is Equality? Part 2: Equality of Resources." *Philosophy & Public Affairs* 10, no. 4 (Autumn 1981): 283–345.

Eaton, Ralph. *General Logic*. New York: Charles Scribner's Sons, 1931.

Else, Gerald. *Aristotle's Poetics: The Argument*. Cambridge: Harvard University Press, 1957.

Feldman-Royle. "Homicide: First Degree Murder." Phoenix, AZ: Feldman-Royle, Attorneys at Law, 2024. Accessed on

Dec. 28, 2024. https://www.feldmanroyle.com/homicide/first-degree-murder/.

Findlay, J. N. "Neoplatonism of Plato." In *The Significance of Neoplatonism*, edited by R. Harris, 23–40. Norfolk, VA: International Society for Neoplatonic Studies, 1976.

Fink, Jakob. "Introduction." In *Suárez on Aristotelian Causality*, edited by Jakob Fink, 1–22. Leiden: Brill, 2015.

Ford, Andrew. *Aristotle as Poet: Song for Hermias*. Oxford: Oxford University Press, 2011.

Franklin, James. *The Worth of Persons*. New York and London: Encounter Books, 2022.

Frede, Michael. "*La théorie aristotelicienne de l'intellect agent.*" In *Corps et âme. Études sur le De Anima d'Aristote*, edited by Cristina Viano, 377–390. Paris: Vrin, 1996.

Freeland, Cynthia. "Accidental Causes and Real Explanations." In *Aristotle's Physics: A Collection of Essays*, edited by Lindsey Judson, 68–71. Oxford: Clarendon Press, 1991.

Freeman, Charles. *A.D. 381*. New York: Overlook, 2009.

———. *The Closing of the Western Mind: The Rise of Faith and the Fall of Reason*. New York: Vintage, 2002.

Fussi, Alessandra. "Aristotle on Shame." *Ancient Philosophy* 35, no. 1 (Spring 2015): 113–135.

Gagarin, Michael. "Self-Defense in Athenian Homicide Law." *Greek, Roman, and Byzantine Studies* 19, no. 2 (1978): 111–120.

Gager, John. *Curse Tablets and Binding Spells from the Ancient World*. Oxford: Oxford University Press, 1992.

Gans, Eric. *Signs of Paradox: Irony, Resentment, and Other Mimetic Structures*. Stanford, CA: Stanford University Press, 1997.

Gendlin, Eugene T. *Line by Line Commentary on Aristotle's De Anima Book III*. Focusing Institute Spring Valley, 2012. http://previous.focusing.org/aristotle/Ae_Bk_3.pdf.

George, Marie. "Would Aristotle Agree with St. John That 'God Is Love'?" *Aquinas Review* 8 (2003): 1–43.

Gerson, Lloyd. *Aristotle and Other Neoplatonists*. Ithaca, NY: Cornell University Press, 2005.

Golden, Leon. "Hamartia, Ate, and Oedipus." *Classical World* 72, no. 1 (September 1978): 3–12.

Goldin, Owen. "Aristotle on Good and Bad Actualities." *The Journal of Neoplatonic Studies* 2, no. 1 (1993): 126–150.

Goodman, Len, and Robert Talisse. *Aristotle's Politics*. Albany, NY: SUNY Press, 2007.

Gould, Thomas. "The Innocence of Oedipus: The Philosophers on 'Oedipus the King, Part III.'" *Arion* 5, no. 4 (Winter 1966): 478–525.

Greenblatt, Stephen. *The Swerve: How the World Became Modern*. New York: Norton, 2011.

Greene, William Chase. *Moira: Fate, Good, and Evil in Greek Thought*. Cambridge, MA: Harvard University Press, 2013. https://doi.org/10.4159/harvard.9780674282421.

Grote, George. *Aristotle*. Vol. 1. London: John Murray, 1872.

Groarke, Louis. *An Aristotelian Account of Induction: Creating Something from Nothing*. Kingston and Montreal: McGill-Queen's University Press, 2009.

———. "Aristotle's Contrary Psychology." *Review of Metaphysics* 69, no. 1 (September 2015): 47–72.

———. "Aristotle's Tyche (τύχη) and Contemporary Debates About Luck." *Metaphilosophy* 55, no. 3 (July 2024): 401–414. https://doi.org/10.1111/meta.12699.

———. "Aristotle: Logic." In *Internet Encyclopedia of Logic*, edited by James Fieser and Bradley Dowden. Accessed on Nov. 5, 2022. https://iep.utm.edu/aristotle-logic/.

———. "Intelligibility Versus Proof: Philosophical Method in Pascal and Descartes." In *Whence Intelligibility?*, edited by Louis Perron, 93–111. Washington, DC: Council for Research in Values and Philosophy, 2014.

———. *Moral Reasoning: Recovering the Ethical Tradition*. Don Mills, ON: Oxford University Press, 2011.

Guthrie, W. K. C. *A History of Greek Philosophy. Aristotle*. Cambridge, UK: Cambridge University Press, 1981.

Hacking, Ian. "Leibniz and Descartes: Proof and Eternal Truths." In *Rationalism, Empiricism and Idealism,* edited by Anthony Kenny, 47–60. Oxford: Clarendon Press, 1986.

Haidt, Jonathan. *The Righteous Mind: Why Good People are Divided by Politics and Religion*. New York, Pantheon Books, 2012.

———. Haidt, Jonathan, and Joseph Craig. "Intuitive Ethics: How Innately Prepared Intuitions Generate Culturally Variable Virtues." *Daedalus* 133, no. 4 (Fall 2004): 55–66.

Han, Pierre. "Recognition in the Odyssey." *Revue belge de philologie et d'histoire* 59, no.1 (1981): 50–55.

Hardie, W. F. R. "Aristotle and the Freewill Problem." *Philosophy* 43, no. 165 (July 1968): 274–278.
Harsh, P. W. "Hamartia Again." *Transactions and Proceedings of the American Philological Association* 76 (1945): 47–58.
Heidegger, Martin. *What Is Philosophy*. Translated by William Kluback and Jean Wilde. New Haven: College & University Press, 1955.
Hey, O. "Hamartia." *Philologus* 83, nos. 1–4 (1927–1928): 1–17, 137–163.
Huismann, Tyler. "Aristotle on Accidental Causation." *Journal of the American Philosophical Association* 2, no. 4 (Winter 2016): 561–575. https://doi.org/10.1017/apa.2016.33.
Imperato, Roberto. *Portraits of Jesus*. Lanham, MD: Hamilton Books, 2020.
Jayne, Edward. *An Archaeology of Disbelief, The Origin of Secular Philosophy*. Lanham, UK: Hamilton Books, 2018.
Jaeger, Werner. *Aristotle: Fundamentals and History of His Development*. 2nd ed. Translated by Richard Robinson. Oxford: Oxford University Press, 1962.
Johnson, Kent. "Luck and Good Fortune in the Eudemian Ethics." *Ancient Philosophy* 17, no. 1 (1997): 85–102.
Johnson, Monte. "Luck in Aristotle's *Physics* and *Ethics*." In *Bridging the Gap between Aristotle's Science and Ethics*, edited by Devin Henry and Karen Nielsen, 254–275. Cambridge: Cambridge University Press, 2015. https://doi.org/10.1017/CBO9780511846397.014.
Judson, Lindsay. "Chance and 'Always for the Most Part' in Aristotle." In *Aristotle's Physics: A Collection of Essays*, edited by Lindsay Judson, 73–99. Oxford: Clarendon, 1991.
Keeler, L. "Aristotle on the Problem of Error." *Gregorianum* 13, no. 2 (1932): 241–260.
Kieran, Matthew. "Tragedy Versus Comedy: On Why Comedy Is the Equal of Tragedy." *Ethical Perspectives: Journal of the European Ethics Network* 20, no. 3 (2013): 427–450.
King, Hugh R. "Aristotle Without *Prima Materia*." *Journal of the History of Ideas* 17, no. 3 (1956): 370–389.
Kirkwood, G. M. *A Study of Sophoclean Drama*. Ithaca, NY: Cornell University Press, 1958.
———. Review of *Hamartia: Tragic Error in the Poetics of Aristotle and in Greek Tragedy* by Jan Maarten Bremer. *The American Journal of Philology* 92, no. 4 (October 1971): 711–715.

Kitto, H. D., *The Greeks*. London: Penguin, 1957.
Knox, Bernard. *Oedipus at Thebes: Sophocles' Tragic Hero and His Time*. New Haven, CT: Yale University Press, 1985.
Konstan, David. *Emotions of the Ancient Greeks*. Toronto: University of Toronto Press, 2006.
Kratz, "How Sexual Reproduction Creates Genetic Variation." In *Dummies: Biology Articles*. Hoboken, NJ: John Wiley & Sons, Inc. 2017. Article last updated 07-05-2017. Accessed on July 18, 2023. https://www.dummies.com/article/academics-the-arts/science/biology/sexual-reproduction-creates-genetic-variation-241752/.
Kraut, Richard. "Aristotle's Ethics." In *Stanford Encyclopedia of Philosophy* (Summer 2018 Edition). Stanford, CA: Stanford University Press, 1997–. Article published May 1, 2001; last modified July 2, 2022. https://plato.stanford.edu/entries/aristotle-ethics/.
Larsen, Kasper Bro. *Recognizing the Stranger: Recognition Scenes in the Gospel of John*. Leiden; Boston: Brill, 2008.
Lear, Gabriel Richardson. *Happy Lives and the Highest Good. An Essay on Aristotle's Nicomachean Ethics*. Princeton, NJ: Princeton University Press, 2004.
Lear, Jonathan. "The Illusion of a Future: The Rhetoric of Freud's Critique of Religious Belief." In *On Freud's "The Future of an Illusion,"* edited by Mary Kay O'Neil, Salman Akhtar, 84–97. London: Karnac, 2009.
Lennox, James. "Aristotle on Chance." *Archiv für Geschichte der Philosophie* 66, no 1 (1984): 52–60.
Lesher, James. "The Meaning of ΝΟΥΣ in the Posterior Analytics." *Phronesis* 18, no. 1 (1973): 44–68.
Lloyd, G. E. R. *Aristotle: The Growth and Structure of His Thought*. Cambridge: Cambridge University Press, 1968.
———. "Chapter 11. Mathematics and Narrative: An Aristotelian Perspective." In *Circles Disturbed: The Interplay of Mathematics and Narrative*, edited by Apostolos Doxiadis and Barry Mazur, 389–406. Princeton, NJ: Princeton University Press, 2012. https://doi.org/10.1515/9781400842681.389.
(Liddell & Scott) Liddell, Henry and Robert Scott, *A Greek-English Lexicon*. Oxford: Clarendon Press, 1940.
Lonergan, Bernard. *Insight: A Study of Human Understanding*. Vol. 3 in *Collected Works of Bernard Lonergan,* edited by Frederick

Crowe and Robert Doran. Toronto: University of Toronto Press, 1992.

Long, A. A. "Aristotle on *Eudaimonia, Nous,* and Divinity." In *Aristotle's Nicomachean Ethics: A Critical Guide,* edited by Jon Miller, 92–114. Cambridge: Cambridge University Press, 2011.

Macfarlane, John. "Aristotle's Definition of *Anagnōrisis.*" *American Journal of Philology* 121, no. 3 (2000): 367–383.

Magee, Glen. "Hegelian Pantheism." In *Models of God and Alternative Ultimate Realities,* edited by Jeanine Diller and Asa Kasher, 421–430. Dordrecht: Springer, 2013.

Martin, Craig. *Subverting Aristotle: Religion, History and Philosophy in Early Modern Science.* Baltimore: Johns Hopkins University Press, 2014.

Massie, Pascal. "The Irony of Chance: On Aristotle's Physics B, 4–6." *International Philosophical Quarterly* 43, no. 1 (March 2003): 15–28.

Mathews, Gareth. "Accidental Unities." In *Language and Logos,* edited by Malcolm Schofield and Martha Nussbaum, 223–240. Cambridge: Cambridge University Press, 1982.

Mayhew, Robert. "Aristotle on Prayer." *Rhizai. A Journal for Ancient Philosophy and Science* 2 (2007): 295–309.

McClymont, John. "Reading Between the Lines: Aristotle's Views on Religion." *Acta Classica* 53 (January 2010): 33–48.

Melzer, Arthur. *Philosophy Between the Lines, The Lost History of Esoteric Writings.* Chicago: University of Chicago Press, 2014.

Menn, Stephen. "Aristotle and Plato on God as Nous and as the Good." *Review of Metaphysics* 45, no. 3 (March 1992): 543–573.

———. "Aristotle, Democritus and the Problemata." In *Aristotelian Problemata Physica,* edited by Robert Mayhew, 10–35. Leiden: Brill, 2015.

———. "Aristotle's Theology." In The *Oxford Handbook of Aristotle,* edited by Christopher Shields, 422–464. Oxford: Oxford University Press, 2012.

Meyer, Susan. "Aristotle, Teleology, Reduction." *The Philosophical Review* 101, no. 4 (October 1992): 798–803.

Meynell, Hugo. *Introduction to the Philosophy of Bernard Lonergan.* New York: Barnes & Noble, 1976.

McGregor, James. *Athens.* Cambridge, MA: Harvard University Press, 2014.

Miller, Fred. "Aristotelian Statecraft and Modern Politics." In *Aristotle's Politics*, edited by Len Goodman and Robert Talisse, 13–32. Albany, NY: SUNY Press, 2007.

———. "Aristotle's Divine Cause." In *Aristotle on Method and Metaphysics,* edited by Edward Feser, 277–297. Basingstoke, UK: Palgrave Macmillan, 2013.

M'Mahon, John. *Aristotle's Metaphysics*. London: Henry G. Bohn, 1857.

Moore, John. *Aristotle and Xenophon on Democracy and Oligarchy.* Berkeley, CA: University of California Press, 1986.

Morrissey, Christopher. "Oedipus the Cliché: Aristotle on Tragic Form and Content." *Anthropoetics* 9, no. 1 (Spring/Summer 2003). E-journal. https://anthropoetics.ucla.edu/ap0901/oedipus

Murray, Robert Jr. "Thought and Structure in Sophoclean Tragedy." In *Sophocles: A Collection of Critical Essays*, edited by Thomas Woodard, 23–28. Englewood Cliffs, NJ: Prentice-Hall, 1966.

Nightingale, Andrea. "On Wandering and Wondering: '*Theôria*' in Greek Philosophy and Culture." *Arion* 9, no. 2 (Fall 2001): 23–58.

———. *Spectacles of Truth in Classical Greek Philosophy: Theôria in Its Cultural Context.* Cambridge: Cambridge University Press, 2004.

Nussbaum, Martha. *Fragility of Goodness: Luck and Ethics in Greek Tragedy and Philosophy*. Cambridge: Cambridge University Press, 1986.

O'Grady, Patricia. *Thales of Miletus: The Beginnings of Western Science and Philosophy*. Abingdon, UK: Routledge, 2016.

Owens, Joseph. "Aristotle's 'Definition of the Soul.'" In *Aristotle: Collected Papers of Joseph Owens,* edited by J. Catan, 109–121. Albany, NY: SUNY Press, 1981.

Pangle, Thomas. *Aristotle's Teaching in the "Politics."* Chicago: University of Chicago Press, 2013.

Parker, Robert. *Athenian Religion*. Oxford: Clarendon, 1997.

Pasnau, Robert. "Divine Illumination." In *Stanford Encyclopedia of Philosophy* (Spring 2020 Edition). Stanford, CA: Stanford University, 1997–. Article published November 2, 1999; last modified May 22, 2024. https://plato.stanford.edu/entries/illumination/.

Peters, Francis E. (F. E.). *Greek Philosophical Terms: A Historical Lexicon*. New York: New York University Press, 1967.

Pollitt, Jerome. *Art and Experience in Classical Greece*. Cambridge, UK: Cambridge University Press, 1972.

Preus, Anthony. *Historical Dictionary of Ancient Greek Philosophy*. Lanham, MD: Scarecrow, 2007.

Price, Simon. *Religions of the Ancient Greeks*. Cambridge: Cambridge University Press, 1999.

Pulleyn, Simon. *Prayer in Greek Religion*. Oxford: Clarendon, 1997.

Rabinowitz, Nancy. *Greek Tragedy*. Oxford: Blackwell Publishing, 2008.

Rand, Ayn. *Ayn Rand Lexicon: Objectivism From A to Z*, edited by Harry Binswanger. New York: New American Library, 1986.

Rapp, Christof. "Aristotle's Rhetoric." In *Stanford Encyclopedia of Philosophy* (Spring 2010 Edition). Stanford, CA: Stanford University, 1997. https://plato.stanford.edu/entries/aristotle-rhetoric/.

Renehan, R. "Aristotle as Lyric Poet: The Hermias Poem." *Greek, Roman, and Byzantine Studies* 23, no. 3 (1982): 251–274.

Richards, David. "Rights and Autonomy." *Ethics* 92, no.1 (October 1981): 3–20.

Rist, John. "The End of Aristotle's *on Prayer*." *American Journal of Philology* 106, no. 1 (Spring 1985): 110–113.

———. *The Mind of Aristotle: A Study in Philosophical Growth*. Toronto: University of Toronto Press, 1989.

Robertson, Noel. "The Concept of Purity in Greek Sacred Laws." In *Purity and the Forming of Religious Traditions in the Ancient Mediterranean World and Ancient Judaism*, edited by Christian Frevel and Christopher Nihan, 195–245. Leiden: Brill, 2013.

Rosemann, Philipp. *Omne Agens Agit Sibi Simile: A "Repetition" of Scholastic Metaphysics*. Leuven, Belgium: Leuven University Press, 1996.

Rosivach, Vincent. "The Tyrant in Athenian Democracy." *Quaderni Urbinati di Cultura Classica* 30, no. 3 (1988): 43–57. https://doi.org/10.2307/20546964.

Ross, David. *Aristotle*. London: Methuen, 1966.

———. *Aristotle's Prior and Posterior Analytics*. Oxford: Clarendon Press, 1965.

Rubel, Alexander. *Fear and Loathing in Ancient Athens: Religion and Politics During the Peloponnesian War*. Translated by Michael Vickers and Alina Piftor. Oxon, OX: Routledge, 2014.

Sachs, Joe. "Aristotle: Motion and its Place in Nature." In *Internet Encyclopedia of Philosophy*, edited by James Frieser and Bradley Dowden. Accessed on July 18, 2023. https://iep.utm.edu/aristotle-motion/.

———. "Aristotle: Poetics." In *Internet Encyclopedia of Philosophy*, edited by James Frieser and Bradley Dowden. Accessed on July 18, 2023. https://iep.utm.edu/aristotle-poetics/.

Schillinger, Daniel. "Politics of Luck." PhD diss., University of Toronto, 2018. https://tspace.library.utoronto.ca/bitstream/1807/89705/3/Schillinger_Daniel_201806_PhD_thesis.pdf.

Schmidt, Robert. *Domain of Logic According to St. Thomas Aquinas.* The Hague: Martinus Nijhof, 1966.

Schollmeier, Paul. "Ancient Tragedy and Other Selves." *Revue de métaphysique et de morale* 103, no. 2 (April–June 1998): 175–188.

———. "Purgation of Pitiableness and Fearfulness." *Hermes* 122, no. 3 (1994): 289–299. http://www.jstor.org/stable/4477021.

Scodel, Ruth. *Sophocles.* Boston: Twayne, 1984.

Sedley, David. *Creationism and Its Critics in Antiquity.* Berkeley, CA: University of California Press, 2007.

Segev, Mor. *Aristotle on Religion.* Cambridge, UK: Cambridge University Press, 2017.

Shields, Christopher. "Soul and Body in Aristotle." *Oxford Studies in Ancient Philosophy* 6 (1988): 103–110.

Silva, Paul. "The Epistemology of Intuition and Seemings." PhD diss., University of Connecticut, 2013.

Sinnige, Theo Gerard. "Cosmic Religion in Aristotle." *Greek, Roman, and Byzantine Studies* 14, no. 1 (1973): 15–34.

Smith, Robin. "Filling in Nature's Deficiencies." In *Essays in Ancient Greek Philosophy, V: Aristotle's Ontology*, edited by Anthony Preus, George Kustas, and John Anton, 295–314. Albany, NY: SUNY Press, 1992.

Solmsen, Friedrich. *Aristotle's System of the Physical World: A Comparison with His Predecessors.* Ithaca, NY: Cornell University Press, 1960.

Sorabji, Richard. "Introduction." In *Simplicius on Aristotle Physics 2*, translated by Barrie Fleet, 1–5. London: Bloomsbury, 2014.

———. "Myths about Non-Propositional Thought." In *Language and Logos: Studies in Ancient Greek Philosophy Presented to G. E.*

L. Owen, edited by Malcolm Schofield and Martha Nussbaum, 295–314. Cambridge, UK: Cambridge University Press, 1982.

Stinton, T.C.W. "Hamartia in Aristotle and Greek Tragedy." *Classical Quarterly* 25, no. 2 (1975): 221–254.

Struck, Peter. "Animals and Divination." In *Oxford Handbook of Animals in Classical Thought and Life*, edited by Gordon Lindsay Campbell, 310–323. Oxford: Oxford University Press, 2014.

Timotin, Andrei. "Porphyry on Prayer: Platonic Tradition and Religious Trends in the Third Century." In *Platonic Theories of Prayer*, edited by John Dillon and Andrei Timotin, 88–107. Leiden: Brill, 2016.

Van Braam, P. "Aristotle's Use of Hamartia." *Classical Quarterly* 6, no. 4 (1912): 266–272.

Verdenius, W. J. "Traditional and Personal Elements in Aristotle's Religion." *Phronesis* 5, no. 1 (1960): 56–70.

Von Campenhausen, Hans. *The Fathers of the Latin Church*. Translated by Manfred Hoffman. Stanford, CA: Stanford University Press, 1969 (c. 1964).

Von Fritz, Kurt. "ΝΟΟΣ and Noein in the Homeric Poems." *Classical Philology* 38, no. 2 (1943): 79–93.

———. "Nous, Noein and Their Derivatives in Pre-Socratic Philosophy (Excluding Anaxagoras) Part I." *Classical Philology* 40, no. 4 (1945): 223–242.

———. "Nous, Noein and their Derivatives in Pre-Socratic Philosophy (Excluding Anaxagoras) Part II." *Classical Philology* 41, no. 1 (1946): 12–34.

Waldock, A. J. A. *Sophocles the Dramatist*. London: Cambridge University Press, 1951.

Wales, Katie. *Dictionary of Stylistics*. Oxon, OX: Routledge, 2014.

Webster, Thomas Bertram Lon. *Introduction to Sophocles*. 2nd ed. London: Methuen, 1969.

Wedin, Michael. *Aristotle's Theory of Substance: The Categories and Metaphysics Zeta*. Oxford: Oxford University Press, 2000.

Wehrle, Walter. *The Myth of Aristotle's Development and the Betrayal of Metaphysics*. Lanham, MD: Rowman and Littlefield, 2000.

White, F. C. *Plato's Theory of Particulars*. New York: Arno Press, 1981.

———. "Plato's Theory of Particulars." *Apeiron* 17, no. 2 (1981): 138–140.

Whitman, Cedric. *Sophocles: A Study of Heroic Humanism.* Cambridge, MA: Harvard University Press, 1951.

Whitmarsh, Tim. *Battling the Gods: Atheism in the Ancient World.* New York: Vintage, 2016.

Wilson, John. *Thinking with Concepts.* Cambridge: Cambridge University Press, 1963.

Ziguras, Jakob. "Aristotle's Rational Empiricism: A Goethean Interpretation of Aristotle's Theory Knowledge." PhD diss., University of Sydney (Australia), 2010.

Index

A

active mind, 65, 110, 112; vs. passive mind, 156–157; as pure actualization, 156; as unmixed, 129, 132. *See also nous*

actualization: and the active mind, 156–157; and divine imitation, 154–156; and efficient and final causality, 154–155, 157, 159; and *eudaimonia*, 156; fullness of, 158; as movement from potentiality to actuality, 153

A.D. 381 (Freeman), 16

Adkins, A. W. H., 265–266. *See also hamartia*

Advancement of Learning, The (Bacon), 373

Aesop, 286–287, 369

Agamemnon, 98, 164, 283

agathos, 285–287, 305, 314

agency: divine, 170, 238–239, 283; human, 110, 188, 284, 326, 362; moral, 189–190, 205, 285–286; in *Oedipus*, 284, 287, 306, 362; of the soul, 116, 144; sources of, 169, 193; supernatural, 232; of unmoved movers, 114, 116. *See also atê*

agitation of wit, 13, 373, 375

agnosticism (Aristotle's), 16, 40. *See also* atheism; secularism

akrasia, 314–317, 324, 363

Alexander of Aphrodisias, 44, 65, 188, 386, 395

Alighieri, Dante, 95

ambrosia, 82–83

Anabasis (Xenophon), 32, 34

anagnôrisis, 180, 245, 354, 377–382. *See also* discovery

anamnêsis. *See* recollection (Platonic)

Anaxagoras, 20, 76, 136, 209; on the impassive and unmixed mind, 129–130

anthropomorphism, 53, 104–105, 129, 176
anti-realism (metaphysical), 177, 213
Aphrodite: and *anagnôrisis*, 378; and Aristotelian induction, 397; encounter with Helen (*Iliad*), 375–377; and rapid insight, 389–392; two levels of (Socrates), 80
Apology (Plato), 209, 258
Aquinas, Thomas, 163; on parricide, 321–324
Archaeology of Disbelief (Edward), 16, 19
aretê, 383
Aristotelian corpus, 10–11, 30, 249; and Andronicus of Rhodes, 6, 37; compilation of sources, 6; inconsistencies in, 55, 58, 161–162, 247, 400; influence of editors on, 8, 27, 37, 249; uncertain chronology of, 37
Aristotelianism, 13, 92; commitment to Greek pagan religion, 16; original spirit of, 209; and Platonism, 20, 48, 96
Aristotelian school: anonymous students and followers, 6–8; disagreement on religious matters, 6, 171, 400; evidence of religious commitment, 26–27
Aristotle: as a "closet heretic," 20; as an empiricist, 96, 237; esoteric vs. exoteric, 42–47, 55–56; as a monotheist, 44, 52, 68, 70–71, 97–98; as a practising pagan, 49, 58–59, 67, 70, 95; as a religious man, 22–24; as a secret atheist, 42, 47, 52, 54–55; secularist interpretations of, 16–22, 49, 54–55; as a synoptic thinker, 4, 5, 8–10, 101, 178. *See also* developmentalism
Aristotle (Barnes), 399
Aristotle's Metaphysics (M'Mahon), 15
Aristotle on Religion (Segev), 16
Aristotle and the Theology of the Living Immortals (Bodéüs), 179
Atē, 85, 185, 282–283
atheism: in Aristotle (hidden), 42, 47, 52, 54–55; Enlightenment reaction against Judeo-Christian tradition, 18; and Greek paganism, 18; pejorative implications of *atheos*, 17; vs. philosophy (the holiness of), 70–71; Plato on, 29; of Socrates, 20; trend in Aristotelian scholarship, 16, 167. *See also* agnosticism; developmentalism; secularism
Athena, 26, 59, 65, 129, 230. *See also* cult of the dead
Athens: Athenian law, 301–303; civic life, 30–32,

40, 286, 354; religious
    practices, 40
atomism: and ancient
    materialism, 19; and
    human agency, 188; and
    Platonism, 48
Auerbach, Erich, 378
Augustine, 97, 107, 386; on the
    importance of authorita-
    tive tradition, 3
autonomy, 286–287, 295, 329

B
Bacon, Francis, 373, 375
Barnes, Jonathan, 399
Battling the Gods (Whitmarsh),
    16
Bechler, Zev: on accidental
    causality (in Aristotle),
    210–215; critique of
    Aristotelian science,
    210–211, 225; misinter-
    pretation of Aristotle,
    214–220
Bernabé, Alberto, 91–93
Binswanger, Harry, 97
Birge, Darice, 255
Birth of Tragedy, The
    (Nietzsche), 241, 252
Blondell, Ruby, 253
bloodguilt, 337, 341, 357
Bloom, Harold, 321
Bodéüs, Richard, 16; on
    Aristotle as a sincere
    believer, 23; on Aristotle's
    theology, 29, 57, 83, 97,
    179
Boethius: on agreement
    between Aristotle
    and Plato, 21–22; and

intuition, 386; and predes-
    tination, 190
Bremer, Jan, 263, 273
Broadie, Sarah: on Aristotle
    and prayer, 49, 53–54;
    caricature of pagan piety,
    60–61; desacralization
    of Aristotle, 55; reliance
    on esoteric reading of
    Aristotle, 55–56; on the
    secret, secular Aristotle,
    54, 70; secularized
    interpretation of Aristotle,
    77–78
brutishness, 265, 279
Burkert, Walter, 62
Bush, Stephen, 84
Butterfield, Herbert, 1, 5, 206
Byrne, Christopher, 15

C
Cameron, Alister, 288–289
Cardullo, Loredana, 182
Castriota, David, 359–360
Categories (Aristotle), 149
catharsis: Aristotle's doctrine
    of, 348; in Aristotle's
    treatment of tragedy, 173,
    249–250, 349, 366; as
    cleansing, 339, 349, 368;
    as epiphany, 366, 367; in
    Oedipus, 354, 365; of pity
    and fear, 249, 350–351
causality: accidental, 210–228,
    efficient, 154–159,
    162–171, 215, 365; final,
    154–159, 166–171; four
    levels of, 225–228; and
    happenstance, 226–228;
    material, 143, 177, 217,

221–222; particular, 194–195, 213–219
causes: direct *vs.* indirect, 203–204; the four causes, 193, 402; and luck, 191–193, 200–204, 207–211
celestial spheres, 97, 107, 114–115, 126, 129, 138, 153, 155, 162
censorship: Aristotle's (alleged) avoidance of, 20; Aristotle's support for, 25; Plato's support for 343–345
chance: ancient *vs.* modern notions of, 183; Aristotle's analysis of, 200–210; and causality, 192–193, 216–217; and divine determinism, 187–190; related terms, 182, 200; and science, 198. *See also* fate; happenstance; luck
character flaws: and *hamartia*, 252–253, 264–265, 334, 355–356; and hubris, 355–362 (in *Oedipus*); of Oedipus, 267–268, 280, 288–289, 325; and tragedy, 262, 267–270
Christianity, 17, 68, 397
Chroust, Anton-Hermann, 16, 26; on Aristotle's belief in "inner illumination," 93; on Aristotle's interest in myths, 40–41; on Aristotle as a "profoundly religious man," 22–23
Cicero, 89, 98–100, 179
circularity, 124–125, 158

Closing of the Western Mind, The (Freeman), 16, 95
Cohen, David, 311
Constitution of Athens (Aristotle or student of), 30–32, 40
Cornford, Francis, 73, 183
Craig, Joseph, 326–329
Crisp, Roger, 278
Crowley, Timothy, 133
cult of the dead, 65–67, 394
curse tablets, 56
cuttlefish, 42

D
D'Alembert, Jean Le Rond, 95
Dawe, R. D.: on *hamartia*, 252; on *Oedipus*, 257, 280
De Anima (Aristotle), 24, 45, 47, 64, 105, 109, 131–132, 141
De Caelo (Aristotle), 45
De Interpretatione. See On Interpretation
Demeter: Aristotle's dedication of statue to, 65, 230; feeding ambrosia to Demophoon, 82; Homeric Hymn to, 183
De Mundo (pseudo-Aristotle), 115
de Rijk, Lambertus Marie, 383
design (argument from): Aristotle's (Cicero); 100; from intelligence or nature, 202–204; as striving to resemble God, 126, 152, 157
determinism: Aristotle's rejection of, 188–190, 212–213; and fate, 189–190, 224

developmentalism: contrived chronology of, 37–39, 199; distinction between youthful and mature Aristotle, 75, 96–97, 166–167; theory of Aristotle's turn from (Platonic) piety to science, 36–37, 41–42
didacticism: *vs.* aesthetics in tragedy, 275; in Greek poetry and drama, 271, 403; moral complexity of, 272, 276, 369; in *Oedipus*, 325; statue of Mitys example, 347–348
Diderot, Denis, 95
Dillon, John, 22
Diogenes Laërtius, 30, 79
Diogenes the Cynic, 286
Dionysius of Syracuse, 35–36
Discourses (Epictetus), 79
discovery: and Aristotelian induction, 381–384; as a change from ignorance to knowledge, 180, 354–355; in Homer and the Gospel of Luke, 375–377, 389–398; as "quick-knowing," 384–389; and self-discovery, 245, 247; as sudden enlightenment, 374–383. *See also* agitation of wit; *anagnôrisis*
Divine Comedy (Dante), 95
divine intervention, 86–89, 193, 231–237, 395
divine providence, 24, 43
Dodds, E. R.: amoralist interpretation of tragedy, 348; on *Oedipus*, 251–252, 276, 298; on poetic justice, 259; on Victorian sensibilities, 252, 254, 257

E

Eaton, Ralph, 383
Economics (Aristotle or student of), 27, 35, 163
elenchus. *See* Socrates
Eleusinian Mysteries, 52, 89–90
Emmaus (New Testament), 375–377; and *anagnôrisis*, 378; and Aristotelian induction, 397; and rapid insight, 389–392
Encyclopédie (Diderot and D'Alembert), 95
endoxa: as Aristotle's starting point for investigation, 46, 373–374; as popular consensus, 10, 46, 141; as traditional belief, 56
Enlightenment: animus against religion, 4, 18; opposition between science and religion, 17, 220–221, 227–228, 400; positivist interpretation of Aristotle, 177; reaction against Judeo-Christian tradition, 18; tropes about scientific progress, 40, 217
epagôgê, 65, 375, 380–382, 388, 401. *See also* induction
epistemology (Aristotelian): direct intuition (*nous*), 92; and fate, 227; first levels of understanding, 375, 386; and perceptible forms,

145–146; and religious belief, 397; and religious experience, 388–393; and religious tradition, 375, 385. See also agitation of wit; discovery; induction

esoteric doctrines: vs. exoteric (public) texts, 42–47, 374; interpretations of *Oedipus*, 251; reliance on in reading Aristotle, 54–56

essentialism: caricature of (Aristotle's), 176–177, 211, 217–218; logical principles derived from, 152

eternal duration, 106–112

eudaimonia: and eternal reputation 107, 110, 394; and external goods, 78, 207; as godlike, 156; as good fate, 255; as happiness, 78; and virtuous behavior, 207

Eudemian Ethics (Aristotle), 12, 45–46, 50, 85–88, 168, 232–236

Euripides, 249, 362

Euthyphro (Plato), 62, 303–305

evolution, 109, 118, 121, 133

exile: in *Oedipus*, 244, 293, 335, 337, 339–340; as penalty in ancient Greece, 294

external goods: and fate, 208; from the gods, 208, 227; and *eudaimonia*, 78, 207–208; and honour, 51; vs. internal goods, 46; and prayer, 227–232

F

Fainlight, Ruth, 341

fatal flaw, 253–254, 298, 355. See also hamartia

fatalism, 187–188

fate: and causality, 211, 215, 223; and chance, 189–191, 201–204, 211; and external goods, 78; and free will, 190, 288; gods' influence on, 62, 78, 180–181, 185; good and bad, 77–78, 86, 255, 259; in Greek tragedy, 171, 187, 362, 369; and luck, 182, 193, 196–197, 204–205; and morality, 205, 208–209, 272, 352; in *Oedipus*, 267, 288–289, 318, 334; in pagan Greek culture, 180, 183, 207; and poetic justice, 365; and prayer, 230; religious notions of, 196, 205–206, 209–210, 215, 237; and science, 193–196, 198, 210–211, 222–223; Stoic account of, 189. See also chance; happenstance; luck

Fate(s), 62, 183–185, 187–188

fear (and pity): catharsis of, 173–174, 249, 350, 366; as missing the mark, 278; in *Oedipus*, 352; and tragedy, 258, 347, 348, 351

felony murder, 325

first principles, 82, 92, 126, 386–387

forms (Platonic), 36–37, 103, 124–125

Fortuna. See Fate(s)

fortune. See chance; fate; happenstance; luck

Freeman, Charles, 16, 18, 95
free will, 188, 190, 288
friendship (between gods and men), 24, 55, 64, 67–70
Fussi, Alessandra, 336–337

G

Gagarin, Michael, 301
Gans, Eric, 248
Generation of Animals (Aristotle), 46, 47–48, 119, 142, 157
George, Marie, 168
Gerson, Lloyd: on Aristotle as a Platonist, 48, 96; on developmentalism, 37; on influence of Platonism, 28, 96; on the removal of Platonic elements from the late Aristotle, 39
Glaucon, 60–61
god(s): Aristotle's monotheistic God, 52, 68, 70; as caring parents, 67; definitions of God (Aristotle's), 52, 70, 72, 98, 106; as eternal, changeless, 53; as the guardians of morality, 29, 61; imitation of, 103, 110; loyalty and friendship with, 24, 63–64, 67–69, 77; mythological, 113–114, 129, 140; philosophy as imitation of, 70; polytheism *vs.* monotheism, 71, 97–98; self-contemplating god, 53, 57–58, 67, 74; as thought-thinking-thought, 52, 72, 154, 397. *See also* monotheism; unmixedness; unmovedness
Golden, Leon, 261
Gorgias (Plato), 258, 290
Gould, Thomas: on Aristotle's interpretation of tragedy, 337, 343; on Aristotle's *Poetics*, 333; on Aristotle's use of *miaron*, 330–334; on debate surrounding *hamartia*, 277, 334; on *Oedipus*, 253
Greek paganism: Aristotle's acceptance of, 16, 21, 28, 56–57; in civic life, 30–33; cult of the dead, 64, 66, 394; and fate, 171, 180, 186; inspiration in, 236; magic and superstition in, 56; and mythology, 16, 81, 176; piety as virtue in, 23, 52, 78; polymorphousness of, 18, 56, 62, 207; relationship with the gods, 76–78, 98, 185–186; religious experience in, 375, 388; role of prayer in, 49, 52, 62–64, 231–232; supernatural revelation in, 396; temple worship, 16, 28
Greek tragedy: Aristotle's account of, 242–246; best type of plot in (Aristotle), 258–260; catharsis in, 173–174; critiques of Aristotle on, 267–270, 275–276; and fate, 171, 187; and *hamartia*, 261–264, 267; and

(religious) happenstance, 272; happy tragedies, 247–250; intellectualist vs. moralist interpretations of, 252, 261; moralistic readings of, 252–255
Grene, David, 256, 296
Grote, George, 53
guilt: absolving of (Oedipus), 314–315; collective, 340–342, 357; and fate, 267; four levels of (Aristotle), 306; and *hamartia*, 274–275; and hubris, 284; of Oedipus, 282, 296, 301–302, 334; and parricide, 321–326; and shame, 336–337

H
Hades, 64–67, 361, 394; cult of the dead, 65; individual immortality, 65
Haidt, Jonathan, 326–329
hamartia: Aristotle's use of the term, 261–265, 274, 277; as error vs. character flaw, 252–253, 266–267, 334; as missing the mark, 262, 277–279; in the Mitys story, 348; as moral ignorance (Aristotle), 264, 321; moral vs. amoral sense of, 263–265, 273–276; in *Oedipus*, 267–268, 276, 280, 310; as sin (New Testament), 351
Han, Pierre, 379
happenstance: and accidental causality, 189, 222, 226–228; as chance, 182, 207; and *eudaimonia*, 207; and human agency, 188; and luck, 235; and poetic justice, 202; vs. science, 210–211, 221–222; and tragedy, 266–267, 269, 272
happy tragedies, 248–251, 257, 343, 378
hepatomancy, 33
Hesiod, 30, 82, 106, 186
Hippo, 17–18
historia, 74
holiness, 15, 71
Homer: and *anagnôrisis*, 378–379; Aristotle's comments on, 30, 164; and *atê*, 283; depiction of gods, 114, 129; encounter between Aphrodite and Helen (*Iliad*), 375–377, 389–392; use of prayer, 27
homoeomerous, 135
hubris: ancient Greek view of, 281–282, 284, 359; interpretations of (in *Oedipus*), 251, 321; and the Mitys story, 369; of Oedipus, 303, 319, 355–358, 360; and pride, 279; sexual (in ancient Greek thought), 311
Huismann, Tyler, 199, 216
hupokeimenon, 121
Hutton, James, 377
hymn(s): Aristotle's comments on, 30; and catharsis, 368; and Greek religious practice, 62; for Hermias (Aristotle), 23, 51–52, 394

I

ignorance (moral), 264–265, 316. *See also akrasia; hamartia*

Iliad (Homer): and Agamemnon, 98; and Aphrodite, 375–379, 390, 395; and *atê*, 283; as the prototype of tragedy, 174

illumination (mental): and Aristotelian induction, 382–383; as first stage of knowing, 385–389; in Homer and Luke, 398; and mystical practices, 90. *See also epagôgê*

imago dei, 103, 402

imitation: of divine actualization, 154–156; of divine eternity, 106, 110; of divine immateriality, 137, 149; of divine unmovedness and unmixedness, 130, 132, 135–136; philosophy as (of God), 70, 72; and piety, 54, 77, 80, 103, 160, 178

immateriality: and the active *nous*, 140; Aristotle's belief in, 96, 124; and Aristotle's self-thinking god; 55–56, 138–139, 153; definition of, 137; of forms, 145–146, 148–150; and perception, 141–142; of the soul, 116, 141–145. *See also* metaphysics (Aristotelian)

immortality: Aristotle's belief in, 23–24, 43, 47–48; Aristotle's statue dedications, 65–66; and divine imitation, 110; and reproduction, 109, 118; of the soul, 76, 93

induction: and *anagnôrisis*, 379, 382; in Aristotle's epistemology, 92, 242; criteria of, 387–388; and *epagôgê*, 380; and mental illumination, 382; moral side to, 383; in science, 380–381; similarities with religious experience (in Homer and Luke), 389–394. *See also epagôgê*

infinity, 138–139, 172–173, 201

inspiration: beneficial aspects of, 86–87; as divine influence, 84–86; and fate, 234–235, 237; in Greek paganism, 237; negative form of in tragedy, 85–86; Socrates' theory of, 84, 346

intuition: infallibility of, 387; and moral judgment, 327; as non-discursive reasoning (*nous*), 74, 92, 375, 385; theory as, 374

Ion (Plato), 84

J

Jaeger, Werner: denial of Platonic elements (in Aristotle), 39; and developmentalism, 36–39, 41; rejection of esoteric/exoteric thesis, 44–45

Jayne, Edward, 16, 19–21

Johnson, Kent, 191–192, 194

Johnson, Monte Ransome, 182, 235–236

Judeo-Christian tradition: concept of God, 98, 152, 159; Enlightenment reaction against, 18; influence of Aristotelian metaphysics on, 374

K
karma, 206, 227; moral aspect of, 261, 370; in *Oedipus*, 341, 355; as poetic justice, 254, 258
King, Hugh, 134
King Midas, 50
Kirkwood, G. M.: on *hamartia*, 273–274; on *Oedipus*, 280
Knox, Bernard, 280–281

L
Laplace, 224
Larsen, Kasper Bro, 378
Last Will and Testament (Aristotle's): on freeing slaves, 287; on friendship between men and women, 287; statue commissions, 26, 59, 65, 230
Laws for Man and Wife (Aristotle), 27
Laws (Plato), 29
leisure, 161, 176, 370
Littman, Robert, 341
Lloyd, G. E. R., 37, 124–125
Lonergan, Bernard, 387
lottery: and causality, 191, 201; and fate, 195–197; and prayer, 231
love: as cause of motion, 160; and prayer, 49; and relationships with the gods, 69, 77, 206, 235–236; spiritual *vs.* carnal (Socrates), 80
luck: ancient *vs.* modern notion of, 182–183, 186–187; and causality, 190–194; and chance, 201–204; and divine intervention, 207–208, 235–237; as epistemological ignorance, 191–192; good *vs.* bad, 182, 195–197; and happenstance, 227, 235; and moral agency, 204–206; in *Oedipus*, 296, 299; and prayer, 228–231; *vs.* reason, 210; related terms, 182, 200; as religious inspiration, 233; and science, 197–198, 214–215, 222–223. *See also* chance; fate; happenstance

M
Macfarlane, John, 180
Magna Moralia (Aristotle), 58, 69, 78, 85–87, 182, 232–233
marriage, 10, 27, 184, 292
Martin, Craig, 1
Massie, Pascal, 193
materialism, 18, 19, 401
mathematics: and abstraction, 149–150; eternal truths of, 111; and Platonic forms, 124–125; and science, 218; and unmovedness, 125–126

Mayhew, Robert: on Aristotle and prayer, 49, 53–54, 228–232; on divine intervention, 208
McClymont, John: on Aristotle's piety, 23–24; on Aristotle's traditional beliefs about the dead, 66, 394; on Aristotle's unanswered questions, 28–29
McGregor, James, 303, 334
mean (Aristotelian), 277–280. *See also sôphrosunê*
medieval scholastic tradition, 18, 57, 90, 374
megalopsychia, 362–363, 366
Meineck, Peter, 356–357
Melzer, Arthur: on Aristotle's esoteric and exoteric writings, 42–44; discounting contrary evidence, 43–44, 48; on the secret, atheistic Aristotle, 47
Menn, Stephen, 104, 159
metaphysics (Aristotelian): God as final cause, 100, 103; monotheism of, 70–71; philosophy as divine imitation, 70, 72; Platonic and religious aspects of, 19, 96, 100–106; technical version of, 107, 121. *See also* divine imitation; eternal duration; god(s); immateriality; immortality; unmovedness
Metaphysics (Aristotle), 46, 58, 81–82, 134, 138, 160–163, 166, 188, 198–199, 211–212
mêtis, 320, 362, 383
miaron, 330–331, 333–334, 339
miasma, 326, 331–332, 345
Miller, Fred, 162, 167
mimēsis, 70, 344
miracles, 204, 210, 237, 374
M'Mahon, John, 15
monotheism: Aristotle's belief in an intellectualized god, 44; Aristotle's definition of god, 52; god as a thinking principle, 70; impossible friendship with god, 68; *vs.* polytheism (in Aristotle), 71, 97–98
moral behaviour: ancient Greek beliefs about, 180, 210, 221, 227; Aristotle's views on, 23, 61, 111, 320; and *eudaimonia*, 255; and hubris, 359; in *Oedipus*, 288–289, 303, 310
Morrissey, Christopher, 246–248, 251
Movement of Animals (Aristotle), 116, 165
Murray, Robert, 271–272
music, 90, 246, 350
mystery cults, 18, 31, 62, 88, 92
mythology: Aristotle's views on, 24, 175–176; and Aristotle's popular works, 394; and fate, 187; and *Oedipus*, 243; and pagan revelation, 81–84; representation of the divine, 106–107

N

Nemesis, 184–185
Neoplatonism: on Aristotle, 48, 58; higher and lower levels of piety, 80; and non-discursive intuition (*nous*), 74; and prime matter, 122–123, 133; similarities with Aristotle's metaphysics, 100, 103
New Testament, 351, 373–379, 390, 393, 397
Nicanor, 26, 59, 237
Nicomachean Ethics (Aristotle), 45, 49, 66–67, 76, 102, 190, 236, 264, 267, 278, 306–308, 311, 316, 368
Nietzsche, Friedrich: amoralist account of Greek tragedy, 272, 302; difference from Aristotle, 370; impact on the classicist imagination, 252; and *Oedipus*, 241
Nightingale, Andrea, 72, 366–367, 369
nihilism: as un-Aristotelian, 190, 209, 370; and happenstance, 227–228; interpretation of *Oedipus*, 272. *See also* Nietzsche
nous (active): as direct intelligence, 380; as divine, 88, 105, 126, 153; as eternal, 64, 76; and immateriality, 153; as non-discursive intuition, 74, 92; *vs.* passive mind (*nous*), 64, 67, 109, 131–132; of the rational soul, 140; as unmixed, 129–132; as unmoved, 116, 126. *See also* active mind

O

O'Grady, Patricia, 104
Oderberg, David, 194–195
Odyssey (Homer), 379
Oeconomica. See Economics
Oedipus at Colonus (Sophocles), 255–257, 272
Oedipus Rex. See Oedipus Tyrannos
Oedipus Tyrannos (Sophocles), 242–245; amoralist interpretations of, 251–255, 310; Aristotle's commentary on, 245–250; esoteric and exoteric interpretations of, 251–261; and *hamartia*, 252–253, 265–269, 310, 355–356
On Colours (Aristotelian author), 128
On Divination (Cicero), 179
On Divination in Sleep (Aristotle), 88, 396
On Fate (Alexander of Aphrodisias), 188
On Fate (Cicero), 179
On Generation and Corruption (Aristotle), 106, 124, 134, 165, 167–168
On Interpretation (Aristotle), 188, 190
On Prayer (Aristotle, disputed), 50
On the Common Life of Husband and Wife (Aristotle), 27

On the Heavens (Aristotle), 50, 134
On the Universe (pseudo-Aristotle), 26, 50, 129, 160, 206
On the Usefulness of Belief (Augustine), 3
On Virtues and Vices (pseudo-Aristotle), 50
organon, 194

P

Pangle, Thomas, 183
Parker, Robert, 52
parricide: ancient view of, 326–330; and exile (of Oedipus), 335–336; as an involuntary act (Aquinas), 322–323; moral and legal implications of, 321, 325; Oedipus' crime of, 298–299, 316–317, 324
paterfamilias, 163
Peirce, Charles Sanders, 387
Peters, F. E., 317
Phaedo (Plato), 45, 48, 208–209
philosophy (Aristotelian), 35, 37, 47, 87; as beginning in wonder, 174–175; as divine imitation, 70, 72, 136; holiness of, 71; as an intellectual form of prayer, 81; as intensification of the religious impulse, 71; of mind, 145–146, 150; as mystical illumination, 56; as observation of religious rites, 75–76; scope of, 57; as *theôria*, 73, 369; as "thought-thinking-thought," 72
Philoxenus, 50
Phocylides, 50, 79
phronêsis, 45, 320, 363, 383
physics, 29, 193, 195, 218–219
Physics (Aristotle), 19, 46, 166, 168, 182, 183, 188, 190–192, 199–205, 223
piety: Aristotle's attitudes towards, 23, 28–29, 50–52, 70; caricature of, 60–61; and divine imitation, 103, 159, 178; higher and lower levels of, 80; intellectualized forms of, 54, 63, 70–71, 76–78; traditional Greek notions of, 61, 65, 297. *See also* imitation; prayer
pilgrimage, 72–73, 366–367. *See also theôria*
pity. *See* fear
Plato: Aristotle's disagreements with, 47, 65, 217, 349, 367; and catharsis, 348–350; and censorship, 343–345; contrasted with Aristotle, 39, 92–93, 97, 104; influence on Aristotle, 19–23, 27–28, 73, 82, 374; on morality, 61–62, 275; and moral impurity, 331–332; and *Oedipus*, 297; tripartite division of the soul, 317
Platonism: and divine imitation, 176; extrication of from Aristotle's thought, 39; and recollection

(*anamnēsis*), 65; similarities with Aristotelianism, 29, 48, 56, 96; theory of forms, 36–37, 103, 124–125; as a way of doing philosophy, 22
Plato's Academy, 28, 93, 96, 141
Plotinus, 57, 74, 97, 101
Plutarch, 65
poetic justice: Aristotle's views on, 259–260, 268; critiques of, 276–277, 321, 337; and happenstance, 202; and karma, 254, 261; in *Oedipus*, 333–334, 347, 365, 367–369; requirements of, 257; Socrates, use of, 258
Poetics (Aristotle), 13, 40, 173, 241–247, 253, 261–267, 273–275, 277, 305, 330, 333, 346, 353, 370, 377
Politics (Aristotle), 32, 45, 50, 107, 165, 228–231, 311, 350, 394
Pollitt, Jerome, 318–319
pollution (moral): in ancient Greek culture, 303, 305, 338; and contagion, 330–333, 341, 346; in *Oedipus*, 377; and purity, 326–328; remedy of exile for, 339. *See also miasma*
polytheism, 44, 71, 98
Porphyry, 80–81, 101, 203
possible worlds, 194–195
Posterior Analytics (Aristotle), 41, 92, 132, 198–199, 381, 387

prayer: Aristotle's attitudes towards, 23, 50, 58–59, 78–79; definition of, 49; in Greek pagan tradition, 49, 62–63; higher and lower forms of, 80; intercessory, 23, 26, 36, 49, 373; non-religious reading of references in Aristotle, 228–231; petitionary, 52–55, 59–62, 79, 225; philosophy as intellectual form of, 81
premeditation, 301, 309
Price, Simon, 32, 34
prime matter, 108, 133–135, 158
principle of non-contradiction, 136, 151–153, 386
Prior Analytics (Aristotle), 379
probability, 183, 381
Problemata (pseudo-Aristotle), 33–34, 41, 91
Proclus, 74, 97
Progression of Animals (Aristotelian author), 144
Protrepticus (Aristotle), 75–76, 88, 102
providence: Aristotle's belief in, 24; divine, 43, 99; and fate, 181, 227, 234; and a self-contemplating god, 159
Psellus, Michael, 90
pseudo-Aristotle, 34, 50, 115, 160, 206
Pulleyn, Simon, 59, 63–64, 79
purity inscriptions, 338–339
Pythagoreanism, 30, 41, 45, 73, 173, 317

R

Rabinowitz, Nancy Sorkin, 355–356
Rackham, H., 321
reasoning from examples, 241–242
recollection (Platonic), 65, 401
Renehan, R., 51–52
reproduction (biological), 109–110, 118–120, 143, 216
Republic (Plato), 60, 258, 285, 343–346
resurrection, 390, 393–394
reward and punishment (divine): Aristotle's attitudes towards, 44, 180, 227; Greek pagan belief in, 61, 181, 227, 230–232, 369; and luck, 196; moral dimensions of, 186, 202, 205, 209–210; and poetic justice, 254, 258
Rhetoric (Aristotle), 81, 182, 190–191, 351, 360
Richards, David, 284–287, 294
Robertson, Noel, 338–339
Rosemann, Philipp, 159
Rosivach, Vincent, 290–291
Ross, W. D.: on *aporiai* in Aristotle, 56–57; on Aristotle as a firm monotheist, 44; on flashes of insight, 383, 388
Rubel, Alexander, 354

S

Sachs, Joe: on catharsis in Aristotle's treatment of tragedy, 173–174; on *hamartia*, 262, 264; on moralistic interpretations of tragedy, 253–254, 257; on *Oedipus*, 281, 306; translations of Aristotle, 248, 259, 262
Sale of the Philosophers (Lucian), 44
Sappho, 65
Schillinger, Daniel, 192
Schollmeier, Paul: on catharsis, 249; on happy tragedies, 250–251; on pity and fear, 351; on plot lines in tragedy, 250
science: Aristotle as champion of, 97, 161, 177; coexistence with religion (in Aristotle), 96, 101, 181, 209, 224; critique of Aristotelian (Bechler), 211–214, 217 218; and developmentalism, 36, 39–41; explanatory limits of, 193–199, 210–212, 218–224; four causes of, 193; opposition between religion and, 17, 220–221, 227–228; Peripatetic paradigm of, 35; rules and principles of, 181, 198–199, 212, 219
Scodel, Ruth, 288
sea battle, 188
Second Alcibiades (Plato), 79
secularism: absence of in ancient Greece, 25, 30–36; anachronistic interpretations of, 33, 35, 44, 49, 77–78; Aristotle's alleged,

16, 20, 54–55; caricature of paganism, 60; and modern notion of luck, 183, 186–187, 227, 233–235
Segev, Mor, 16, 17
self-movement, 56, 112–117, 119, 122. *See also* unmovedness
Sense and Sensibilia (Aristotle), 131
shame: and hubris, 311, 360; and moral impurity, 327–328, 330; in *Oedipus*, 296, 335–337, 359, 365; and spiritedness, 310
Sinnige, Theo Gerard, 96–97
slavery, 285–287, 295–296, 340, 359
Smith, Robin, 193
Socrates: accusation of atheism, 20, 28; on drama and poetry, 344–346; and *elenchus*, 56; and fate, 208–209, 239; good *daimon* of, 2, 208, 239; on inspiration, 84; on levels of religious observance, 80; on philosophy as beginning in wonder, 174; and poetic justice, 258, 344; and prayer, 79; as a religious figure, 2, 12; way of life, 4
sophia, 78
Sophocles: aesthetic sensibilities of, 338–339; audience expectations of, 271–272, 291, 294, 369; intentions (in *Oedipus*), 243, 261, 276, 283, 314; literary genius of, 298, 343; moralistic reading of Greek tragedy, 255, 343; moral temperament of, 256–257; and poetic justice, 257–258; as a virtue ethicist, 314, 355
sôphrosunê, 317–319, 325, 358
soul: as divine, 47, 56, 88; as final and efficient cause of the body, 164–165; greatness of, 362–365; immateriality of, 96, 116, 141, 143–145, 157; immortality of, 43, 47, 76, 93, 109; Plato's tripartite division of, 318; as rational, 120–121, 140–144; as unmixed, 130–132, 135, 141; as unmoved, 56, 116–117, 119, 130, 141. *See also nous* (active); unmixedness; unmovedness
spiritedness, 284, 302, 310, 315–316
spontaneity, 166, 204, 209, 226
Stinton, T. C. W.: on character flaws and errors, 269–270; criticism of Aristotle, 270; on *hamartia*, 263–265, 267; on moralizing interpretations of tragedy, 252; on *Oedipus*, 268, 298–299
strategy (religious), 70–81
substance: divine, 138–139; as *homoeomerous*, 135; and immateriality, 137, 140, 147; perceptions *vs.* concepts, 149; in

syllogisms, 152; thought as, 47, 109; unmovable, 115, 121–123. *See also* metaphysics (Aristotelian)
substrate, 121–123
Subverting Aristotle (Martin), 1
Summa Theologiae (Aquinas), 322
supernatural, the: in ancient Greece, 60, 161; and discovery, 376, 390, 395–396; as final or efficient cause, 171; and inspiration, 84, 87, 232; in *Oedipus*, 361; and prayer, 62
Swerve: How the World Became Modern, The (Greenblatt), 16
syllogisms, 152, 198, 365, 383–385
Symposium (Plato), 1, 75, 286
Symposium (Xenophon), 80

T
technê, 45
Theaetetus (Plato), 174
theology (Aristotelian): ambiguity of, 100; exposition of, 83, 95–97; loose, 56; as problem-solving, 57; rival to Plato, 104; as a science, 392; unfinished state of, 55, 67, 70
theôria: and contemplation, 81, 92, 176–177; and God, 100, 156, 368; philosophy as, 73, 369; and pilgrimage, 73, 366–367; religious aspect of, 72; and theatre, 74, 365–367, 370

theory: as activity of the divine, 71–73; and contemplation, 81; of luck, 191; of mind, 148; philosophical, 76
thumos. *See* spiritedness
Timotin, Andrei, 80–81
Topics (Aristotle), 24, 28–29, 141
triangularity, 150
tuchē, 183, 185, 205
tyranny: ancient Greek concept of, 290–292; and hubris, 356–357; and immorality, 297–298; of Oedipus, 293–296, 320, 340; tyrant vs. king, 291, 295

U
universals, 153, 218–221, 324
unmixedness: in the active and passive mind; 131–132; of God, 127, 133, 139; god-like properties of, 127–128; of prime matter, 133–134; and purity, 135–136
unmovedness: of the active *nous*, 116; and agency, 114–116; and divine imitation, 115, 126, 130; of God (as an unmoved mover), 112, 118, 125, 160; and immaterial principles, 151; and mathematical objects, 125–126; and Plato's forms, 124; of souls, 117, 119–121; and substance, 122–123; unmoved movers, 114–118, 124–126, 151–153, 162

V

virtue ethics: Aristotle's, 51, 152, 155, 277–279, 312; Sophocles', 314, 355
von Fritz, Kurt, 378, 384–385
votive statues: Aristotle's commission of, 26, 59, 65, 107, 230; in Greek paganism, 62

W

Webster, Thomas, 314
Wehrle, Walter, 38
Whig Interpretation of History, The (Butterfield), 1, 5
Whitman, Cedric, 274–277
Whitmarsh, Tim, 16, 17–18
Wittgenstein, 217
wonder: aesthetics of, 173–174; in Aristotle's philosophy, 174–177; incommensurability of, 171–172; philosophy as beginning in, 174; and tragedy, 348, 366
Woodruff, Paul, 356–357
Works and Days (Hesiod), 185

X

Xenophanes, 30, 129
Xenophon, 32, 34, 79–80, 238–239

Z

Zeus: friendship with gods, 69; in Hesiod, 186; prayer and sacrifice to, 34, 51, 79; religious activities in honour of, 31; reward and punishment, 186; statues commissioned by Aristotle, 26, 59, 65, 230
Ziguras, Jakob, 378, 384

Philosophica
Series Editor: William Sweet

The *Philosophica* series presents essays by contemporary authors who offer philosophical reflections on current societal, cultural, artistic, religious, and political questions. A forum for debates, meetings, discussions, and rigorous expression of thought, *Philosophica* is the agora where ideas meet.

Previous titles in this series

Réal Fillion, *The Elective Mind: Philosophy and the Undergraduate Degree*, 2021.
Robert Major, *Mes conversations avec Claude*, 2019.
Maurice Henrie, *Donc je suis*, 2018.
Maurice Henrie, *Le poids du temps*, 2017.
Richard Feist, Chantal Beauvais and Rajesh Shukla (eds.), *Technology and the Changing Face of Humanity*, 2015.
Normand Baillargeon and Christian Boissinot (eds.), *Hockey and Philosophy*, 2015.
Charles Le Blanc (ed.), *Laïcité et humanisme*, 2015.
Carol Collier, *Recovering the Body: A Philosophical Story*, 2013.
Réal Fillion, *Foucault and the Indefinite Work of Freedom*, 2012.
Thomas De Koninck, *Questions ultimes*, 2012.

For a complete list of University of Ottawa Press titles, please visit:
www.Press.uOttawa.ca

www.ingramcontent.com/pod-product-compliance
Lightning Source LLC
Chambersburg PA
CBHW052009290426
44112CB00014B/2180